Art in Brighton 2015

Created by
Alison & Torben Krog

Every time you look through this book, I hope you find something extraordinary that fires your imagination, touches you soul, and brings you joy. I know I do

Alison Krog
Editor

Art in Brighton 2015

First edition printed 2015 in the United Kingdom.

A catalogue record for this book is available from the British Library.

ISBN 978-0-9928543-1-7

Published by Kemp Street Productions. For more copies of this book, please email: info@artymagazines.com
Tel: 01273 670426

Designed and set by
Kemp Street Productions.
www.artymagazines.com
Printed in Great Britain.

Acknowledgements

With our gratitude to the talented community of artists, creators and makers in and around the city of Brighton & Hove who continue to support every Arty venture with unerring faith and passion. We are privileged to know you.

A huge thank you to Dominic Vacher at Four Corners Print for his advice and expertise.

Thanks also to our super-skilled proof-reader Sarah Dyson, and to Dan Murrell, who re-touched the images so brilliantly. You are stars.

Front cover artwork by Ian Hodgson (page 92).

CONTENTS

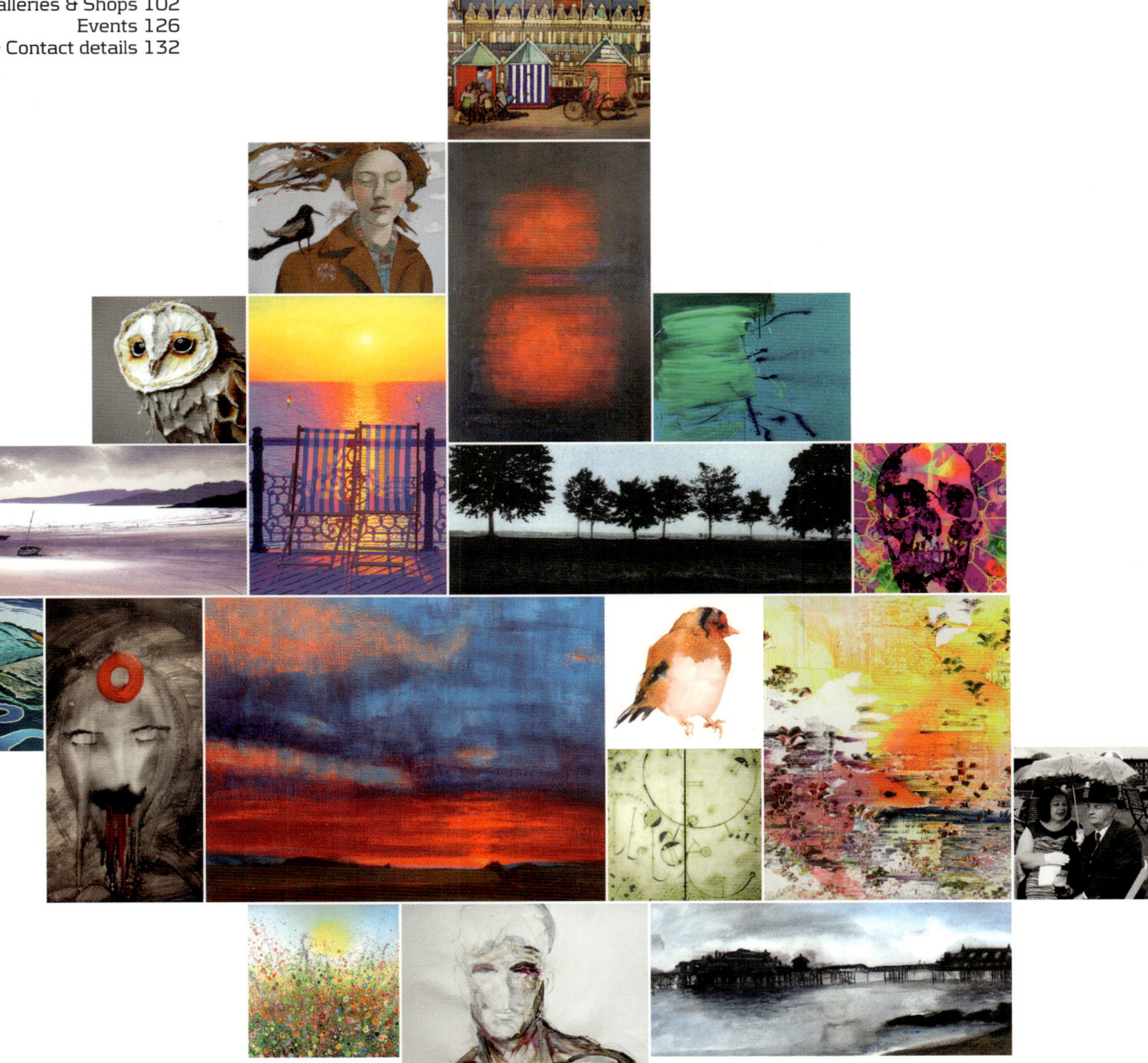

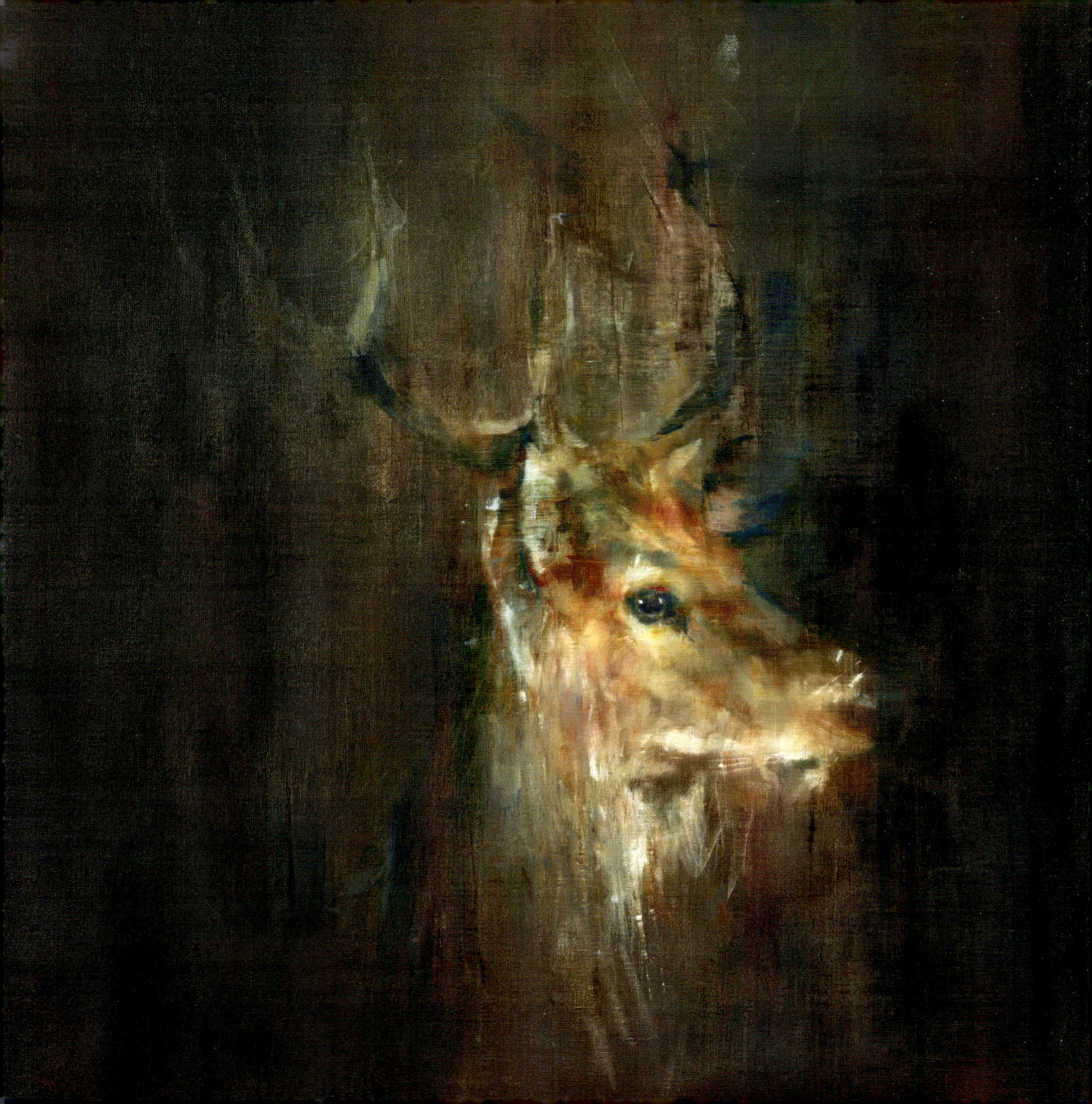

ARTISTS

Exciting and diverse artworks by the city's top artists, photographers, creators and makers

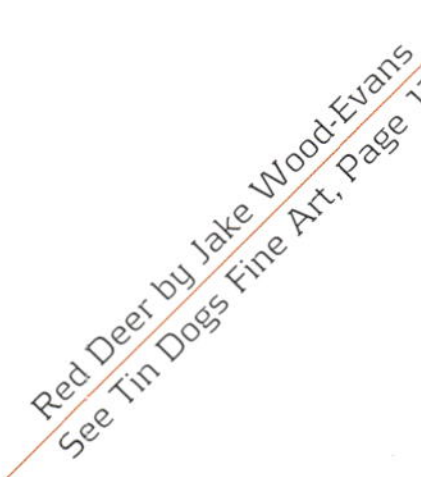

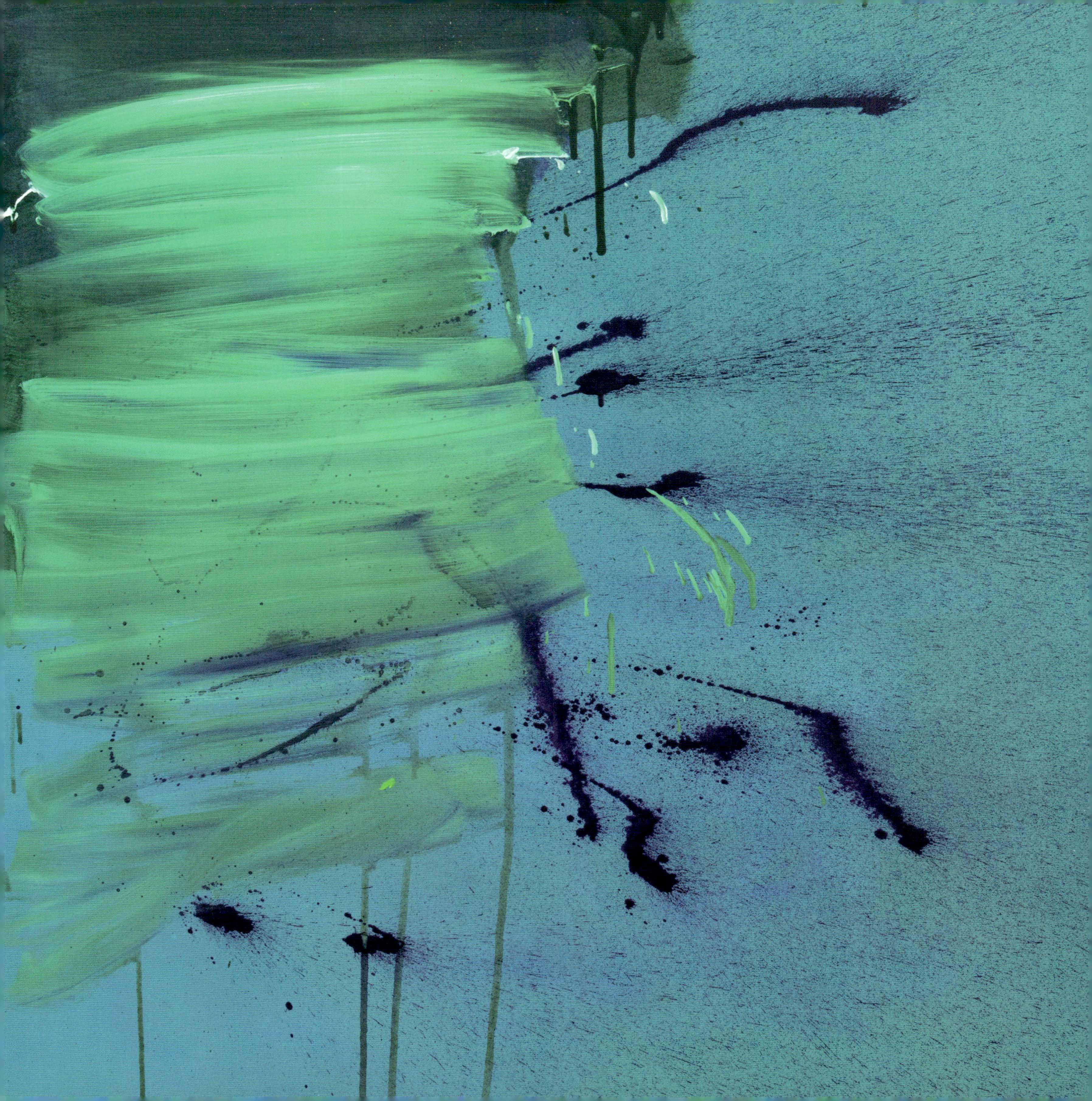

Geoff Hands

Artist
www.geoffhands.co.uk

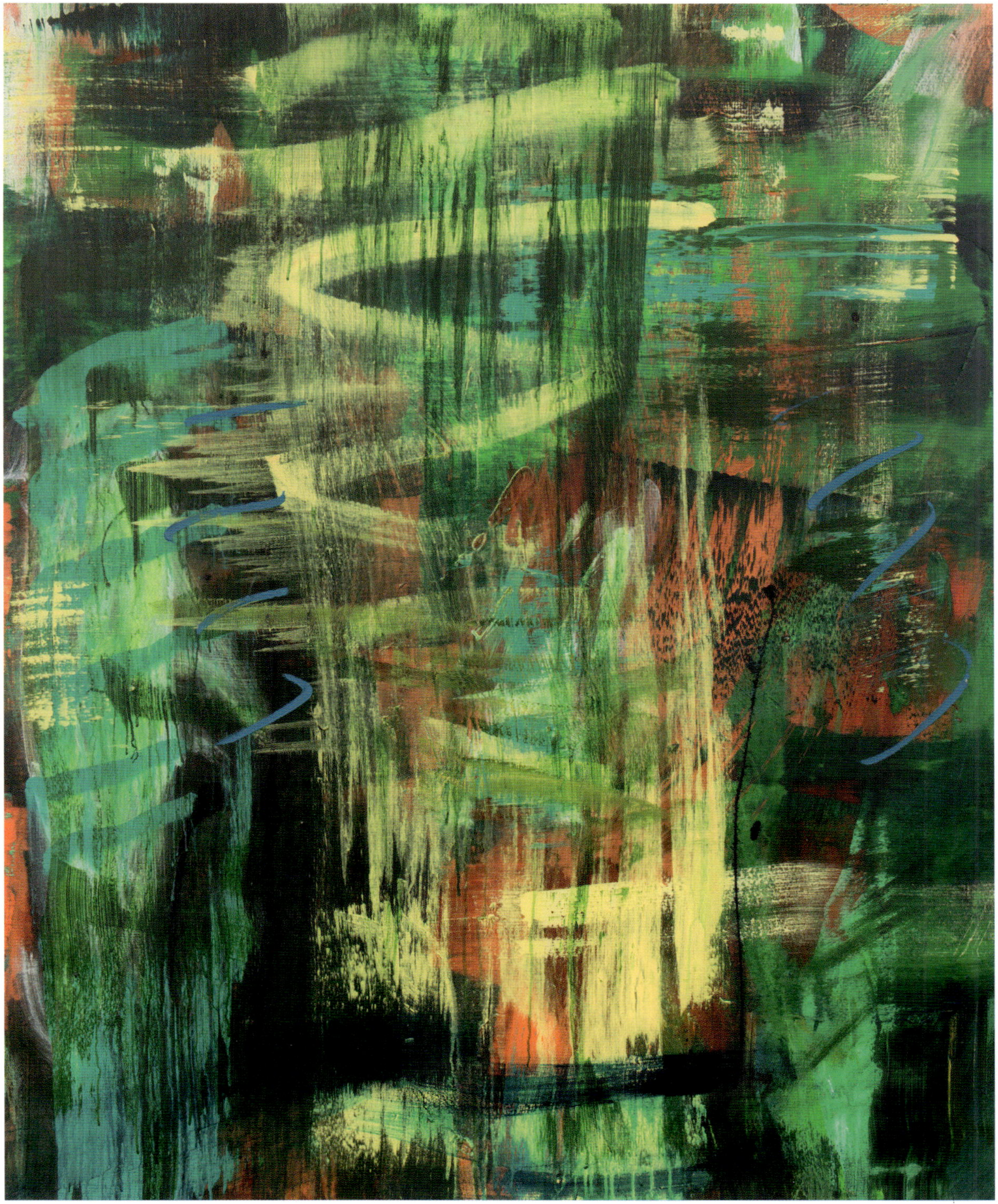

Clockwise from top left: Shropshire II 2014; Untitled 2014; Shropshire Improvisation (small) V 2014
Opposite page: Sea 2014

Geoff Hands' work continues to explore the painterly language of abstraction. Whether the paintings are developed from sea or landscape subjects, the work creates a dialogue between purely abstract decisions rendered in colour, shape and quality of mark.

His most recent work investigates a memory of Shropshire woodland from his earliest studies as an artist, although he considers the series of paintings – on canvas and paper – as occupying the present rather than the past.

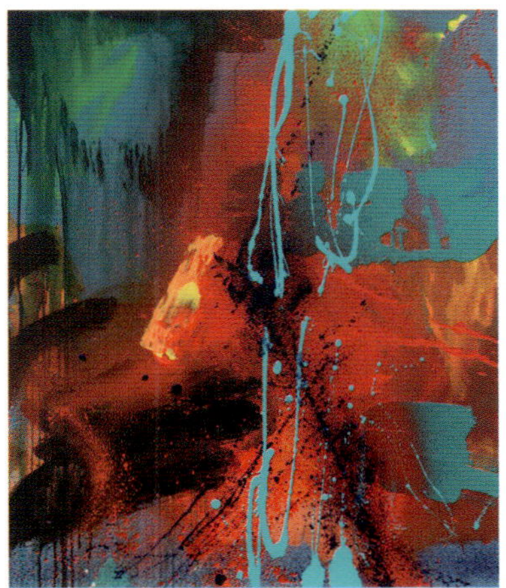

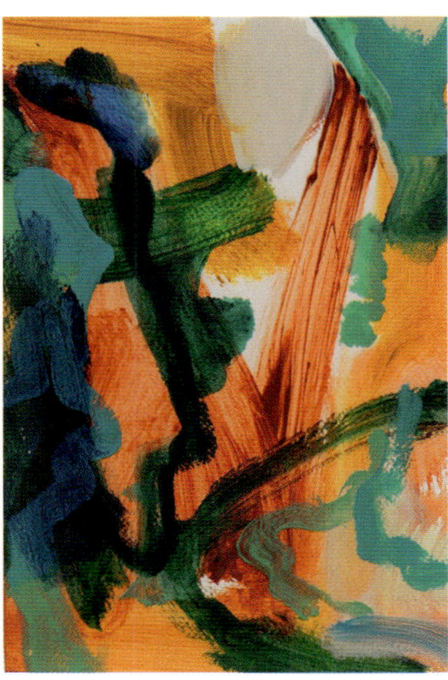

Vincent Donlin

Artist
www.vincentdonlin.co.uk

Clockwise from top left: Metro Deco; Spring & the Amex Building; Arches 2014; Grand Painting 4

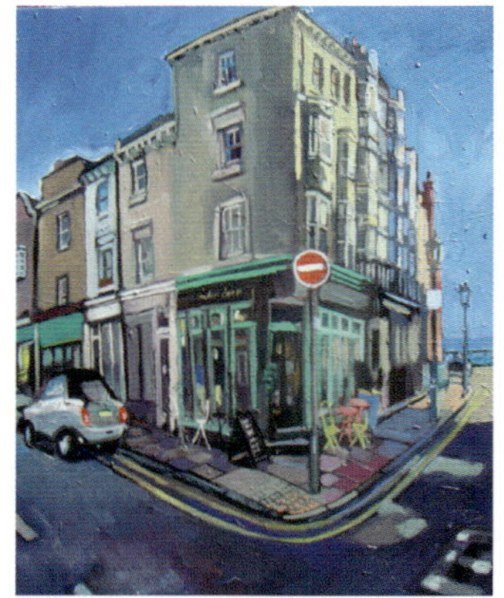

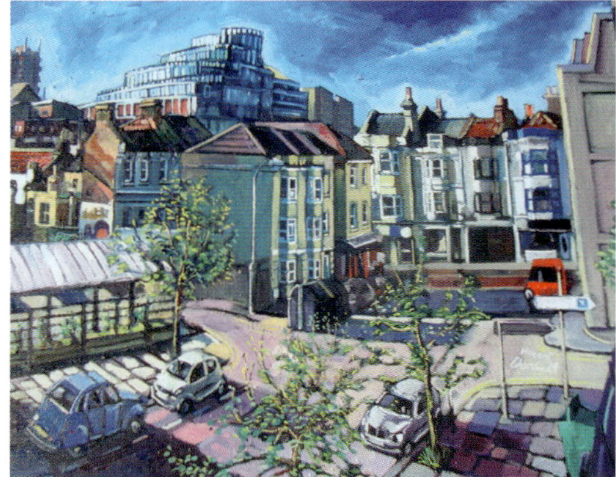

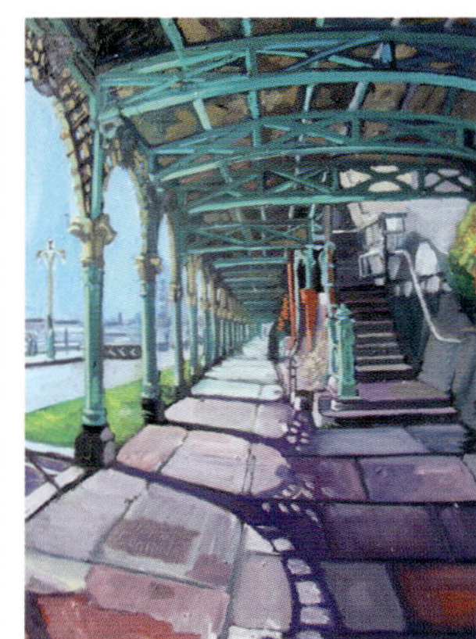

Vincent Donlin's work spans over three decades since he started painting in the early Seventies.

Vincent is largely self-taught, but was lucky enough to meet and be taught by the late visionary artist Donald Pass at Upbury Manor Secondary School. He later attended Medway College of Design, where he completed a foundation course.

After leaving Medway, Vincent met artists Stephen and Simon Postgate, Billy Childish, Sexton Ming and Charles Thompson. He also wrote poetry, which was published by Charles Thompson, co-founder of the 'Stuckists' group. His poem appeared in Charles's *Cheapo* magazine, printed on Mr Thompson's own printing press.

During the early Eighties, Vincent and fellow artist and friend, sculptor Stephen Postgate, spent time working together in Wales, where they were based in Stephen's father's cottage in Llandeilo – painting, sharing ideas, dole cheques, tomato-paste flapjacks, beer and canvas.

Later, in London, Vincent and Stephen lived in various places around Westbourne Park and Notting Hill Gate, eventually settling in 'The Old School House' in Hammersmith. They continued painting large-scale canvases using paint taken from skips, powder-paint mixed with washing-up liquid and sized with wallpaper paste on calico. Miraculously, some of this work has survived and is in remarkably good condition. It can be seen on his website.

The present artworks are painted on canvas or wood, using an acrylic underpainting and building up the picture using linseed oil glazes and finished in oil paint.

Vincent's paintings can be viewed later in the year at iO Gallery on Sydney Street (page 106) in Brighton's North Laine, and also Uden Estate Agents at 88 Dyke Road, Brighton.

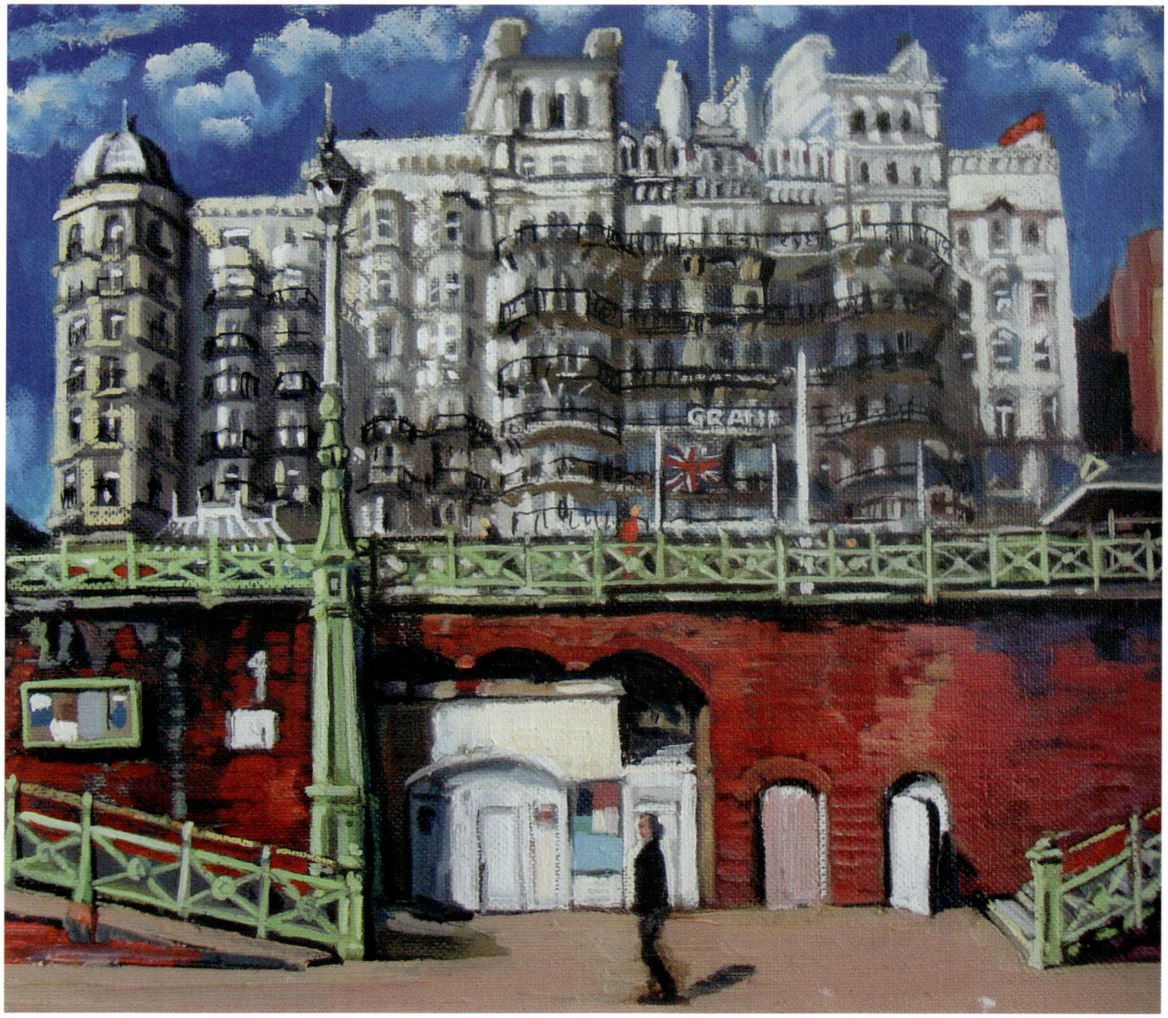

Heike Roesel

Artist
www.heikeroesel.co.uk

Clockwise from top left:
A Motley Assortment; Magic Mountain; Ulysses - Sail or Return

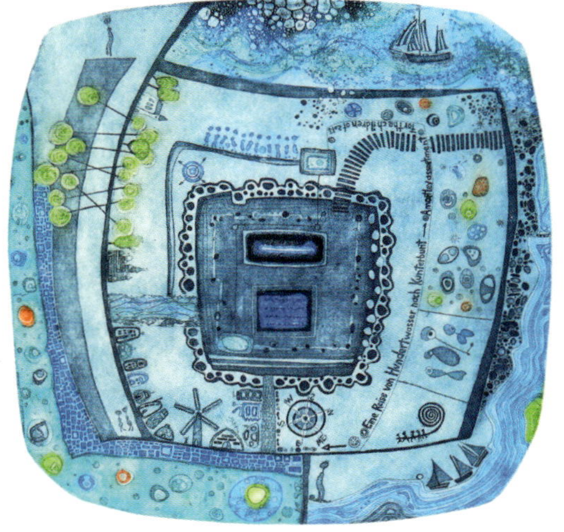

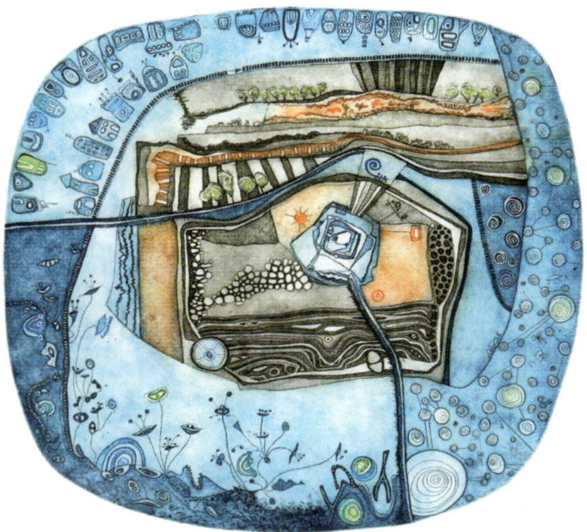

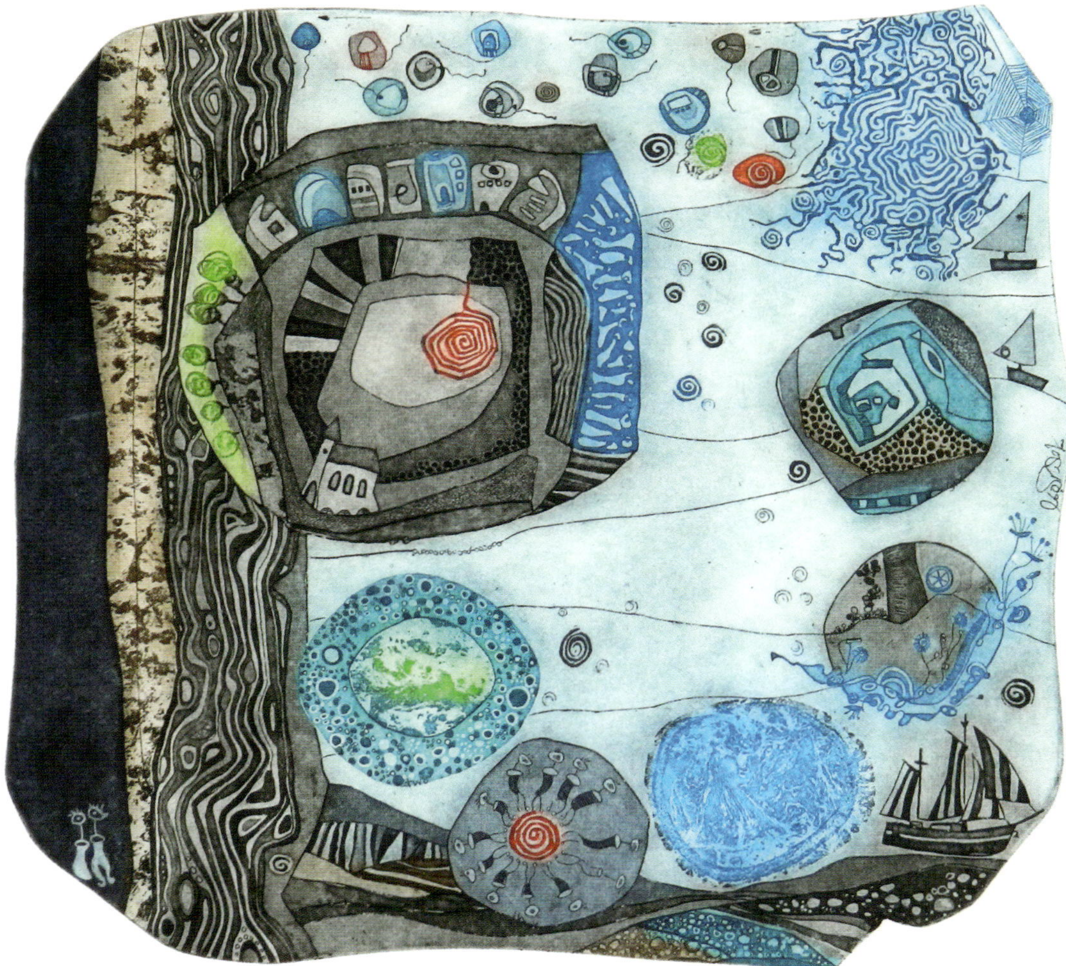

With her etchings and watercolours, Heike Roesel aims to inspire the observer's imagination to create a personal journey through the imagery. She loves to be told the 'stories' that emerge this way, and in some cases they have inspired another image.

I wish to send people's minds on a joyful wander, to find new aspects in my imagery every time they look

Themes for Heike's etchings are often inspired by her surroundings, both geographical and social. From an initial idea, she develops an image by looking at the shapes, colours and forms involved, and also by taking into account any social implications that occur. But it is her intuitive response to the scenery that creates Heike's individual interpretation of the subject. The focus in her artistic work has always been to bring life to these composed 'worlds of their own', which otherwise would not exist.

Since 2010 Heike has been working with acrylic resist techniques. The etching process has a strong influence as a creative tool in its own right, and plays a major part in developing Heike's imagery.

Locally Heike's etchings are on sale in Brighton's iO Gallery, Sydney Street (page 106) and at Bellis Gallery, Kings Road (page 118).

Mark Glassman

Artist
www.markglassman.org.uk

Clockwise from top left:
Rocks; Head 300; Mountains; Boats 102

Mark Glassman's paintings are an abstraction from the landscape of East Sussex – specifically Bishopstone and Seaford – which forms the inspiration for all his work.

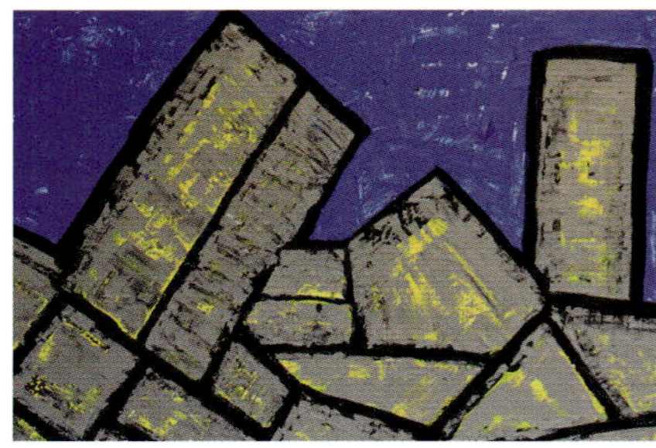

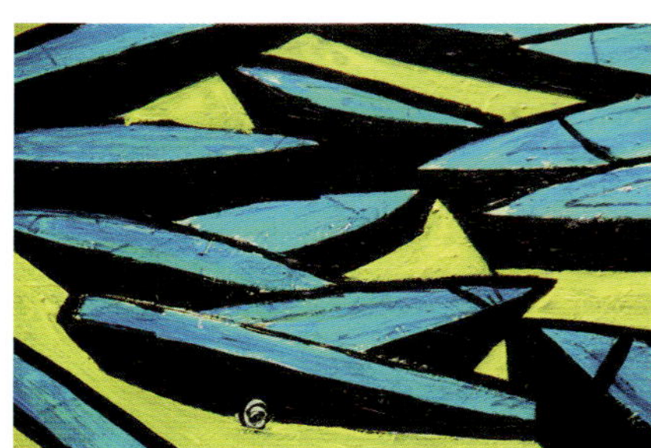

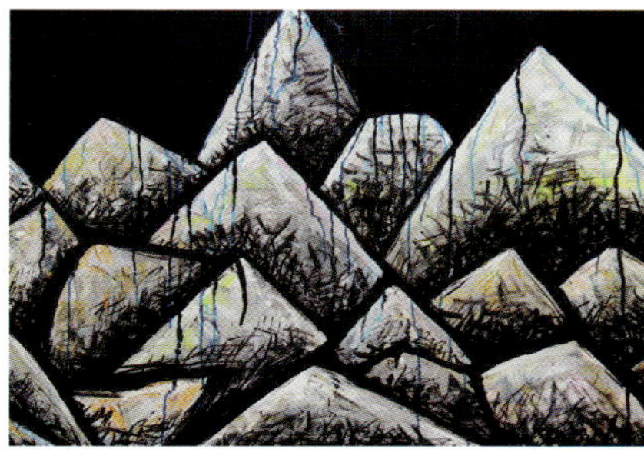

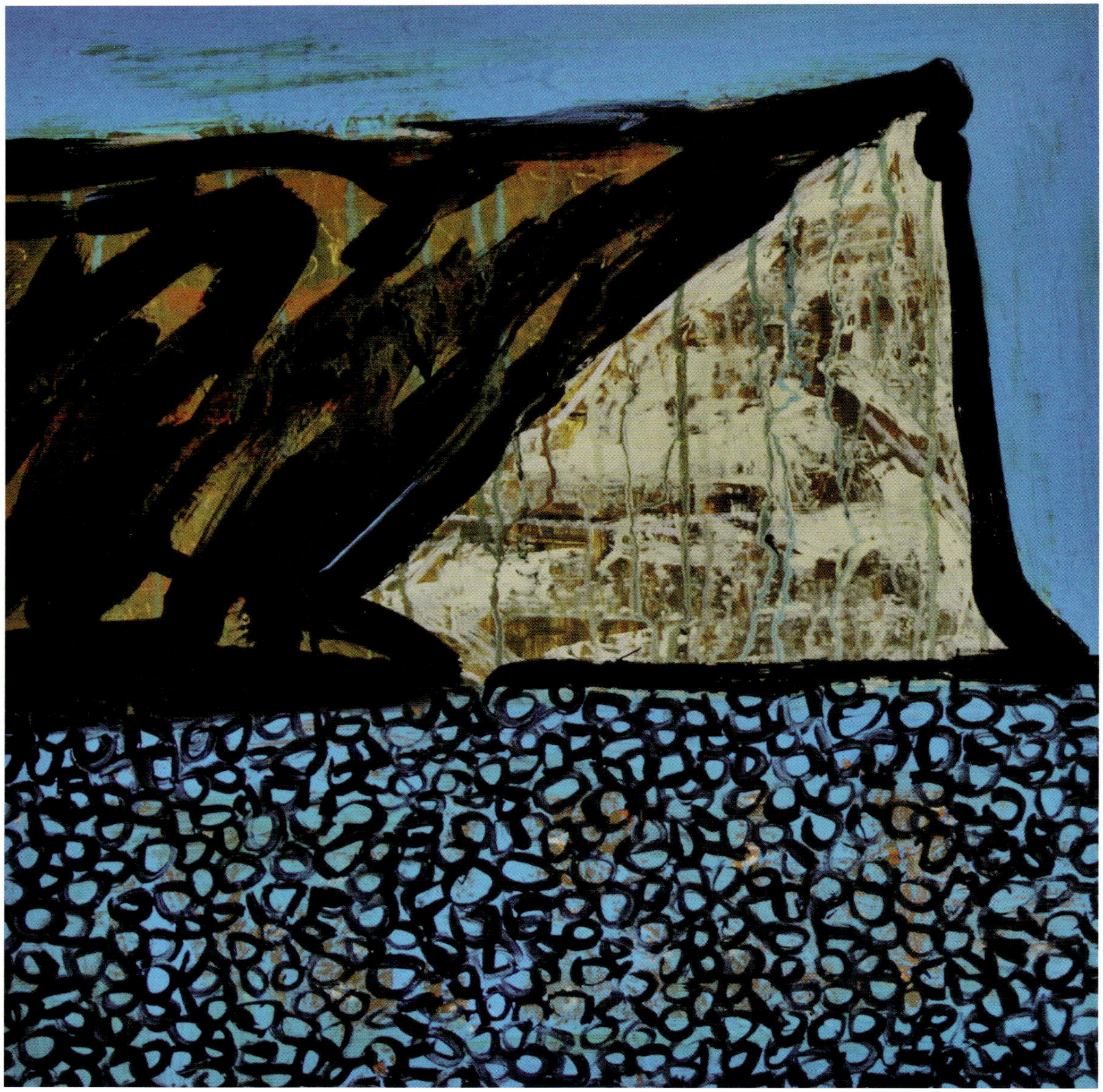

I love Mark Glassman's work. I have his painting of a Norman country church, its pointed hat tower stark against the fields and sky as I see it whenever I go past. He has a strong, evocative and highly original style when painting Sussex: its cliffs, seaside, fields and lanes. His record of a time and place on the Sussex coast has to me an unparalleled truthfulness and graphic beauty

Serena Thirkell
Local sculptor, Lewes

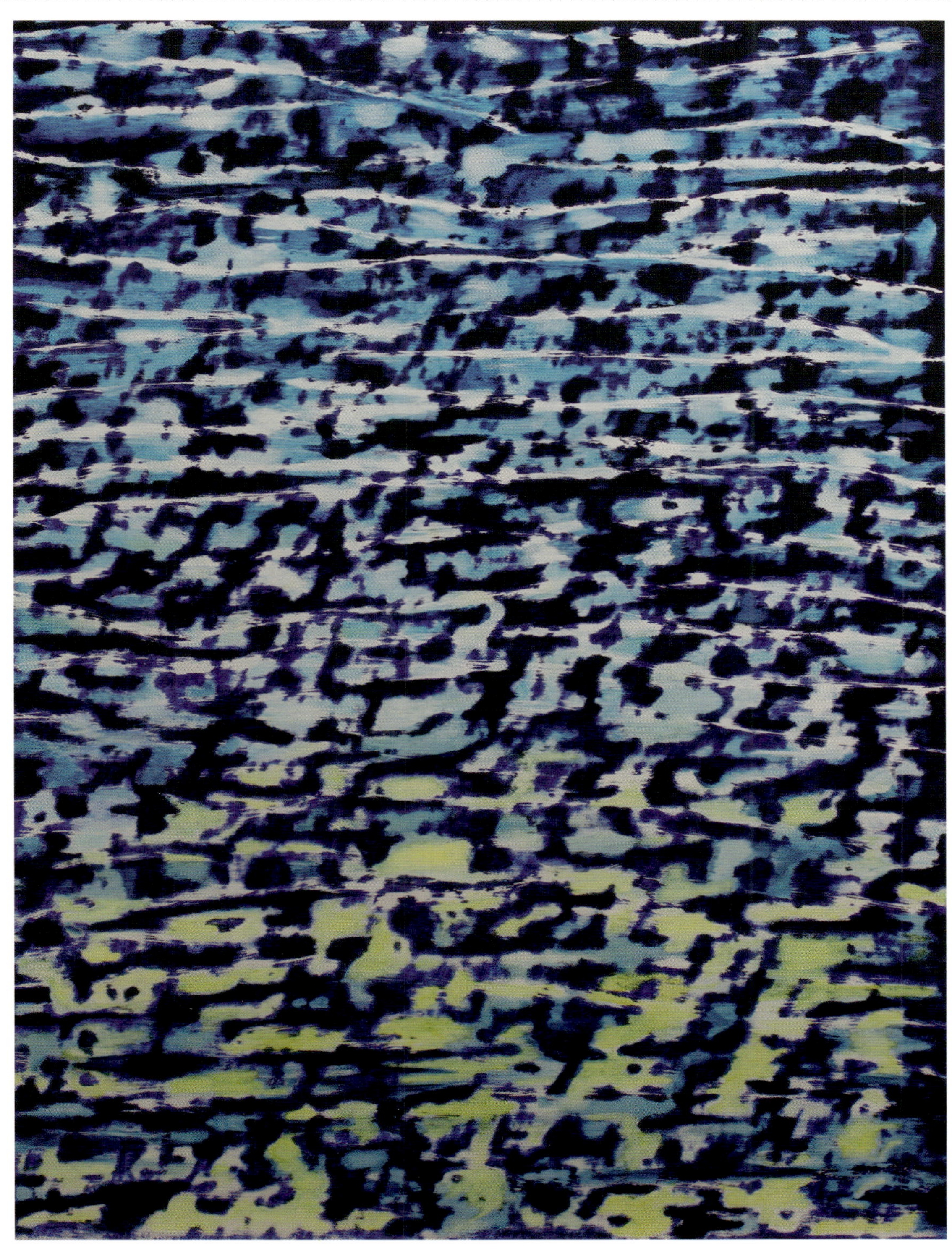

Val Fawbert

Contemporary Artist
www.valfawbertcityretreat.com

This page, top to bottom: Paddlers (100cm x 70cm);
The Terrace (120cm x 80cm)
Opposite page: Rush Hour Brighton Station (100cm x 100cm)

Brighton-born contemporary palette knife artist Val Fawbert creates impressions of the city – in town and by the sea – on deep-edged canvas using acrylics.

I try to capture the very essence of: "That's Brighton, I guess!"

The process – skimming and scraping with the knife – produces a simplicity of line that characterises her striking figurative work. Energised by the cutting edge of the knife, the movement of sculptural figures emerges. This results in a kinetic experience for artist and viewer, encouraging them to identify with the moment. Spatial awareness is crucial to Val's composition, with characters arriving and departing from the canvas. Economy of colour and restraint is often demanded by her identifiable palette to produce the typically leaden skies merging with the coastline.

Studying at University of Brighton, with a Major in Art Education, Modern Sculpture, Drama and The Visual Arts, has led to her exhibiting in Europe and most recently London's Brick Lane. Val will be participating in the May 2015 Artists Open Houses Festival as a member of Hove Arts.

Visitors are welcome to her garden studio and gallery in Hove by appointment (see page 133).

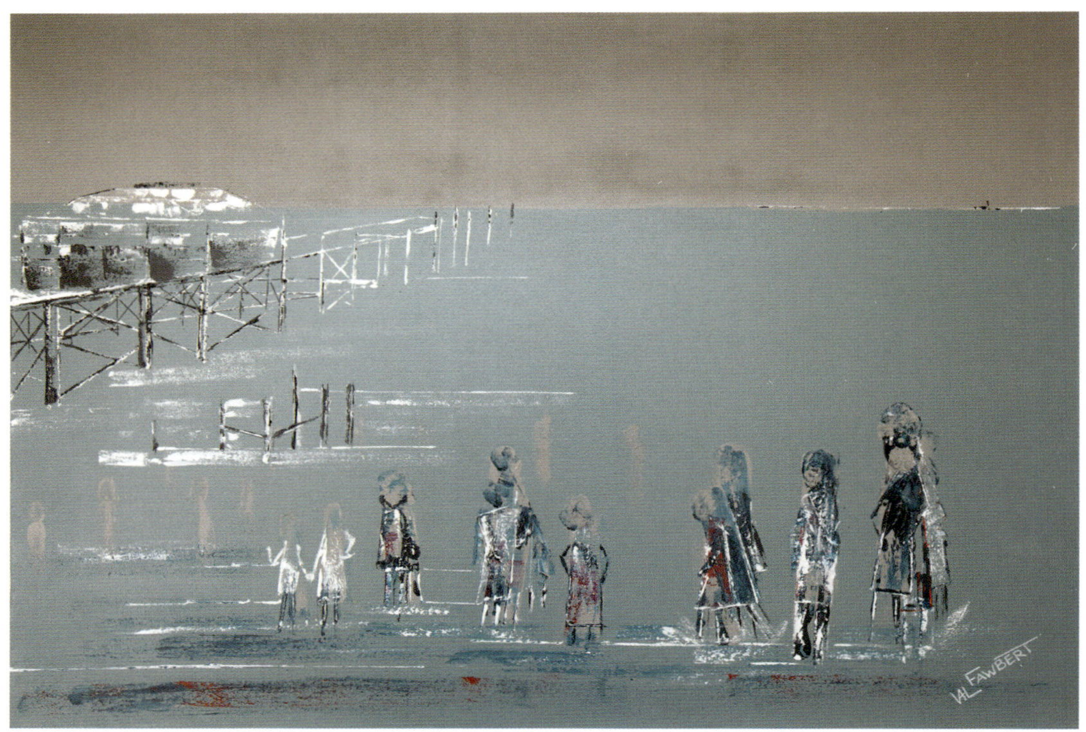

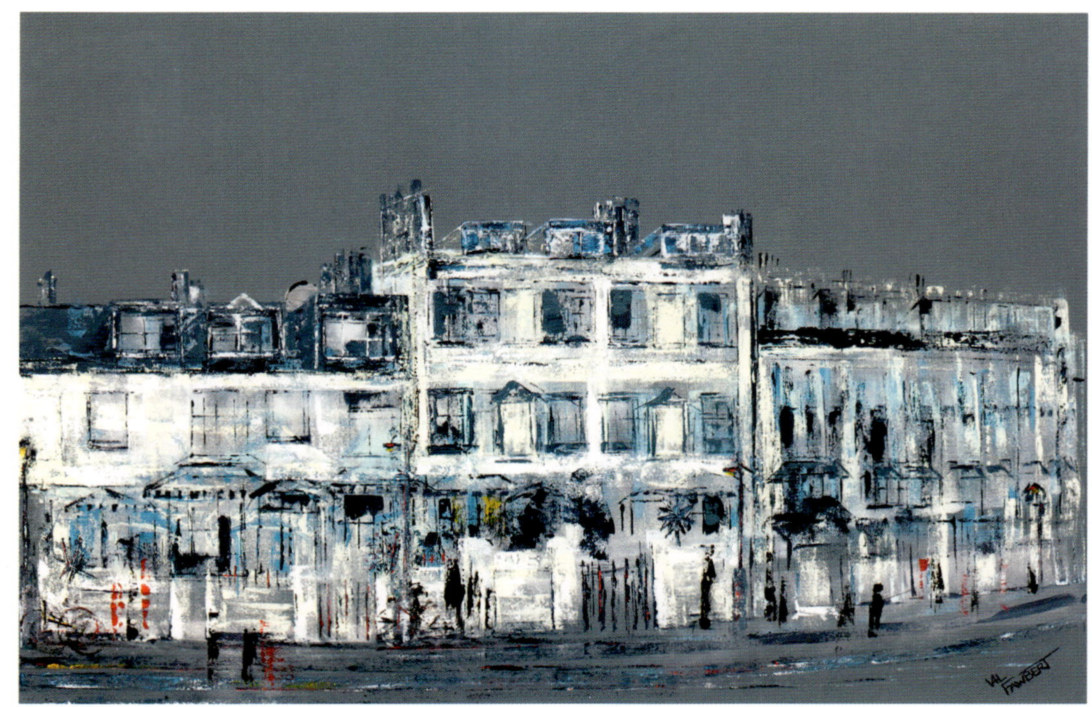

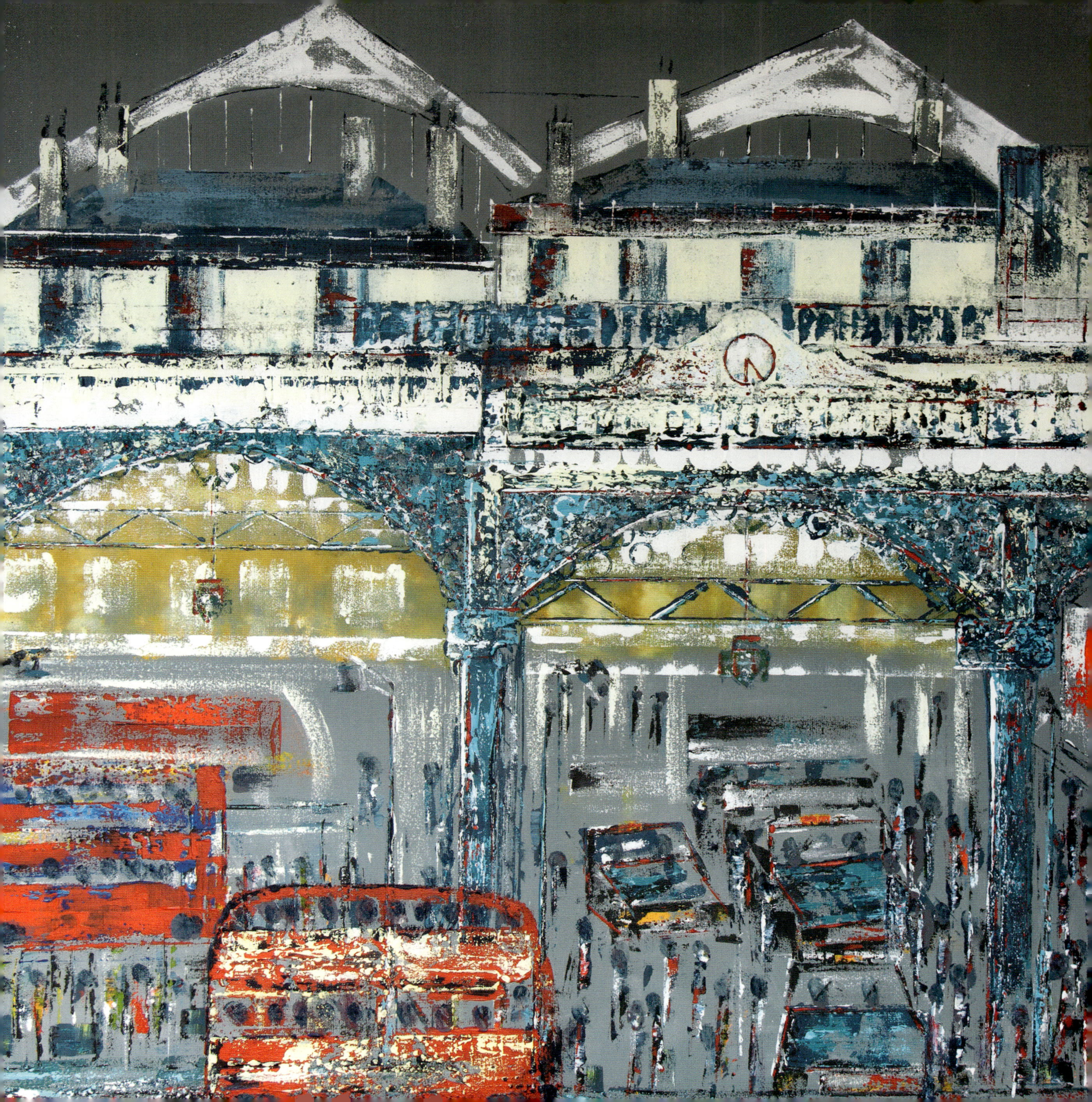

Heinz Michael Kalkbrenner

Digital Art & Photography
www.hmkdigitalartphotography.net

Clockwise from top left: Magic Stones; Colour Fields; Night Flowers; Idea of a Ship; Northern Light; Pyramid Rainbow
Opposite page: Growth Work

He explores limits and possibilities of different materials and procedures by combining analogue and digital art production methods

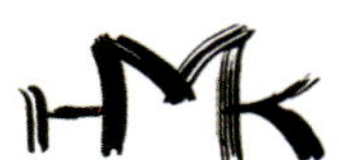

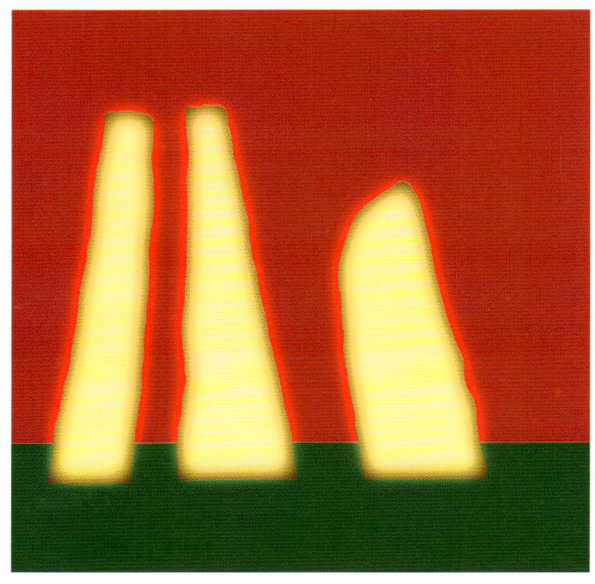

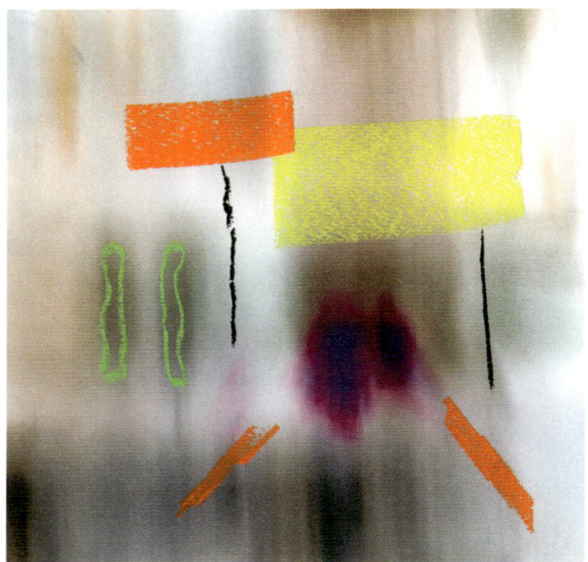

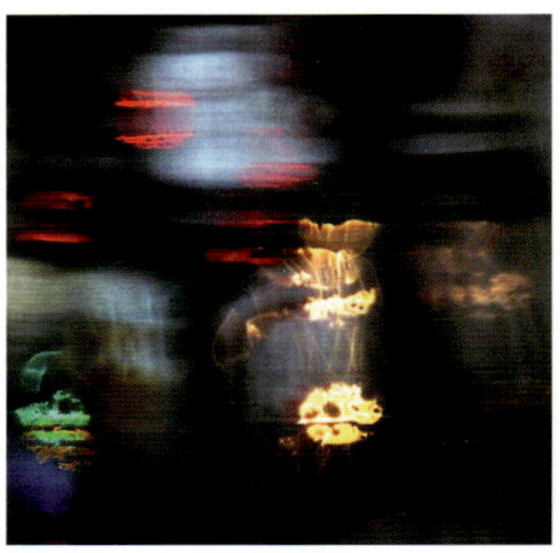

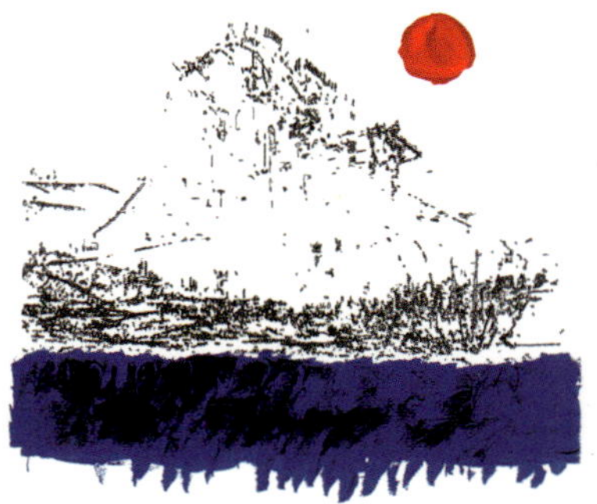

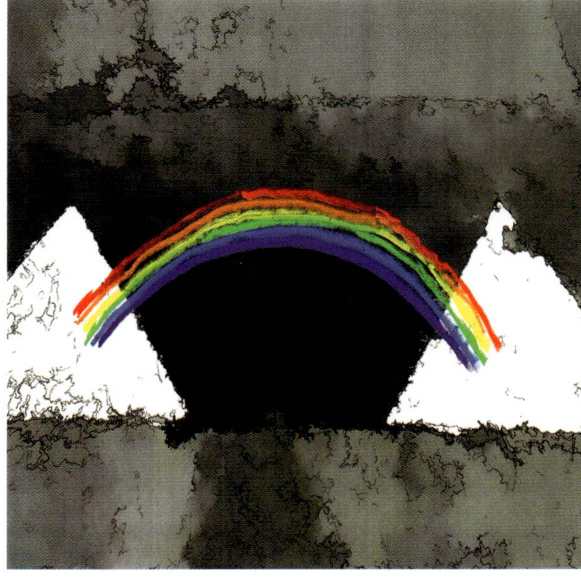

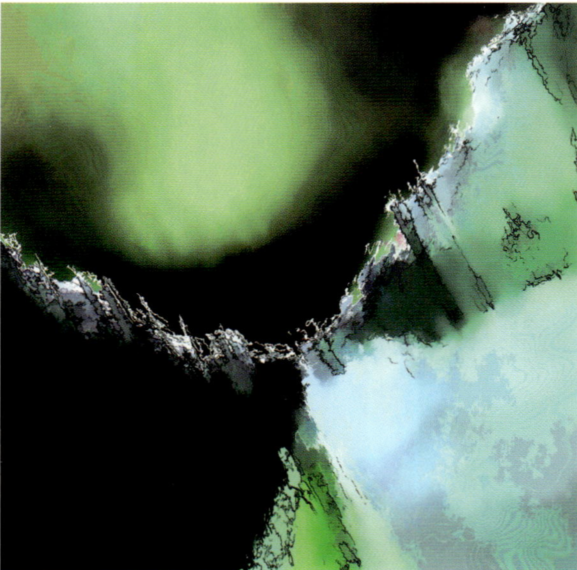

Visual artist Heinz Michael Kalkbrenner creates fine art prints by following an abstracting process that can retain figurative elements and may also have a meditative focus. He explores the limits and possibilities of different materials and procedures by combining analogue and digital art production methods. Structure, colour and light are important.

The artist offers limited editions of fine art prints as well as art greeting cards and art calendars, sold online via his website, at various Artists Open Houses in May and at Christmas and other exhibition venues.

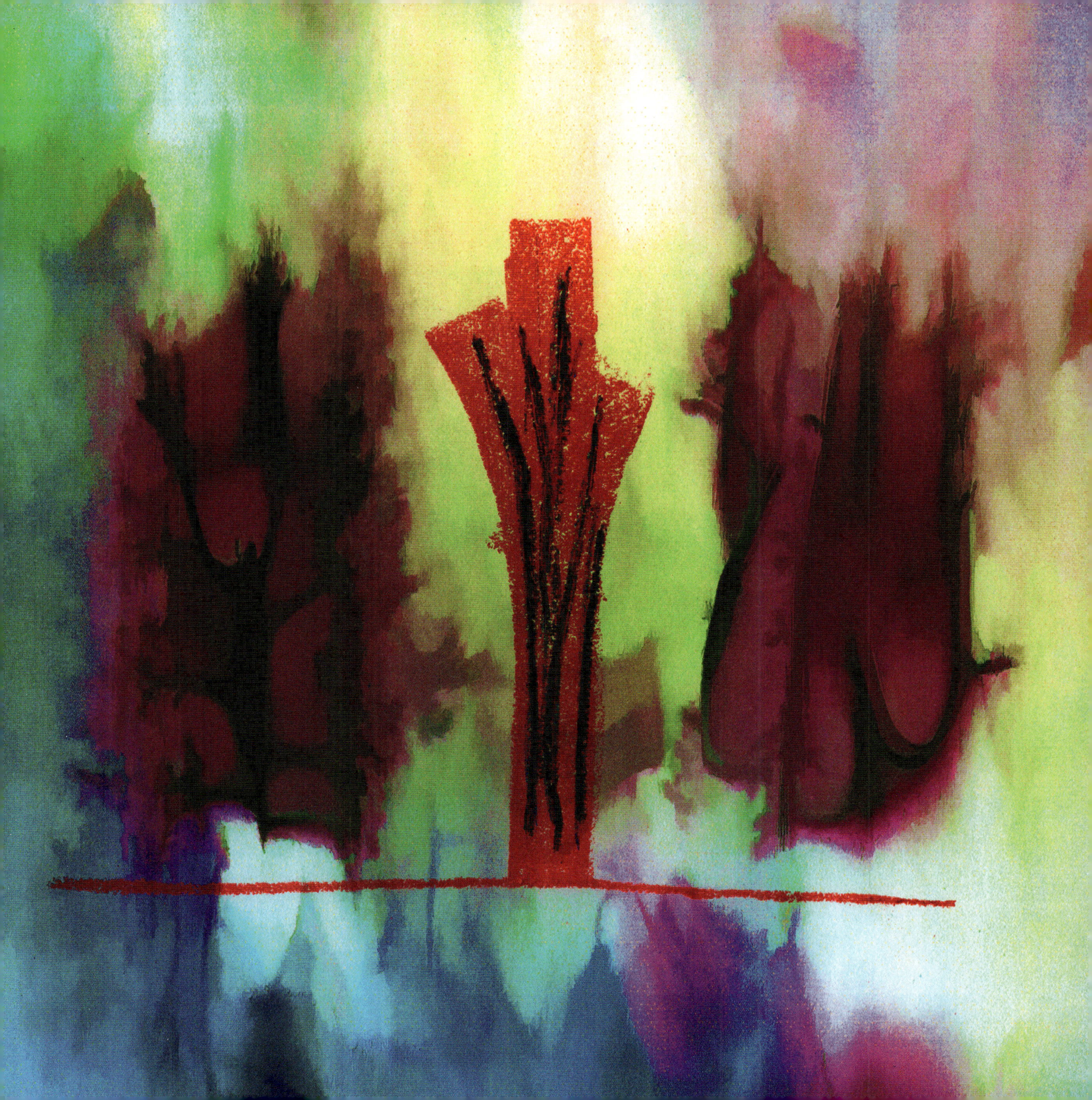

Jay Collins

Artist
www.kemptownartistsgallery.com

Clockwise from top left:
Hove 12; Decorative Hove; Brighton Graffiti; St Dunstan's

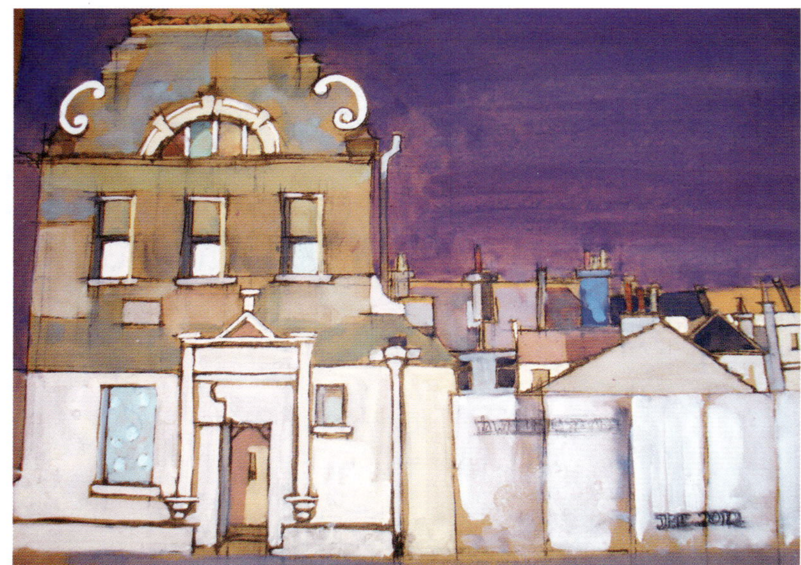

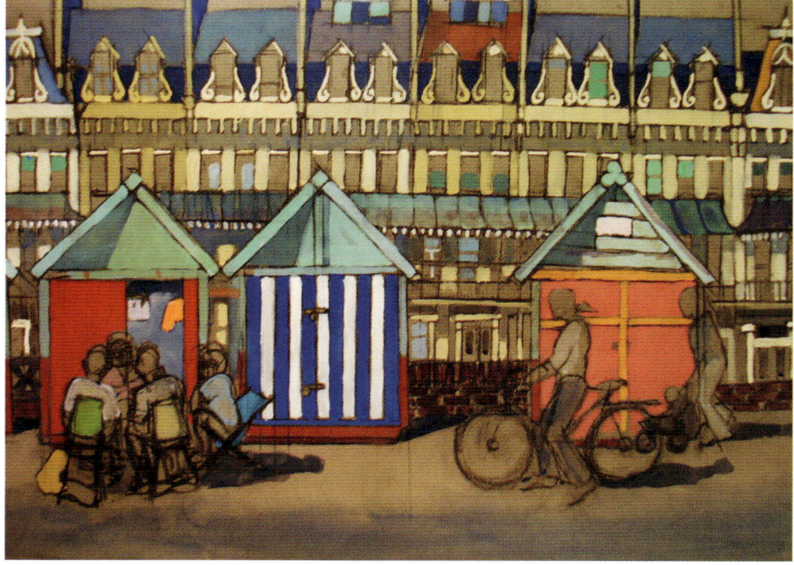

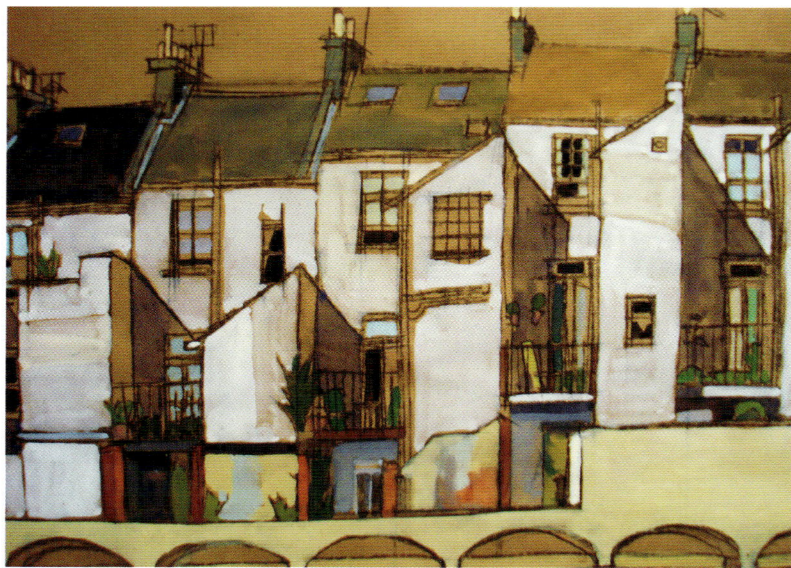

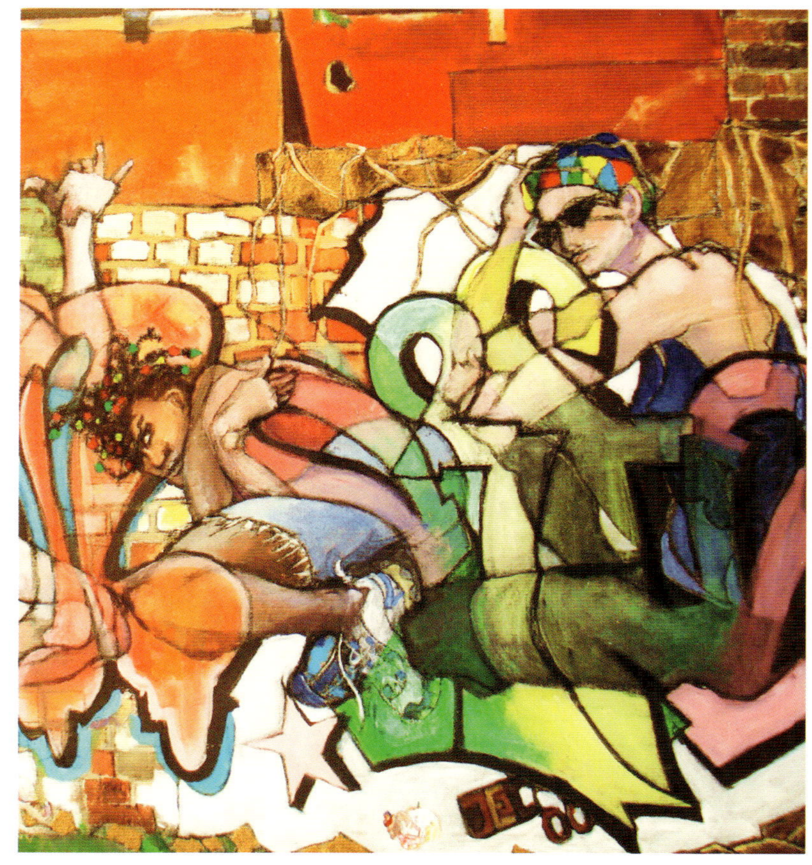

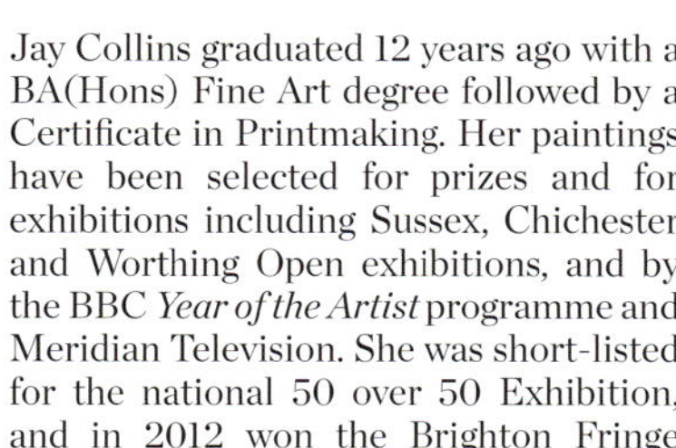

Jay Collins graduated 12 years ago with a BA(Hons) Fine Art degree followed by a Certificate in Printmaking. Her paintings have been selected for prizes and for exhibitions including Sussex, Chichester and Worthing Open exhibitions, and by the BBC *Year of the Artist* programme and Meridian Television. She was short-listed for the national 50 over 50 Exhibition, and in 2012 won the Brighton Fringe Visual Arts Prize. As a local artist, Jay was among the first in Kemptown in 2002 to open her studio to the general public each year during the May Brighton Festival. She contributes colourful illustrations to the pub series in *Viva Brighton* each month. Her continued fascination with the eccentric, historic and those places that have a story to tell is apparent in her latest paintings.

Clockwise from top left: Red Deer by Jake Wood-Evans; Freedom by Warren Fox; Bacchanalia II by Chris Kettle

Tin Dogs Fine Art

TIN DOGS Fine Art PRINTERS OF PEDIGREE

14 St Johns Road, Hove BN3 2FB
www.tindogs.com

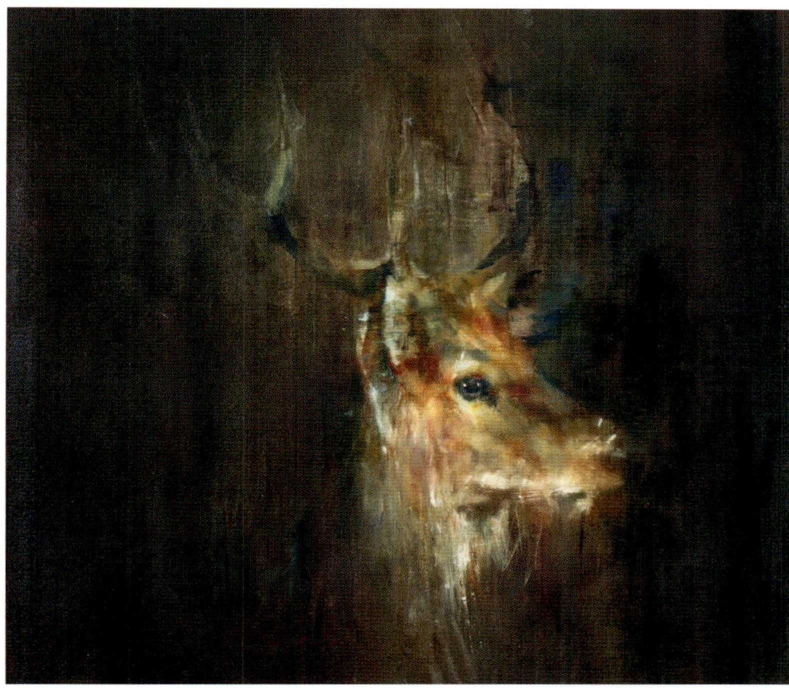

Tin Dogs Fine Art (or Tin Dogs for short) is a bespoke giclée and screen printing company catering for the high-end art creation and replication market. Collectively, the company's staff have more than 20 years' relevant experience in the professional printmaking field.

After working for a major art printing company for 17 years, the Tin Dogs team decided to start a new printing workshop outputting top-quality work, but also providing a more bespoke, personal and creative experience for the artists, paying particular attention to detail and having utmost respect for the original artworks.

Tin Dogs has produced prints for various art publishers and galleries, including the Tate and the National Portrait Gallery, artrepublic, ink_d gallery, Prescription Art and L and S Printing to name a few. The company's reproduction work includes artworks by Picasso, Patrick Caulfield, Bridget Riley and Roy Lichtenstein.

Tin Dogs specialises in digital giclée printing and screen-printing, combining the two processes to create high-quality bespoke images and limited-edition print runs. This pairing of techniques is in demand from contemporary artists, artists' estates needing to reproduce classics, and art publishing houses. They print on various substrates, including: poster papers; high-quality, heavy-weight fine art papers; canvas; glass; aluminium and even mirrors.

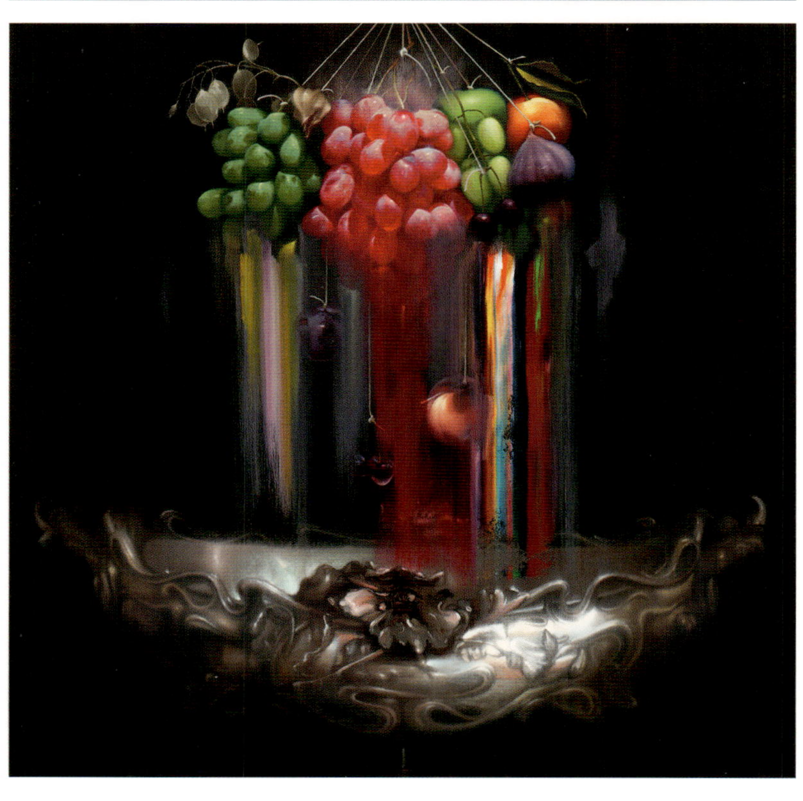

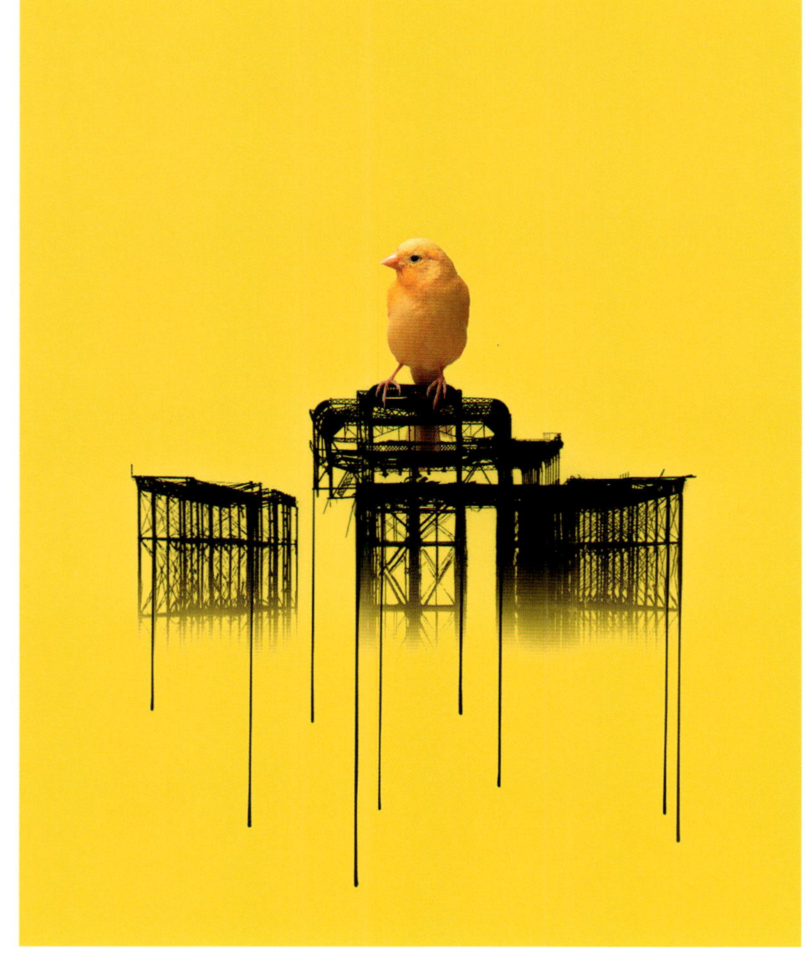

Yvonne Coomber

Artist
www.art5gallery.com

This page from left: Heart of the Forest; Longing
Opposite page: You're Gorgeous

Painting for Yvonne Coomber is evidently a love affair. Her work is a celebration of all that is good in the world.

Her evocative, dreamy, rainbow-drenched paintings sing of wild tumbling hedgerows, tangled meadowlands, open moorlands and magical forests. They whisper of love. Every image has the capacity to instantly transport the viewer to an effervescent place of happiness that is literally saturated in joy. A place where paint smiles.

The materials Yvonne uses are extremely important. A mixture of oils, inks, glosses, acrylics, glazes, fine glitter and gold leaf are applied in a multitude of layers. Washes are built up to form a work that is infused with colour. Paintbrushes, sponges, rags, palette knives and fingers are all used to create the finished piece. The result is a kaleidoscopic, jewel-like composition of rich pigments that prismatically open up to reveal the radiance and beauty of nature.

Yvonne always works outside, so lacy ice and howling gales have as much influence on the final painting as scorching sunshine and gentle breezes. The weather in a very direct way dictates how and where the paint falls. The creation of each piece is a very physically demanding process that requires her all. The initial marks are an energetic dance around the canvas, and they burst with raw emotion and passion. In the early stages she throws, rubs, dribbles and pours radiant washes onto linen, responding to internal and external landscapes as they unfold themselves. However, in the final piece there is also a quiet calm and peacefulness present in each image. A place for the soul to rest. Spontaneous and instinctive, the paintings demand risk, courage and a weaving of magic out of what emerges. Surrendering to the canvas, she touches the place where mystery lies.

Yvonne was brought up on a farm and spent much of her childhood in Ireland, her mother's homeland. Inspired by the world and all it contains, she travelled widely in her twenties, with a thirst for exploration and discovery. She spent time living and working in Australia, Africa and Europe. One of her most formative journeys was spent with a horse-drawn community in England, discovering ancient, sacred and forgotten parts of our land.

Her spirit of curiosity and deep enquiry led her to pursue a degree in Philosophy and Literature at Brighton University. A formal fine art training in Sussex was the springboard for Yvonne's creativity. She now lives in Devon with her husband – and fellow artist – Mike Boyer and has four children.

Yvonne Coomber's work is exhibited nationally and internationally, and is held in a number of private and corporate collections around the world. Her work can be found at ART5 Gallery, Brighton (page 109), where she will have a solo show of new work in April this year.

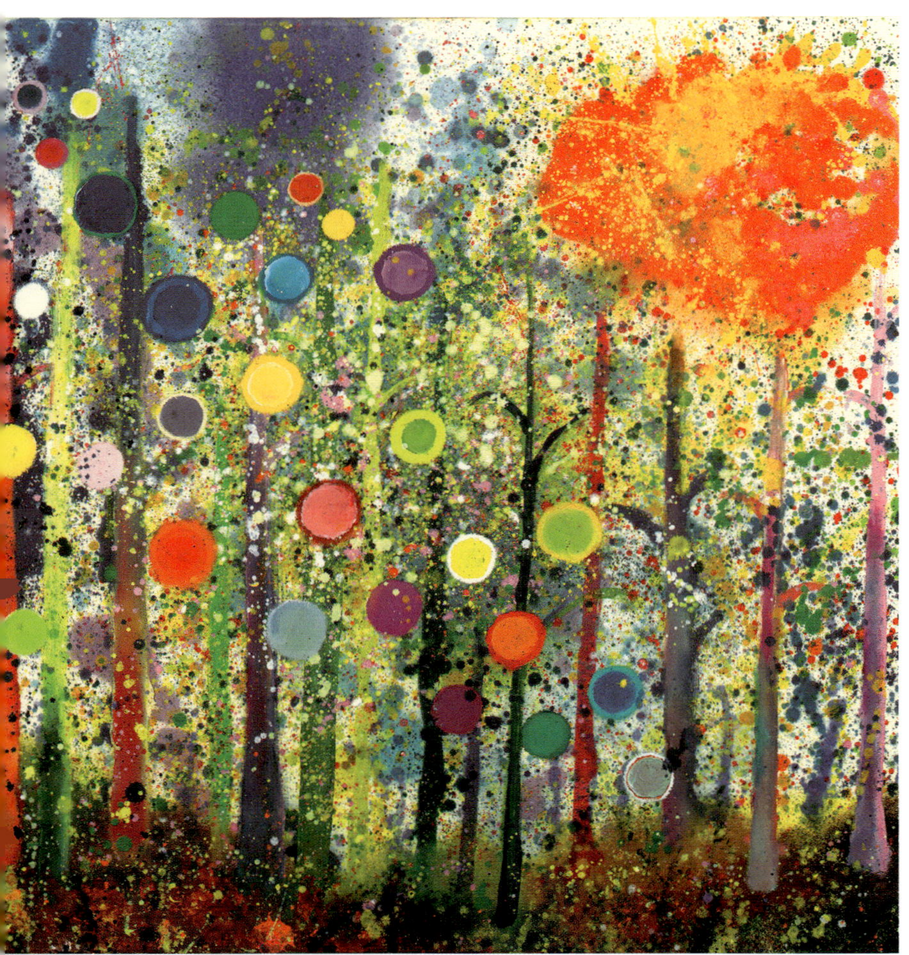

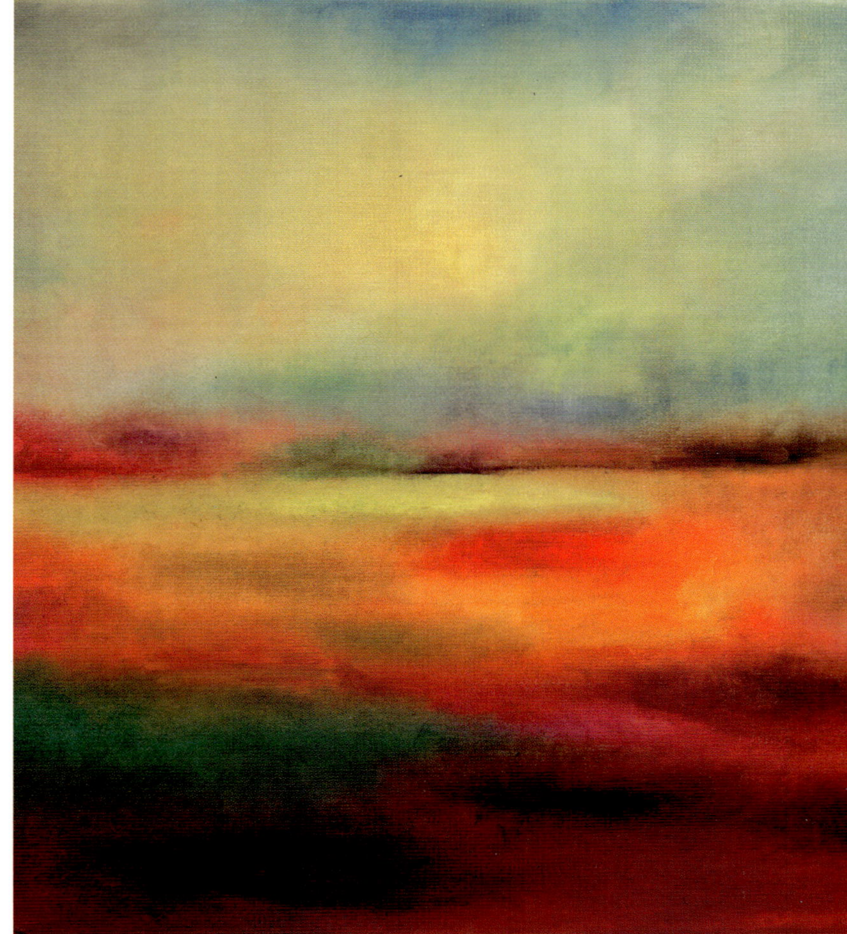

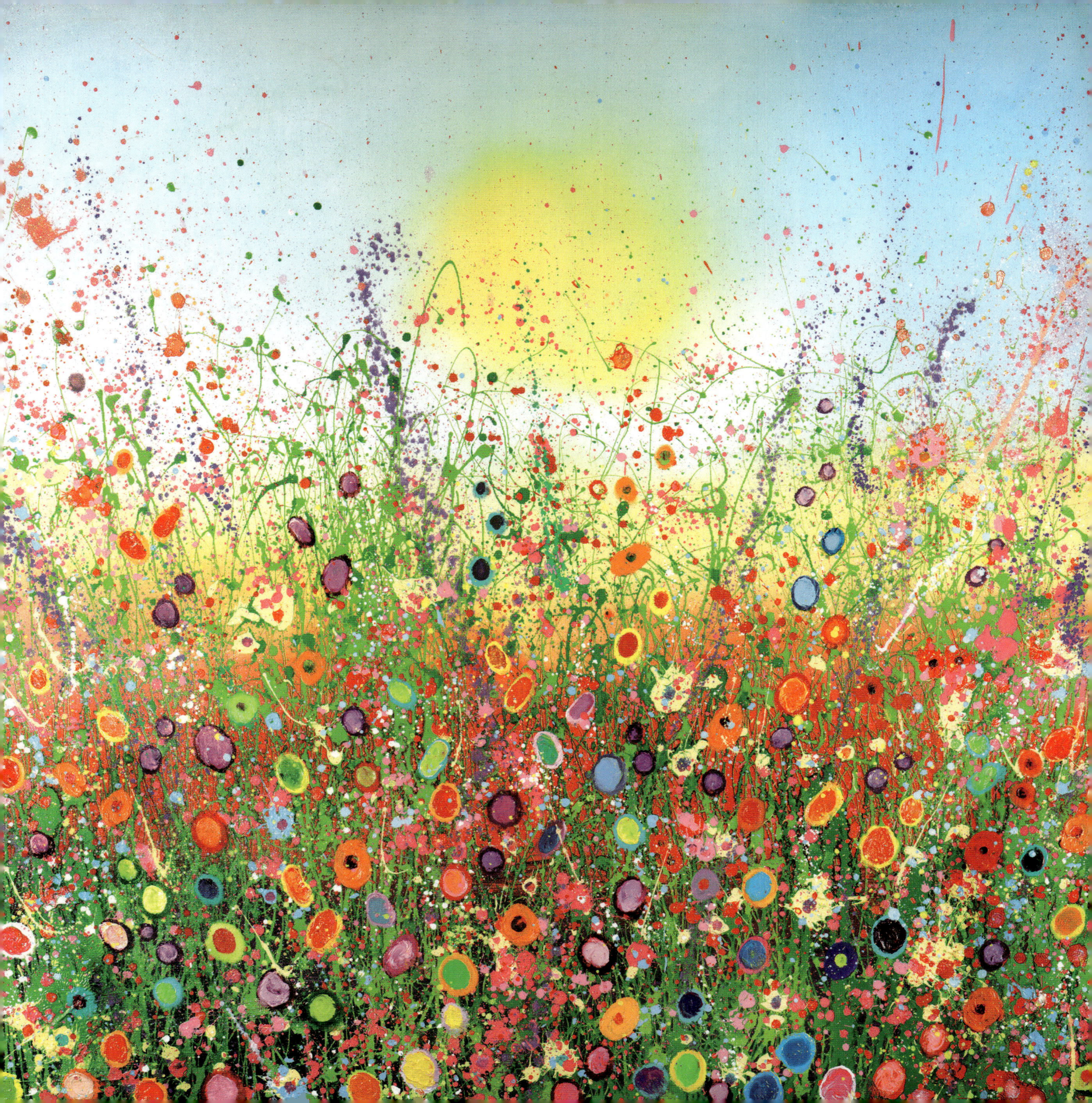

Kate Osborne

Artist
www.kateosborneart.com

Clockwise from top left:
Goldfinch; Barn Owl; Robins; Booth Museum Bugs; Fieldfare

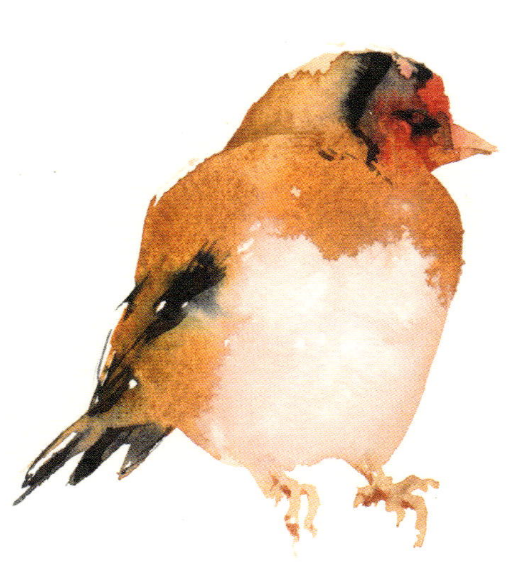

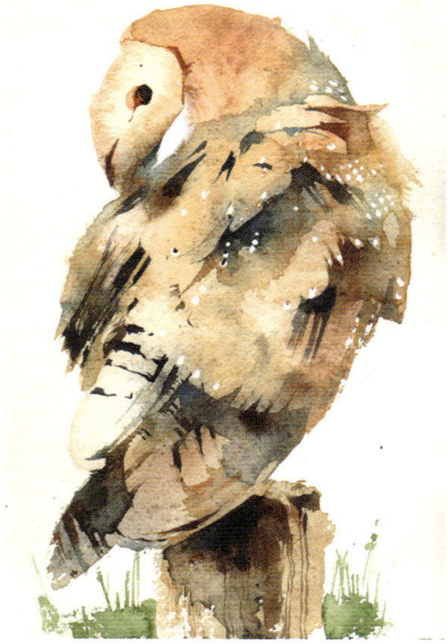

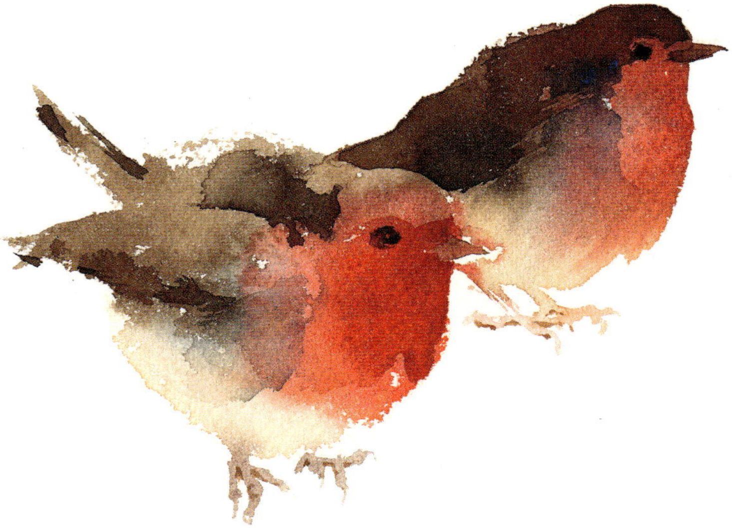

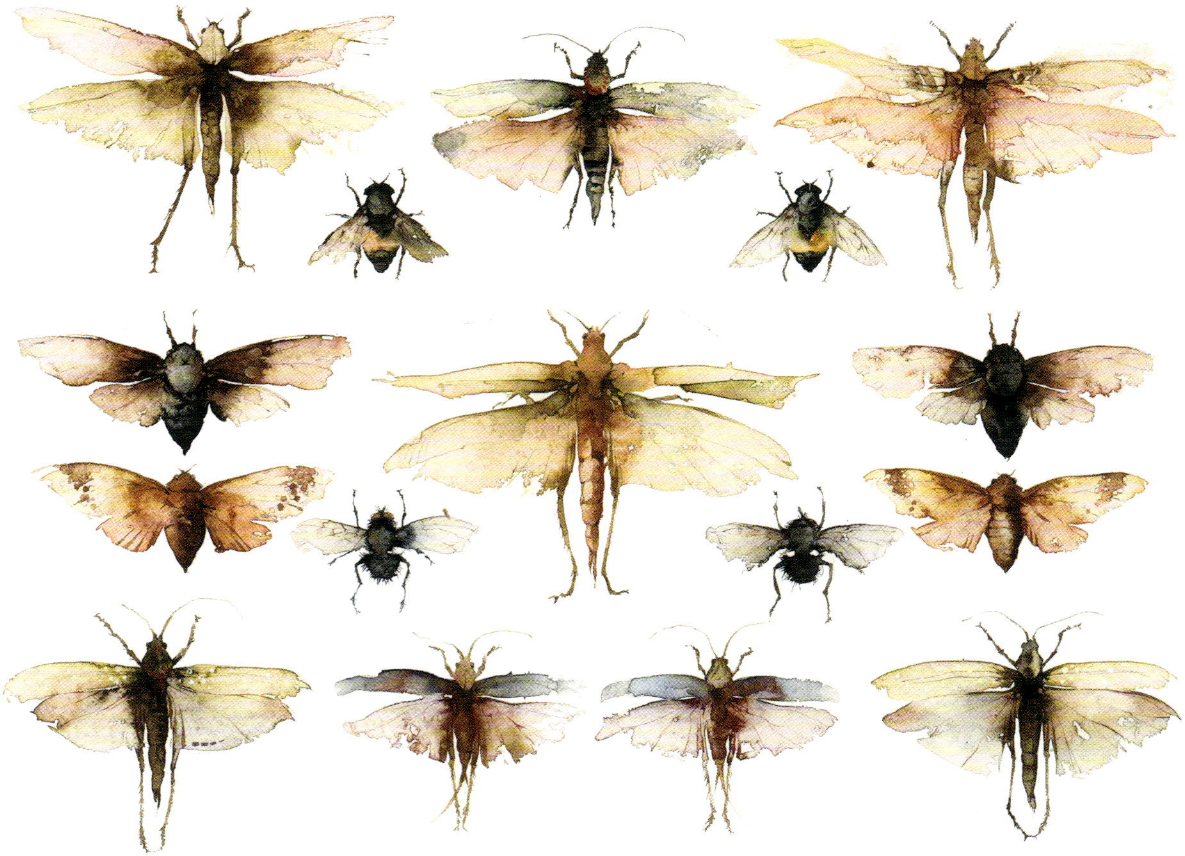

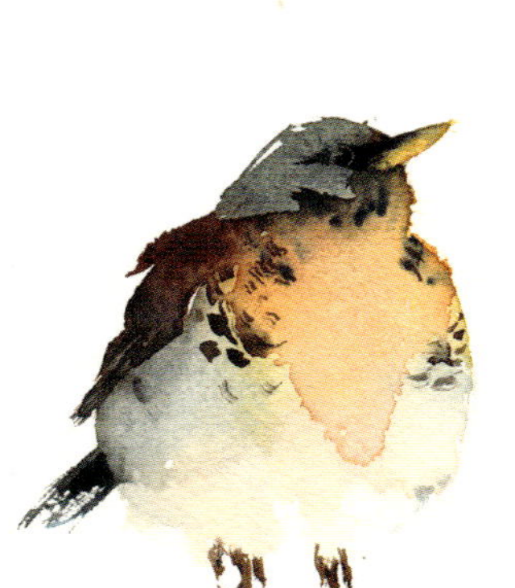

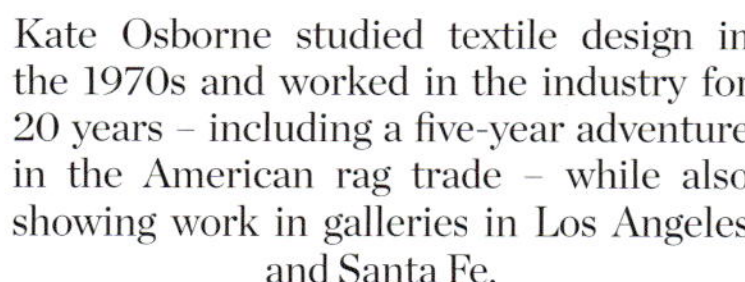

Kate Osborne studied textile design in the 1970s and worked in the industry for 20 years – including a five-year adventure in the American rag trade – while also showing work in galleries in Los Angeles and Santa Fe.

She has lived in Brighton for the past 30 years, moving from illustration and textile design to painting, and now also paints in oil. Whether painting still life, animals or landscape, Kate brings a rich sense of colour and energy to her work.

Exhibitions include the Royal Institute of Painters in Watercolour, the Society of Wildlife Artists and Brighton Artists Open Houses. Kate is also represented by Spa Galleries Tunbridge Wells, Nicholas Bowlby, and Yellow House Art Licensing. Her work is available as high-quality giclée prints, and is also licensed for use on greetings cards, tins, ceramics etc.

Suzanne Breakwell

Clockwise from top left:
Barn Owl; Hare; Wren & Foliage; Wren, Coal Tit & Blue Tit

Paper Artist/Maker
www.suzannebreakwell.com

The inspiration for Suzanne Breakwell's exquisite paper sculpture comes from an overwhelming love and fascination with the natural world. She spends much of her spare time outdoors walking and observing the character and detail of the flora and fauna she finds. Her aim is to capture a unique and playful character within each of the pieces she makes.

Suzanne studied HND Photography at Bradford & Ilkley Community College, and then a BA(Hons) Technical Arts Design for Film & Theatre at Wimbledon School of Art, London, graduating in 2000. She currently exhibits and sells her work at selected galleries throughout the UK, contemporary art and craft fairs, and her website (above). She was awarded the Peer Prize at MADE Brighton craft and design fair 2014.

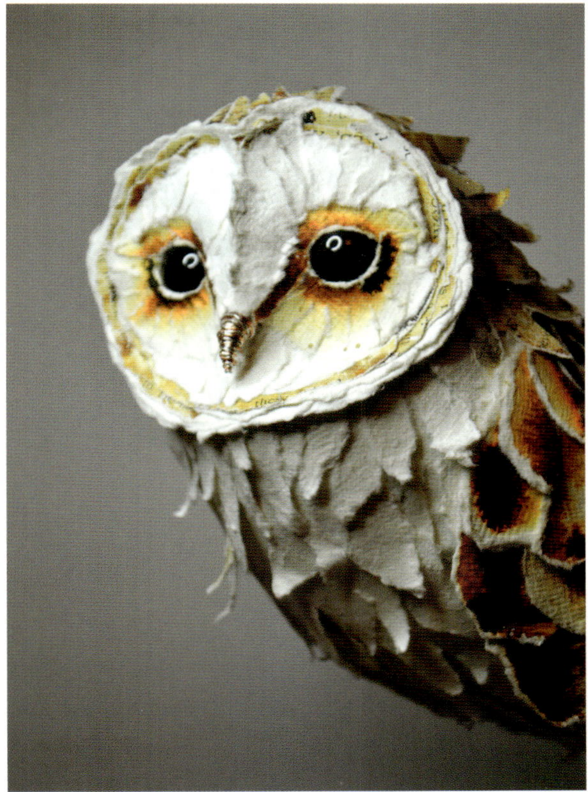

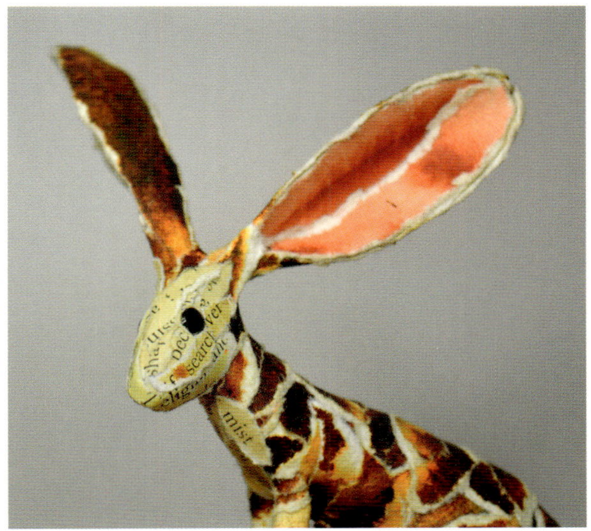

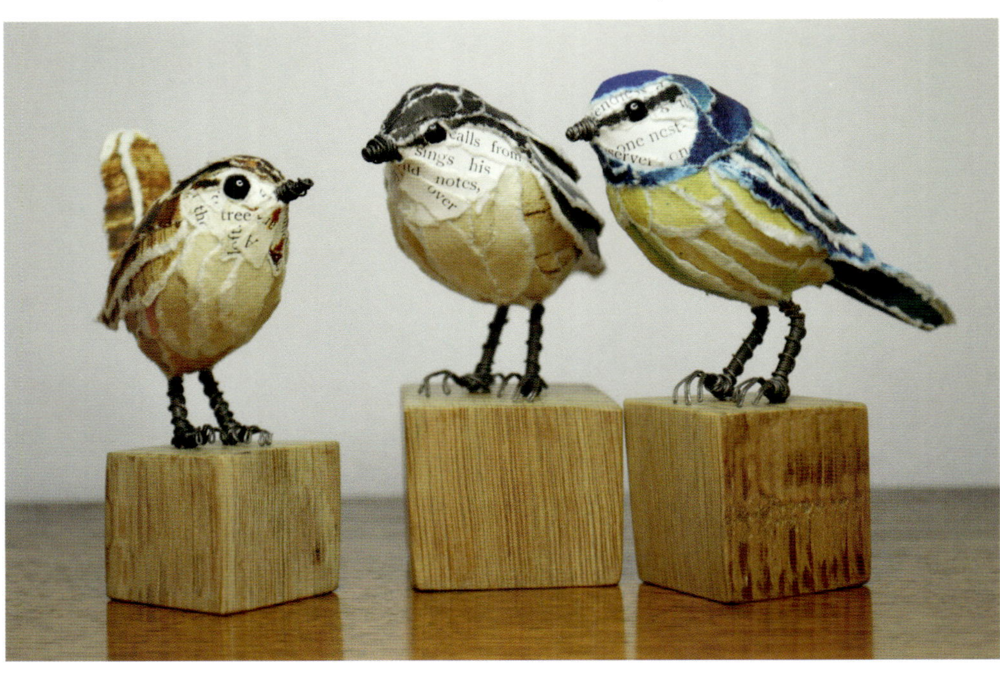

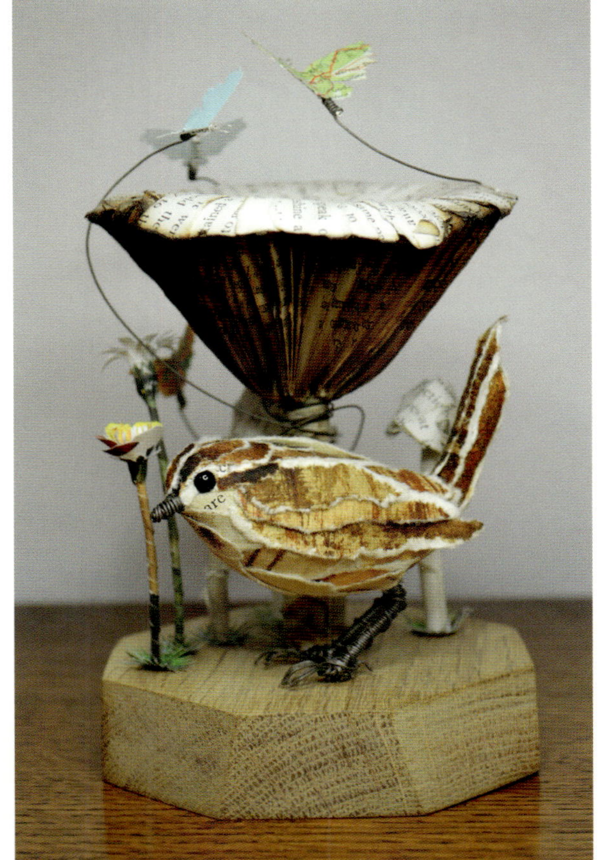

Leila Godden

Artist
www.leilagodden.com

Clockwise from top left:
Coastal Intervention 901; Elemental; Deep and Golden

Leila Godden AUA is an associate member of the United Society of Artists, regularly exhibiting in London as well as galleries in Brighton, Chalk Gallery in Lewes (page 112), and elsewhere in the UK. She specialises in seascapes and abstracts with exquisite textural qualities.

The paintings evolve through a process of improvisation, where artist interacts with materials, leading and following as marks are made and layers are unveiled.

Her source of inspiration is her connection with the sea. The vast panorama of changing light, dramatic weather and powerful water, framed by rocks solid with history, yet transient with time and the rhythm of the earth. The minutiae of rock pools juxtaposed against the expansive sweep of sea and sky. A completeness incorporating time and space, stillness and movement.

Her paintings seek to recreate this connection, and to evoke a personal response in you, the viewer. She aims to create art that will touch you more deeply than just a pretty picture.

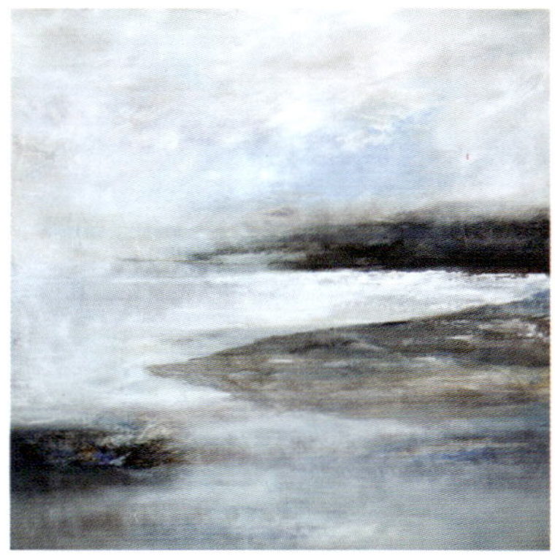

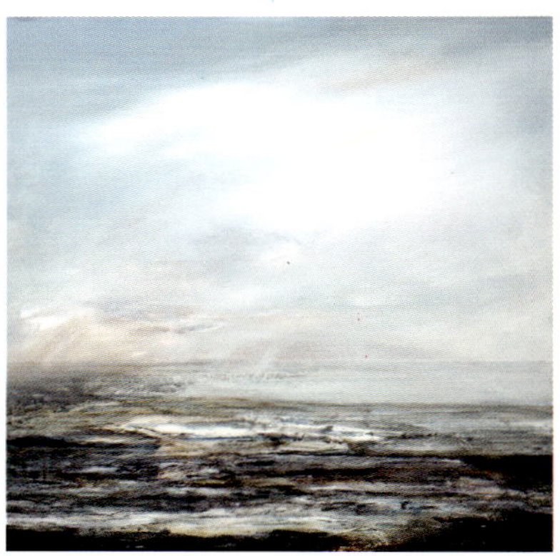

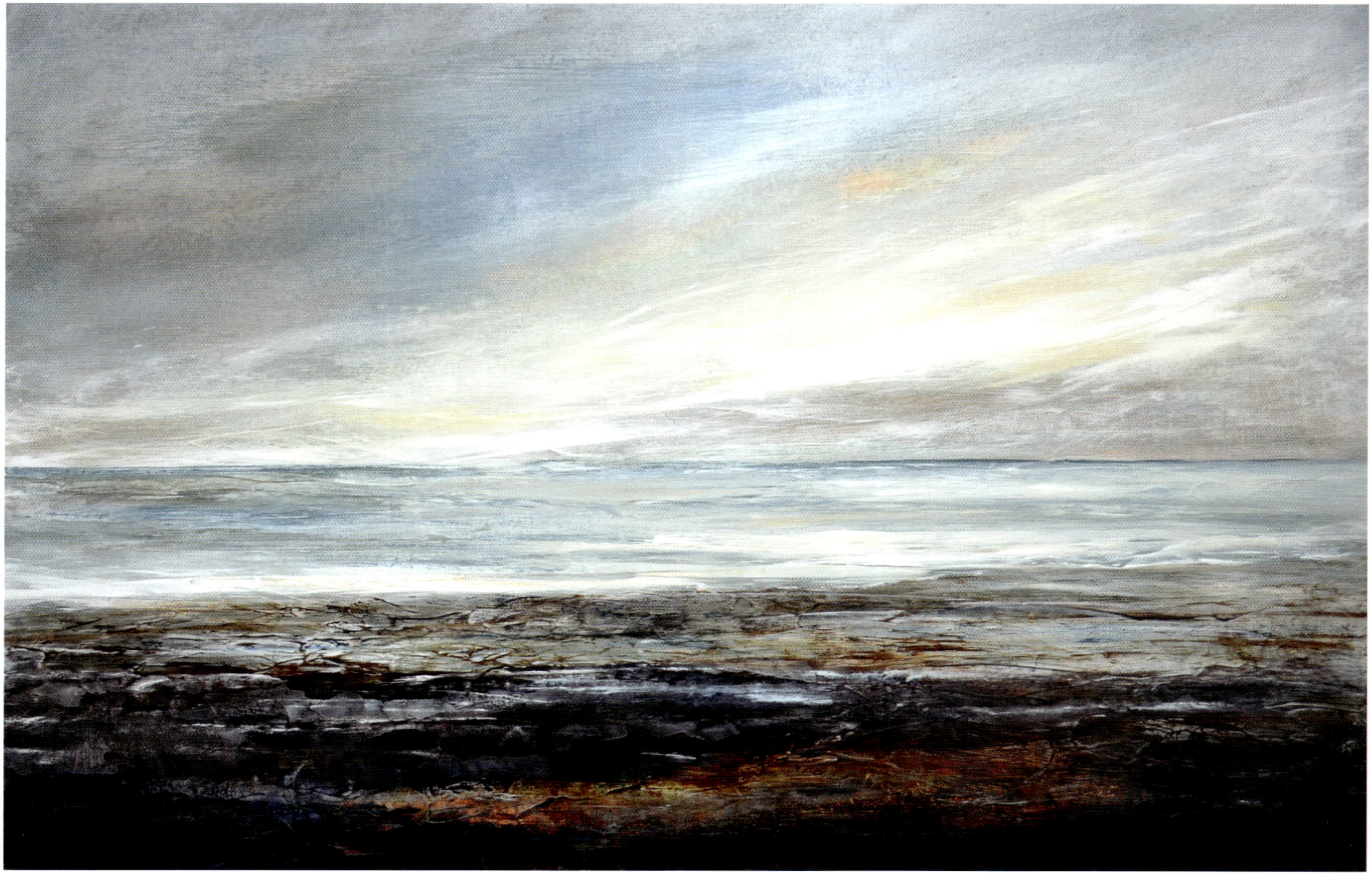

George Antoni

Artist
www.georgeantoni.net

Clockwise from top left:
Coastal Intervention 3; CU 404; CU 412; CU 405; CU 403

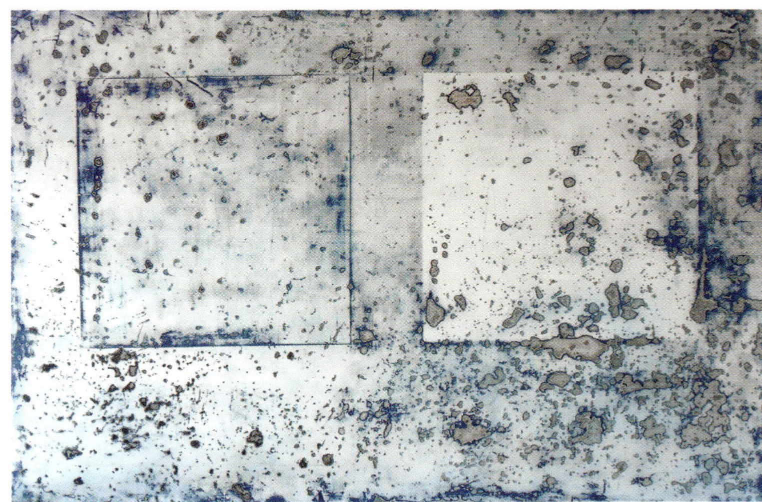

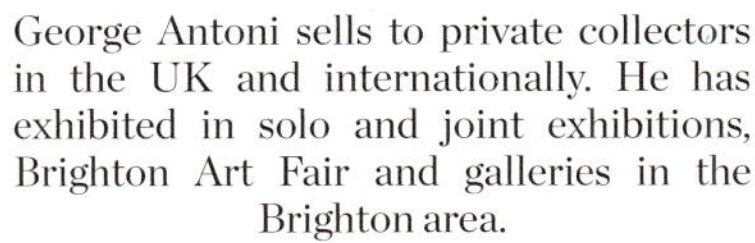

George Antoni sells to private collectors in the UK and internationally. He has exhibited in solo and joint exhibitions, Brighton Art Fair and galleries in the Brighton area.

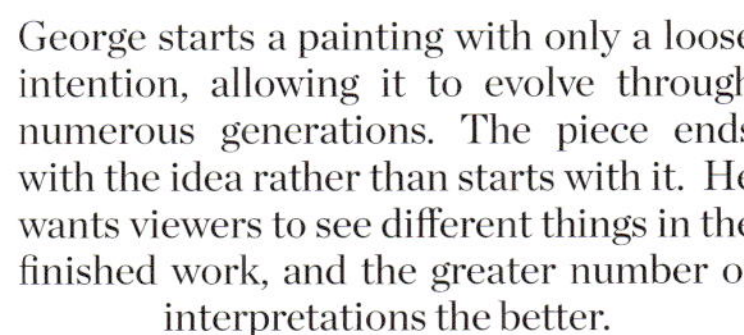

George starts a painting with only a loose intention, allowing it to evolve through numerous generations. The piece ends with the idea rather than starts with it. He wants viewers to see different things in the finished work, and the greater number of interpretations the better.

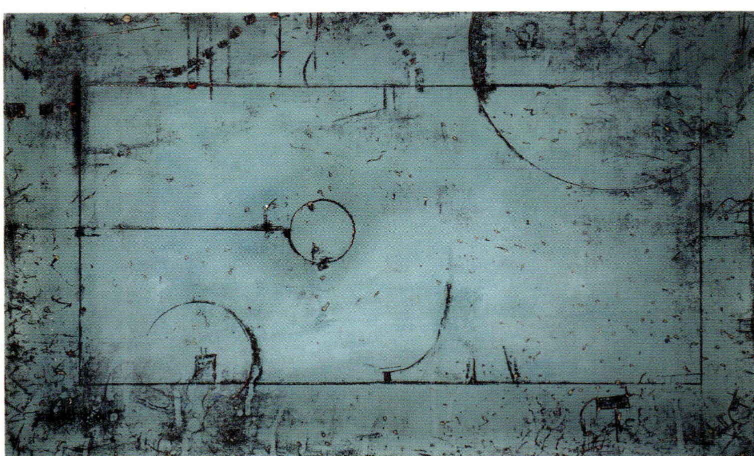

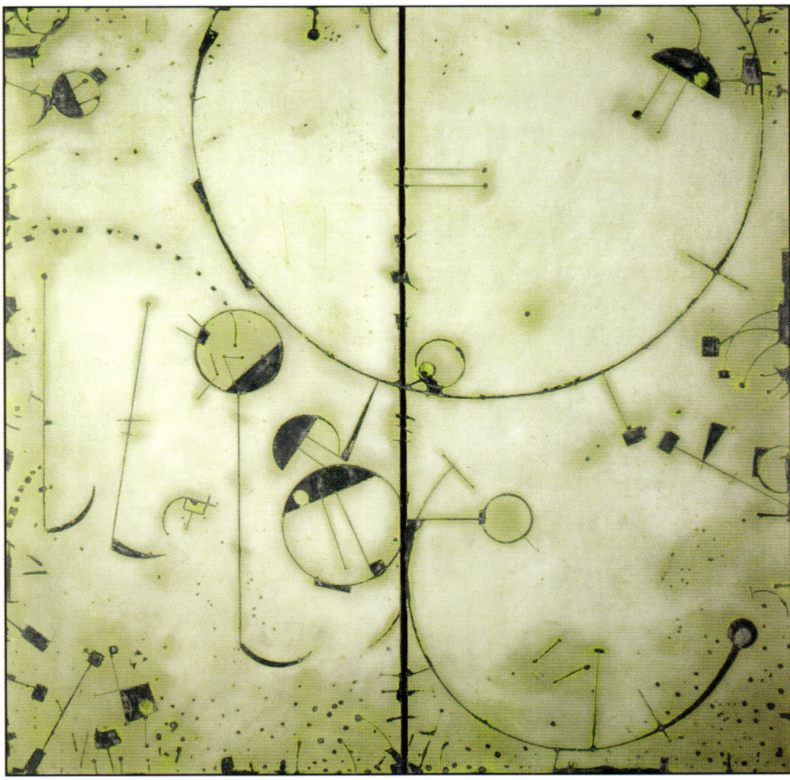

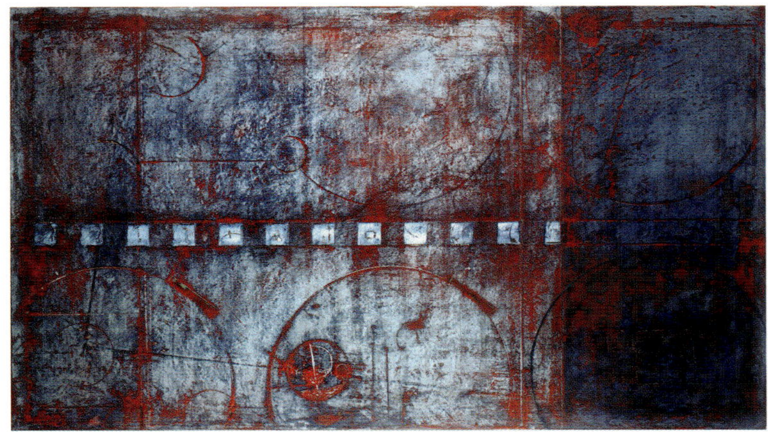

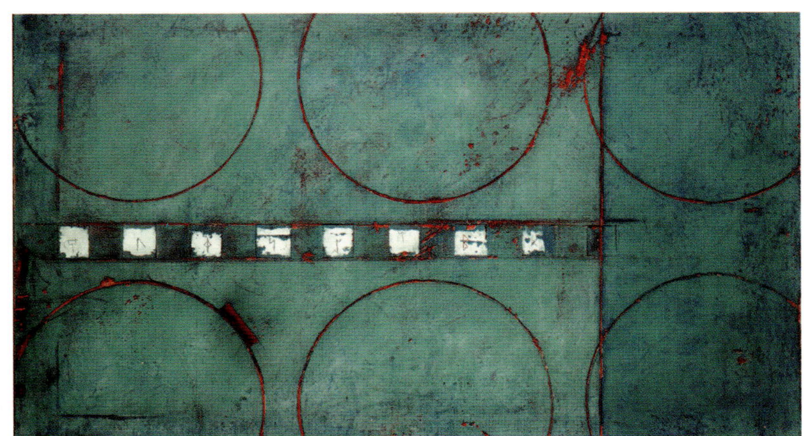

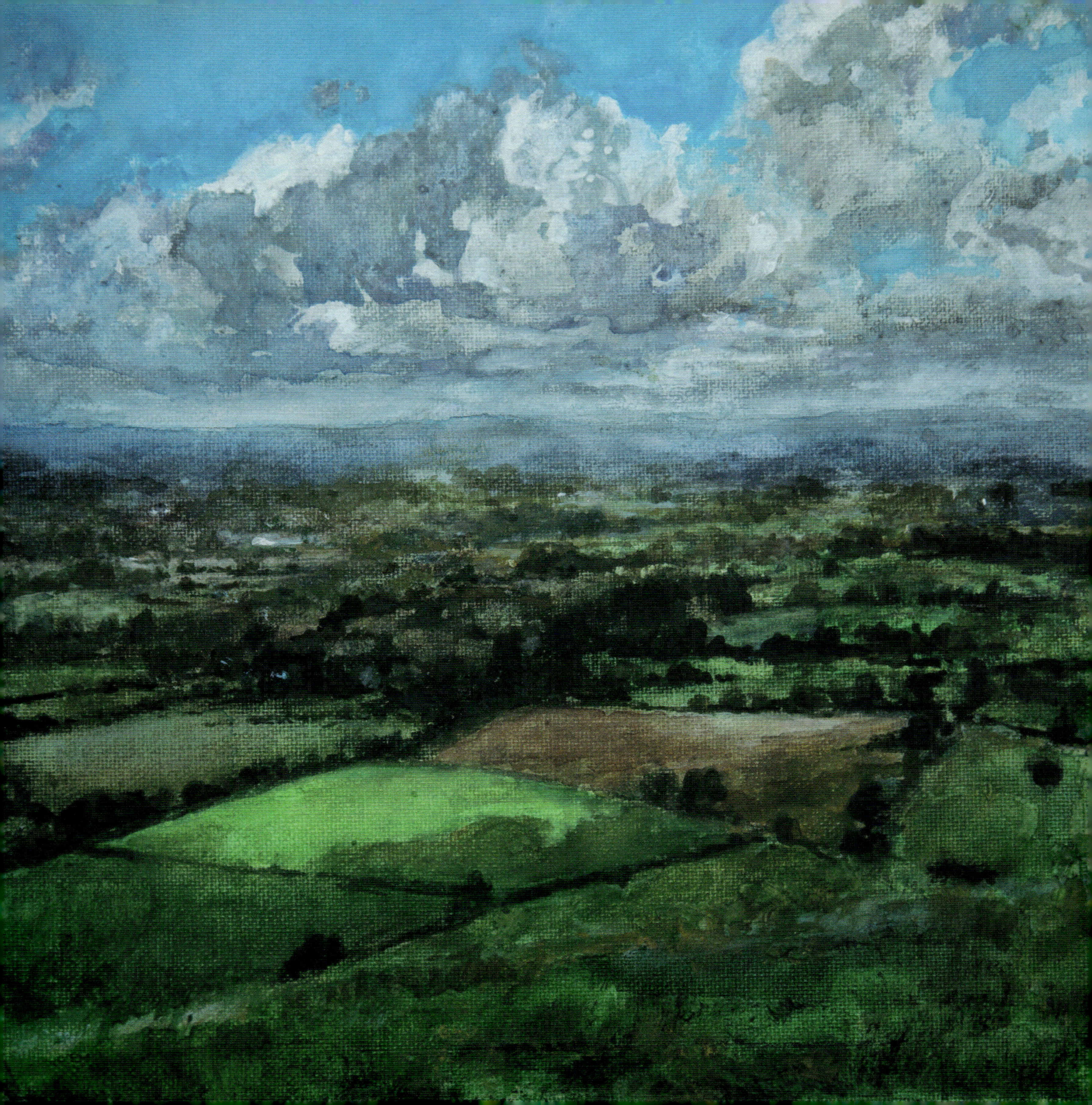

Rob Ollerenshaw

Artist
www.artymagazines.com

Clockwise from top left: Devil's Dyke in Winter; Hove Beach at Sunset; Hove Sunset
Opposite page: Sussex Weald

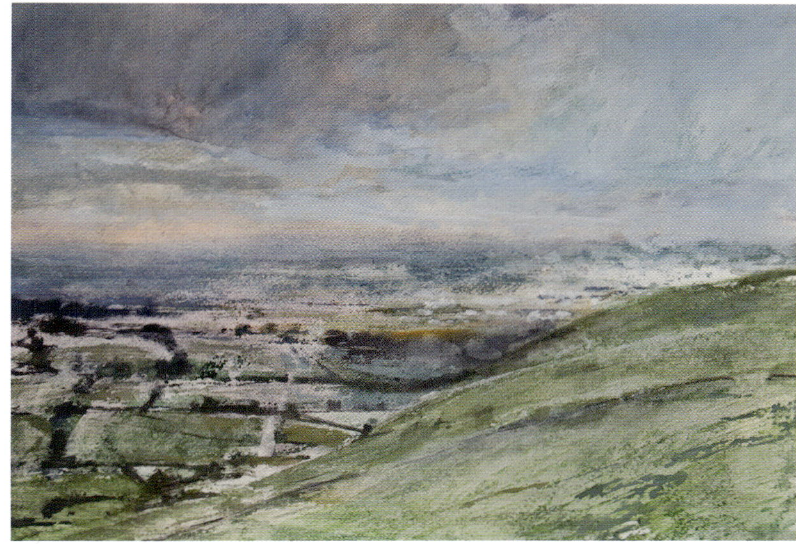

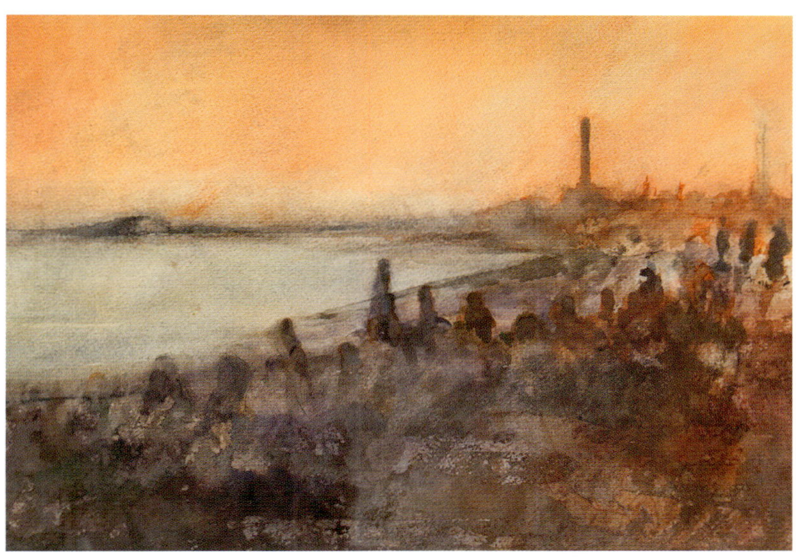

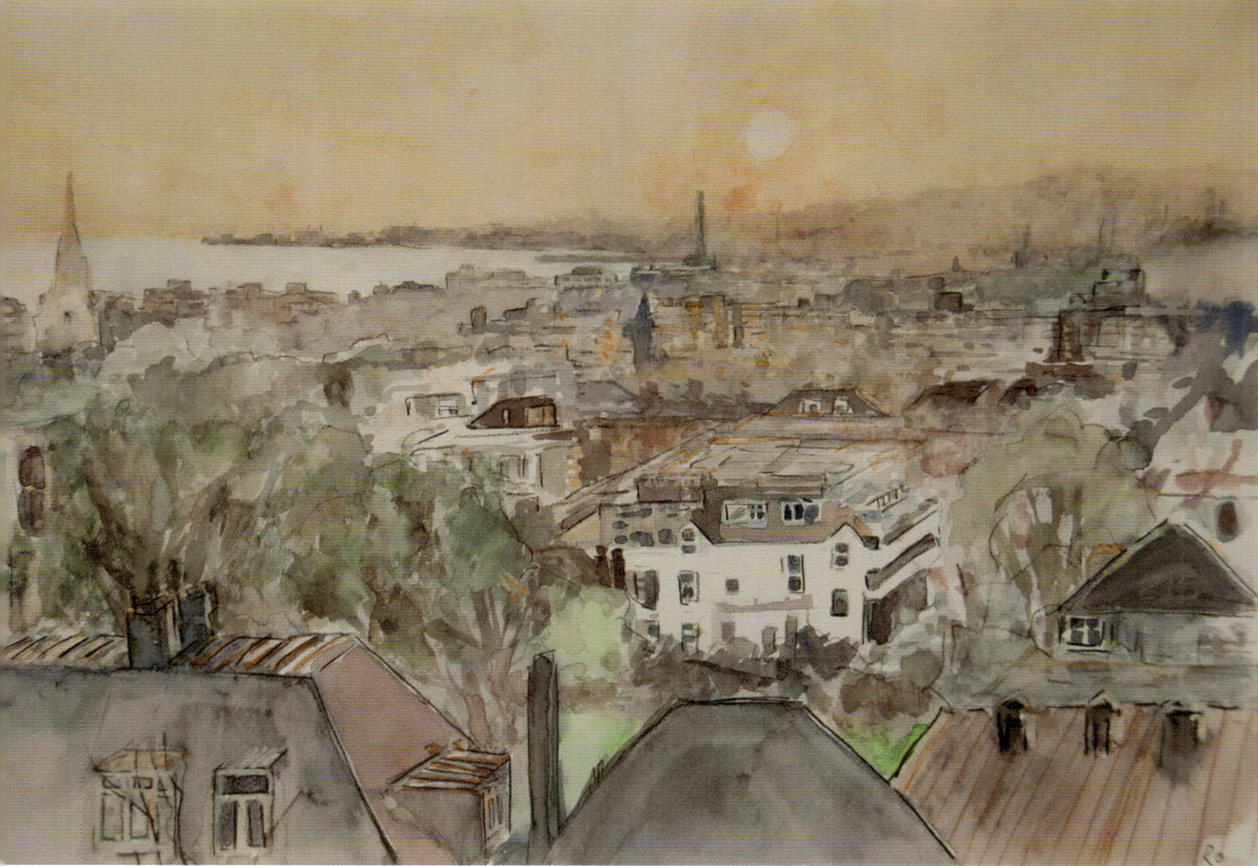

The city of Brighton and Hove, and the Sussex shoreline and countryside, provide endless inspiration for local artist Rob Ollerenshaw. He uses a variety of media – watercolour, gouache, pastel, inks and wax – working on paper, canvas and board.

Rob's paintings are a synthesis of light, colour and texture and a personal impression of a particular place and time. Each painting is a challenge to portray his experience of the scene – the fluctuation of light and shadow and the movement of people coming and going.

A fine art graduate, Rob regularly exhibits in Brighton's Artists Open Houses. He also paints the landscape of Brittany in France, where he has exhibited several times.

Claire Harrison

Artist
www.claire-harrison.co.uk

Clockwise from top left:
Migration 1; Looking Up to the Sky; Helenium; Spirals

Claire has been passionate about art and nature since she was a child. After graduating with a Fine Art degree in 2001, she had her first solo show in 2002 at Farnham Maltings. This exhibition's popularity led to her being offered a studio, and Claire was based in Farnham until 2009, when she relocated to West Sussex. Since 2001, she has successfully exhibited in many solo and selected group exhibitions across the UK, including frequent appearances in London art fairs.

> *To Claire, landscape is a beautiful ecosystem where organisms are reliant upon each other*

Claire enjoys sharing her enthusiasm for art, and has taught for more than 10 years; running demonstrations, talks and workshops for various audiences. She regularly teaches at Guildford Institute and Evolution Arts, Brighton, and also mentors fellow artists.

Claire creates brightly coloured images of nature from a viewpoint that we do not normally see; her inspiration is taken from the plants and insects around her.

This research is developed into paintings of oil, mixed media, ink or watercolour that show the pattern and order hidden within nature. To Claire, the landscape is a beautiful ecosystem where organisms are reliant upon each other.

Claire's work reflects the vivid colours of nature; she combines different elements of the landscape so that we reconsider nature as a perfectly ordered mechanism.

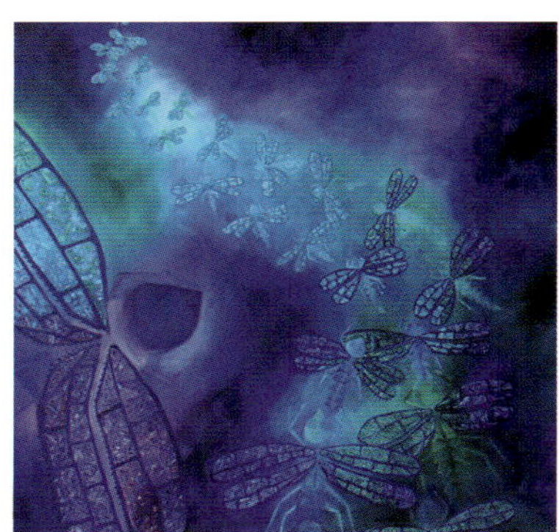

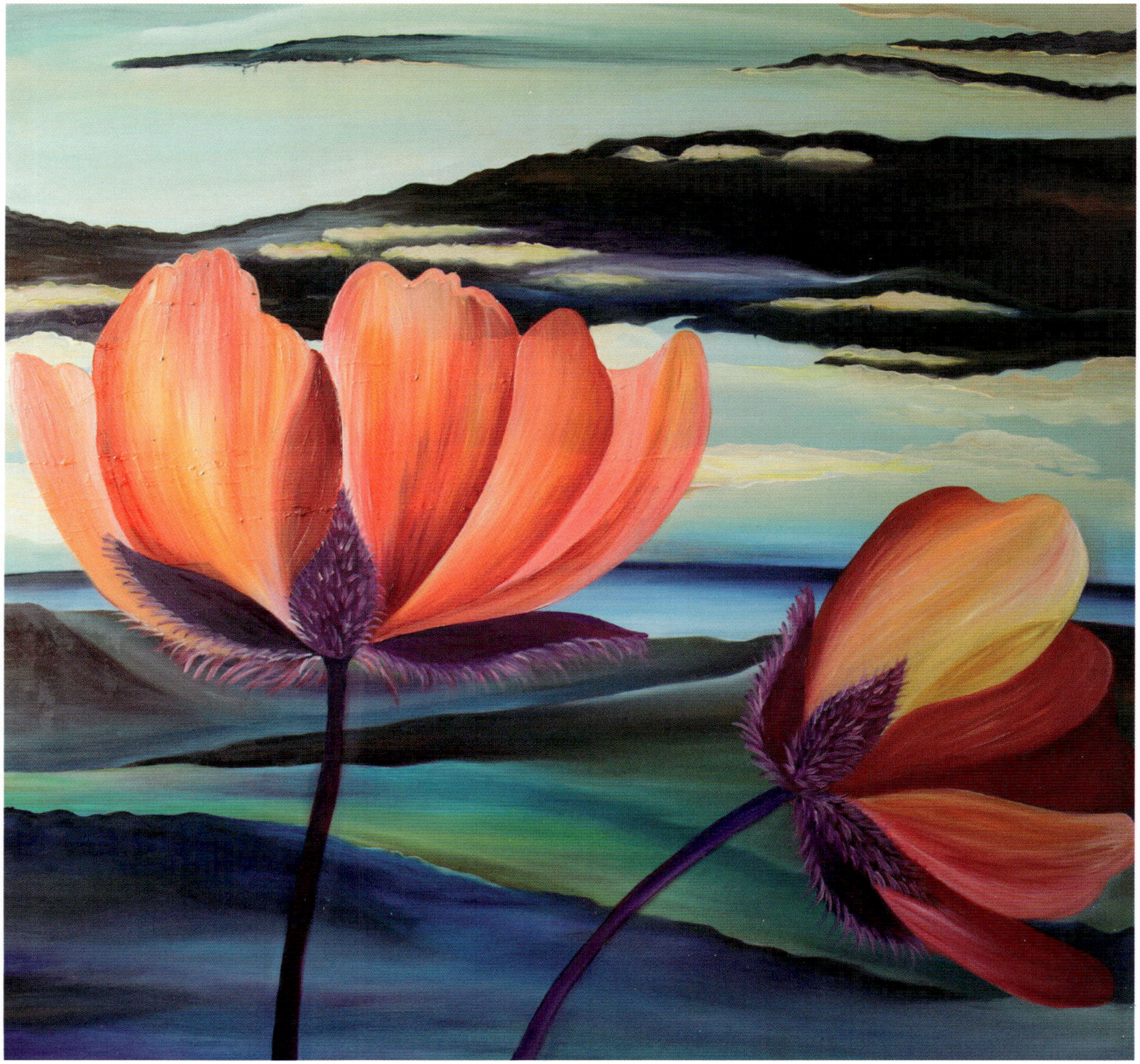

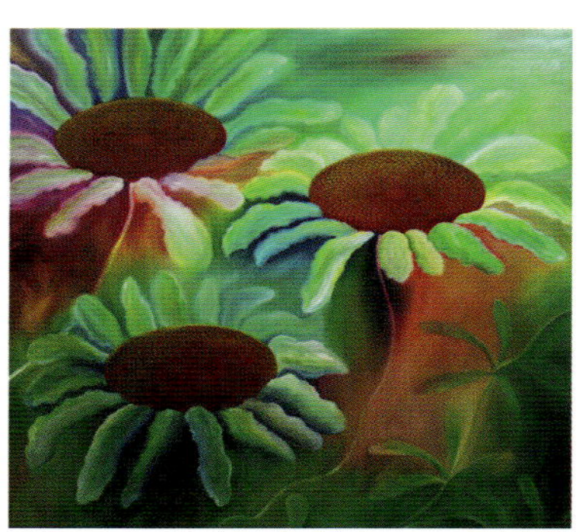

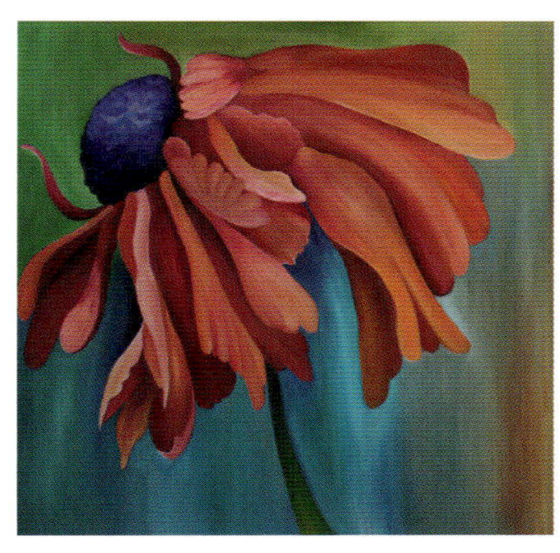

Stephanie Else / Glass in Fusion

Clockwise from top left:
Pink & Black; Mileage; Rainbow Flower; Aqua Scape

Artist
www.glassinfusion.co.uk

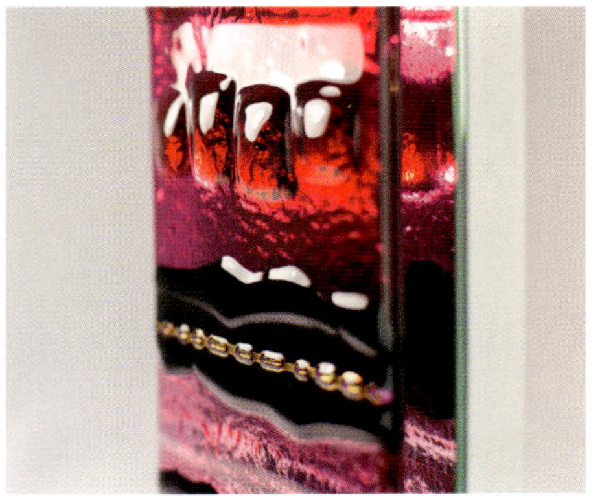

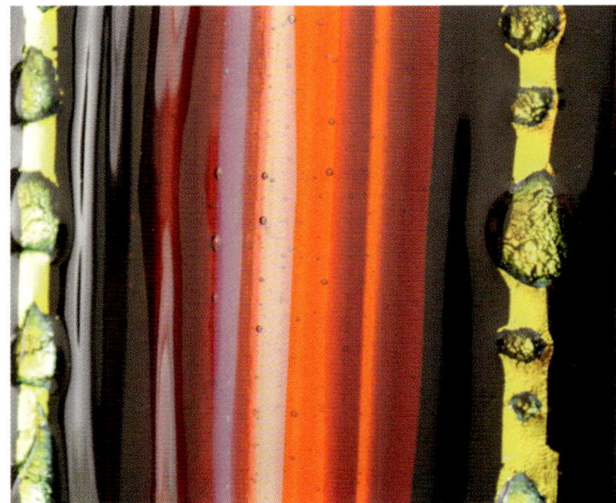

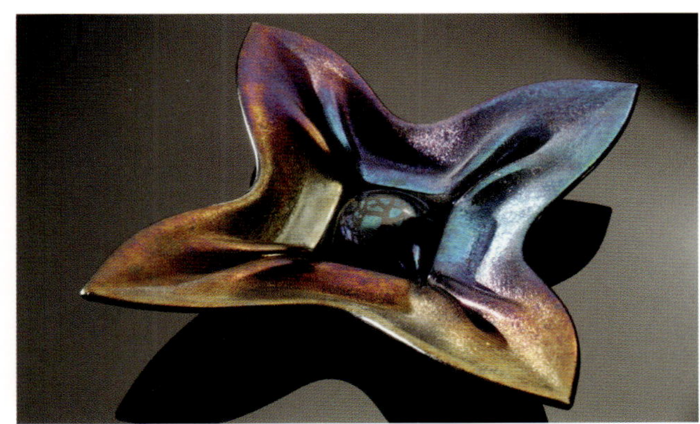

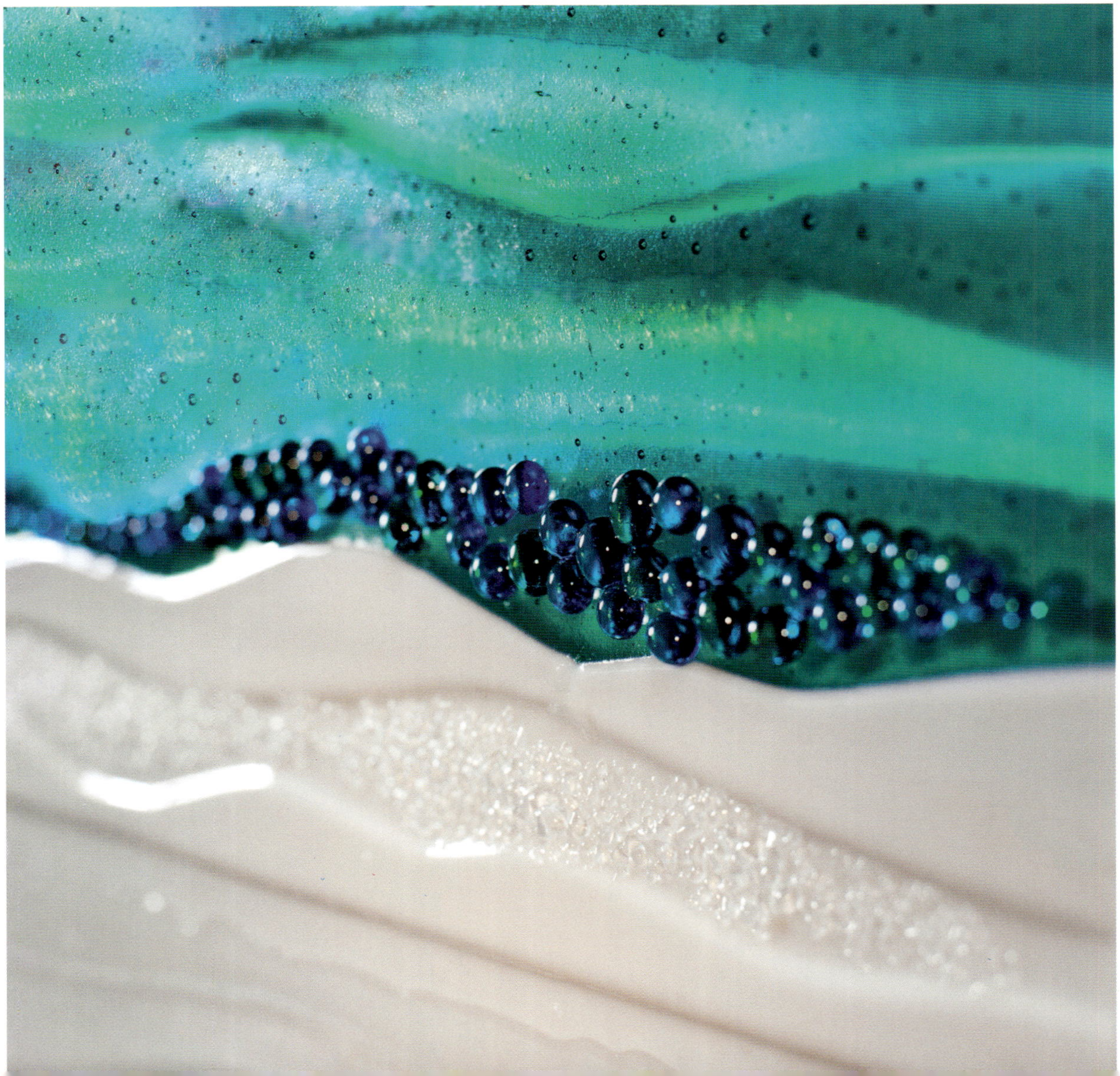

Stephanie Else specialises in making beautiful contemporary glass designs using a variety of kiln-forming techniques. Working with a combination of transparent and opaque glass, she adds metals, foils and lustres to produce a stunning range of both decorative and functional works of art and jewellery.

Inspired by the glass itself, Stephanie combines surface texture, pattern and colour within the glass to create beautifully tactile pieces while exploiting the natural translucent and jewel-like qualities it possesses.

I enjoy the unpredictability of my work – never knowing exactly what a finished piece will look like when it comes out of the kiln, and the fact that no two pieces can ever be the same

As well as exhibiting her work in galleries, Stephanie has also completed numerous commission pieces and interior design projects. She offers a bespoke service and is happy to discuss any design ideas you may have. Stephanie also enjoys sharing her extensive knowledge by running a series of fun and informative glass-making courses, details of which can be found on her website (above).

Patrick O'Donnell

Contemporary Visual Artist
www.patrick-odonnell.co.uk

Clockwise from top left:
Origins 17; Hybrid 9; Hybrid 2; Hybrid 4

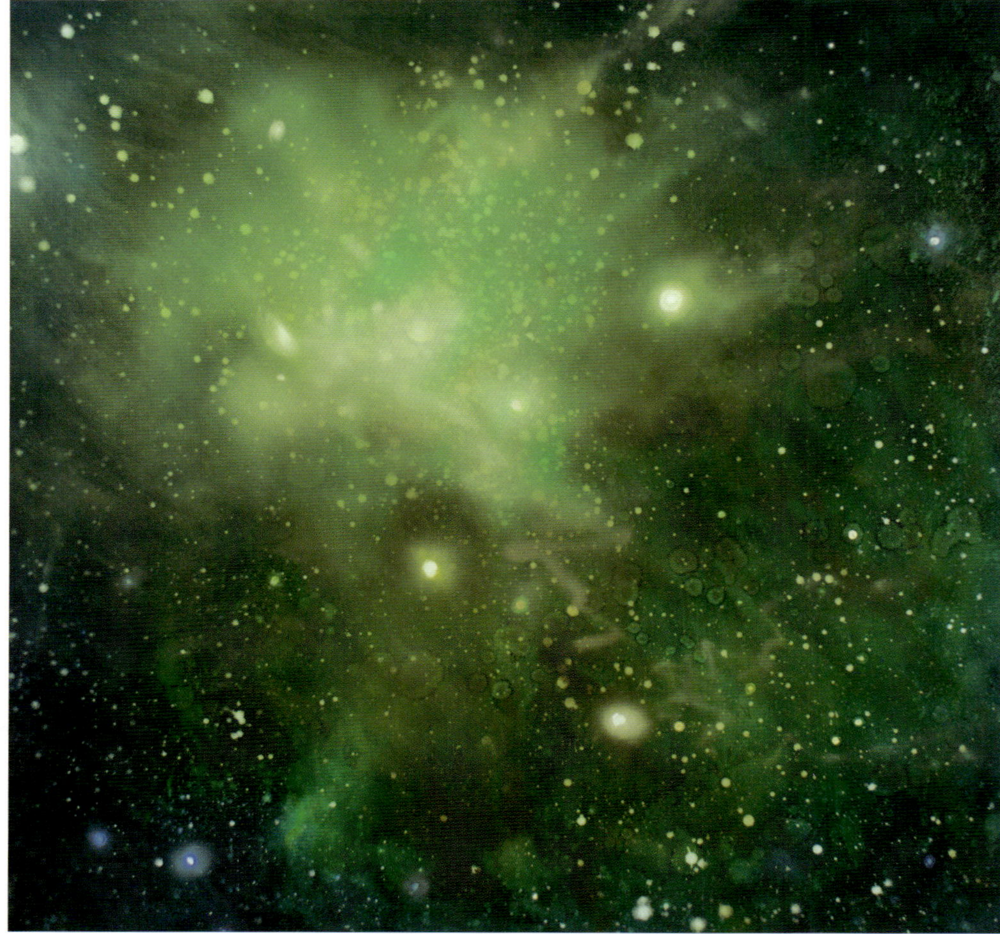

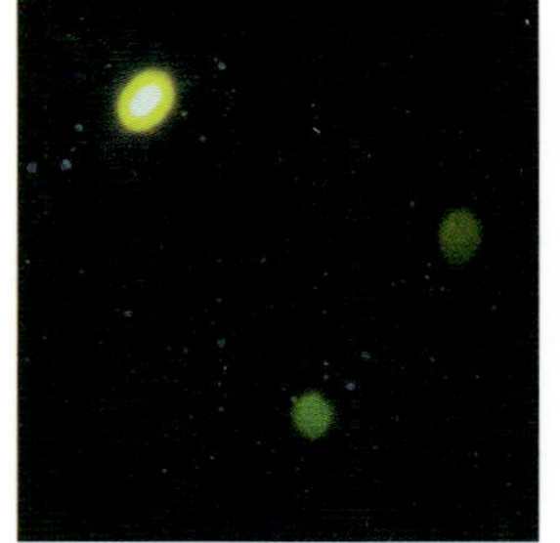

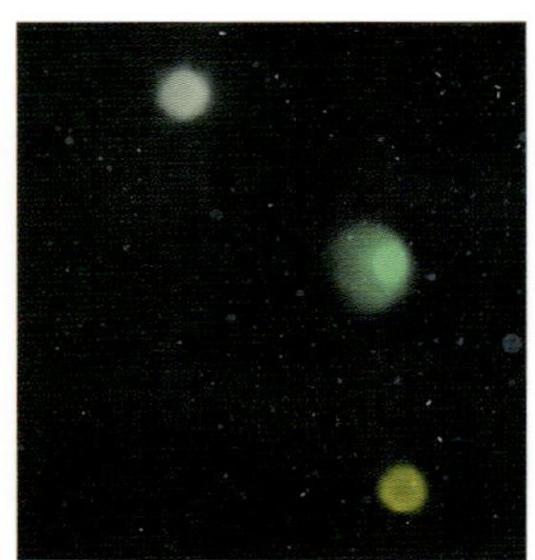

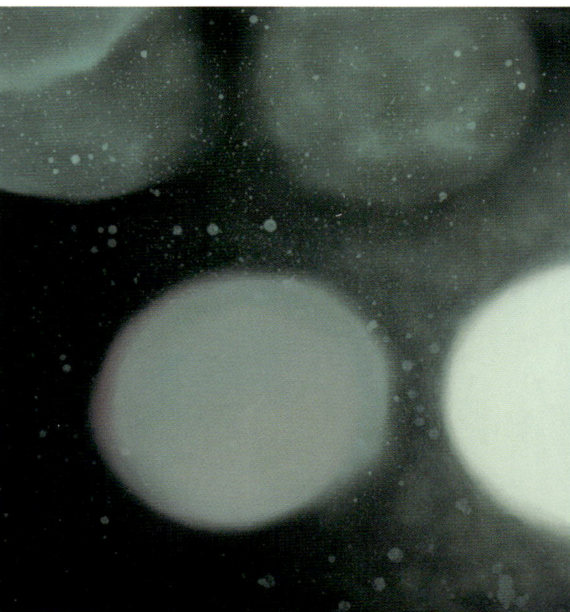

Through his focus on light, colour and abstract shapes, Patrick O'Donnell's oil paintings and ink works explore notions of transition, ideas of perception and our place in the cosmos.

His current body of work – the Origins series – displays Patrick's interest in space and cosmic imagery. He responds to the images beamed down from the Hubble Telescope, with its spectrum of colours, gestures and marks from the myriad densities of dust and gas. Referencing Daniel Altschuler's statement: 'Look at your hand. It is made of atoms. These atoms did not always exist; they were produced inside stars', his paintings explore cosmic atoms as building blocks for our very existence through the medium of oils. With a nod to post-war Abstract Expressionism and its European counterpart Tachisme, the paintings begin life on the floor with loose applications of thinned medium applied with plant sprayers and new celestial images reveal themselves in the painting process.

Running parallel to the Origins series, the Reconstruction series adopts the technique of grisaille (tonal under-painting). This series explores how light indicates human presence. Based on stills taken from various crime-related television programmes and, in particular, transitional shots between pivotal scenes, the titles play with the idea of reconstructed moments. Dark bands at the top and bottom frame the action like a wide-screen TV. They deal with reconstructed light, created and operated by the human hand. The term 'bokeh' has been defined as 'the way the camera lens renders out-of-focus light'. Anything that isn't in the depth of field loses clarity and becomes blurred. These paintings bring forward those out-of-focus parts to take centre stage, as it is these transient moments that allow the imagination to complete the scene. The human presence is suggested; but in what form we do not know.

The Hybrid paintings combine the two approaches adopted in the Origins and Reconstruction paintings and offer an otherworldliness resting somewhere between the familiar and the unfamiliar. These paintings display a renewed interest in abstraction and experimentation with translucent layers of oil paint and medium.

Patrick is showing a range of these paintings in his solo exhibition entitled 'Wavelengths' at The Education Centre, Homerton University Hospital NHS Foundation Trust, Homerton Row, London, until June 2015. For further details see www.homerton.nhs.uk/about-us/art-in-the-hospital/wavelengths-patrick-odonnell-at-homerton/

Kellie Miller

Artist
www.kelliemiller.com

Clockwise from left:
Stillness; Niche; What Lies Beyond

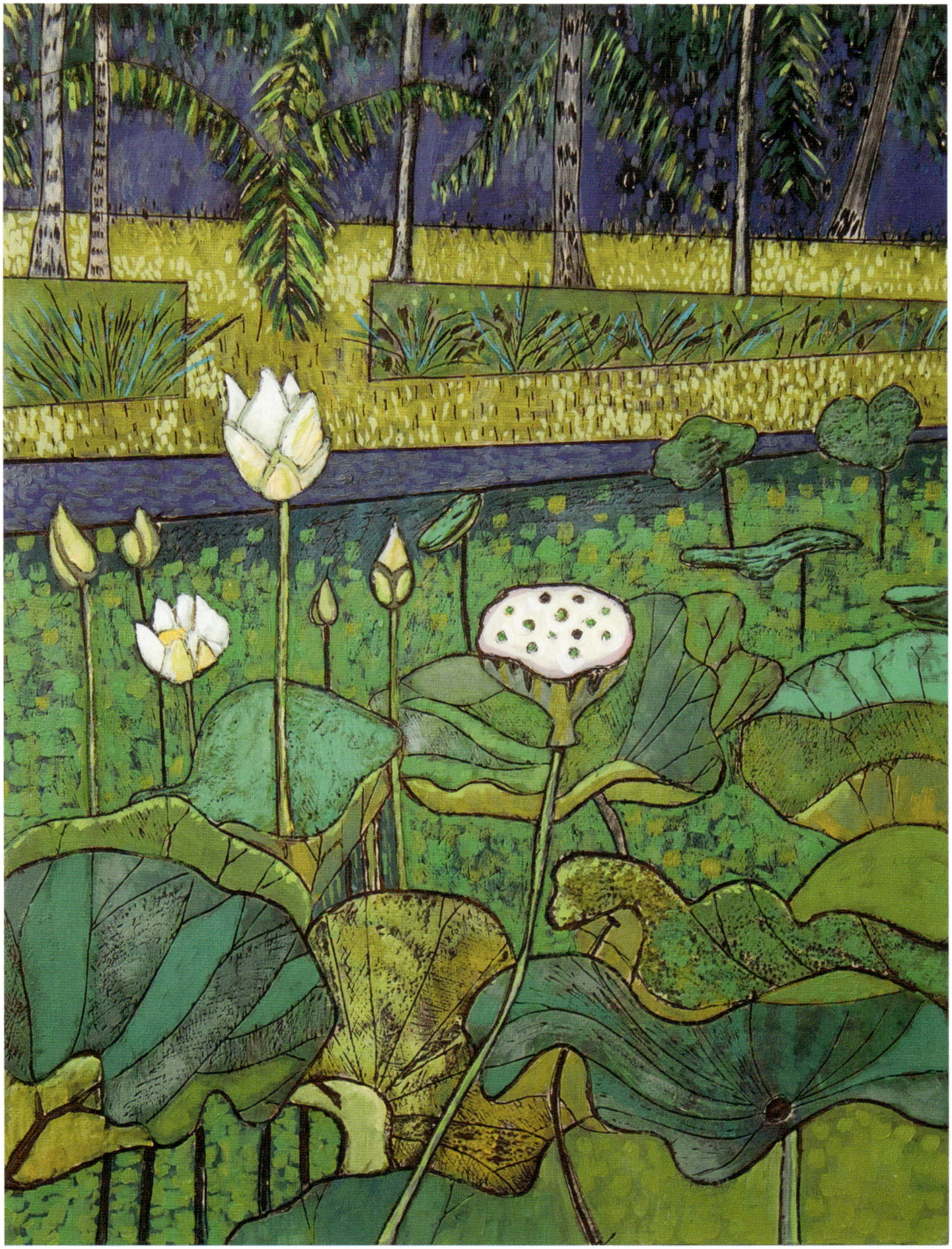

Kellie Miller's work is inspired by nature and travel, depicted in either a direct or abstract way. She has a talent for conveying her subject matter and messages in a simplistic manner, yet her approach and the method of construction of her work is far from simple.

Her unique pieces, which can require up to 27 stages to complete, are tactile carved paintings. They can be a montage of places she has visited, where she absorbs the imagery and atmosphere of a place and then translates them into her pieces.

Kellie's work is distinctive in perspective, materials, texture and colour. Her works are also reflective, calm and approachable, often invoking in the viewer the need to reach out and touch them.

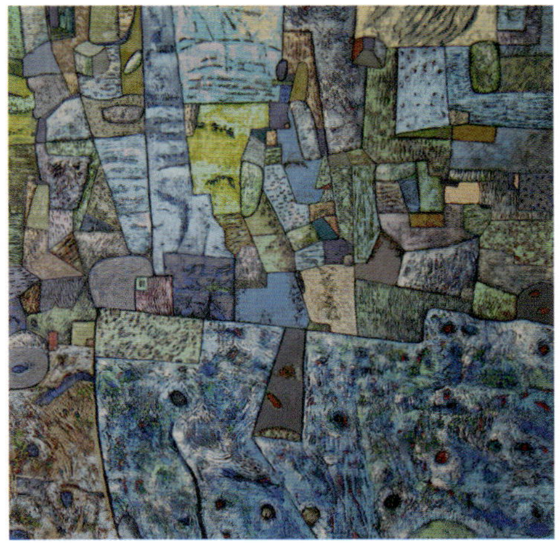

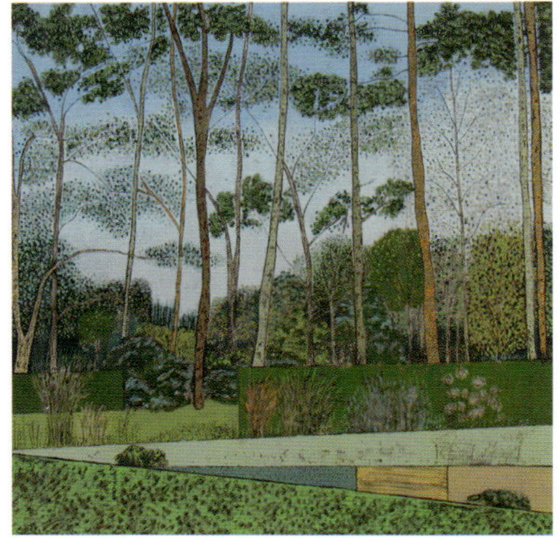

Louisa Crispin

Artist
www.louisacrispin.co.uk

Clockwise from top left: Lichen on Hawthorne iii, Sissinghurst; Lichen on Birch v; Lichen on Crack Willow; Lichen on Crab Apple

I'm captivated by the way lichen grows and enjoy searching for just the right stick

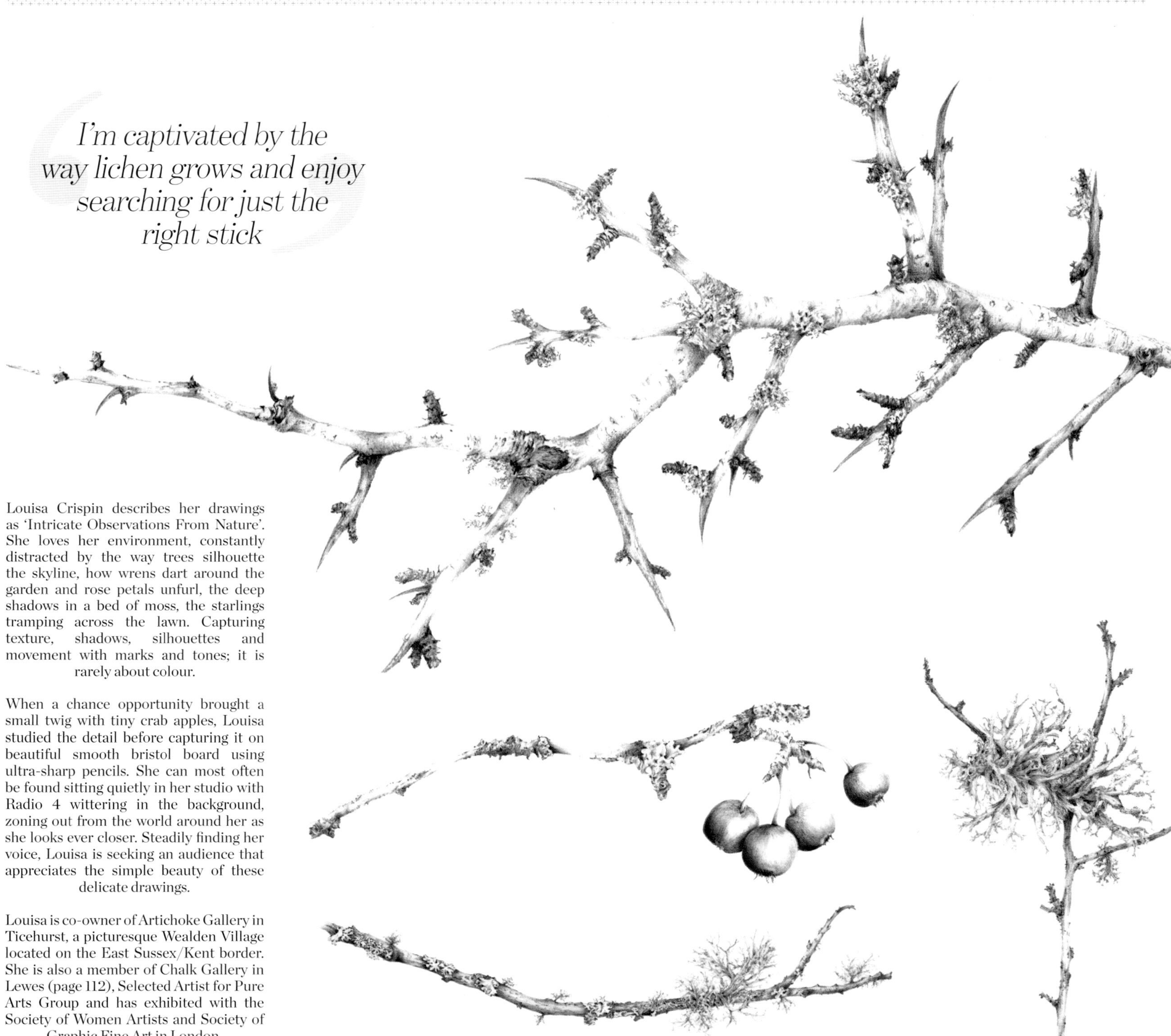

Louisa Crispin describes her drawings as 'Intricate Observations From Nature'. She loves her environment, constantly distracted by the way trees silhouette the skyline, how wrens dart around the garden and rose petals unfurl, the deep shadows in a bed of moss, the starlings tramping across the lawn. Capturing texture, shadows, silhouettes and movement with marks and tones; it is rarely about colour.

When a chance opportunity brought a small twig with tiny crab apples, Louisa studied the detail before capturing it on beautiful smooth bristol board using ultra-sharp pencils. She can most often be found sitting quietly in her studio with Radio 4 wittering in the background, zoning out from the world around her as she looks ever closer. Steadily finding her voice, Louisa is seeking an audience that appreciates the simple beauty of these delicate drawings.

Louisa is co-owner of Artichoke Gallery in Ticehurst, a picturesque Wealden Village located on the East Sussex/Kent border. She is also a member of Chalk Gallery in Lewes (page 112), Selected Artist for Pure Arts Group and has exhibited with the Society of Women Artists and Society of Graphic Fine Art in London.

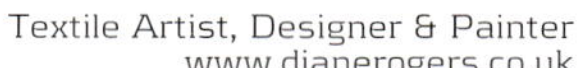

Textile Artist, Designer & Painter
www.dianerogers.co.uk

Clockwise from top left:
Crazed/Abersoch; Pebble Tangle; Pebble Channel; Float Tangle

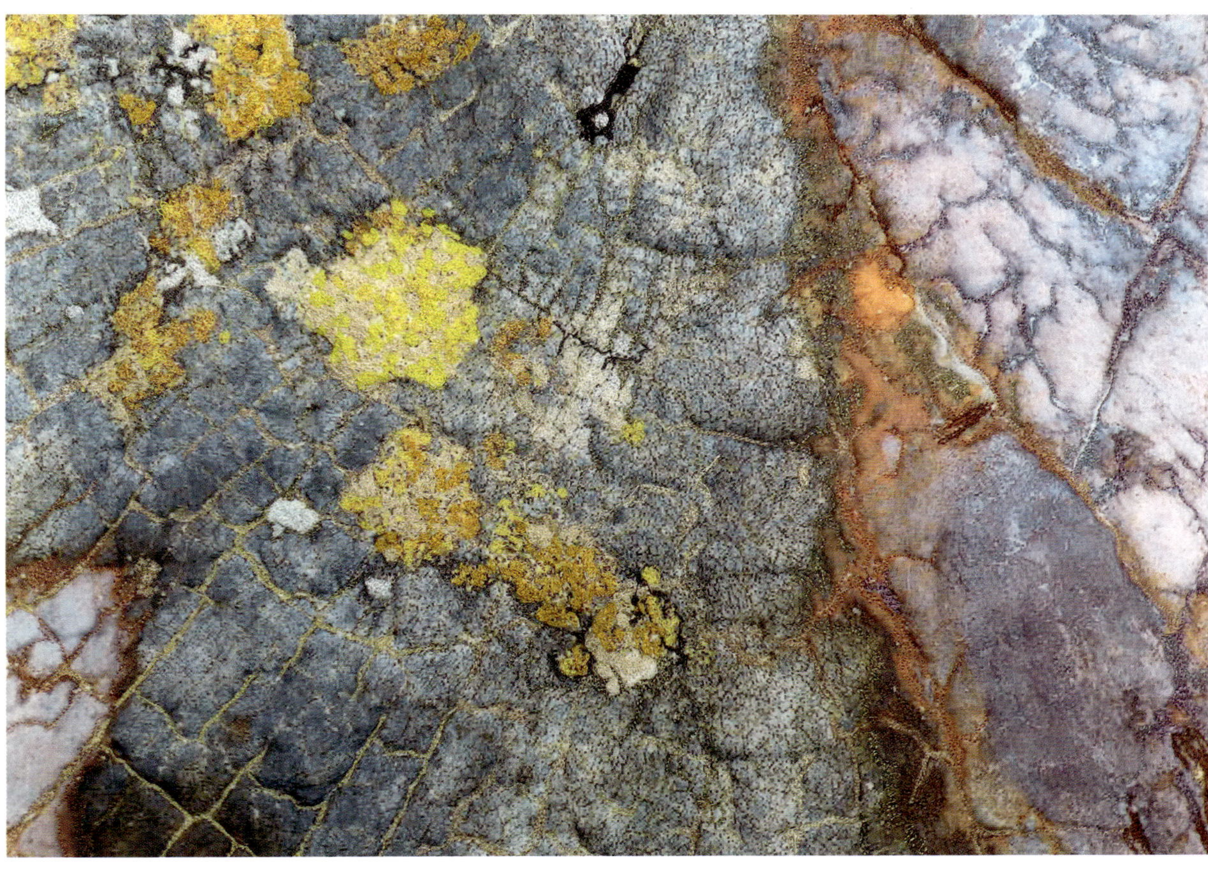

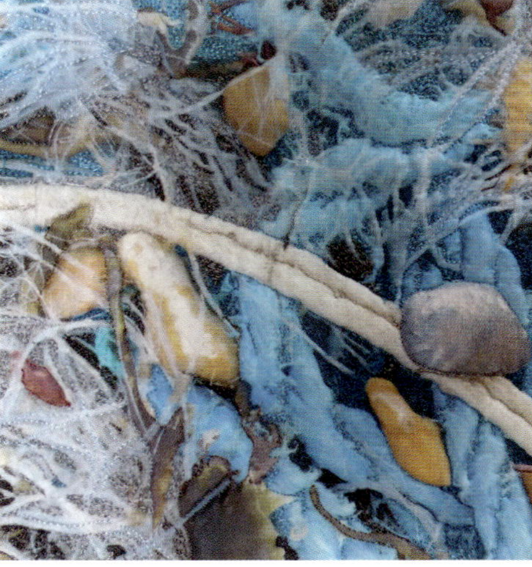

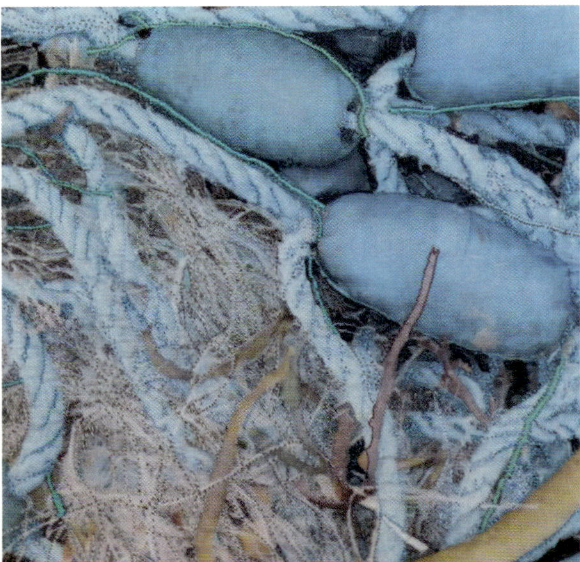

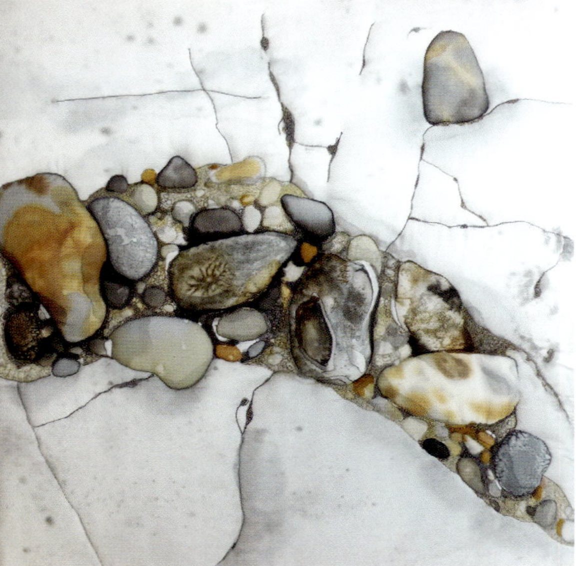

Diane is a textile artist, designer and painter. Having gained a degree in printed textiles at Loughborough, Diane moved to Brighton and worked for many years as a freelance print designer before producing her original pieces of textile artwork.

Diane is drawn to the beauty that is caused by the passage of time and exposure to the natural elements. She is interested in the ever-changing influences of man upon our natural spaces. The process of change is present within the array of rocks and eroded surfaces found along beaches and coastlines. Destruction, neglect and decay reveal interesting shapes, textures and patterns that provide inspiration for her artwork.

The various techniques used to create her textile artwork include hand-painting or printing onto silk, then quilting using machine free embroidery and embellishment by hand-stitching. This creates texture and raised areas in relief, and gives a realistic, compelling, tactile quality to each piece.

Diane exhibits at art fairs and galleries in London and the South East. In May 2015 she is taking part in an exhibition in Tampa, Florida, USA. As a member of the Fiveways Artists group, Diane curates and exhibits at Media Conflux during the Artists Open House Festival in May.

Diane is now also a member of the Sussex Guild and she will be taking part in some of the art and craft fairs held throughout the year.

John Link

Artist
www.johnlink.co.uk

Clockwise from top left: Hermione & Mamillius, The Winter's Tale; Prospero, The Tempest; Othello; Rosalind, Celia & Touchstone, As You Like It
Opposite page: Silvius, As You Like It

Taken from a longer article by Mary Goody MA, Courtauld Institute for Art

Link's working process allows the characters to grow through an exploratory journey of discovery that leads him into a dialogue with the figures that emerge. Much like an actor finding his way into a part, he strikes up an imagined conversation: "Who are you? Where have you come from? Where are you going?" The dynamic, reminiscent of the Surrealists' method of automatic drawing, partly bypasses conscious planning and lets saturated experience seep onto the canvas

John Link's paintings are born of Shakespeare. A lifelong inspiration for his career in acting, directing and teaching, the characters have now burst onto the stage of a new dimension as he engages with them via the medium of paint. We are met by intense colour, whimsical line, a space that invites us in as if to the set of an imagined drama, a clear sense of design, a look that is hard to fathom, but seems to reel with the weight of what it is to be human.

These works, like Shakespeare's plays, hold a lightness alongside intensity and weave a curious, unexpected line between them. The paintings are colourful, quirky and fun. But in the expressive faces, our first impression is of a pervading melancholia. A sense of being a bit lost or damaged.

Just as Shakespeare entertains us while making a profound analysis of human life, Link's vision is as if in portraying the most serious possible experience of ourselves, he offers up this reflection via the sensual joys of painting and his own delight in it. Colour vitalises and design contains. These cushion the melancholy, make the soul-searching manageable.

Rarely does an artist approach what he is painting in such a thoroughly embodied way – it is a unique perspective. Subject and object come close to collapsing into one.

Notably modest about his lack of art-school training, Link is schooled in the theatre, where visual, imaginative and expressive senses are constantly honed and composition involves characters in 3D. His eye is steeped in the perspective of the stage space and the dramatic simplicity of the effective production.

The more structured paintings are like the play's scenery, with the artist as set designer, imagining spaces to tell the story. Even the forest's trees allow a sense of airy space. The Forest of Arden is a recurring metaphor: a strangely unlimited scene of magical transformations, where characters escape, disguise and cross-dressing reveal hidden truths, and minds are changed.

Link shows us persons who are pondering existence, perhaps on the verge of some liberating insight.

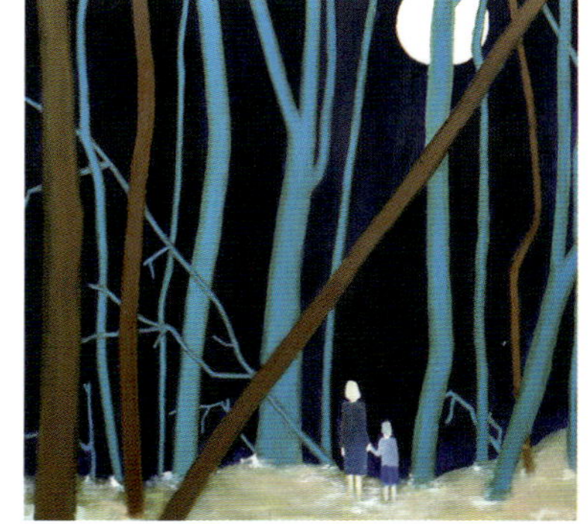

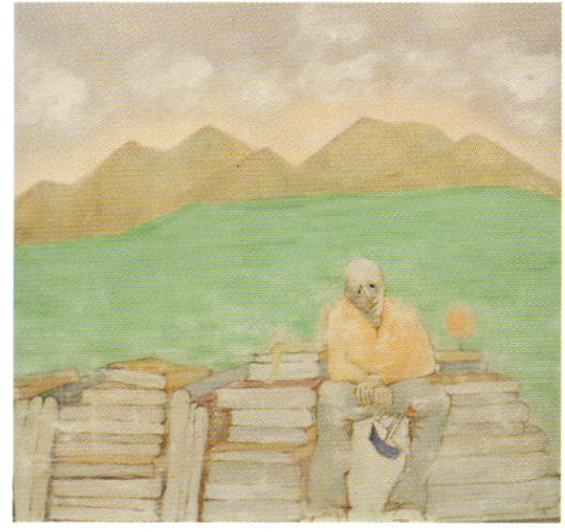

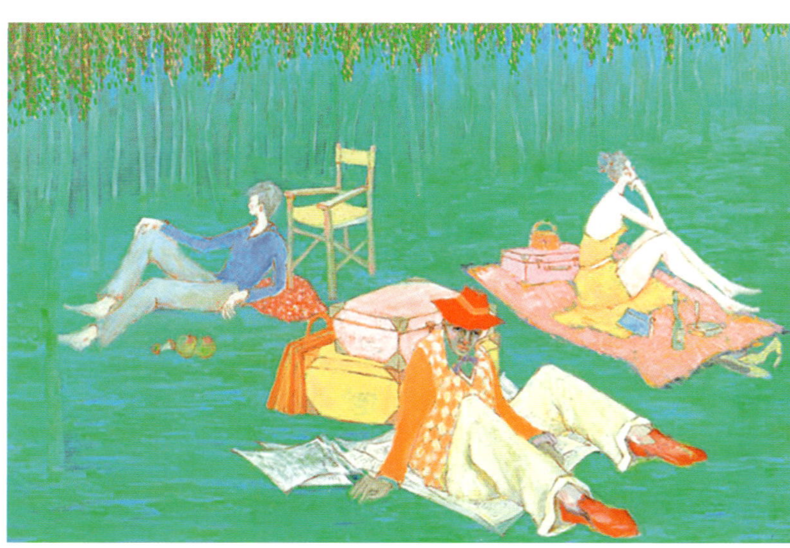

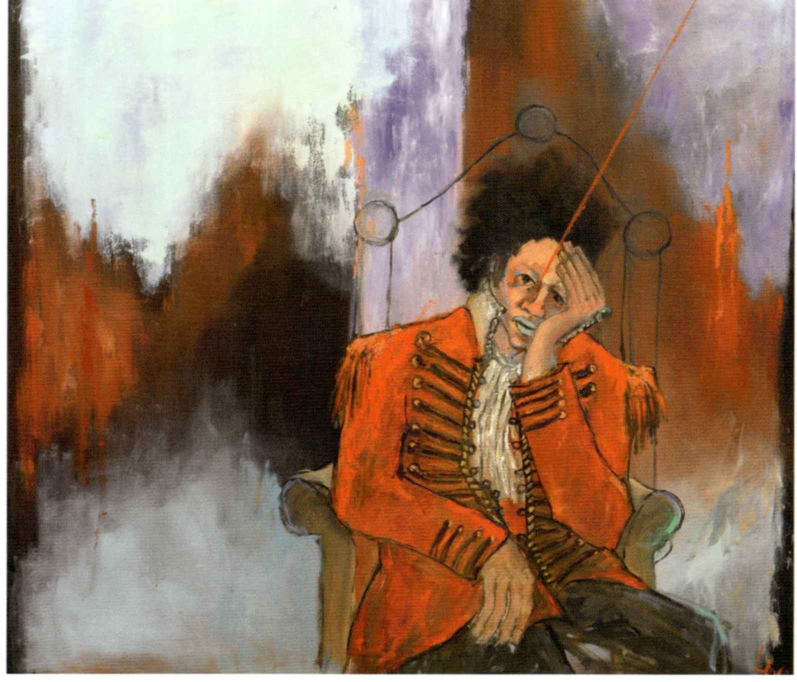

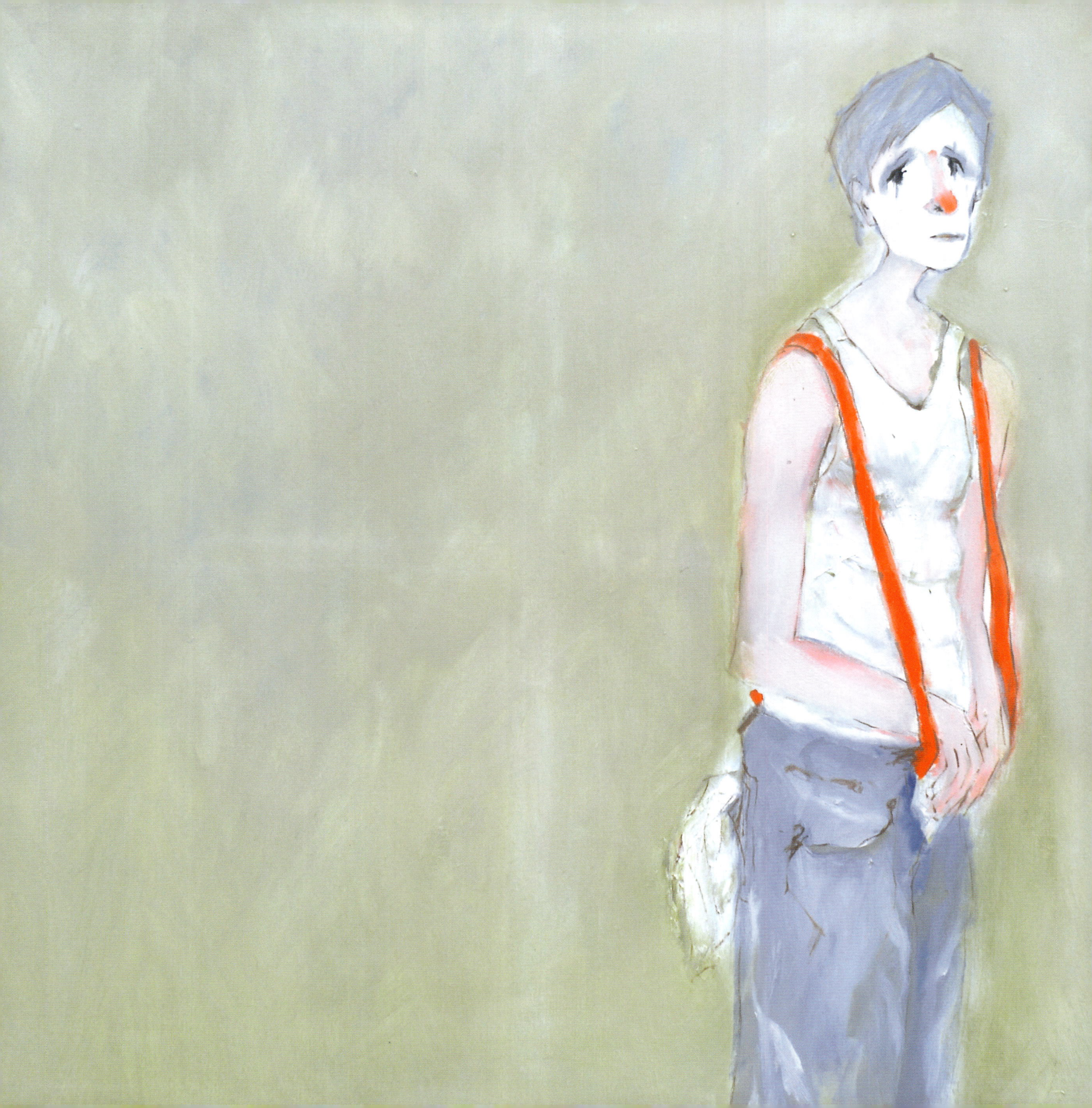

Firb

Artist & Fixer
www.wolfandpigeon.co.uk

Left to right:
Papillon 1; Papillon 2; Papillon 3

Firb describes his work as contemporary paintings based on old-fashioned subject matter. Some are illustrative. Some are more painterly. He can work in a heavy-handed, textured way, or one that is much lighter, using multiple washes. Whatever his technique, the result is always to build up atmosphere and portray a mood.

Although Firb describes his approach as "a fairly standard formula" it's not quite as simplistic as he'd like you to believe. This is an artist who puts a lot of work into researching the different subject matter that inspires him. And the results can be as varied as a sensitive portrait or a bold montage.

Firb is also the force behind contemporary creative arts company Wolf & Pigeon. Be sure to follow him on facebook.com/wolfandpigeon and discover all the exciting stuff that's brewing.

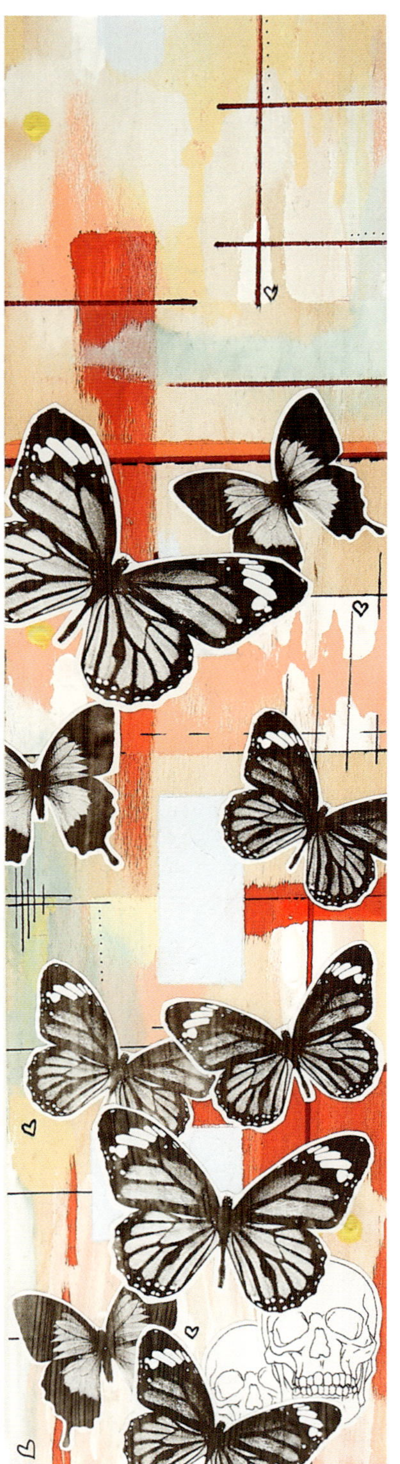

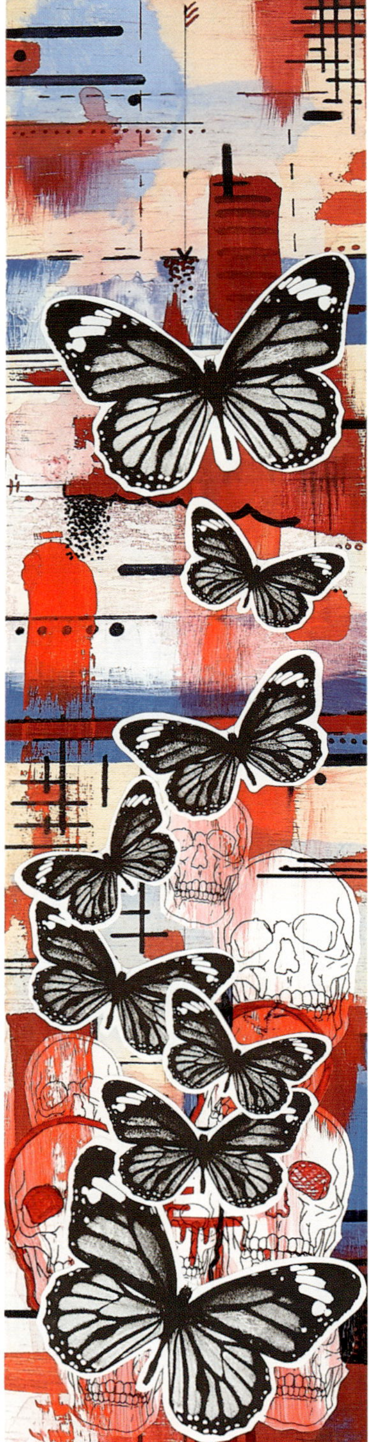

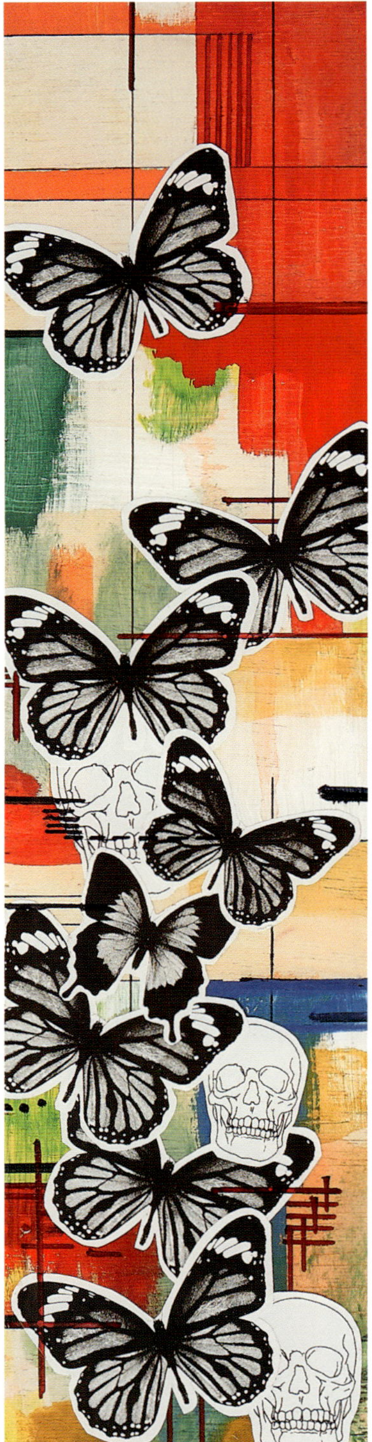

Robin Cooper-Hannan

Artist
www.robincooperhannan.com

Clockwise from top left:
Reverie in Red; Shift in Yellow;
The Selfish Gene; Kinesis; In the Flow

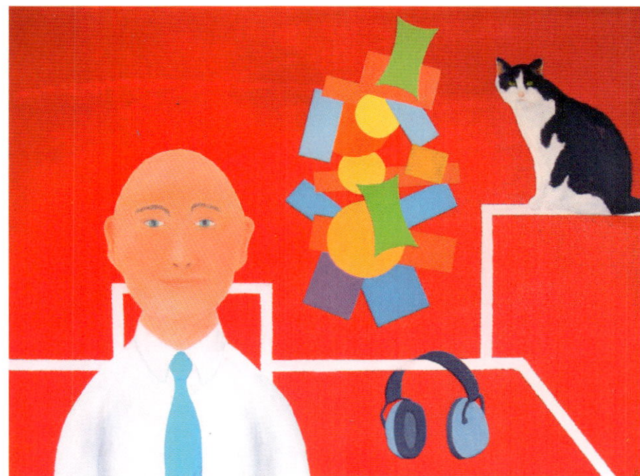

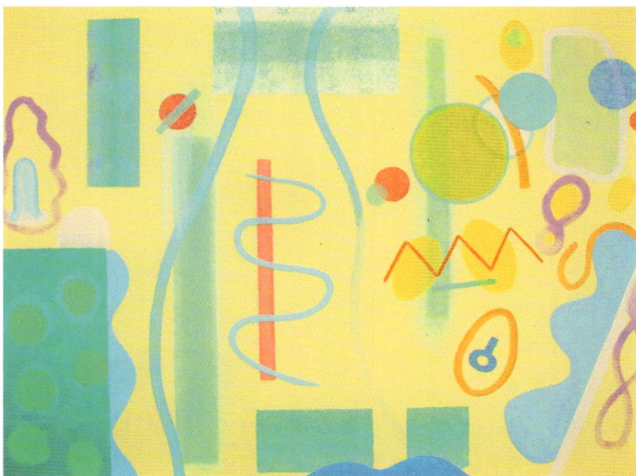

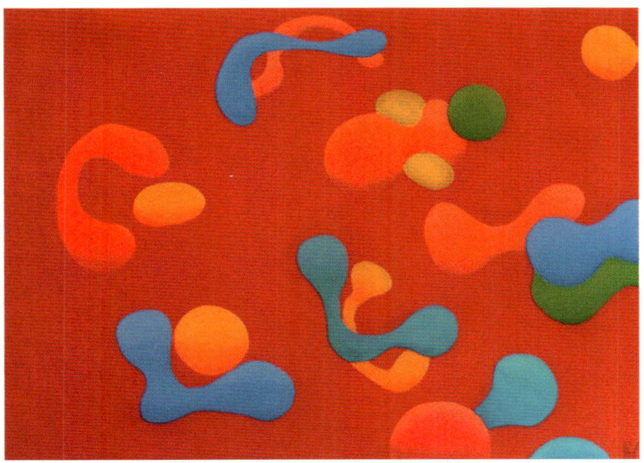

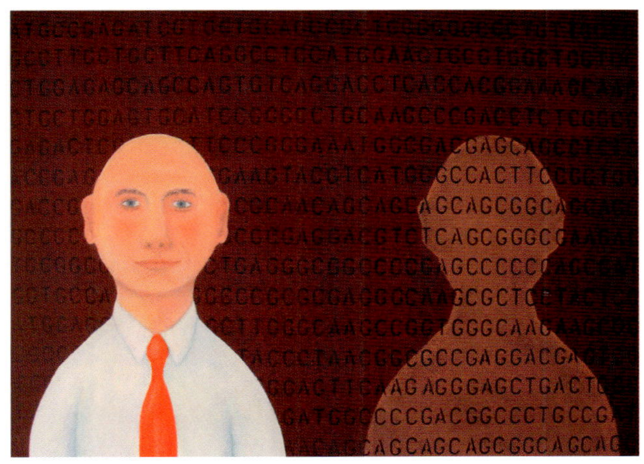

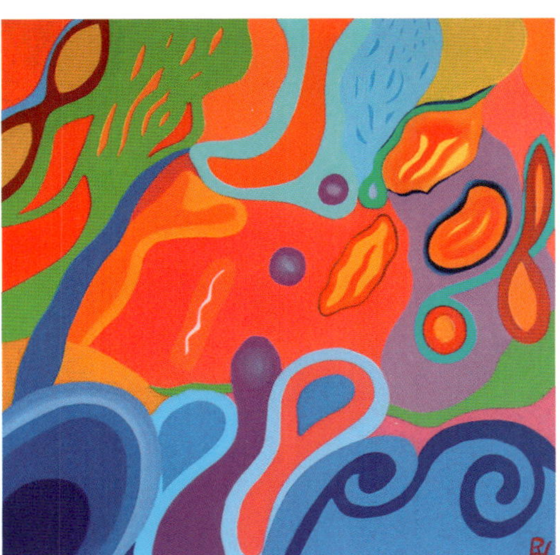

Robin Cooper-Hannan's contemporary oil paintings have a recognisable style embracing art and science. Relationships with the natural world are a recurrent theme. Art and science have more in common than opposition, there is no art without investigation and no science without imagination.

Each work is a journey attaining a resonance, sometimes subtle, sometimes bold. Figurative subjects reflect on identity, while abstract works include dynamics of cellular and sub-cellular worlds, including chromosomes. Composition and colour are key; they act together, allowing the viewer to develop interpretations moving between reality and reflection.

Eve Poland

Artist
www.evepoland.com

Clockwise from top left: Our Lady of the Catnip; Voodoo Kitty; Revenge; Album Kitties

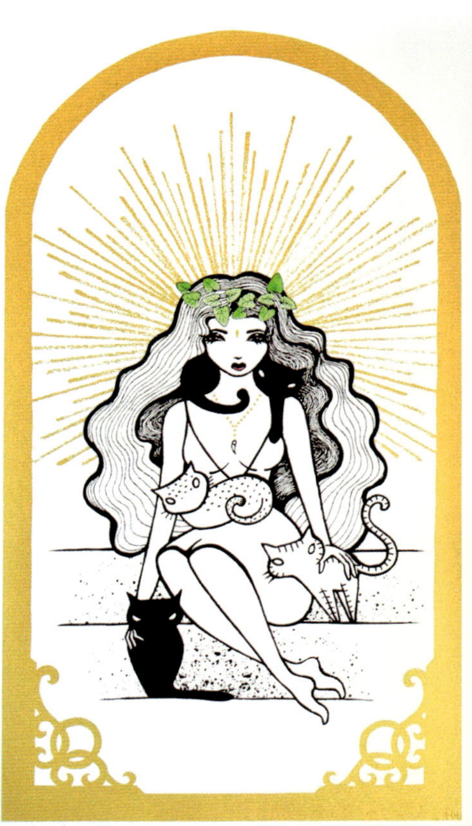

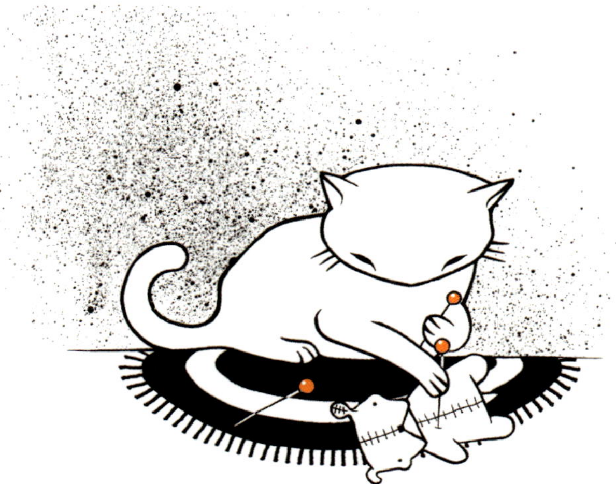

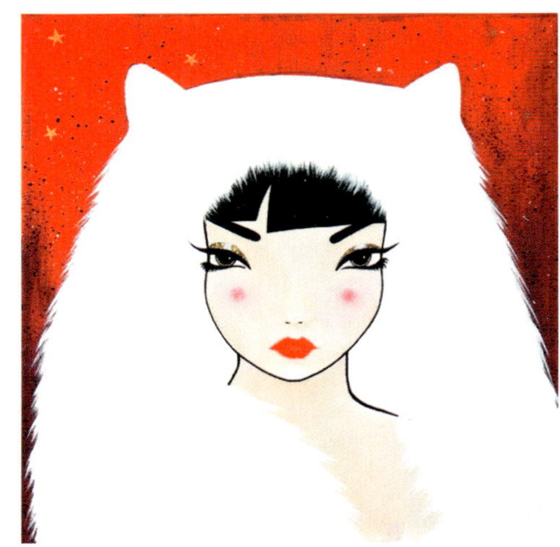

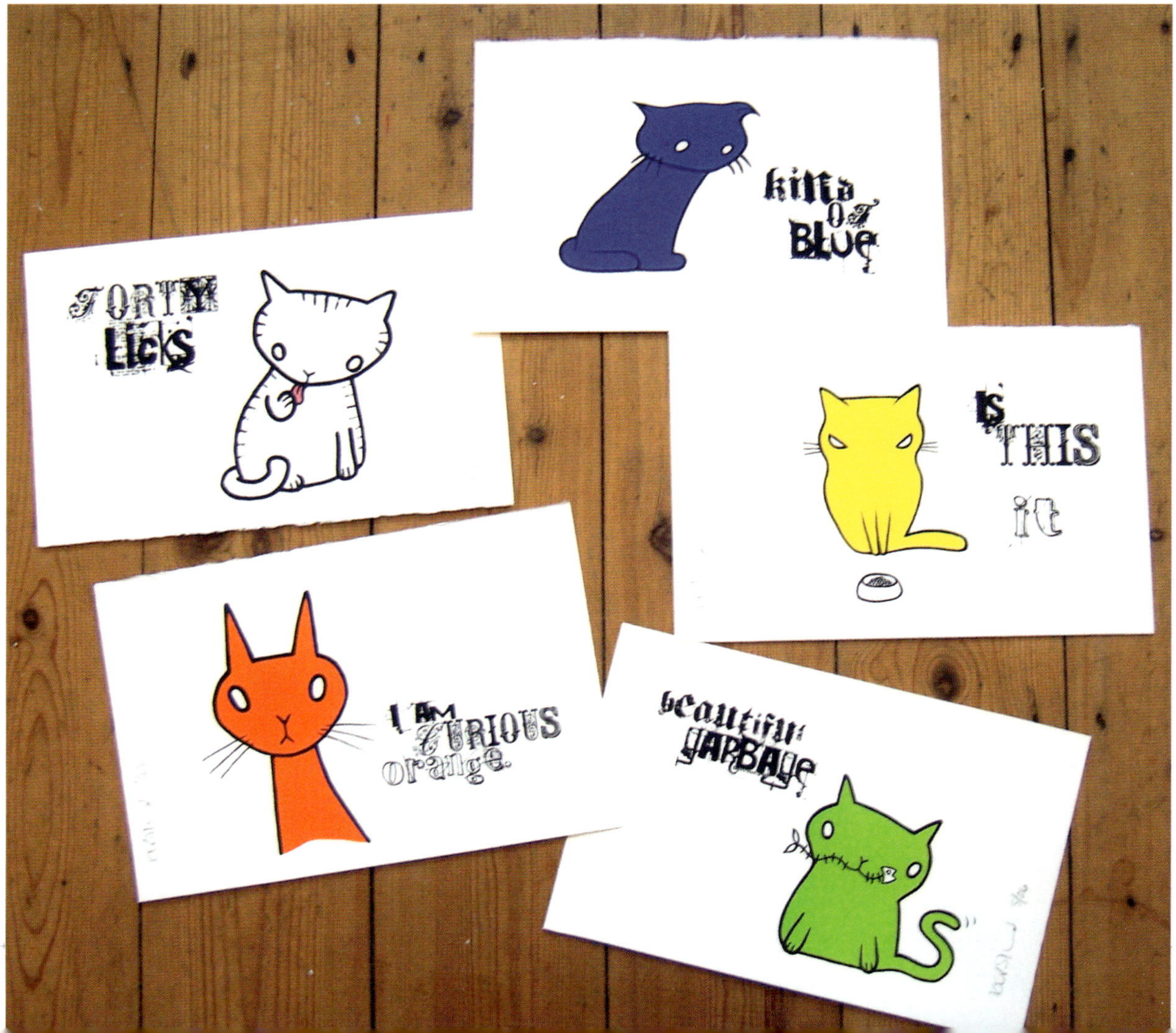

Eve Poland produces paintings and hand-printed silk screen prints in a bold, illustrative style. Her striking original artworks feature twisted kitties and peevish tigers, not to mention lascivious foxy ladies, populating a world where naked nymphettes cavort with obliging octopuses and clever, mischievous kitties will always win out over their cosseted canine counterparts.

Each piece captures the essence of its subject's identity in a deceptively simple execution; Eve employs traditional manual techniques rather than working digitally as she enjoys the characterful imperfections that arise from such handmade processes.

Eve has secured a reputation for intelligent work that reflects her own quirky sense of humour – with an undercurrent of darkness.

Jane Sampson

Artist & Printmaker
www.janesampson.com

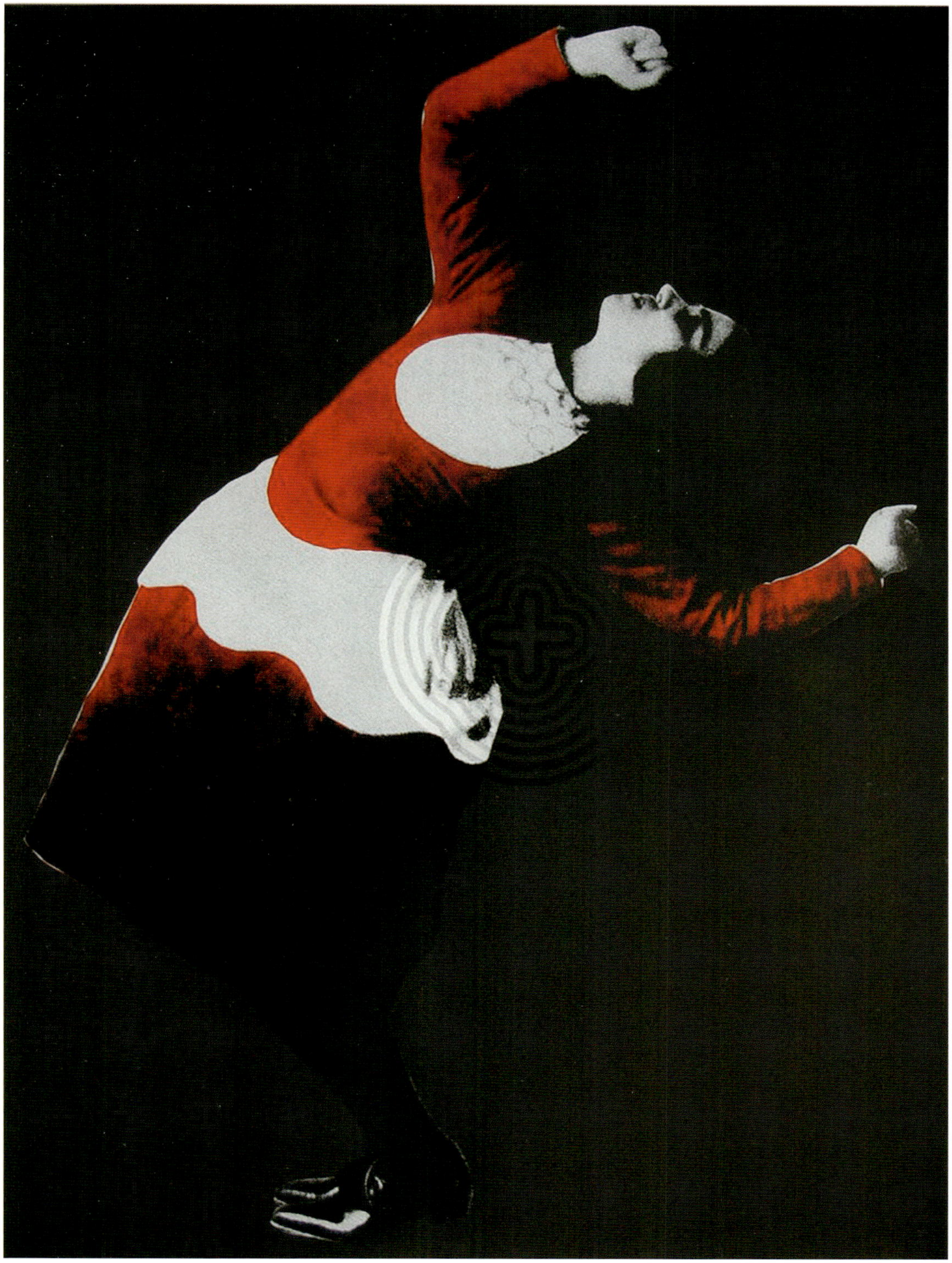

Left to right:
Edge; Solitaire

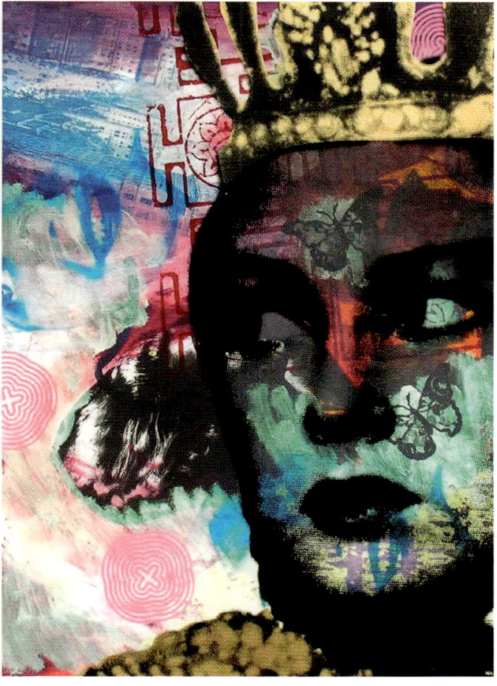

Jane Sampson creates works that contain a narrative using photomontage and collage from many different sources. Often these contain a mixture of found images and also her own photographic or hand-painted images. This library of iconography is constantly being re-used and manipulated through different media. The use of texture, colour and the layering of imagery is central to her work.

A graduate of Exeter University and the Barber Institute of Fine Art, University of Birmingham, Jane moved to Brighton to study printmaking. She carried out research into photomechanical printmaking techniques for Brighton University and is well known for her teaching there, in her own studio Ink Spot Press and at West Dean College (the Edward James Foundation).

Jane exhibits frequently and most recently won the John Purcell prize at the Royal Society of Painter-Printmakers in London.

Ink Spot Press

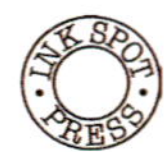

Open Access Fine Art Print Studio, Module B1, Enterprise Point, Melbourne St, Brighton BN2 3LH
www.inkspotpress.co.uk

Clockwise from top left: Bag; Happy customer; Happy weekender; Prints hanging to dry; Assorted letterpress; Printing a length

The team at Ink Spot Press Open Access studio just love to screen print and do letterpress. They can also make linocuts, woodcuts and collagraphs. They like to get their hands dirty making things in an analogue fashion (often quite slowly), but are not above using devious digital tricks to speed the process up and make it more accessible.

If you are interested in learning how to screen print, use type, make books and find out about other printmaking techniques – or you need to get access to screen printing, letterpress, etching and relief printing equipment – then take a look at the Ink Spot Press website (above), or call to find out how to book a course or session in this well-equipped studio (details on page 132).

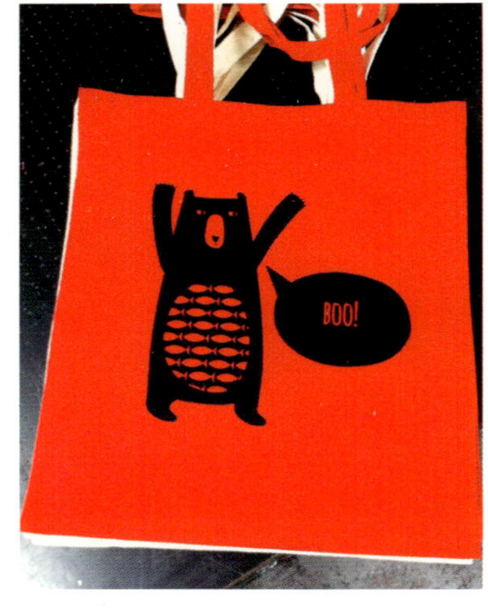

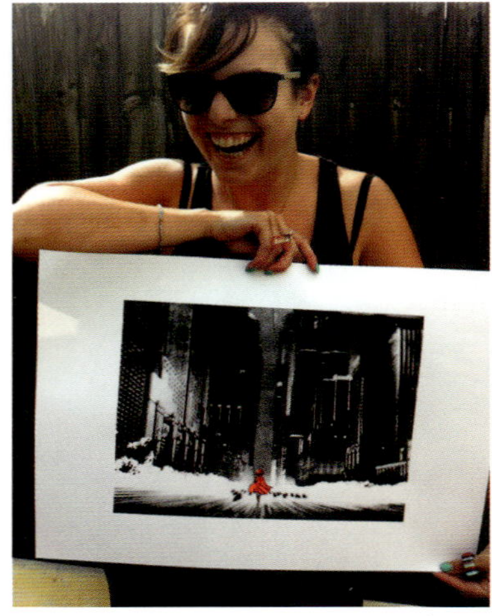

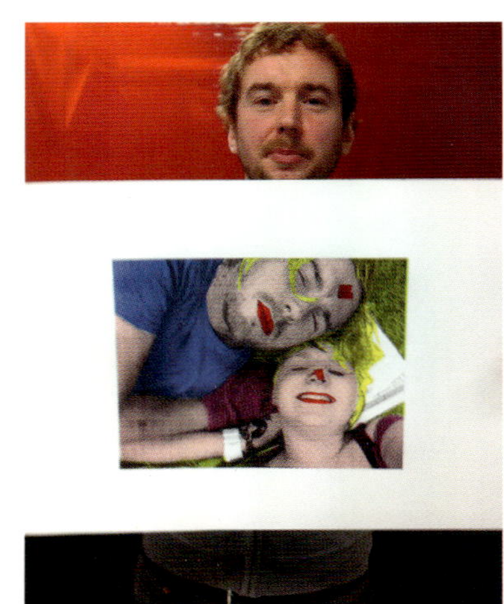

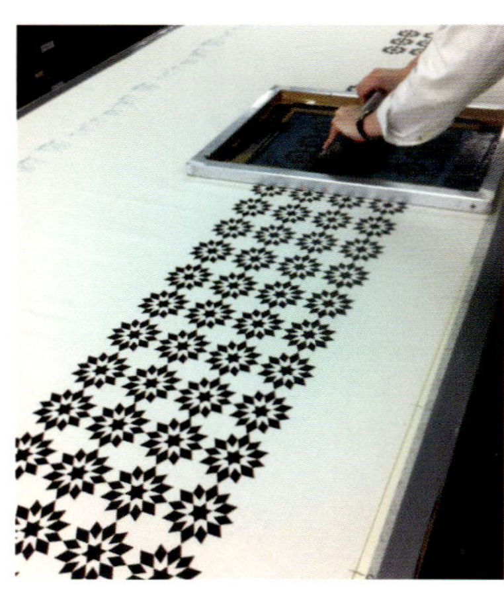

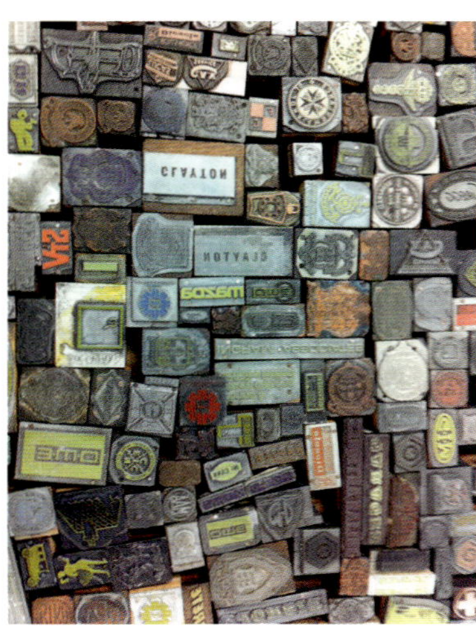

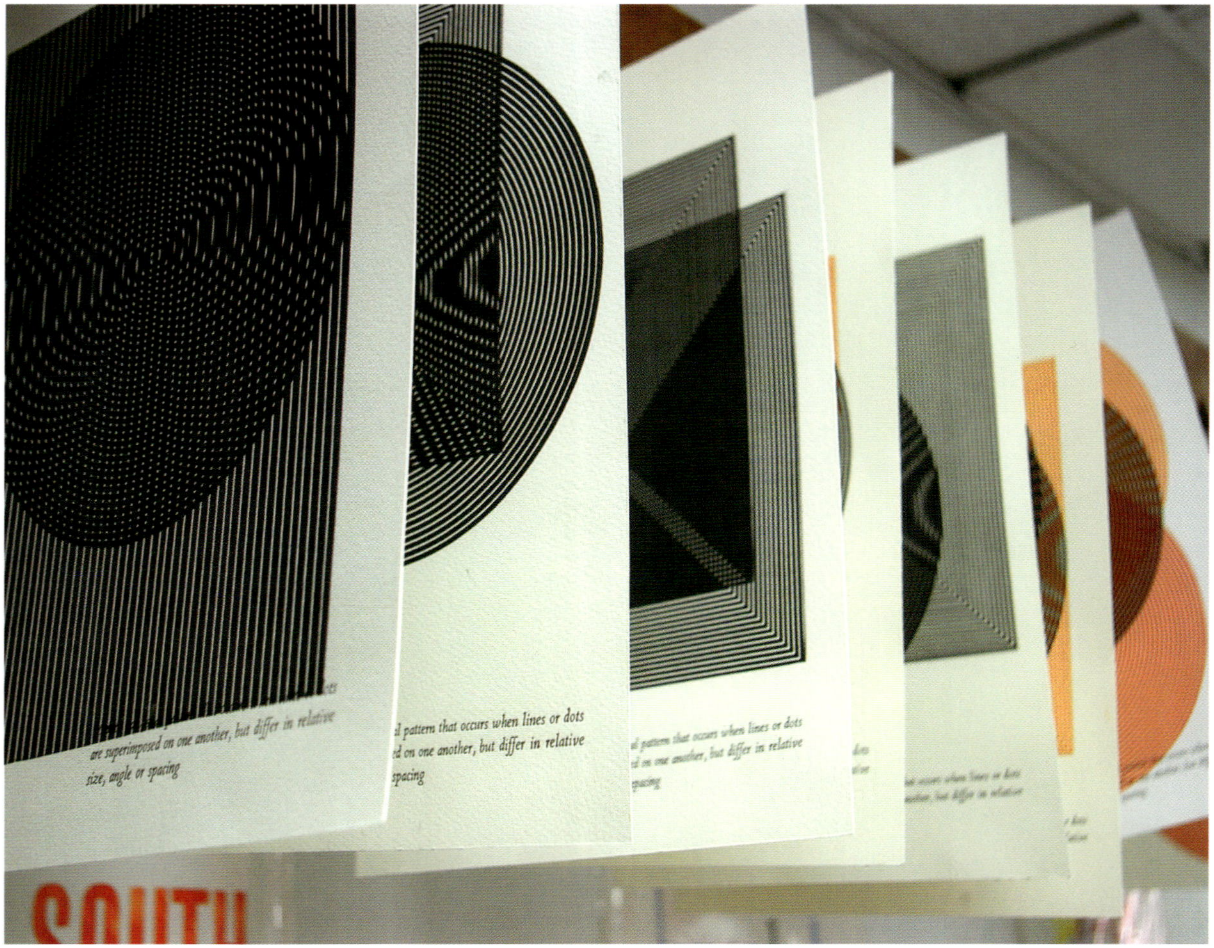

Jill Tattersall

Artist
www.jilltattersall.co.uk

Clockwise from top:
Brighton Glimpses; Leaving Newhaven; Leaving York - again; Lighted Windows

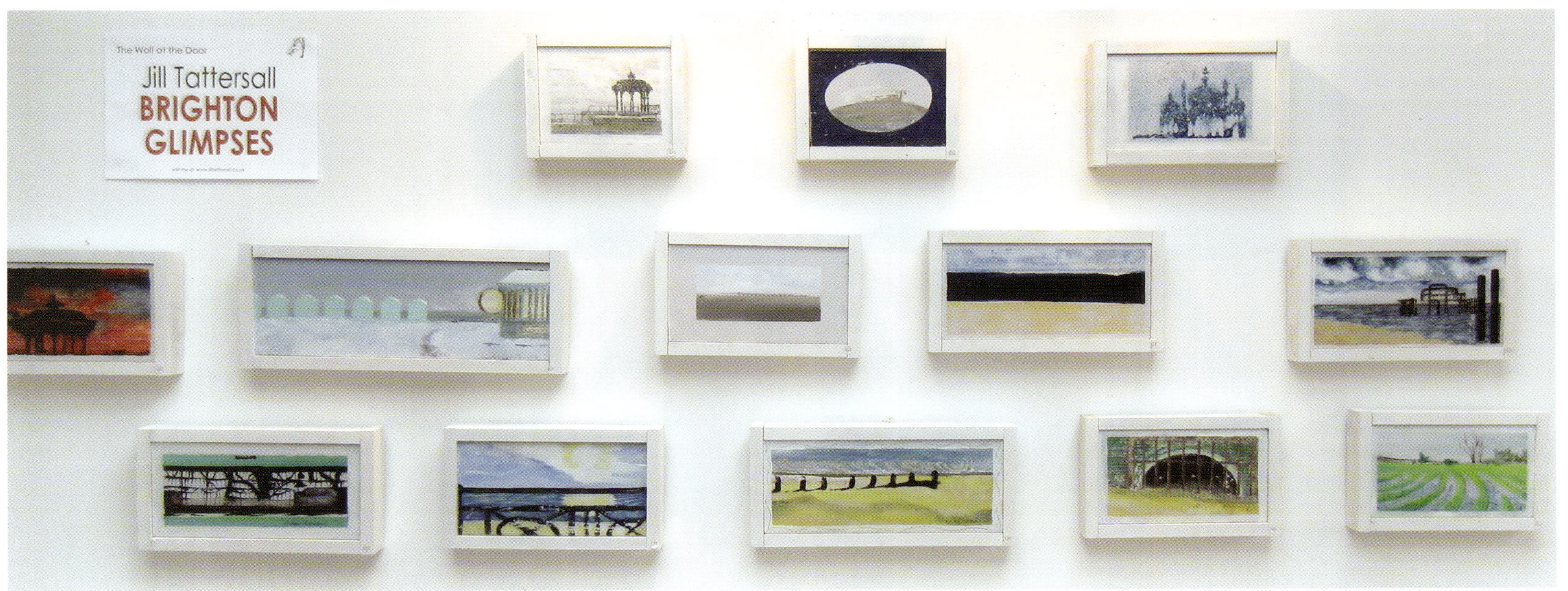

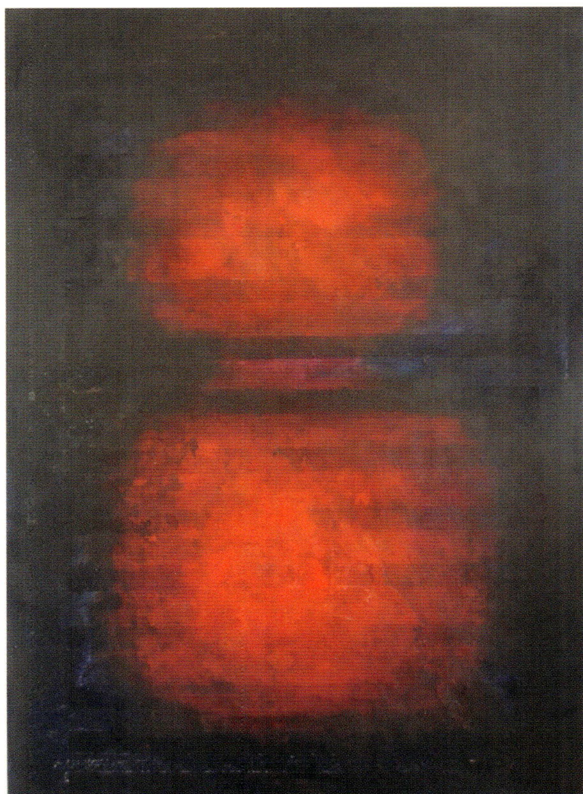

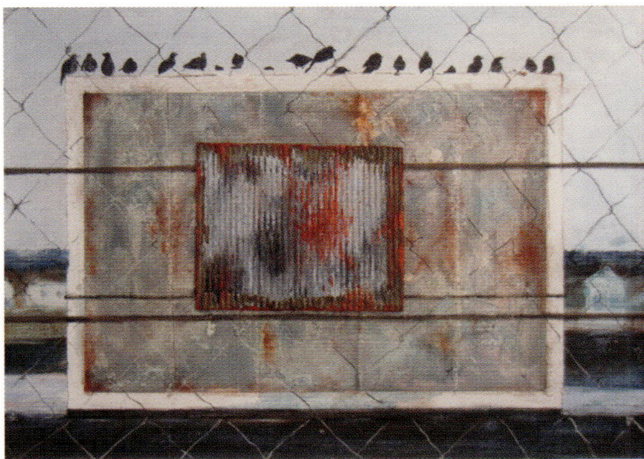

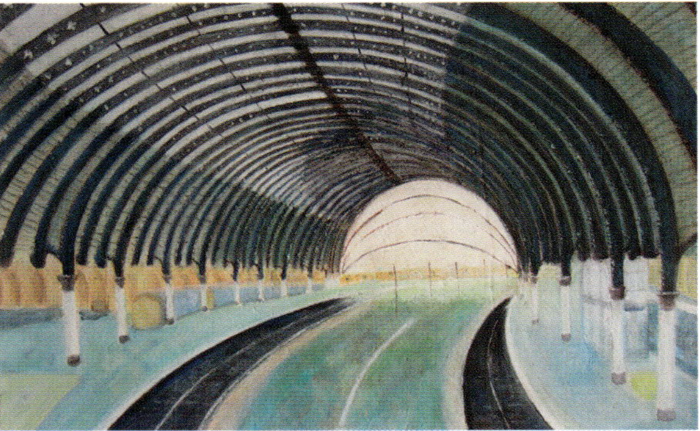

What's art about? What's it for? Jill Tattersall admits she hasn't a clue, after 15 years or so of trying to find out. But we all experience extra-vivid and intense moments. They evaporate quickly, leaving behind a lasting flavour, texture, colour and mood. It's those glimpses Jill tries to capture in visual form.

Often she'll start out by making her own paper, using high-quality cotton fibres. It's time-consuming, but gives each piece a unique and distinctive texture that takes paint in a seductive and unpredictable way. Then she builds up dense, glowing colour – often in many layers – using paints, inks, pigments and dyes. Sometimes a bit of silver or gold leaf asks to be added. She's always experimenting with different techniques and materials. It can all be a bit risky, but things quickly go stale if you always play it safe.

Jill works in Hove (Wolf at the Door). She's shown work in London and all over the place, with many solo exhibitions in private and public galleries. Now she's looking for exciting new projects and collaborations.

Michelle Cobbin

Artist
www.michellecobbin.com

Clockwise from top left: Counting the Breath; Breath Series; Watching the Breath
Opposite page: Space to Breathe

Michelle Cobbin seeks to find balance and harmony in her work, and to create an atmosphere of quiet contemplation. She draws on her yoga and mindfulness practices and her study of Zen calligraphy to inform her work.

Based in Brighton since the 1980s, Michelle studied both Visual Culture and Fine Art at the University of Brighton. 2014 saw her work selected for the East Sussex Open at the Towner Gallery, and shortlisted for the National Open Art Competition and Saatchi Showdown.

Michelle opens her home – 'BareFoot ArtHouse' – during the Brighton Festival as part of Artists Open Houses, and shows with Fourfour gallery at the Affordable Art Fair, Battersea.

Finding balance and harmony to create an atmosphere of quiet contemplation

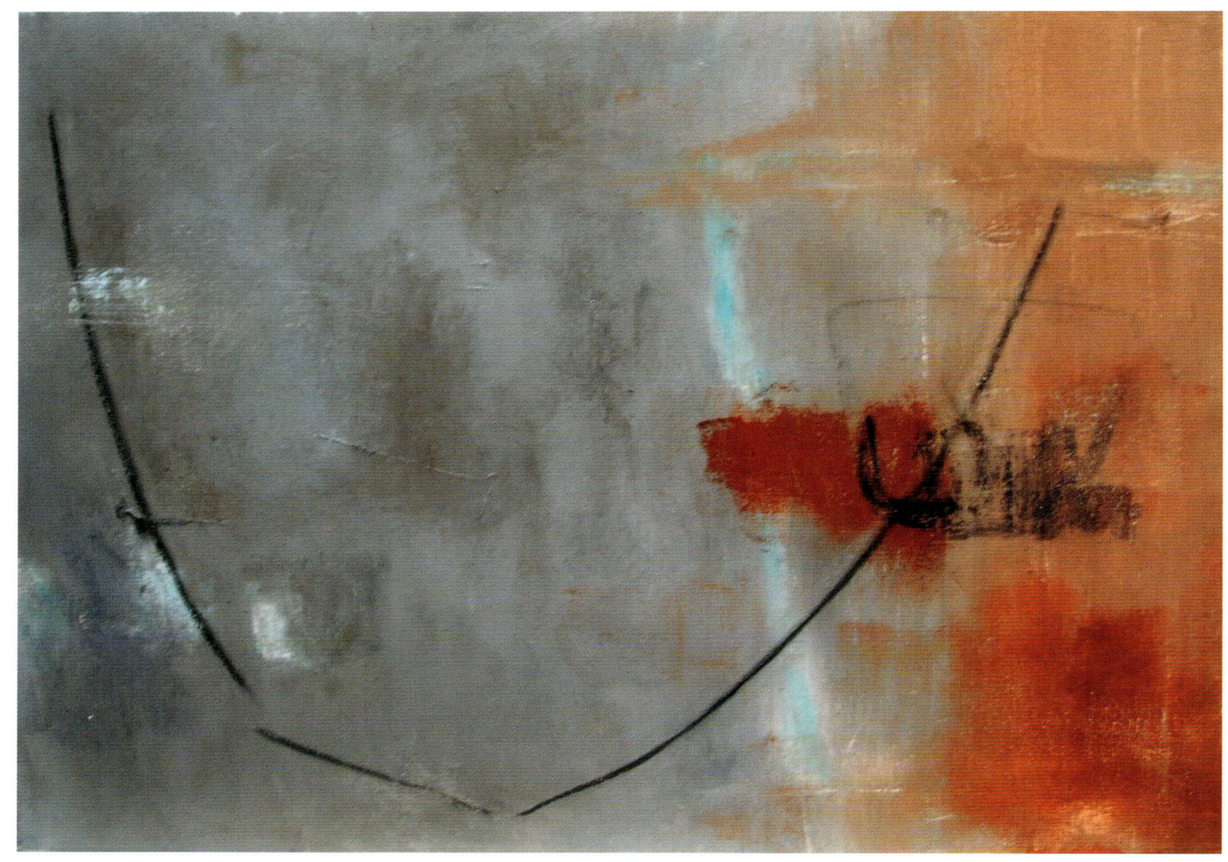

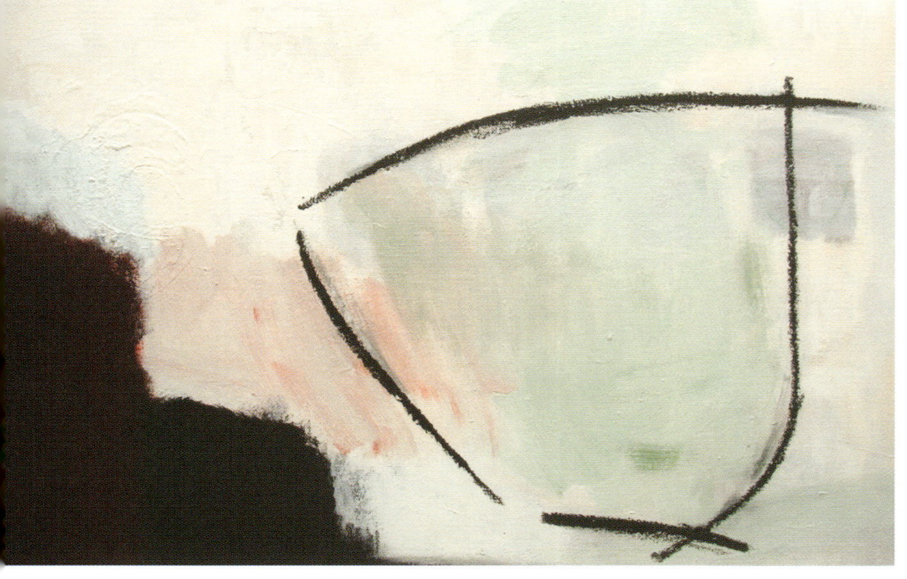

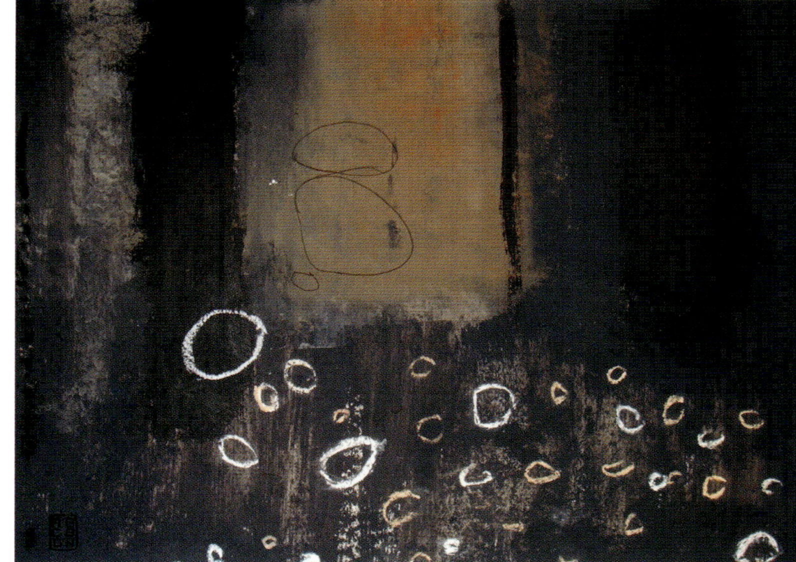

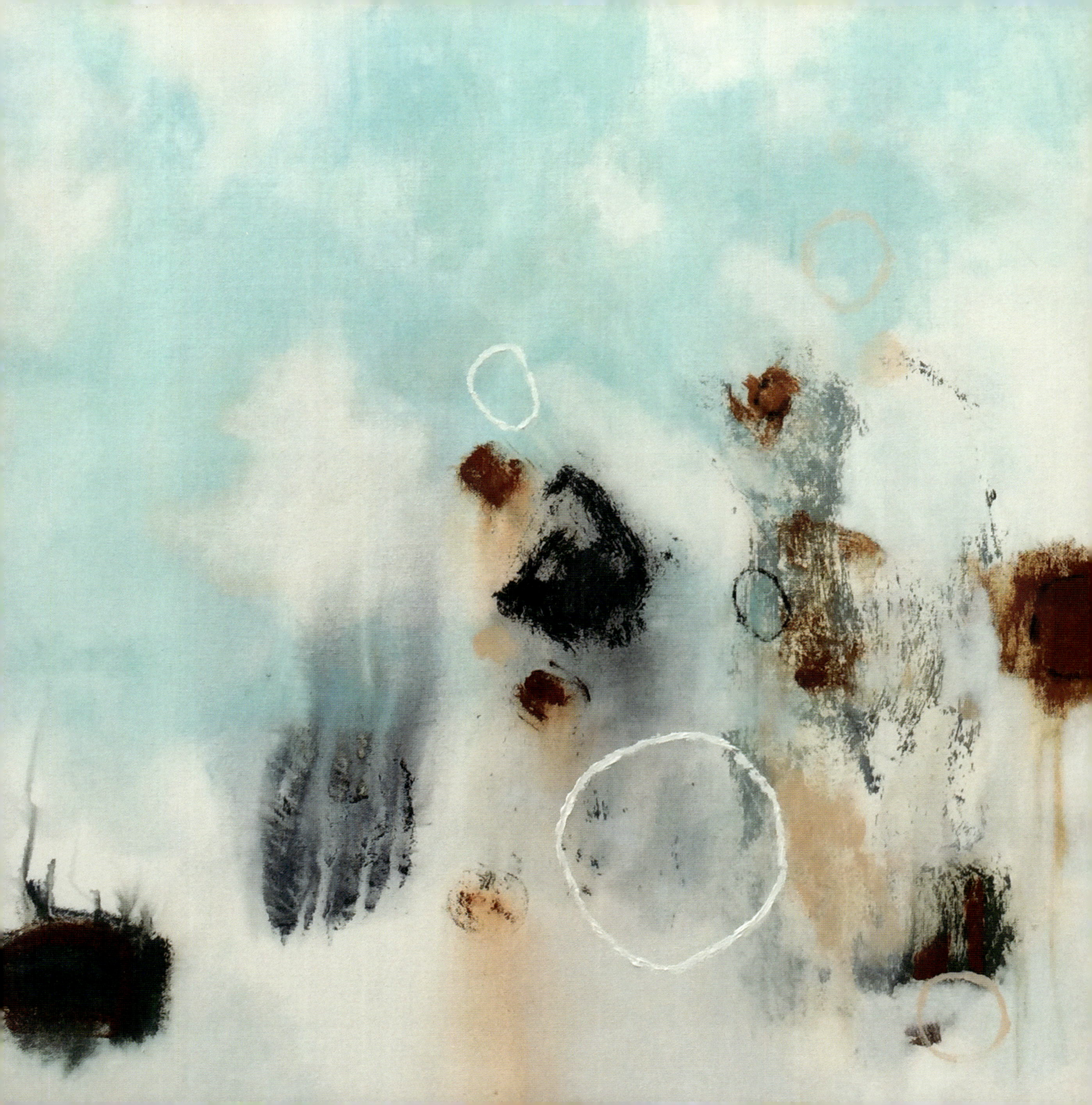

Hiroko Lewis

Artist
www.hirokoart.co.uk

Clockwise from top left:
Profile 2; Spring Glow; Whisper; Willow

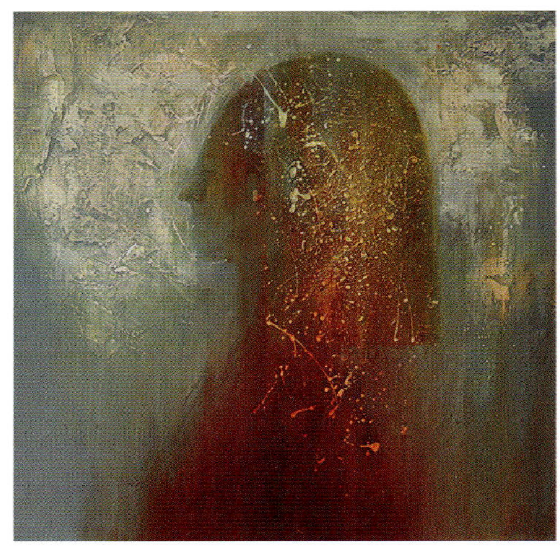

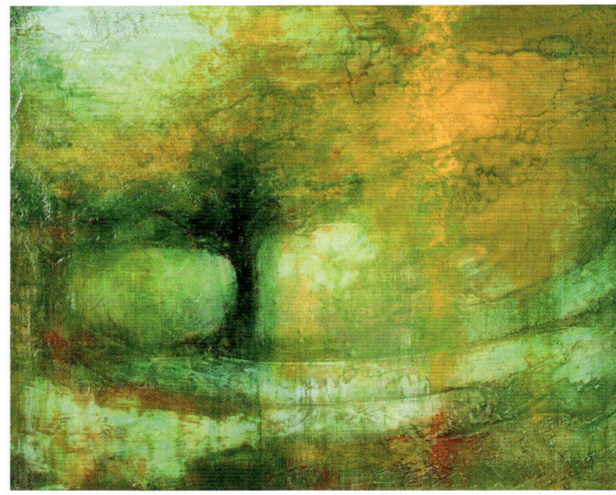

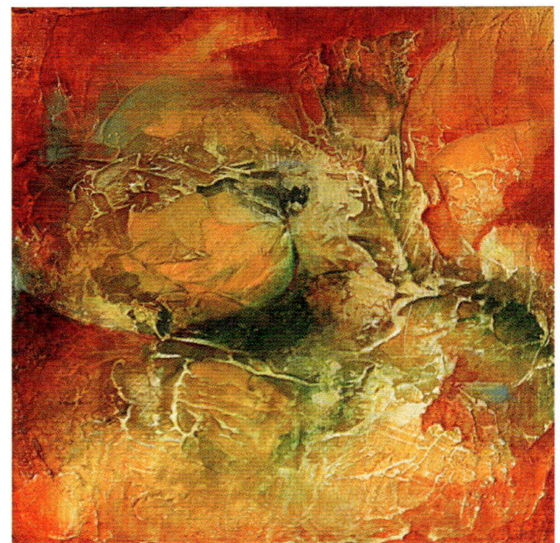

Japanese artist Hiroko Lewis is based in Brighton, where she creates semi-abstract works in oil that draw from and build upon her classical training. Starting with the hint of something remembered or observed, often derived from nature, her work travels to expand these fragments into a new world using a process of repeated construction, destruction, and reconstruction, in search of another sensory reality.

After graduating with a bachelor's degree in Fine Art from Kanazawa College of Art, Hiroko pursued a career as an artist and visual designer in Japan. Since moving to Brighton in 2011, she has focused on fine art, aiming to express and adapt to her new-found environment. Hiroko's work can be seen at Fiveways in Brighton and Hove's Artists Open Houses Festival in May.

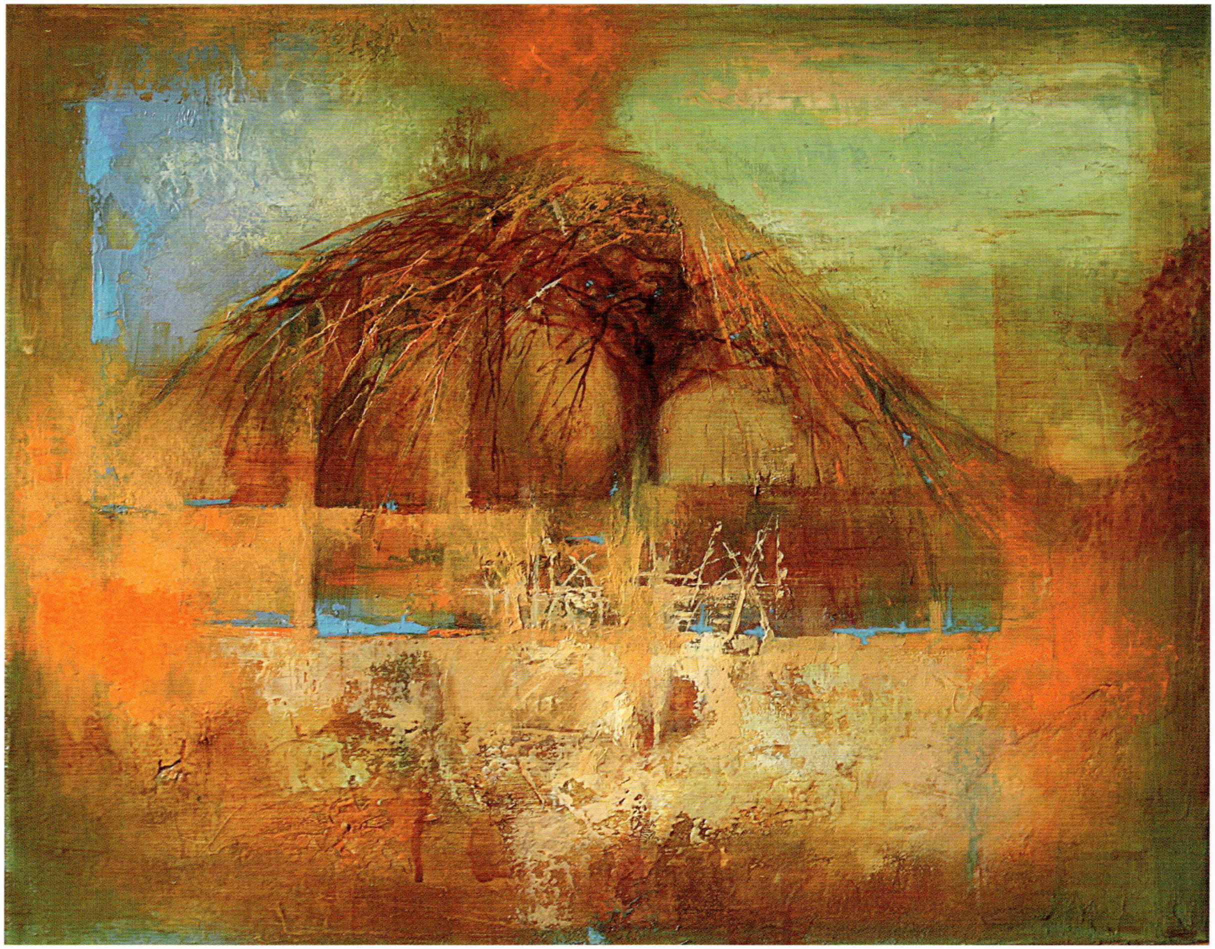

Anne French

Artist & Illustrator
www.artofficial.co.uk

Clockwise from top left: Agnes chair back; Victorian Balloon chair; Faux inlay detail; Vase in the making; Ceramic faux inlay vase; Chair detail, Gorilla talks

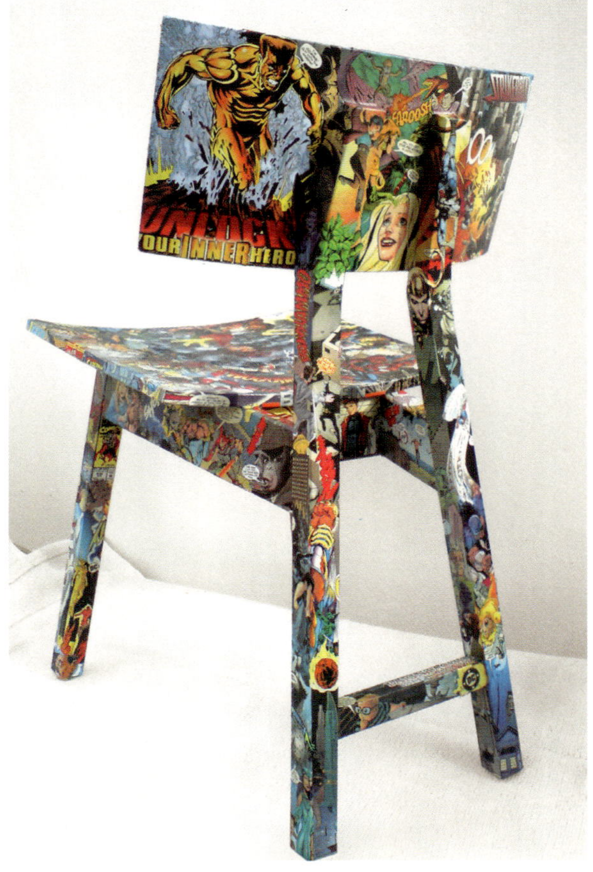

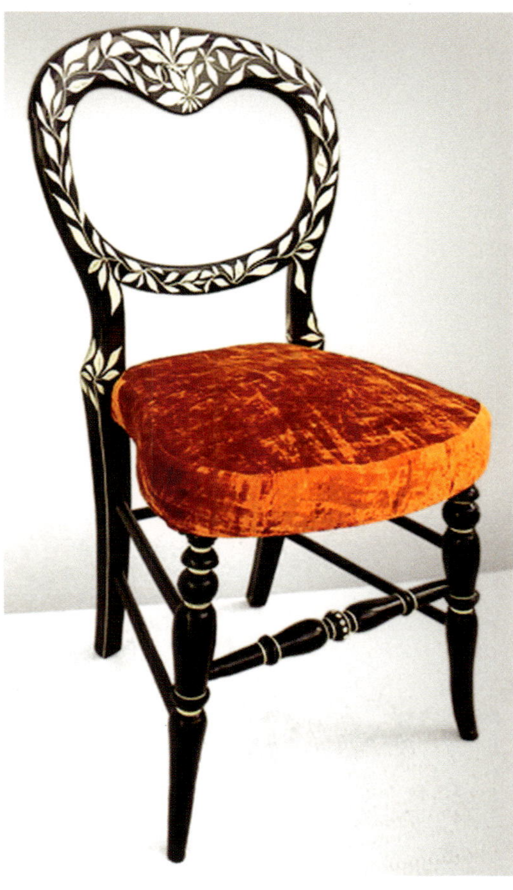

Anne French is self taught, but comes from a family of artists. She left school at a very young age, and went to Paris where she lived and worked for many years. Anne now lives in Brighton and works at the Royal Pavilion.

She has worked in many media – cloth, glass, pâpier maché – and experiments constantly with others. But, in spite of (or perhaps because of) its rather prim, genteel reputation, she finds something about découpage and its extraordinary versatility, fascinating.

Comic characters who have never met find themselves interacting on a piece of charity shop furniture. While an exhibition of antique chests from Rajasthan inspired her to experiment with the 'Faux Inlay' technique, substituting delicate bone inlay pieces with recycled card and string; paint and varnish replacing lacquered wood. Text is scattered parsimoniously. If you take a closer look, these pieces are not quite as they seem at first glance...

One of Anne's comic découpage chairs was chosen as part of the 2010 House Open exhibition in The Regency Town House, Brunswick Square, and the December 2014 issue of *Vogue* magazine featured one of her comic chairs.

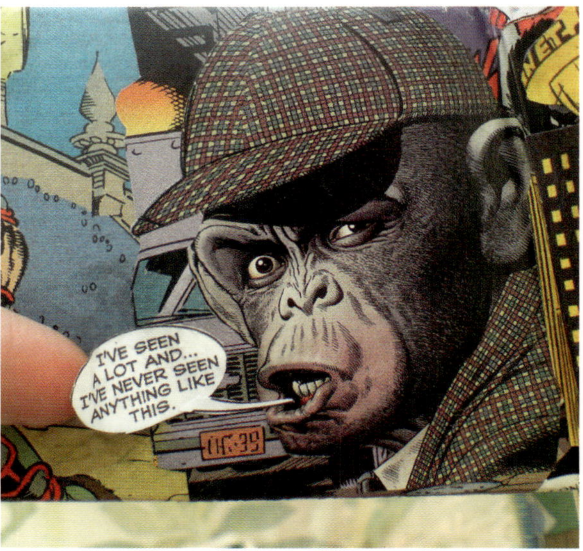

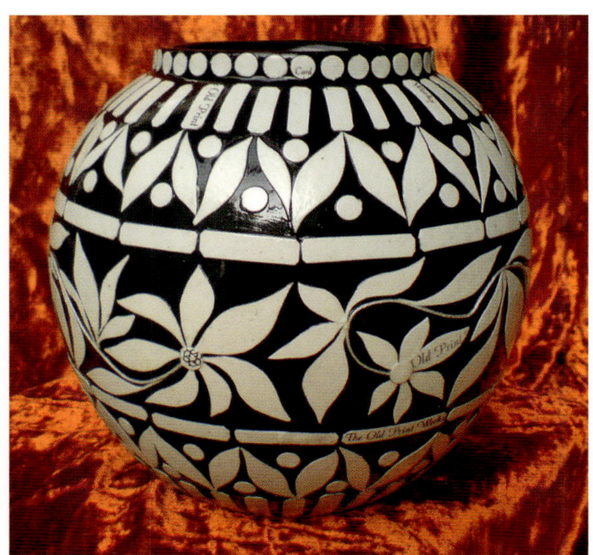

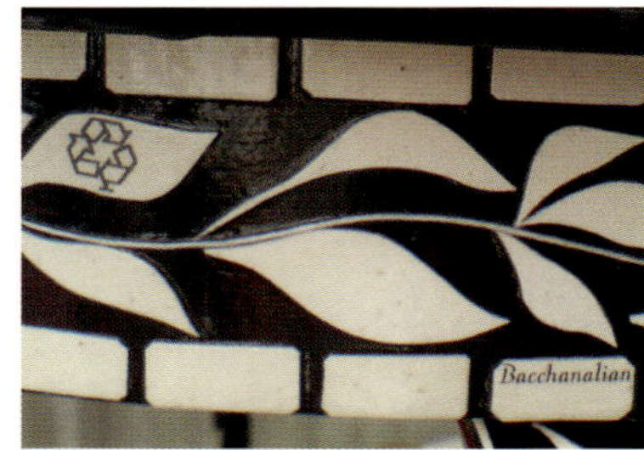

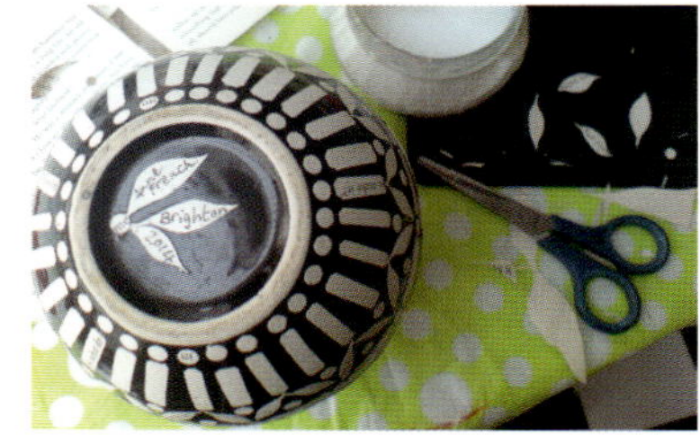

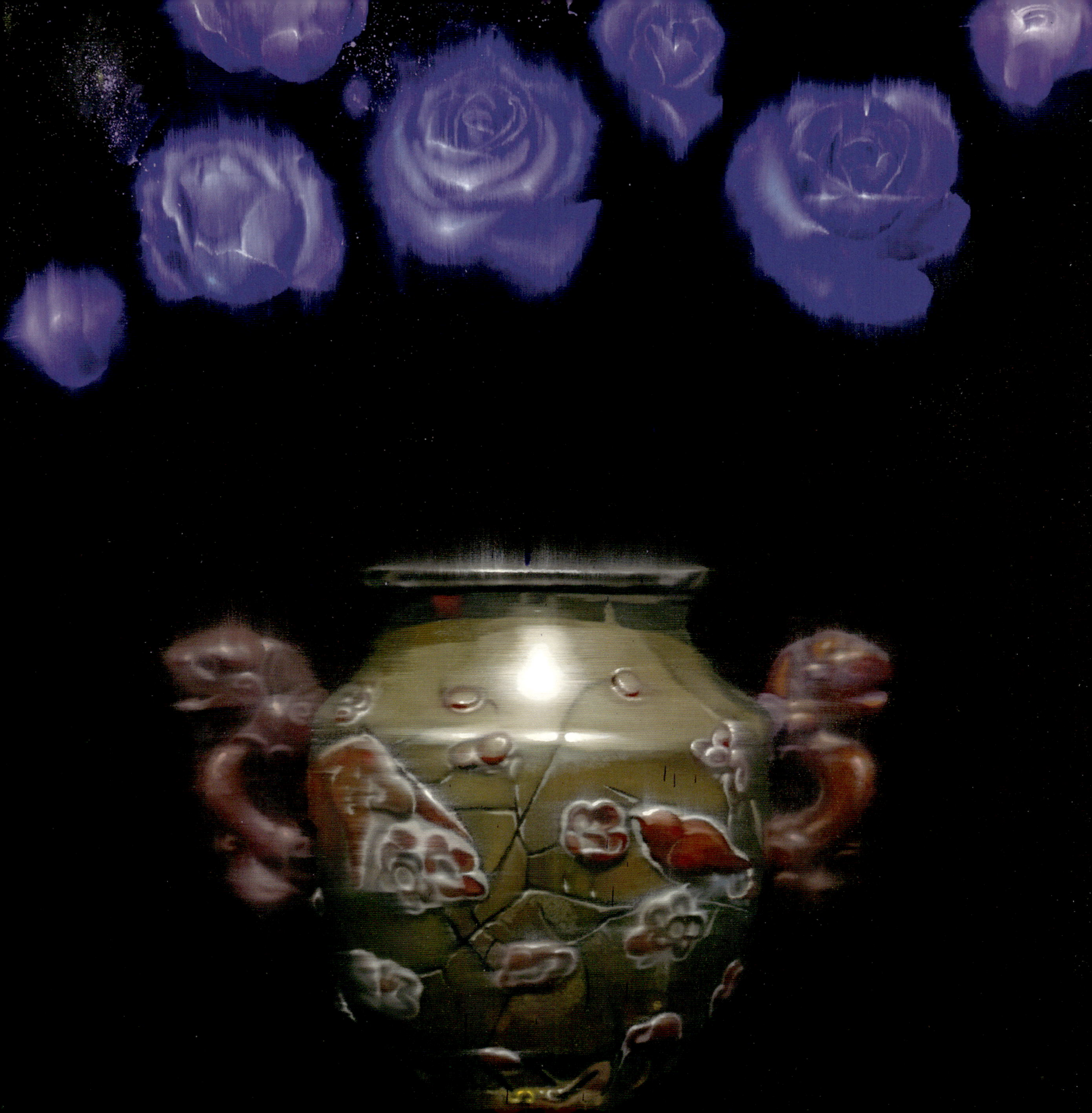

Graeme Richardson-Locke / Eye 4 Colour

Print Studio
www.eye4colourprints.com

Clockwise from top left: ELVIS by Mike Edwards; Metagraf by Ben Allen; I Do Not Play Well With Others by Matt Lambert; Psychedelic Skull by Ben Allen. Opposite page: My Counterpoint II by Chris Kettle

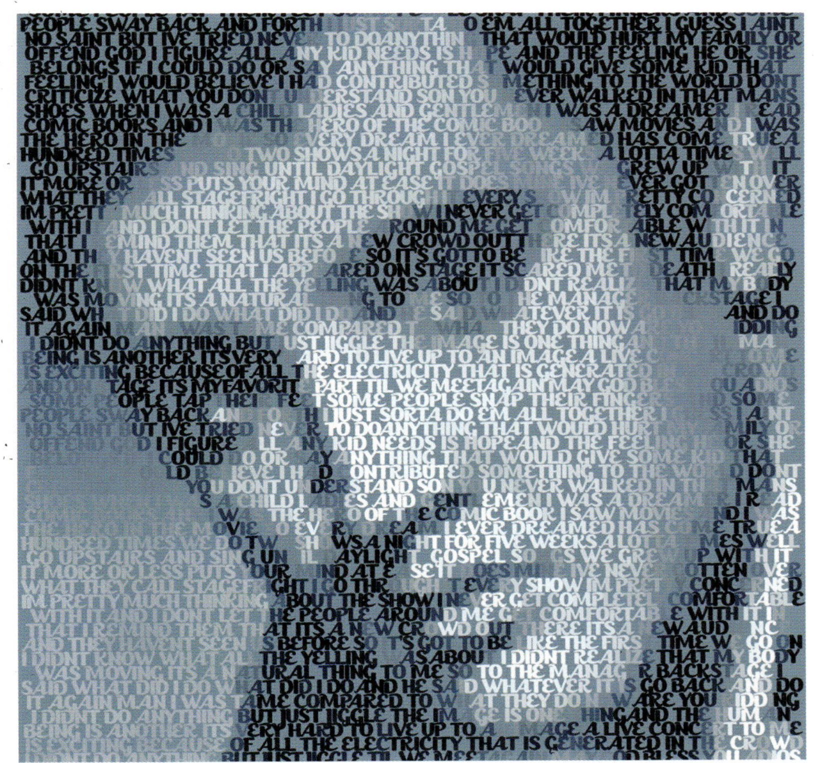

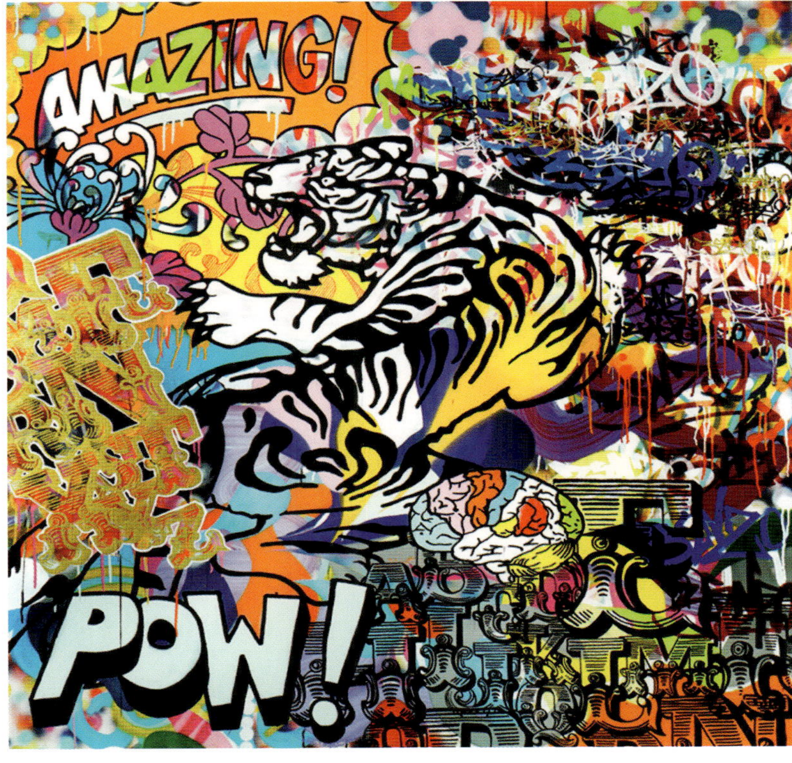

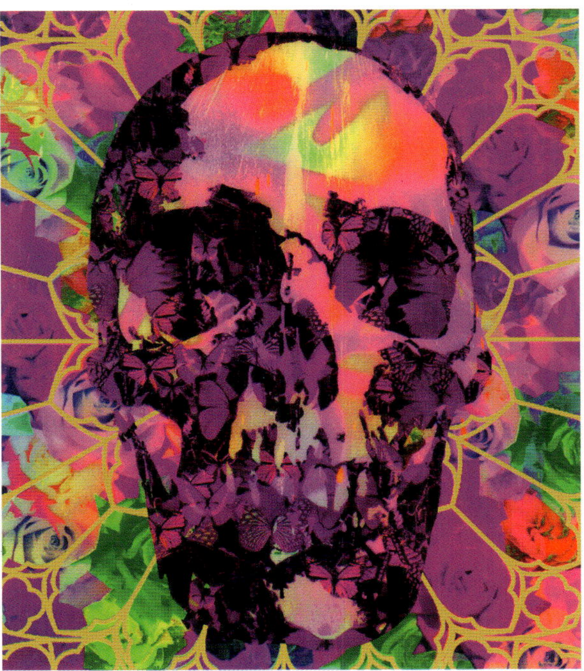

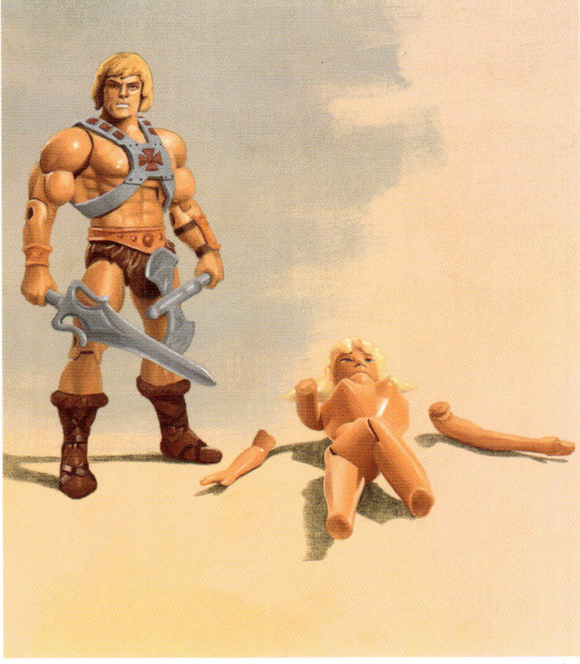

With over 25 years' experience, Graeme Richardson-Locke really understands the finer points of the printing process. And through his company – Eye 4 Colour – he is committed to delivering only the best giclée, screen and lithographic reproductions on the finest papers. From the highest quality scanning to efficient, cost-effective delivery, the service remains the same – personal. If you wish to add something very special, Eye 4 Colour will also manage flocking, foiling, glow-in-the-dark, diamond dusting and high-gloss selective varnishing. Graeme works with fine artists, photographers, art publishers, galleries, graphic designers, interior designers, private commissions and charity organisations. He produces print editions for local artistic luminaries that include Simon Dixon, Chris Kettle, Patrick Bremer, Katty McMurray and Ben Allen.

Eye 4 Colour offers a select range of limited editions online. It is an accredited printer of The Fine Art Trade Guild, giving the reassurance that prints are independently validated and tested to meet the highest expectations set by the Guild.

Frances Bloomfield

Artist
www.francesbloomfield.com

During the past few years Frances Bloomfield has created a significant body of work, which she has exhibited widely. She is now represented by Medici Gallery in London, Saffron Gallery in Battle, Clifton Fine Art in Bristol and Liberty Gallery, who show her work at the major London and international art fairs.

This piece is from the ongoing series – Dialogue Domestique – and has just been selected for *Aesthetica Magazine's* longlist for 2015.

This series explores notions of order and chaos in 'domestique' settings. The 'perfect home' is a powerful contemporary myth – however the home is also the setting for emotional and often disturbing scenarios. The contrast between what is desired or revealed and what may be hidden is often quite extreme. The empty chair could stand as a proxy for the person. It simultaneously creates presence and absence.

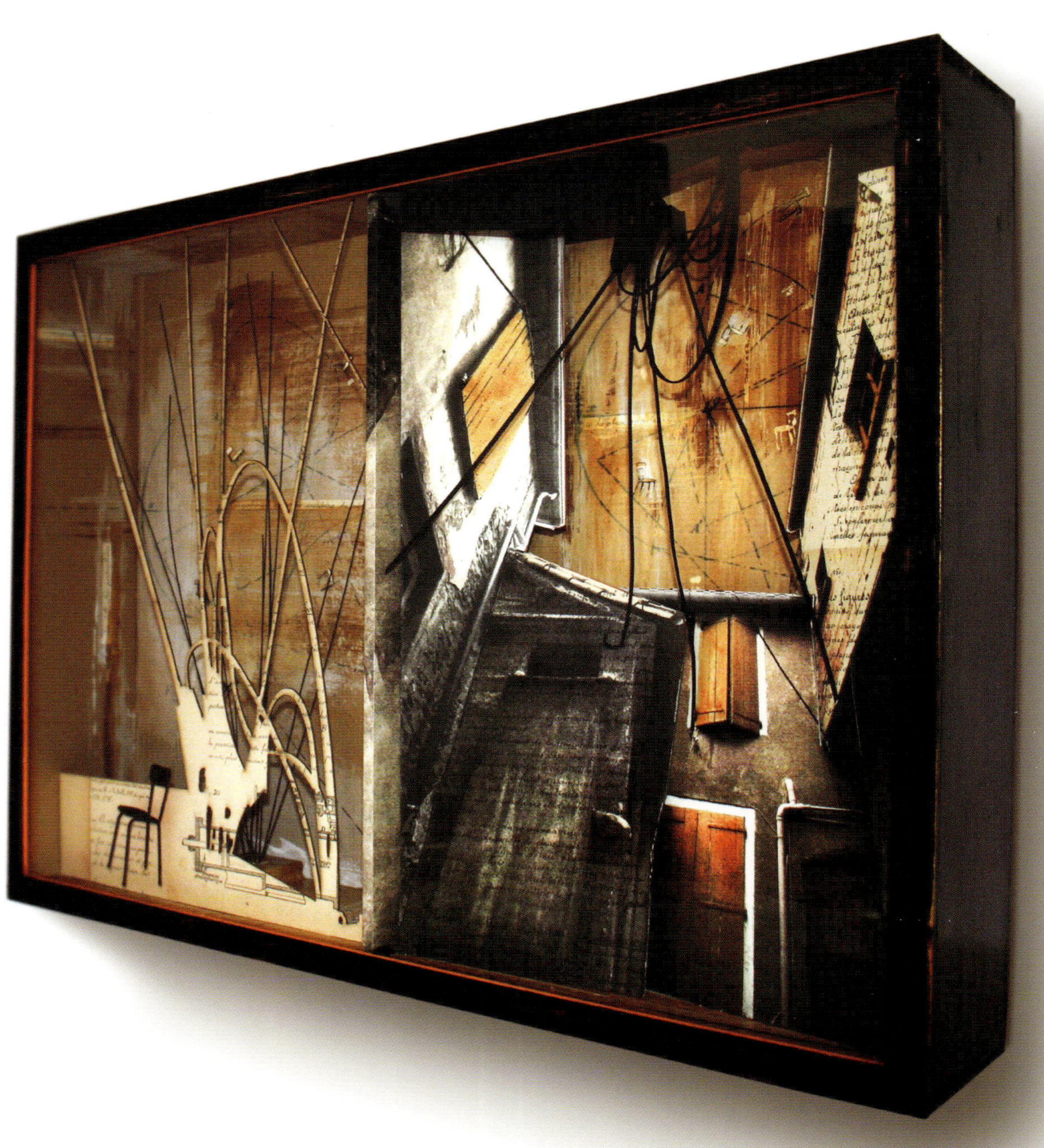

Chris MacDonald

Found Object Sculptor
Art at 24, 24 Foundry Street, Brighton (by appointment)

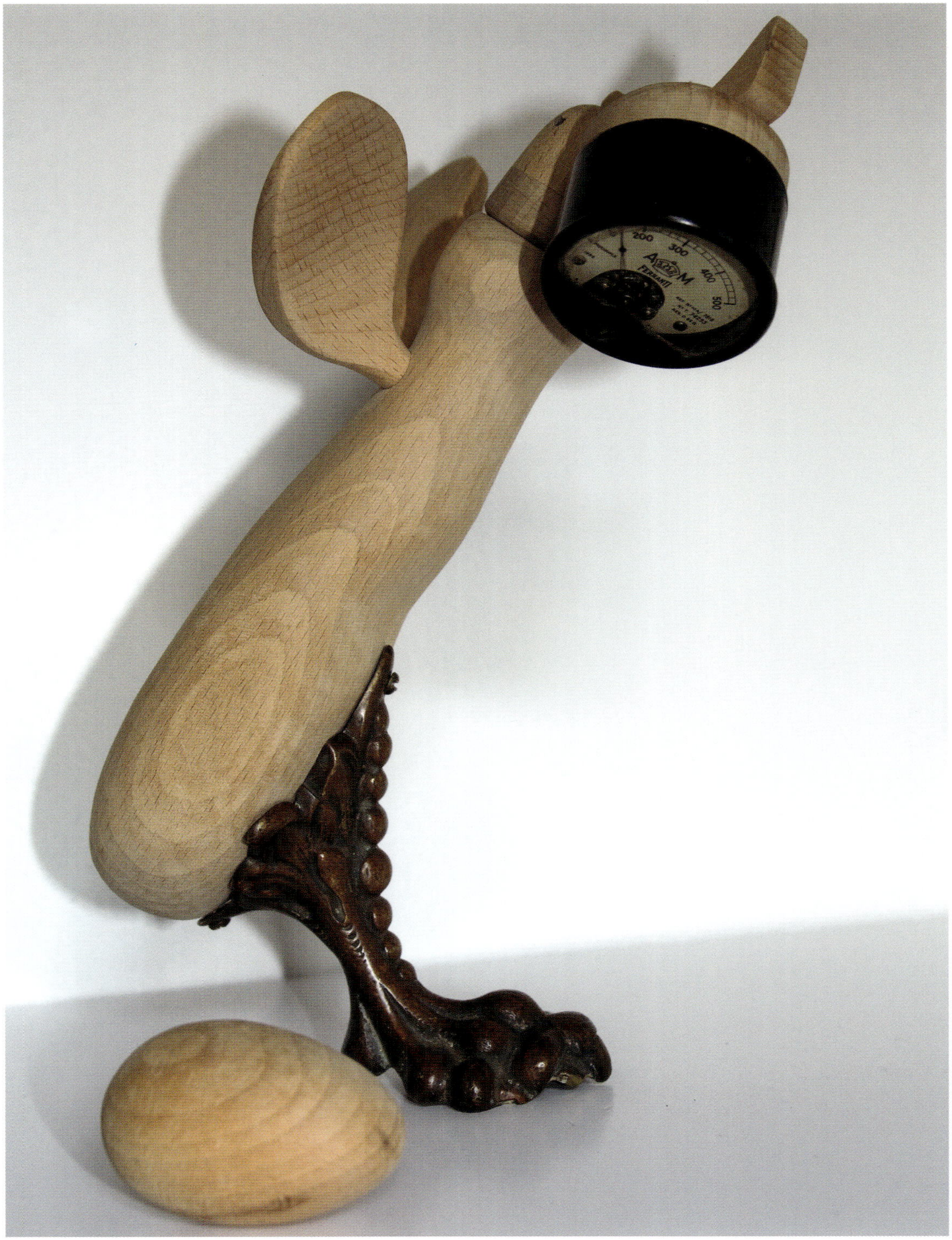

Left to right:
Monoladybird; Flight of Fancy

Chris MacDonald's 'Monoladybird' is staring down intently at the perfectly carved egg that's appeared by its perfectly carved bottom. Its perfectly carved wings are raised in surprise. The sculpture is supported by a single brass foot from a long-discarded piece of furniture. "It would have been no use to anyone but me," observes Chris. Which sums up perfectly what this 'found object sculptor' is all about.

His style is suffused with surreal wit. And if you are looking for a truly original piece of 3D artwork, Chris can transform what most regard as 'rubbish' into artworks that amaze with their imagination and skill.

Chris is one of Brighton's most accessible artists, and you can view his work in his front-room, invitation-only gallery at 24 Foundry Street. Just give him a call (see page 132).

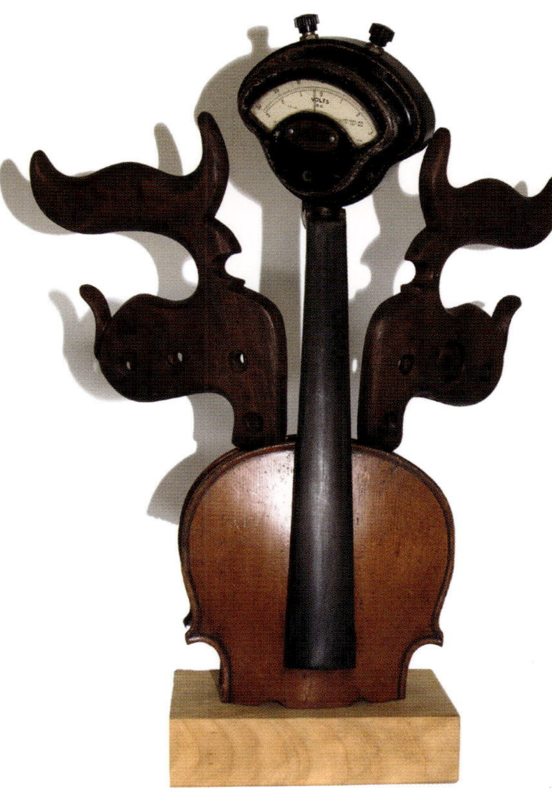

Jessica Zoob

Artist
www.jessicazoob.com

This page: For Joy II
Opposite page: For Joy I

Jessica Zoob now has a range of limited-edition prints available on paper, canvas and Diasec. Also available is a range of textiles, cushions and wallpapers in collaboration with Romo Black Edition. Check out the shop section of her website (above) for further information.

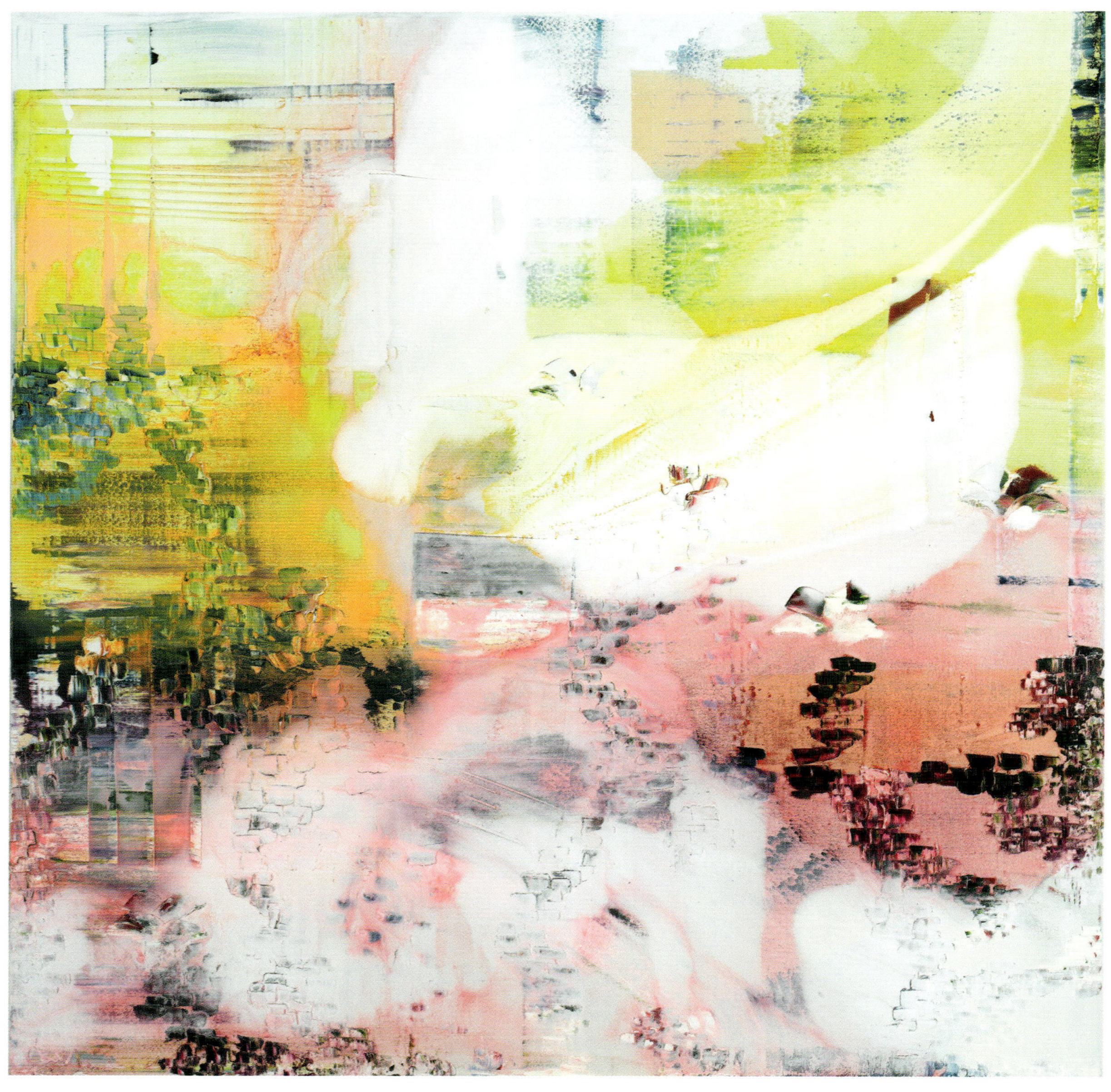

Zoob's use of line, texture and colour recall the work of Gerhard Richter's abstract paintings and the poetic quality of Claude Monet's later works. However, they are rich in imagination with an innate energy and beauty all of their own

Leonie Irvine
Medici Gallery

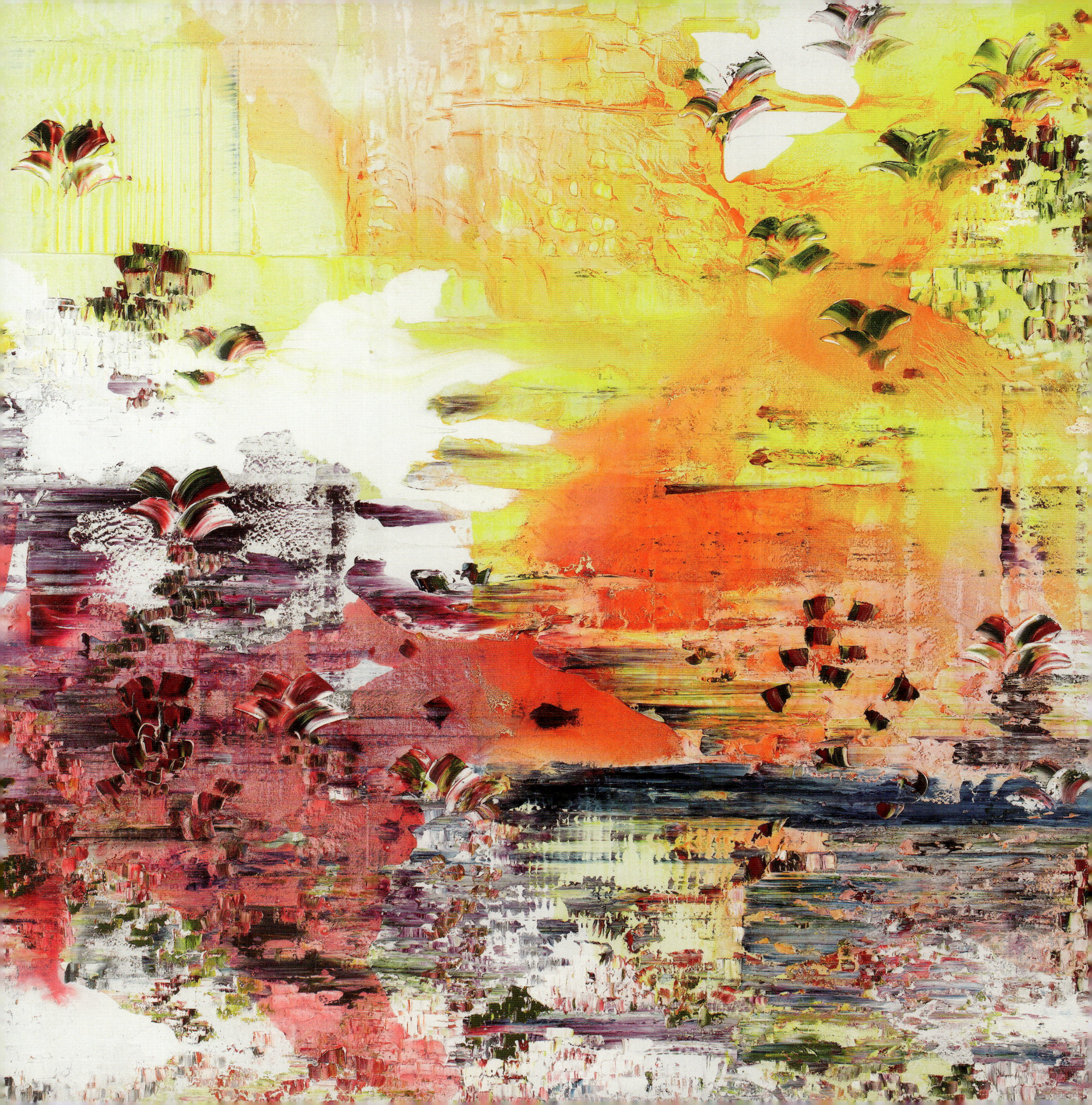

Jude Evans

Artist
www.judeevans.co.uk

Clockwise from top left:
Sands to the West; Harbour; Old Sea Wall; Sands to the East

The South Downs and the Sussex coast have been major influences on the artistic imagination of local artist Jude Evans, inspiring her to create landscape and marine scenes in drawings, paintings and photographs.

A Londoner for many years, Jude studied at Chelsea College of Art, worked at the National Gallery and became assistant editor of *Art Quarterly* magazine. She recently returned to Sussex and is currently exploring digital art by manipulating her photos to create striking graphic images.

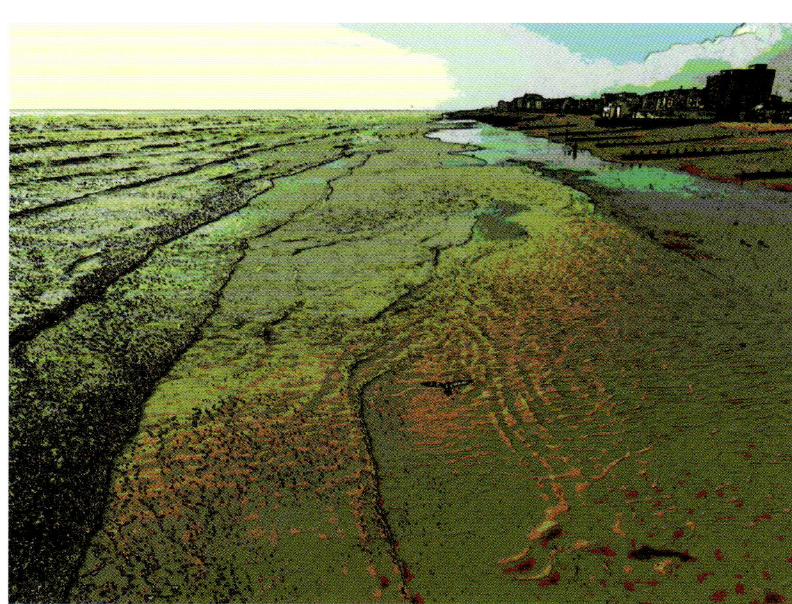

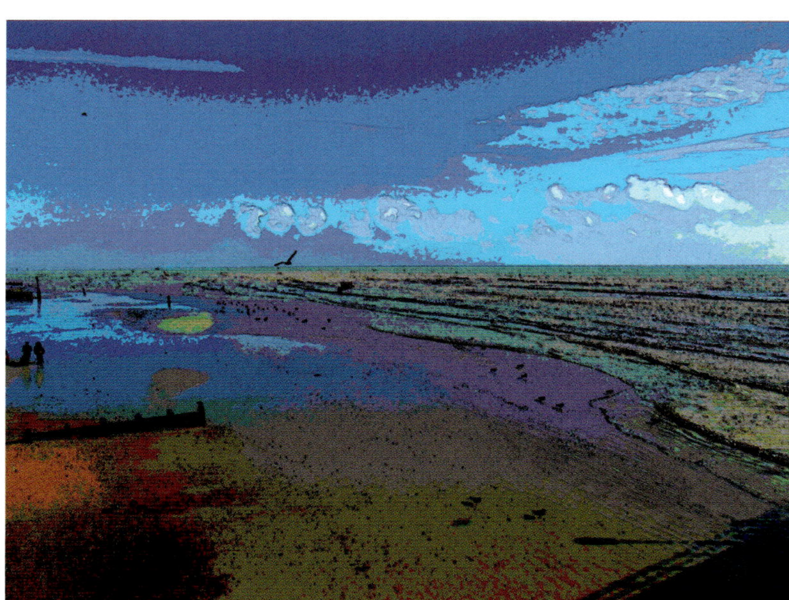

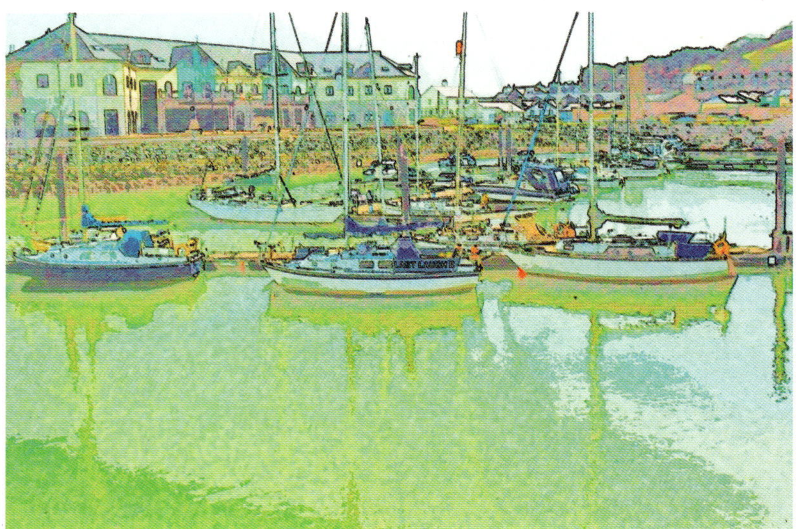

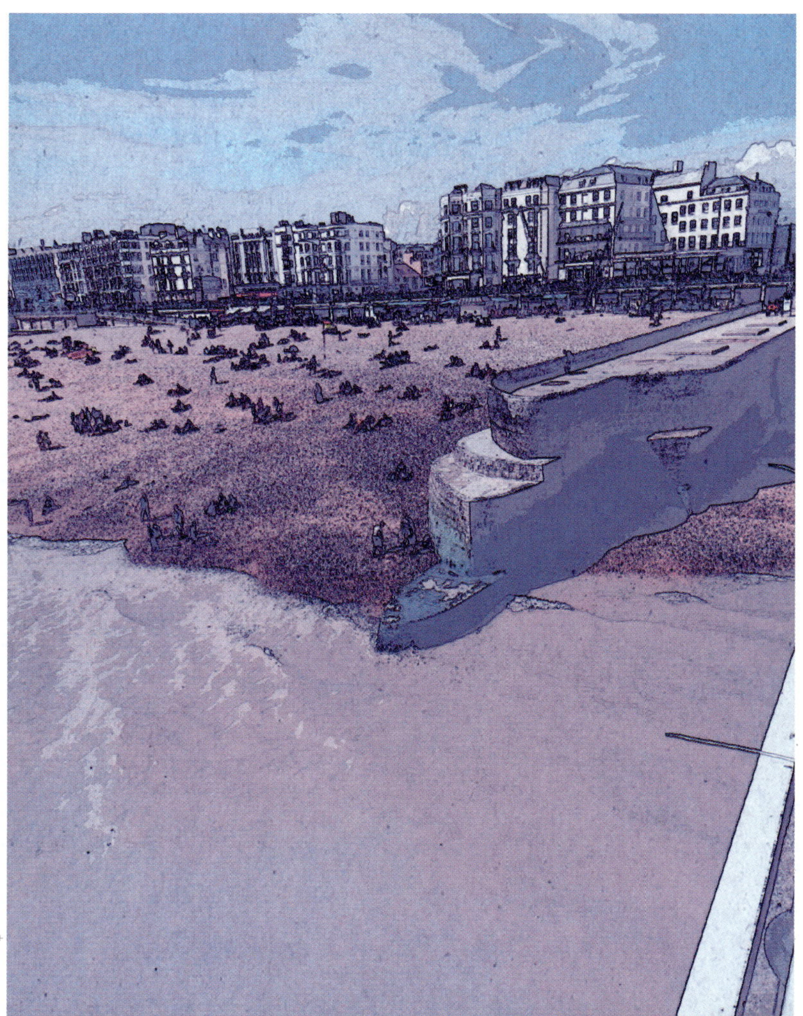

Edith Burtenshaw

Artist
www.edithburtenshaw.com

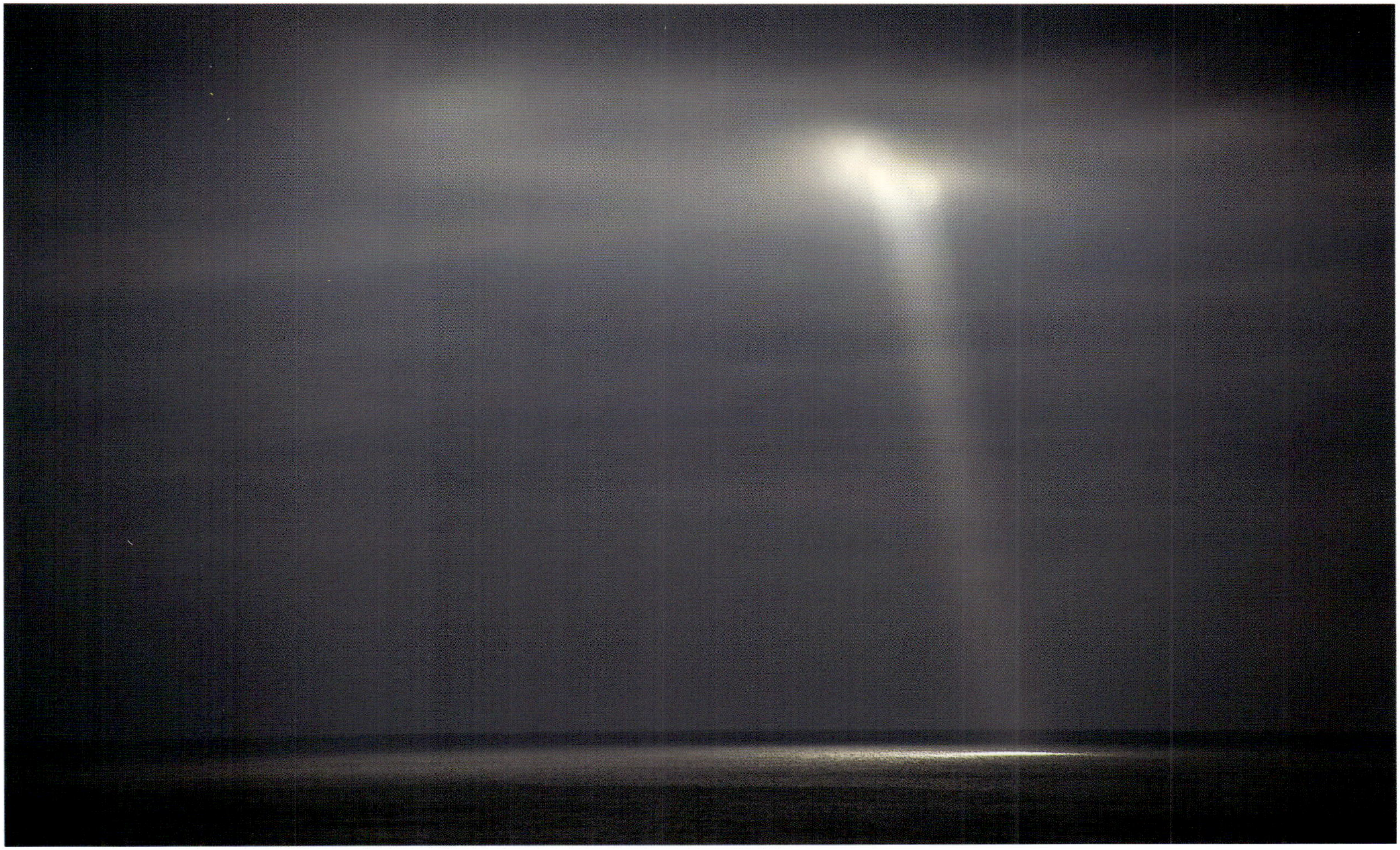

Clockwise from top: No Life Without Light (photograph);
from 'The Tree' series of paintings

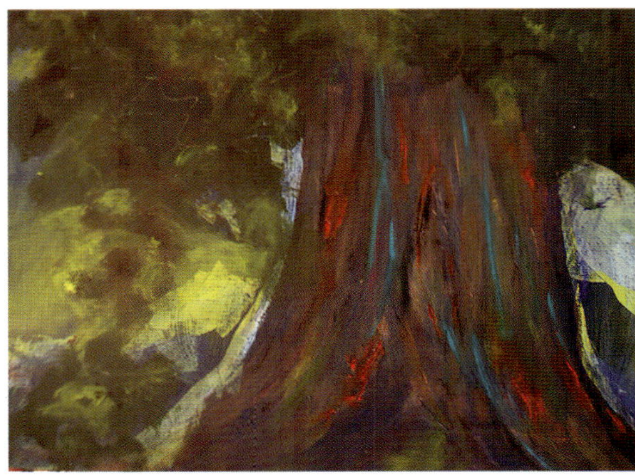

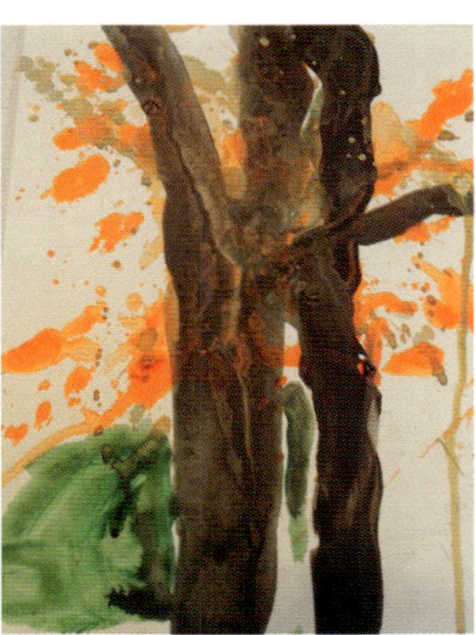

Edith Burtenshaw graduated from the UCA in Farnham, Surrey, with a Fine Art degree. She has recently returned to her love of painting, having spent time successfully expanding her artistic practice into the areas of photography, performance art and film.

Edith's current work explores her favourite subject matter 'The Tree' in all its stages of seasonal change and maturity. Her brushstrokes are bold and energetic, reflecting and representing the strength, energy and colours of her subject.

She will be exhibiting at Namrik Mews, Hove, as part of this year's Artists Open Houses festival.

Betty Shek

Original. Design. Handmade. Vivid Buttons, Felt Art and Upcycled Handmade Jewellery
www.facebook.com/bettyandfriendsartistsopenhouse / www.etsy.com/shop/designedbybettyshek

Top: Handmade Felt Arts & Embroidery Brooches
Below: Fairyland Hand-embroidery Wall Art

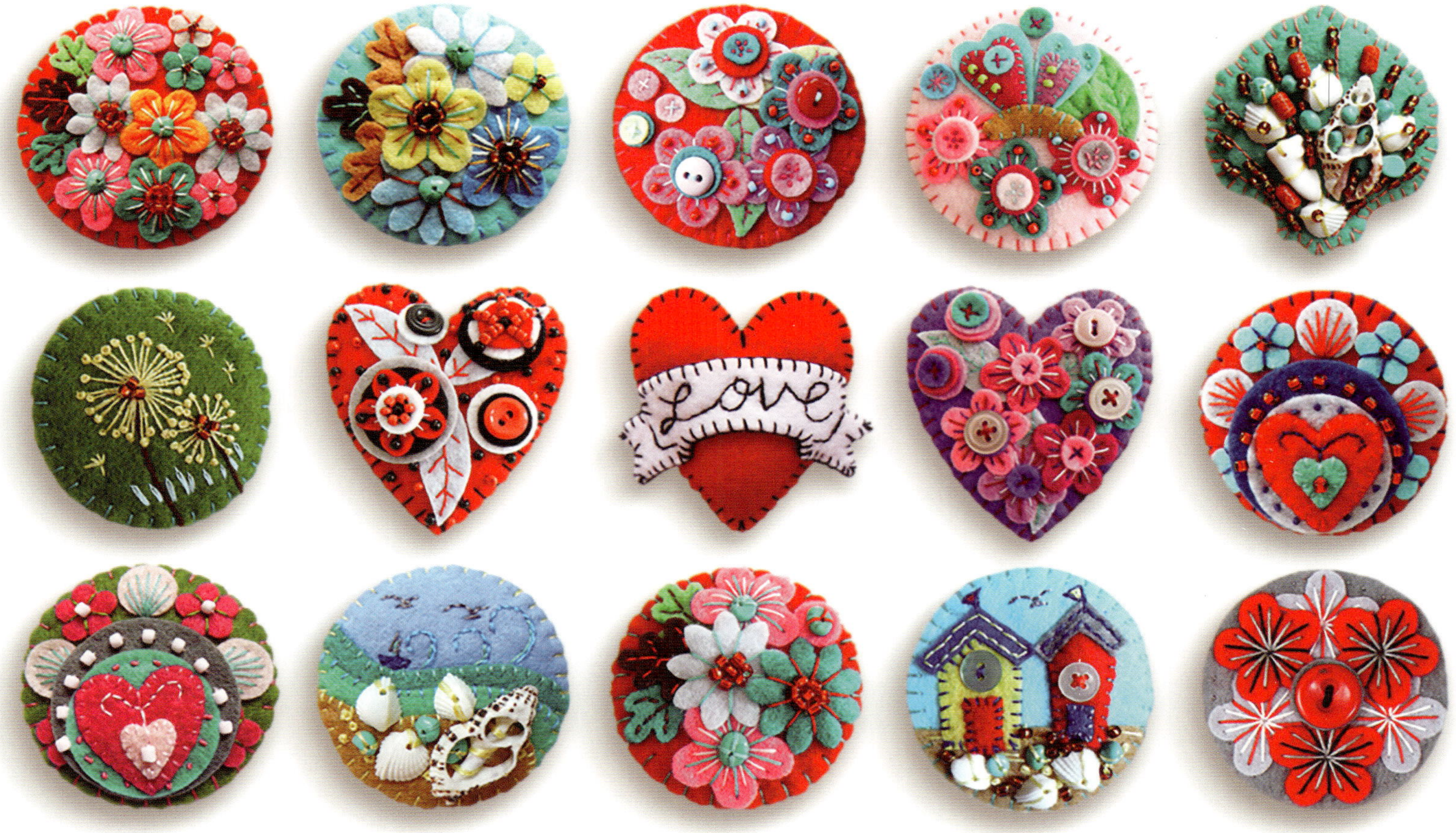

Betty Shek has a background in fashion and textile design, and she enjoys creating unique pieces of felt art, using vintage buttons and up-cycled elements. As a Brighton-based artist, Betty's work is inspired by nature and the surrounding elements.

Her button and found-object jewellery – made from her vast, ever-growing hoard – is always a popular choice, as are her delicate intricate embroideries, which can be enjoyed as brooches or artwork.

Betty's work can be found at iO Gallery, Sydney Street (page 106), in the North Laine and also at the Fishing Quarter Gallery on Brighton's seafront.

Her studio will open in May for the Artists Open Houses event, with a selection of talented artists showing their work. More information can be found on Betty's facebook page (see above).

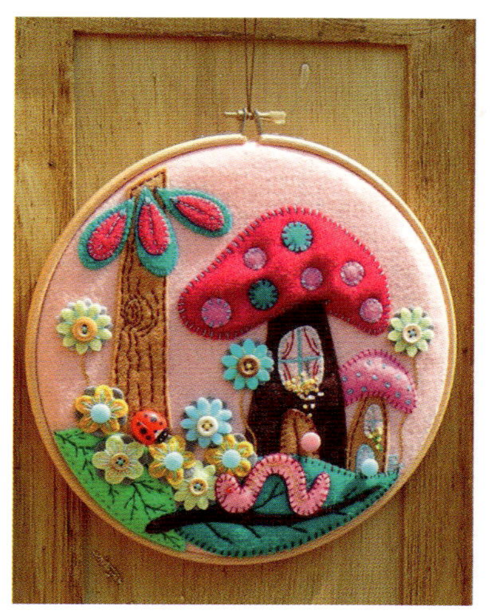

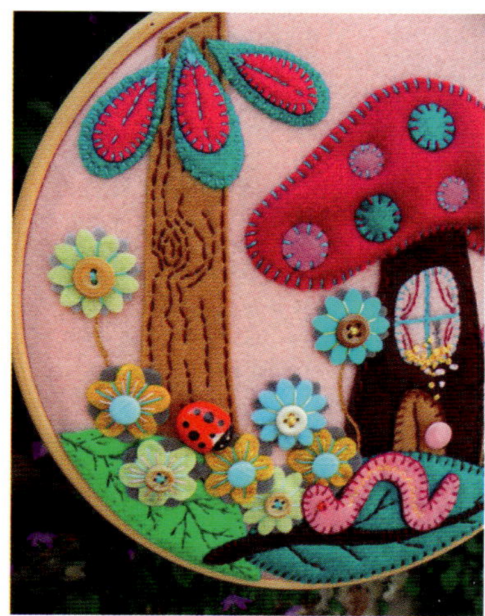

Laura Callaghan Grooms

Mixed Media Artist
tinyurl.com/pdwbpws

Clockwise from top left:
Brighton Seagull; African Butterfly; The First Butterfly; Brighton Butterfly

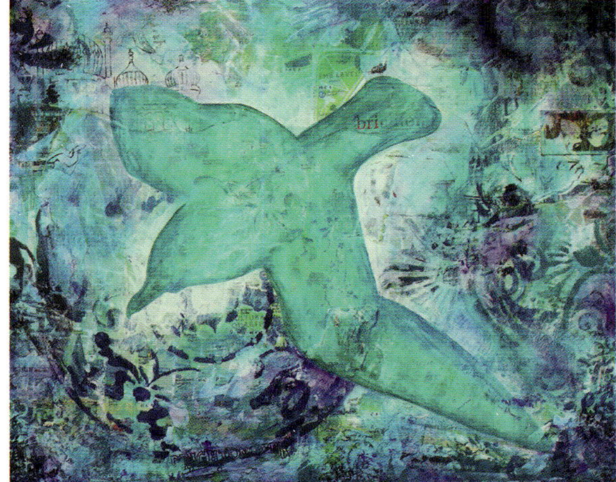

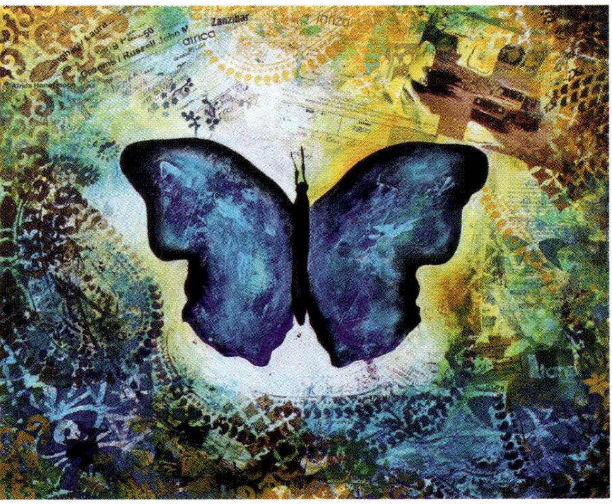

Laura Callaghan Grooms doesn't remember a time in her life when she wasn't painting or drawing. She grew up by the seaside in Thanet, Kent, and remembers a childhood of drawing with pastels in her Nan's garden, felt-tipping every piece of paper she stumbled across, stashing arts materials like treasures in the well-organised chaos of her bedroom, and sketching family members as they sat watching the TV.

Now based in Brighton, her artwork is still inspired by the places she's been and the things she's seen and felt. Using a selection of collaged paper-based ephemera as the basis, she builds up mixed media, found objects and different varieties of paint to create finished canvases with delicate translucent layers. Her work often uses the image, outline or silhouette of butterflies.

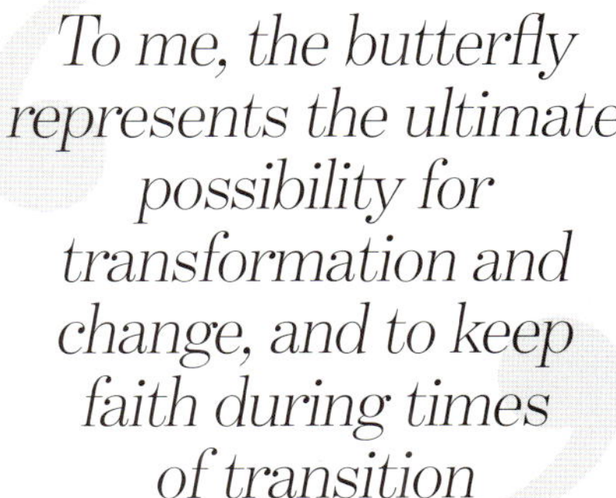

To me, the butterfly represents the ultimate possibility for transformation and change, and to keep faith during times of transition

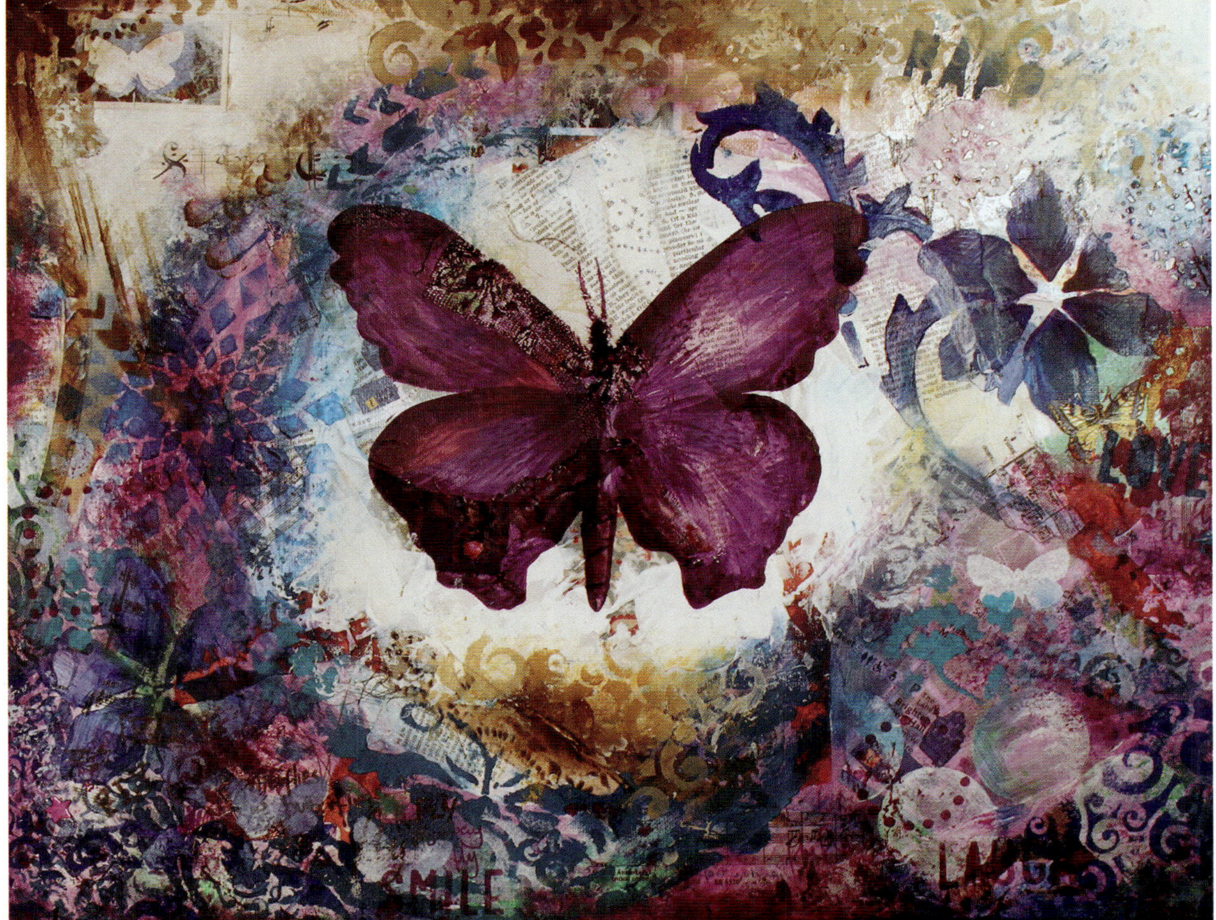

Laura takes commissions, and more examples of her work can be found on Pinterest. For more information, see her contact details (page 133).

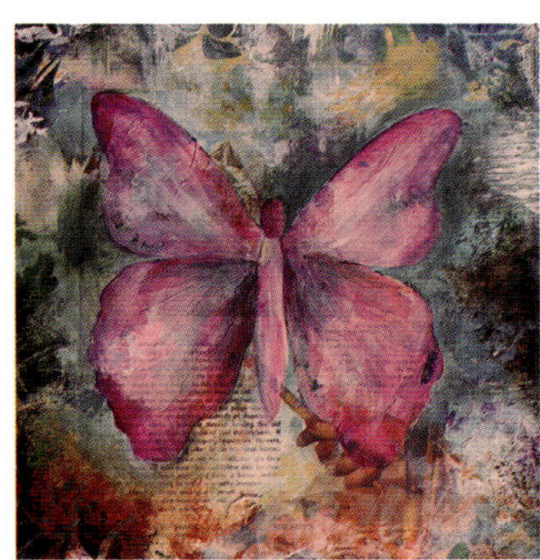

Ian Brown

Printmaker
www.volcaniceditions.com

Pancake Rocks III, 20-colour screenprint (31cm x 46cm) Edition 5, part of a series of 6 prints

My specialist knowledge lies in solar plate etching and the water-based screen process

Ian Brown is a Brighton-based printmaker. He has exhibited widely in the UK and overseas, showing last year in Minneapolis, Milan and the RA Summer Show. This year he is exhibiting in central Tokyo, Keri Keri, New Zealand, and Hangzhou, China (in September) as part of the Impact 9 International Print Symposium.

He has work in collections in the UK and abroad, including the Tate, V&A, Arts Council of Great Britain, and Minneapolis Museum of Modern Art.

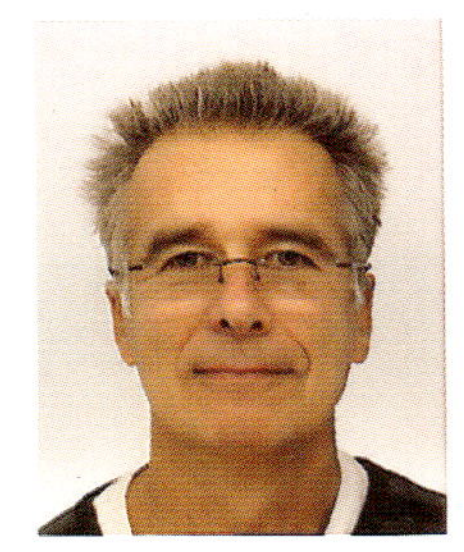

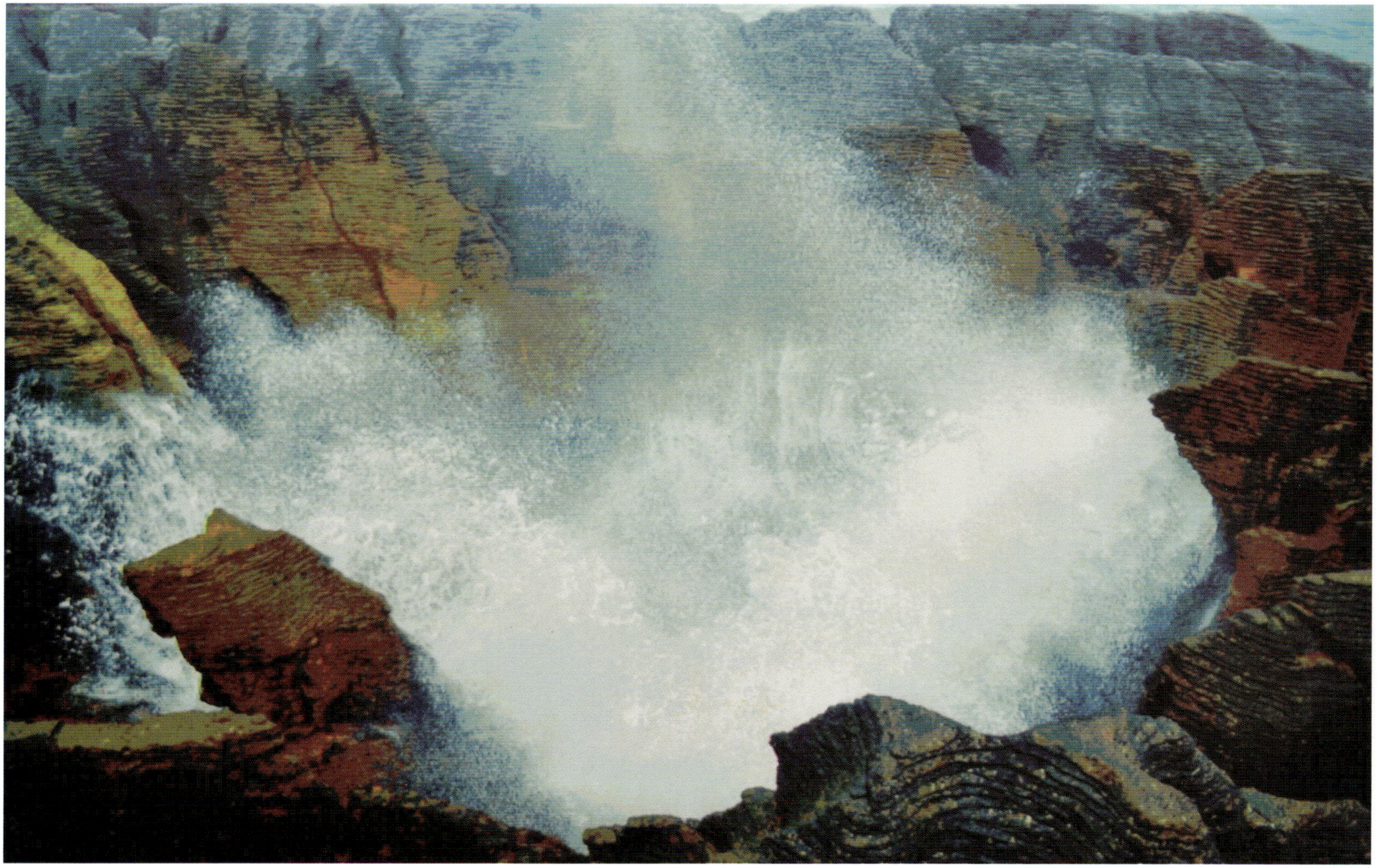

Volcanic Editions

16 Rosehill Terrace, Brighton BN1 4JJ
www.volcaniceditions.com

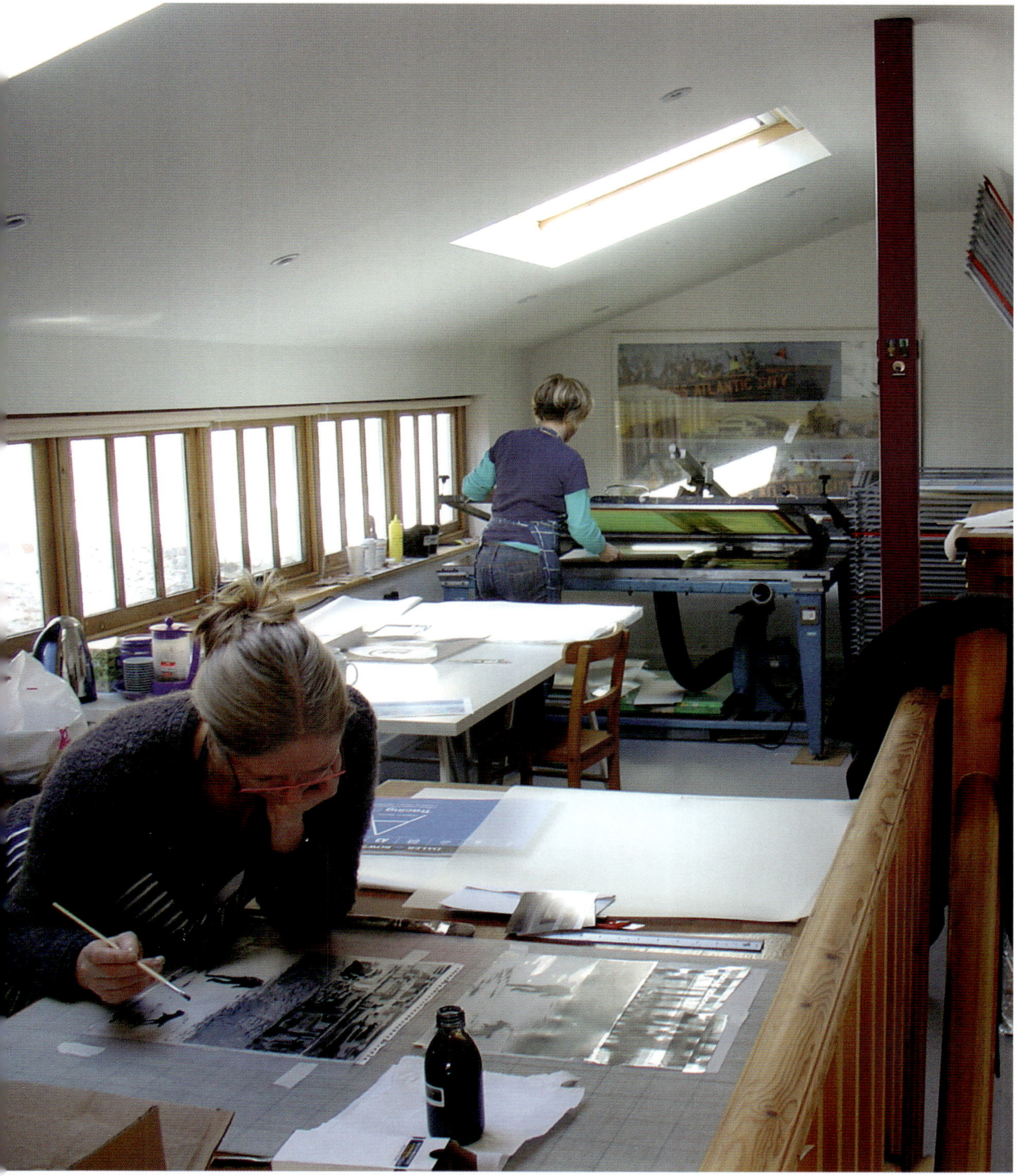

Main image: Screenprinting (first floor)
Inset: Rochat etching press for solar plate etching, drypoint and monotype (ground floor)

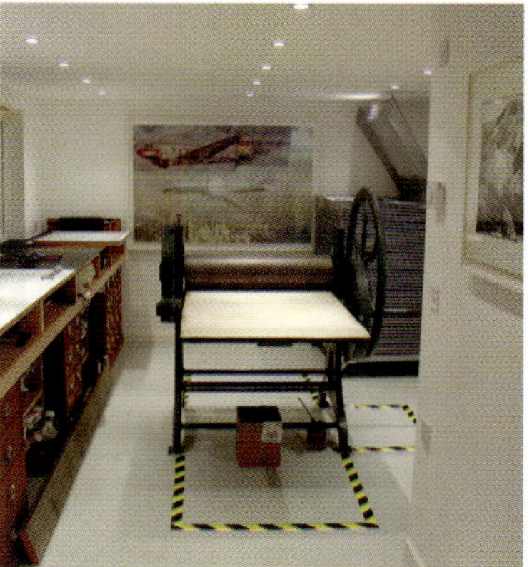

Volcanic Editions was founded in 2010 by Ian Brown. A small workshop on two floors, it specialises in screenprinting, solar plate etching, drypoint and monotype.

Equipment includes a Rochat etching press (32in x 56in), a Marler Elite (30in x 40in) vacuum bed plus the highest quality water-based inks as well as metallics, fluorescents and diamond dust.

Small numbers ensure that artists learning the process get the fullest attention in a relaxed and friendly environment. Over the past four years, work produced in the studio has entered all the major UK open competitions and won prizes at many of them.

As well as weekly access, Volcanic Editions runs a one-week Summer School for screenprinting and a second week for solar plate etching, drypoint and monotype.

Wendy Standen

Artist
www.wendystanden.co.uk

Clockwise from top left:
Amelia Leclercq; Fox; Mother's Prayer

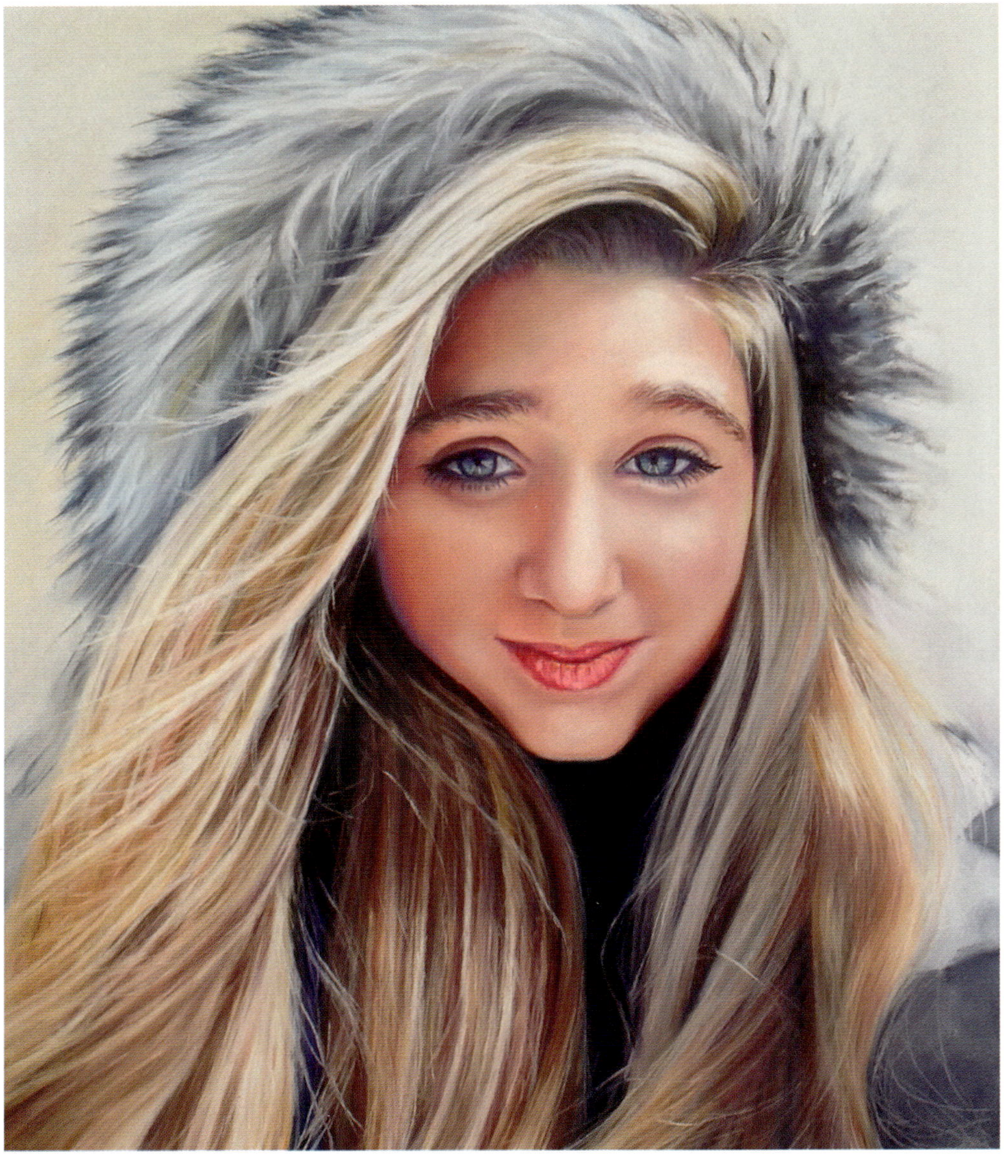

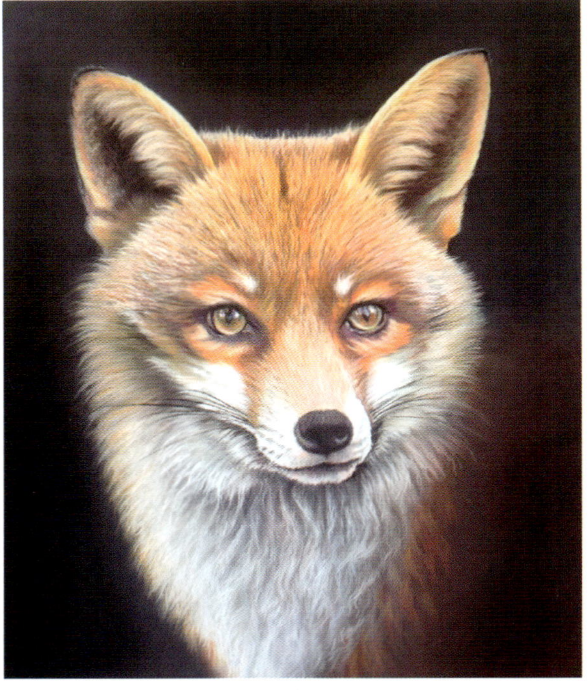

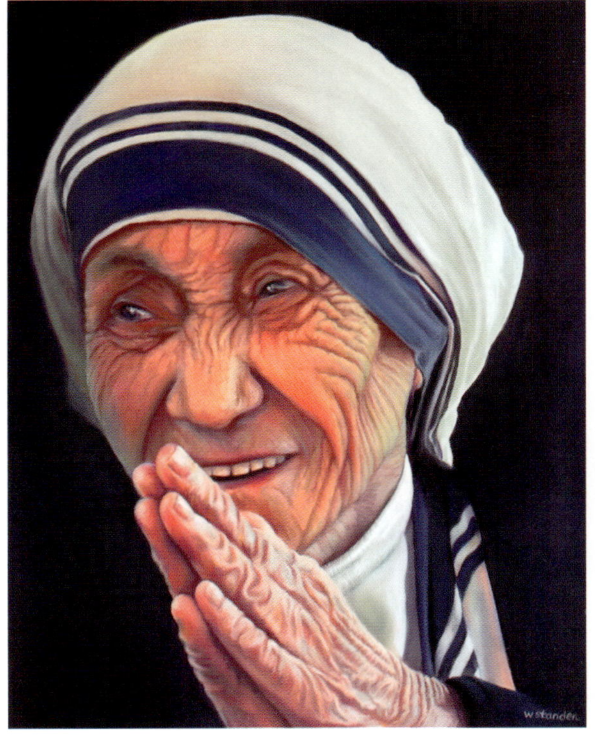

Wendy Standen is an award-winning artist based in Withdean, Brighton. She trained as a teacher specialising in Art and Design and taught for the last 20 years of her career in Brighton primary schools.

Wendy has recently specialised in painting portraits in pastel – human and animal – and also produces work in a range of other 2 and 3D media. Her work has been published in *Artists & Illustrators* magazine and shown in the Mall Galleries, London.

Wendy is a member of several art groups and societies, and is secretary of Ditchling's long-established Attic Art Club. She is currently a director of Shoreham Art Gallery, a collective of more 20 artists, where some of her work is always on show and for sale.

Wendy can be visited by arrangement at her studio in Brighton. She is available for commissions for portraits in pastel.

Clockwise from left:
The Proprietor, Tombstone; Tiger Eyes; Layap Lady

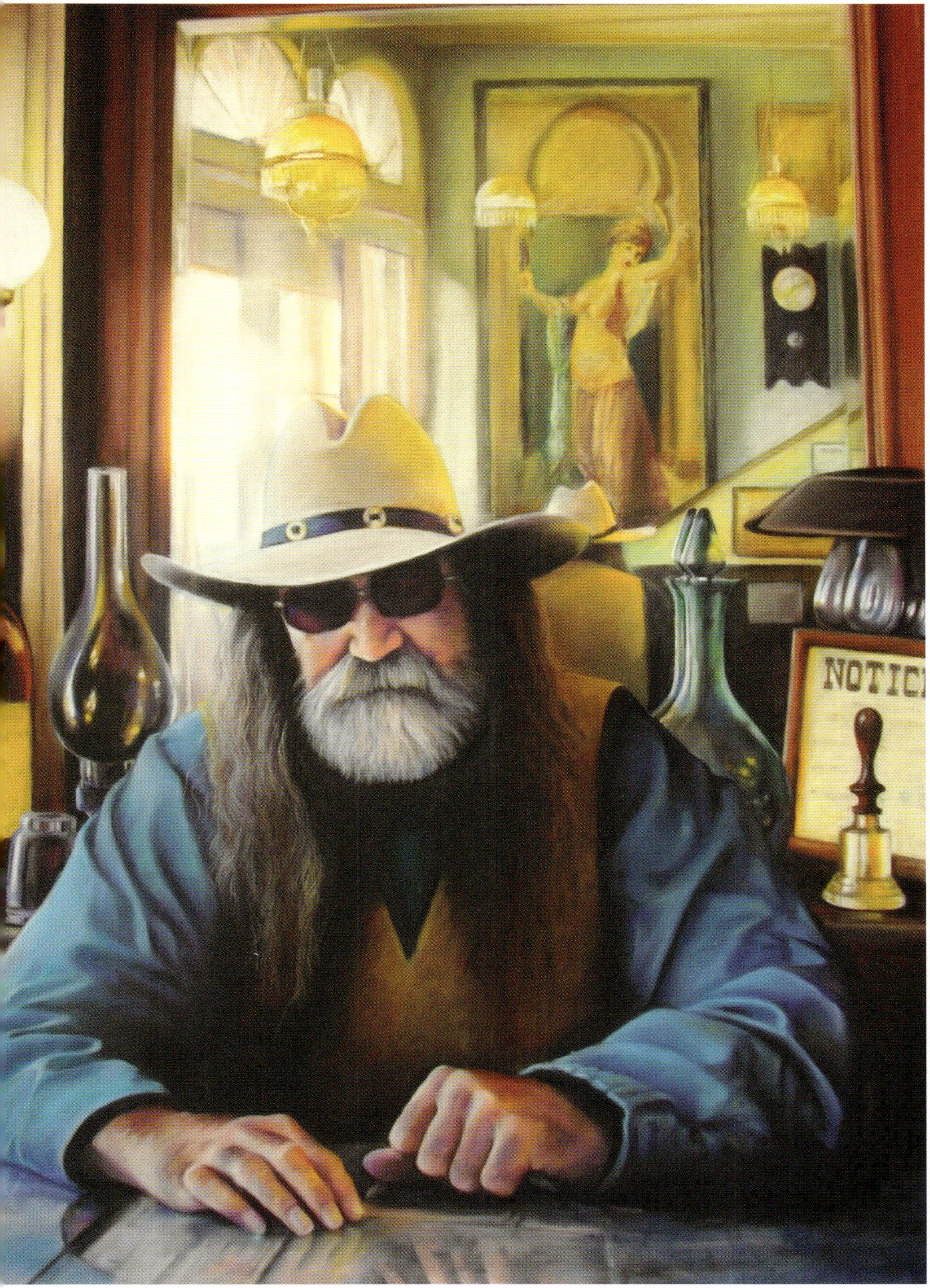

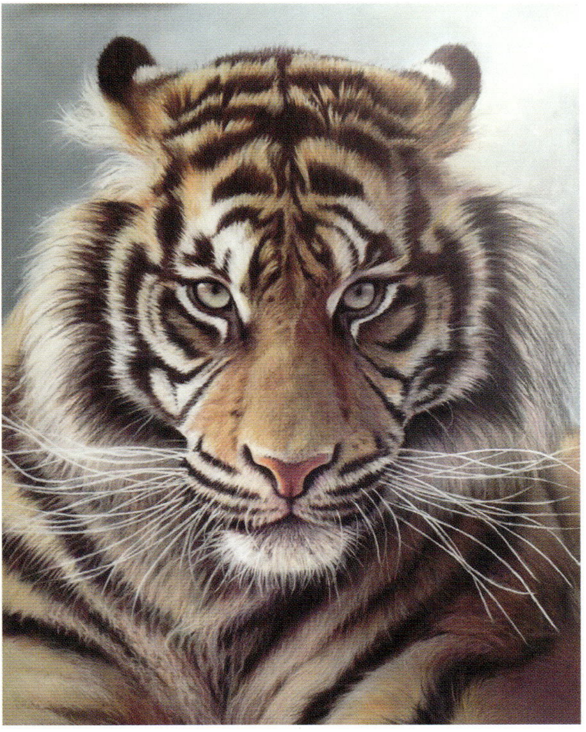

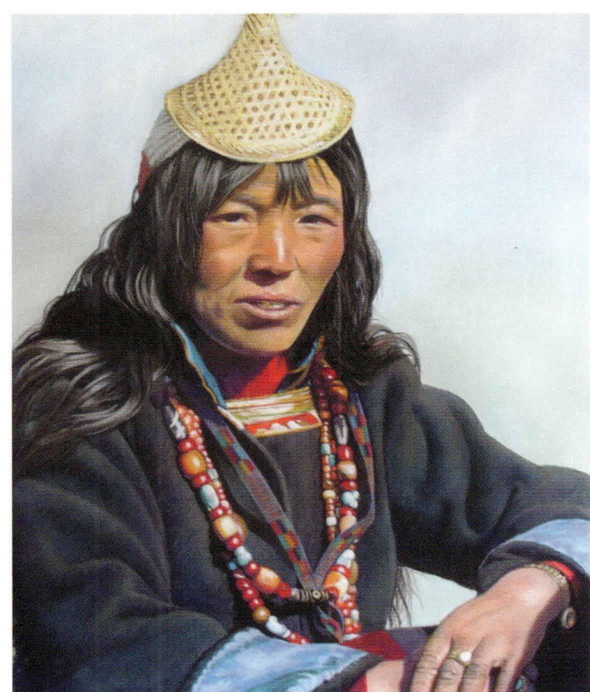

Chanchala Ariyaratne

Jeweller
www.chanchala.co.uk

Clockwise from top: Eric the Half a Bee; My Rusty Heart for all of Time; The Ladybug Invasion

Chanchala makes intricate jewellery from old watch parts. The many characters she creates inhabit a hybrid world of nature and machinery. She's always producing new designs – The Ladybug Invasion (below) is one of the latest.

Her Steampunk-inspired jewellery started with watch and clock parts rescued from the 2004 South Asian tsunami. In addition to her 'upcycled' jewellery involving mechanical bits, she also makes a collection of little stash-away secret lockets, one-of-a-kind clocks with hidden depths and personalised accessories, all with old-world charm and rustic design.

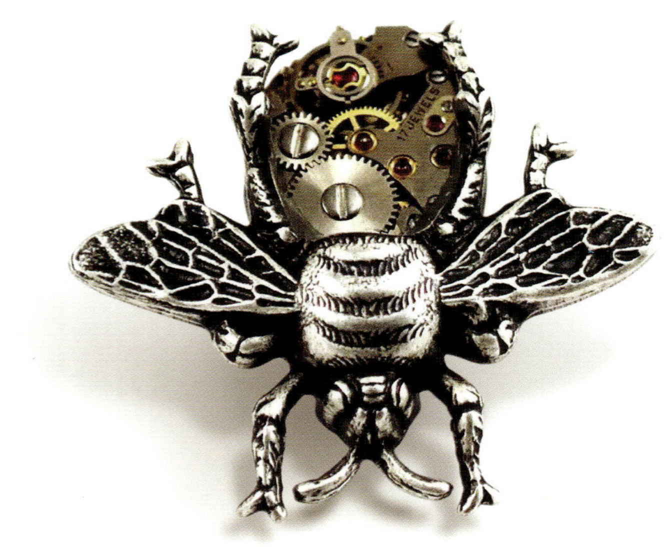

If you were a couple of ladybirds trawling around and came across this mesmerising miniature world of layers upon layers of gears and gems, wouldn't you be tempted to explore?

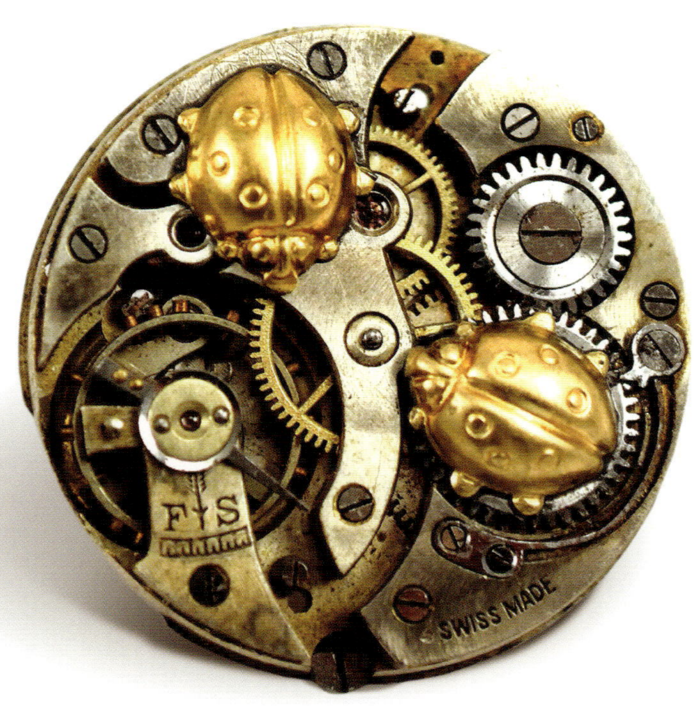

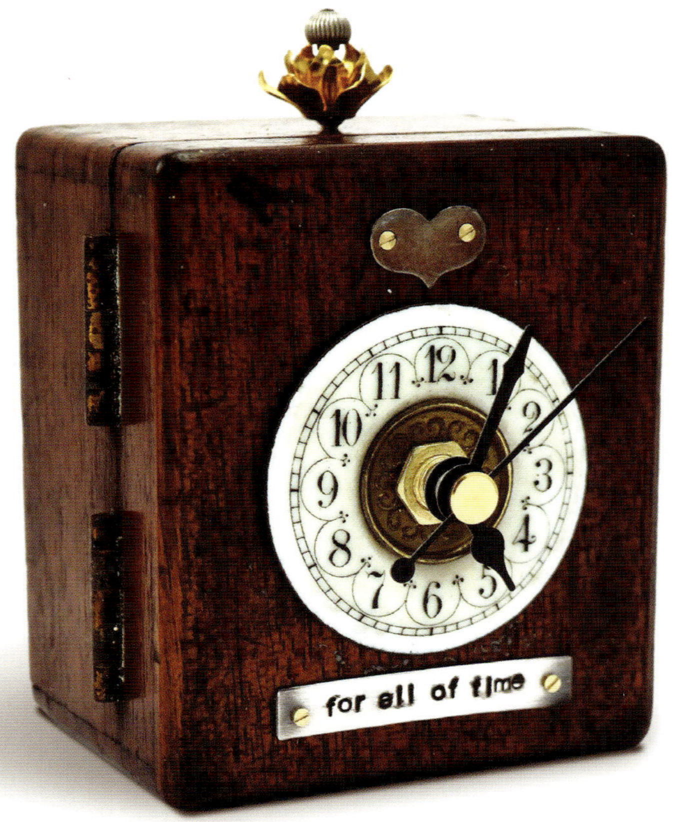

Karl Smith

Sculptor & Jeweller
www.carvedoak.co.uk

Clockwise from top: Oak Dining Table with Pewter Inlay; Earrings and Necklace; 'Caress' Alabaster; The Bench

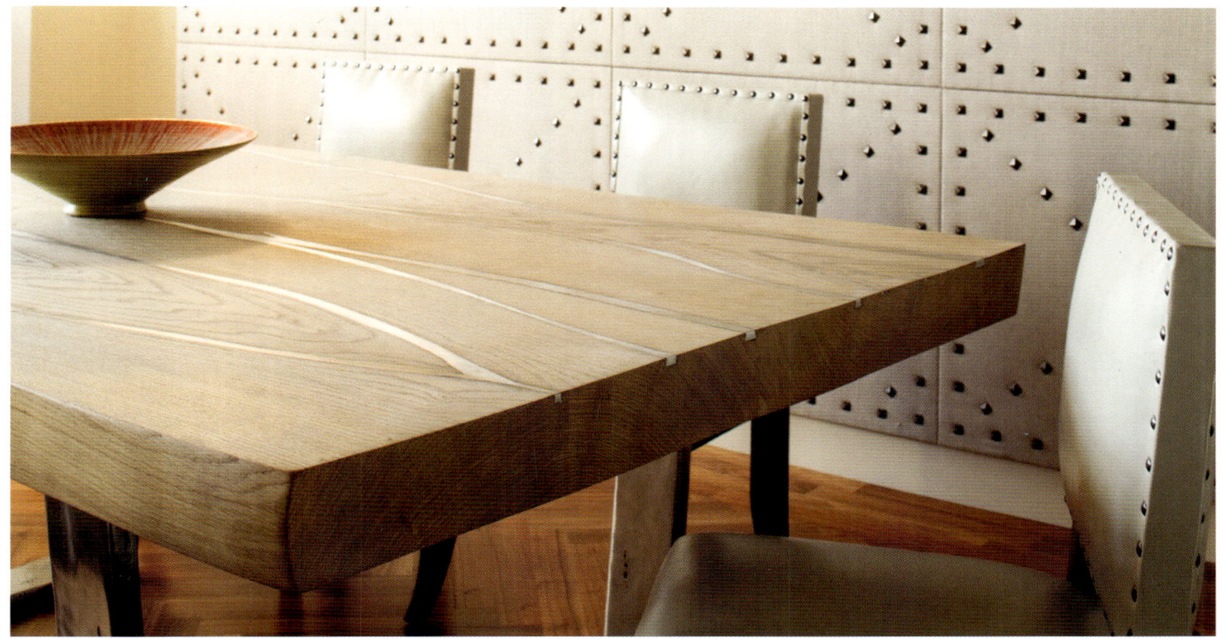

Karl Smith's work is often inspired by his beloved Sussex landscape, the human form and elements from nature. His pieces have a sensual fluid energy and simplicity.

He enjoys working with different media and in different scales, for example the juxtaposition of steel and timber in his epic sculptural furniture, as recently featured in *How to Spend It* magazine. However, he is equally at home carving alabaster into organic forms or creating exquisite heirloom pieces of jewellery.

The slow process, involving hand tools, allows Karl to discover the hidden beauty within the timber or stone that could so easily be lost with the use of power tools. History naturally occurring during the creative process is treasured and explored. These tooled marks are an integral part of his aesthetic.

Karl enjoys working in collaboration with his clients, who have included interior designers such as Intarya, on commissioned pieces. Thus enabling him to create the perfect end product for their environment.

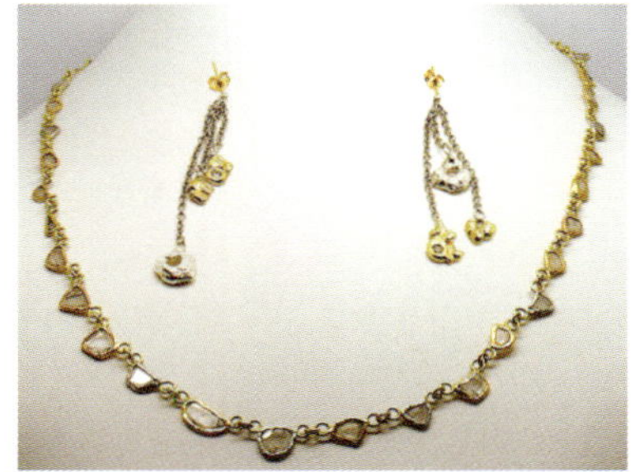

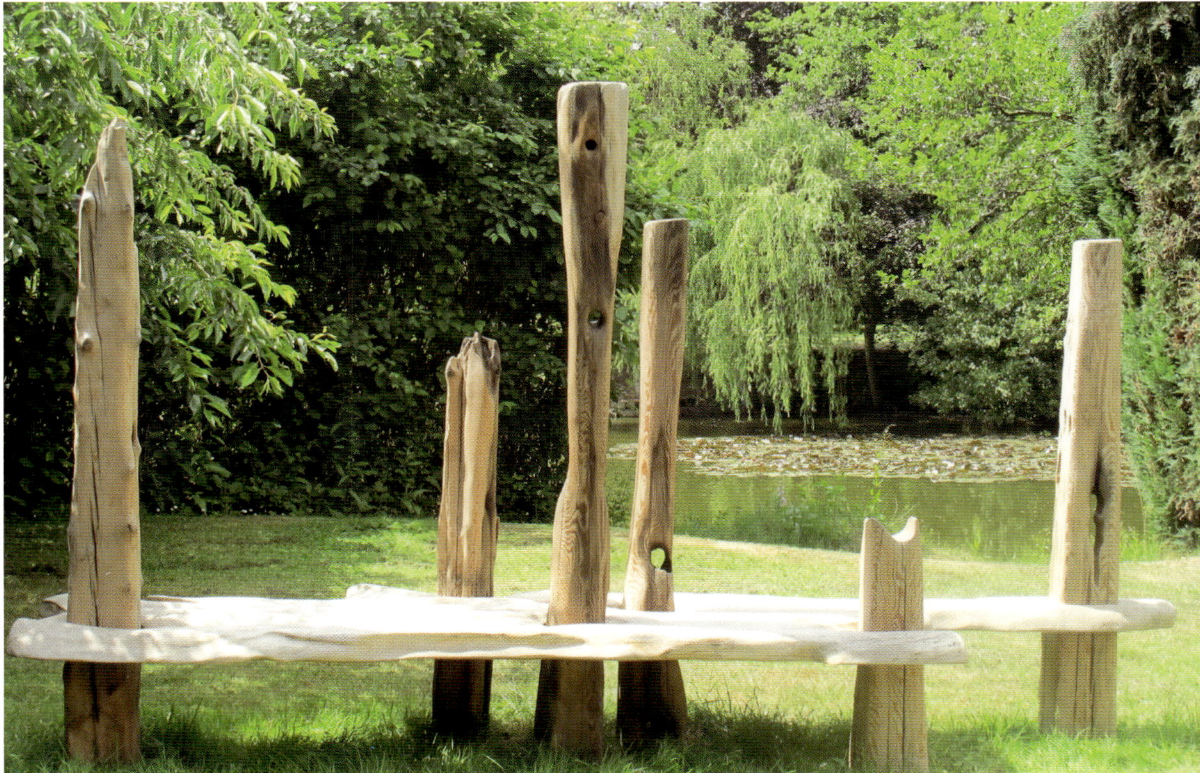

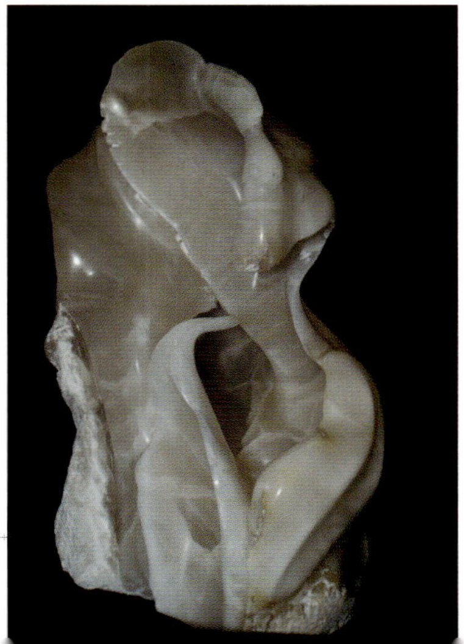

Monika Jakimauskaite

Artist & Accessory Designer
www.moniusia.eu

Clockwise from top left:
Shadow; Devil's Dyke; Fishing

Lithuanian artist Monika Jakimauskaite, who is now based in Brighton, combines photography and textiles to create captivating mixed-media artworks. Applying photographic prints to fabric, she embellishes with embroidery and appliqué, extending details from the image onto the fabric to create perspective or add ornamental touches. Her current colour palette is simple and minimalistic, dominated by pastels and black and white.

Monika has recently started designing handbags, using the same original mixed-media approach. She adds buttons and textile paints to her creations, producing unique and striking results on beautiful accessories for everyday use. The bags feature different designs on each side, giving a choice of ways to wear them.

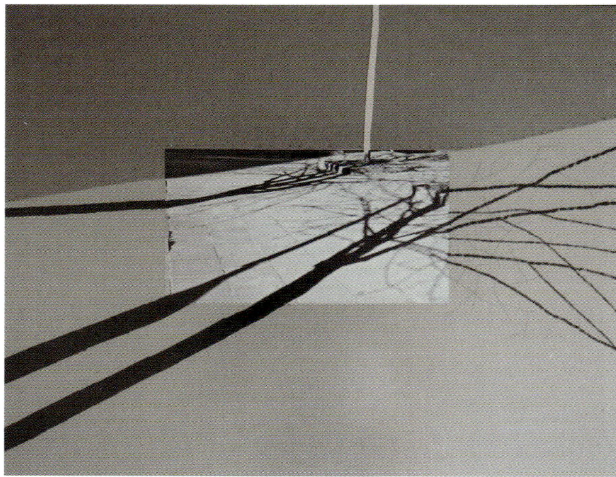

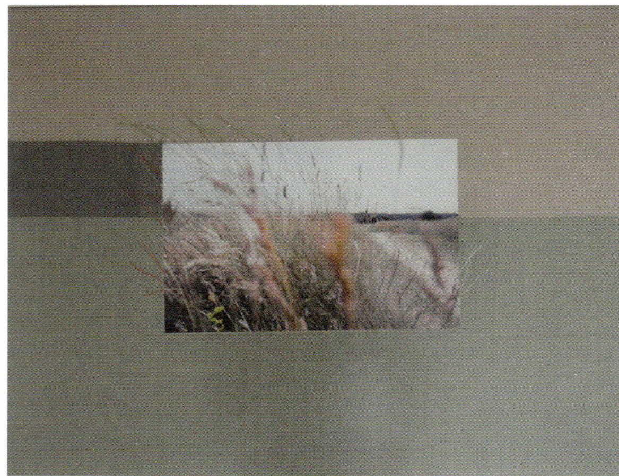

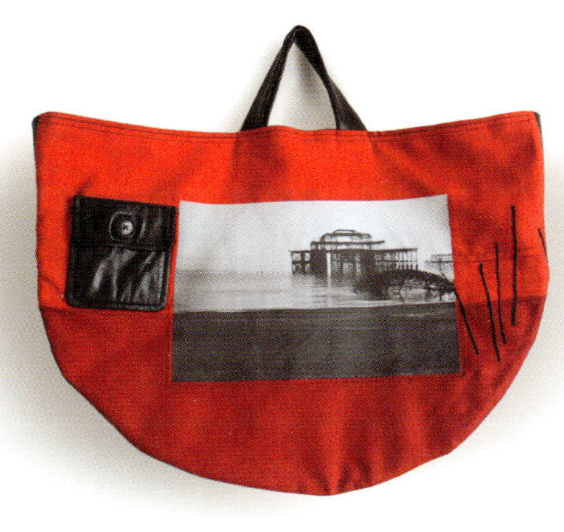

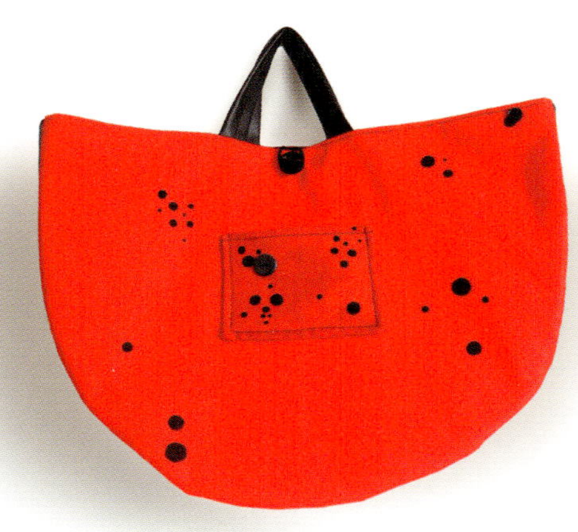

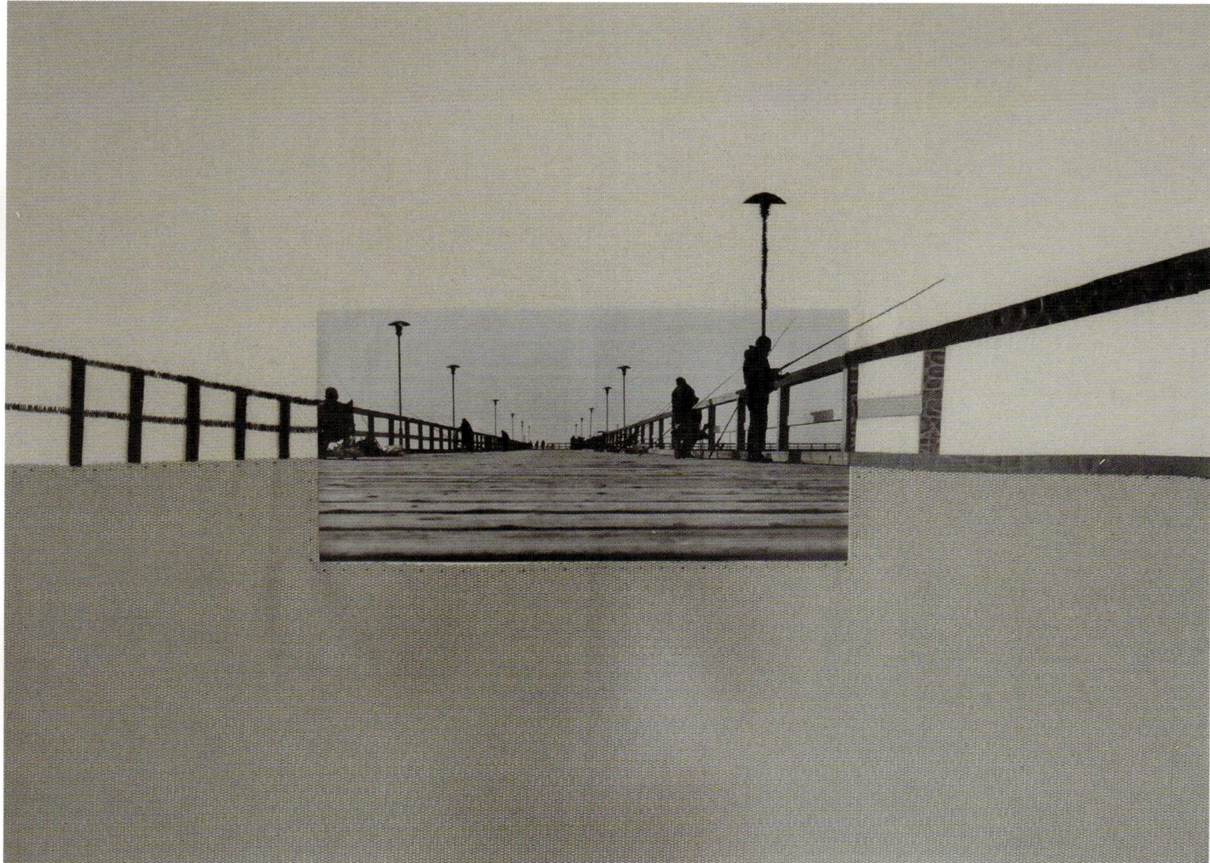

Kris Pawlowski

Documentary & Portrait Photographer
www.krispawlowski.com

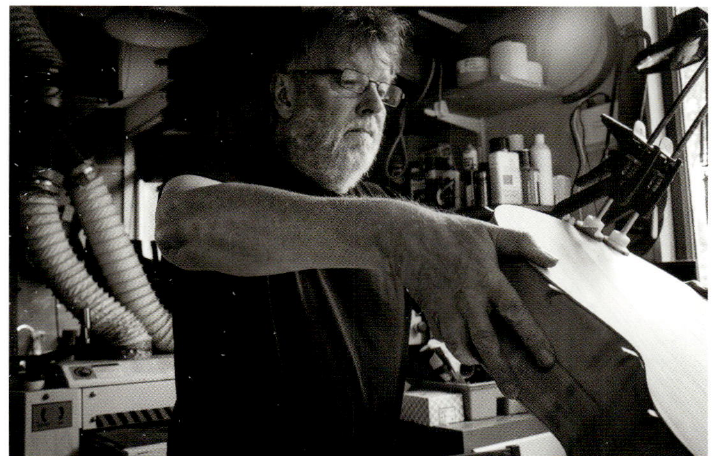

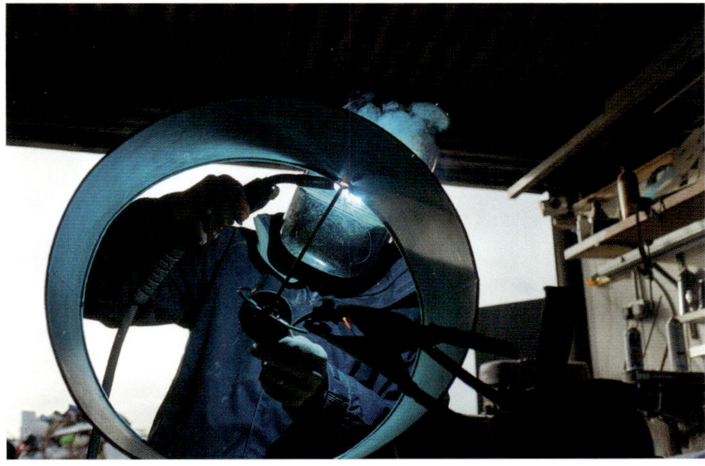

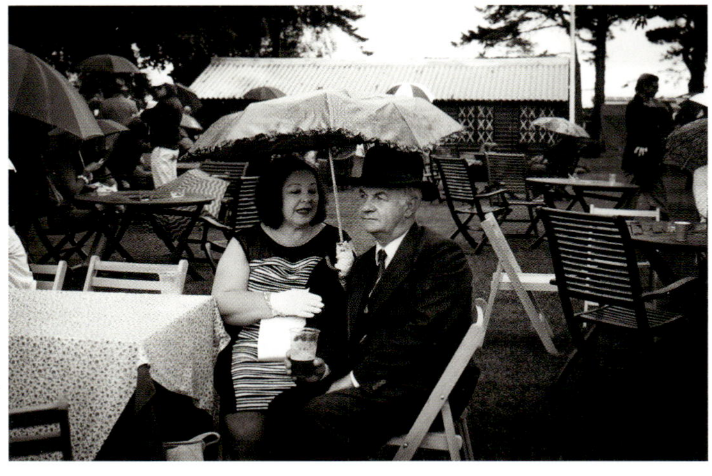

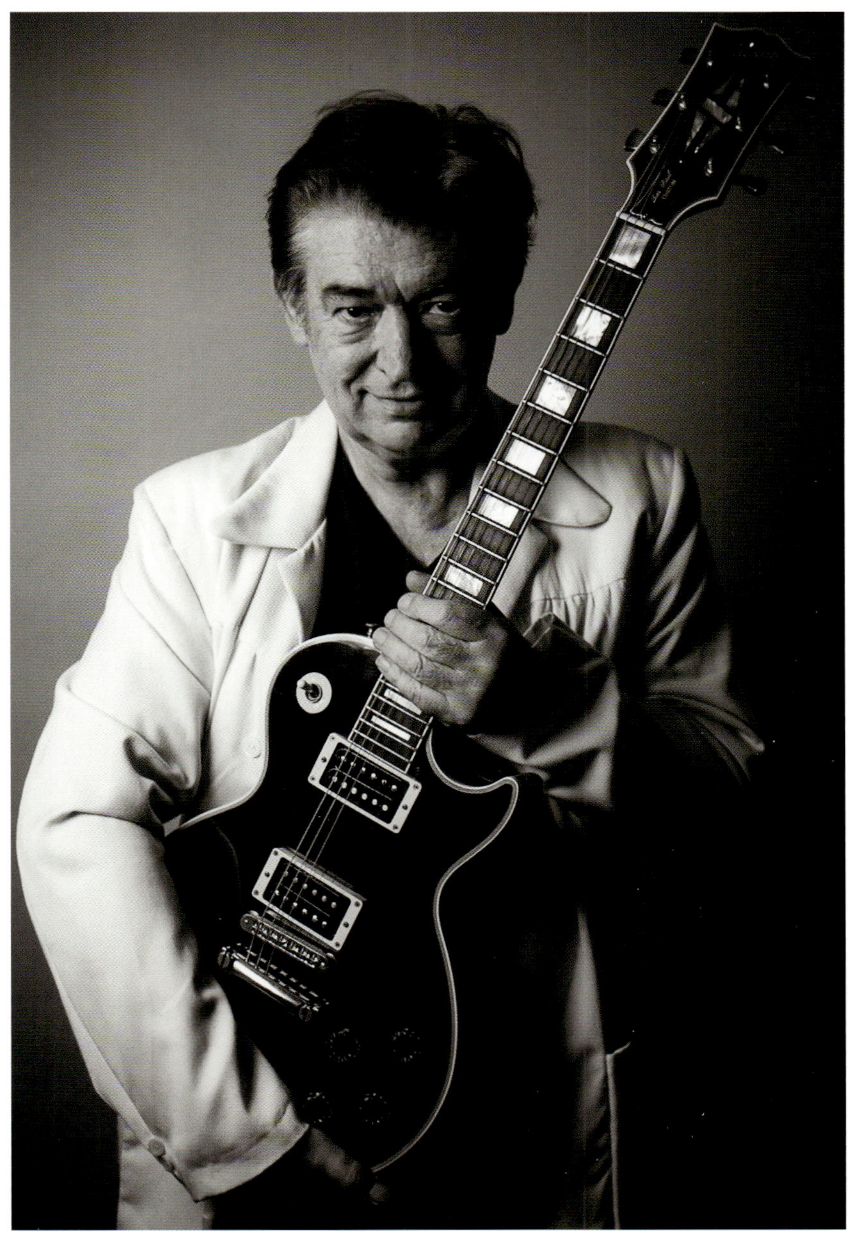

Kris Pawlowski is a Sussex-based photographer who has a passion for photographing artists, craftsmen and musicians. His style is simple, as he aims to capture his subjects in a relaxed and informal way. Kris also specialises in documentary photography and is currently working on two projects that are related to the music business.

Kris will be exhibiting a series of portraits and social documentary photographs in his 2015 Art in Ditchling Open House, which is part of the Brighton Festival Artists Open Houses.

Kim Bodycombe

Artist
www.kimbodycombe.com

Clockwise from top left: Stanmer Woods; Winter Pavilion; West Pier

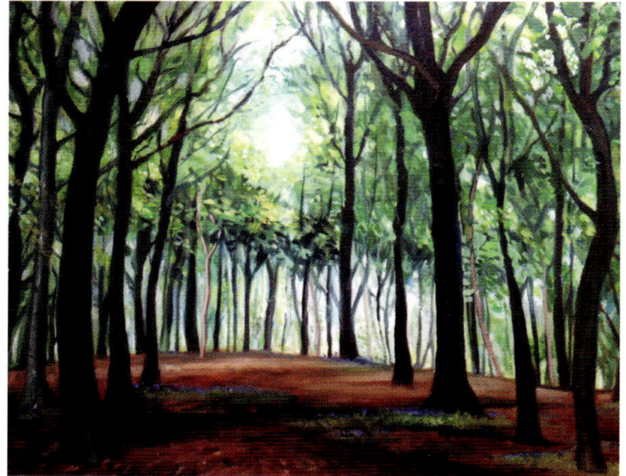

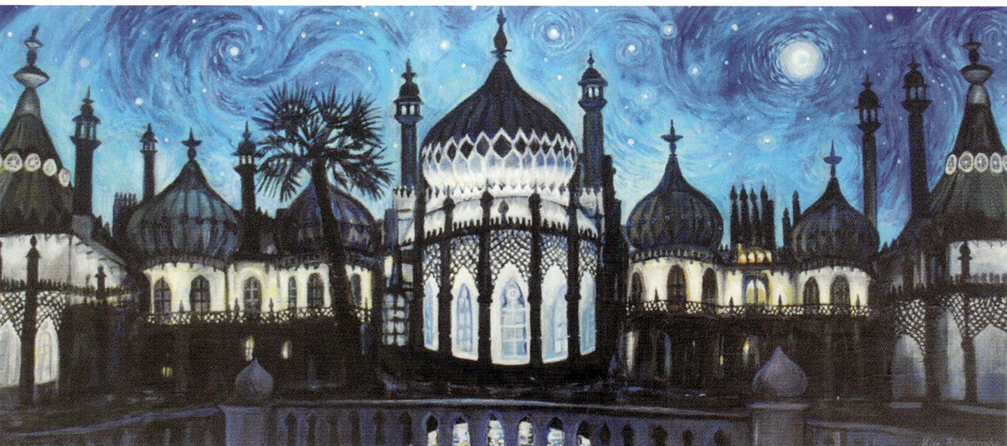

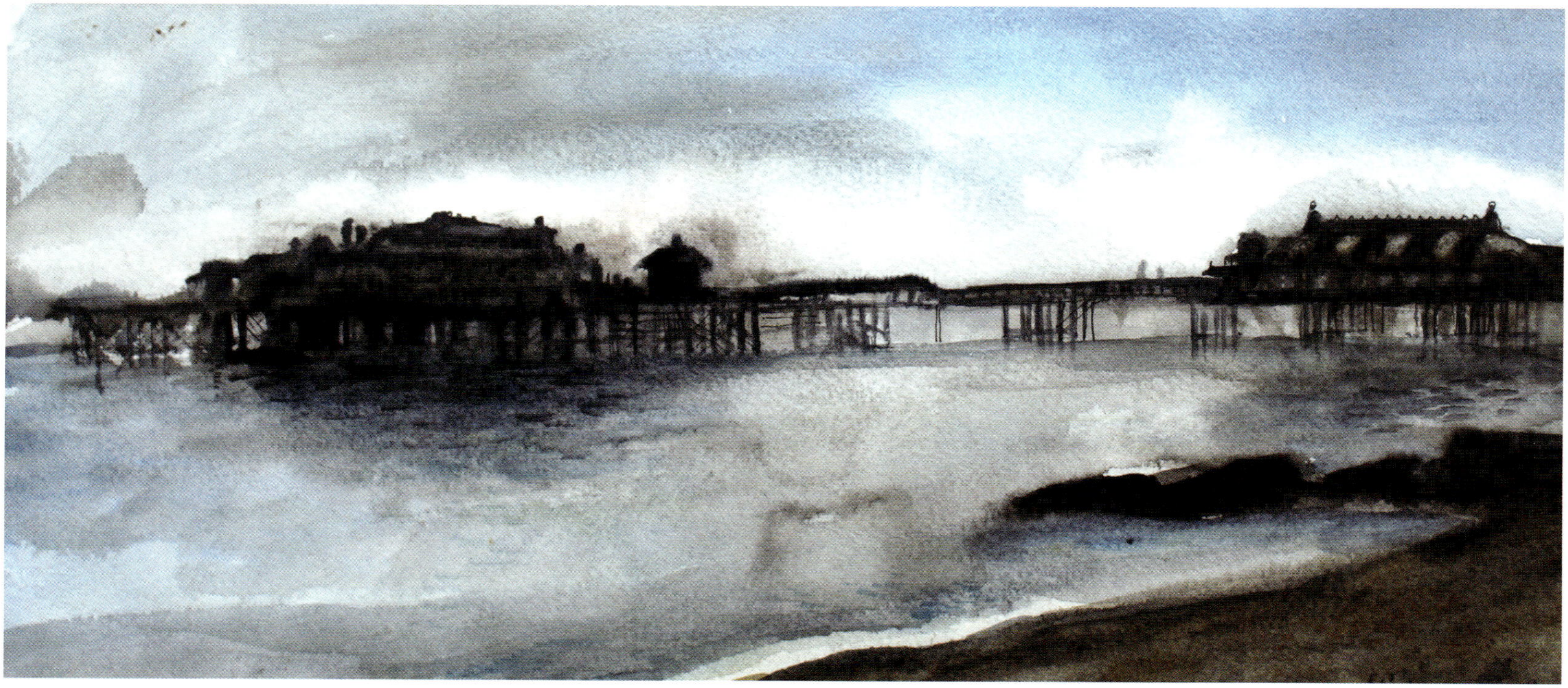

Brighton-based artist Kim Bodycombe came to the city to study illustration, and never left. She clocked up 13 years of teaching art in secondary schools, and a few more of teaching English to language students, before making the leap into full-time painting.

Most days, Kim works from her space in The Open Studios on Brighton beach, so a lot of her recent work has been inspired by the ever-changing coastal landscape. Trees and countryside are also a common inspiration, and Brighton's Stanmer Woods are frequently revisited for plein-air sketches of the changing seasons.

Kim's main influences are Turner and Hockney. She works in oils, acrylics, watercolour, charcoal and pencil, and welcomes commissions (a family portrait or landscape, perhaps), including detailed miniature portraits on pebbles. Visit her website (above) or Facebook page (Art on the Beach) for more information.

David Williams

Clockwise from left:
Lost Island; Little Boat; Secluded Bay: St Ives Harbour Sands

Artist
www.southdownsgallery.co.uk

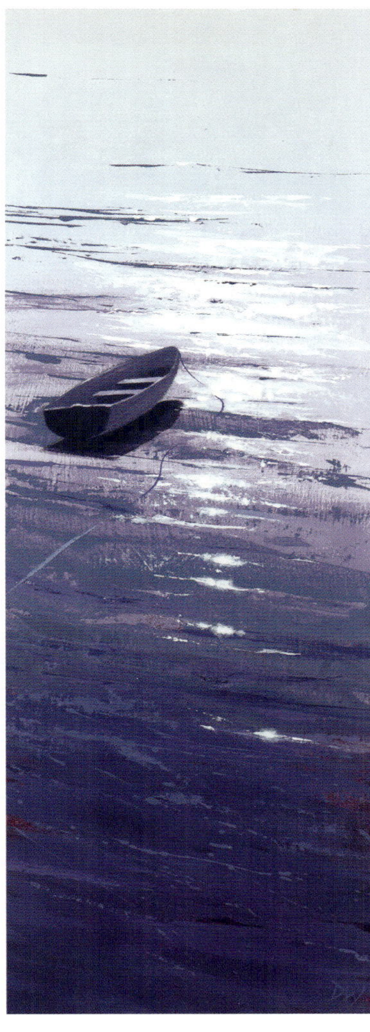

David graduated in Fine Art and Graphic Design at Derby College of Art. He has worked as an art director, graphic designer, illustrator and art therapist in London, and has taught art and design in adult and secondary education. He is a published author of books on design education. He now paints full time. David has been a member of the Fiveways Artists Group since 2006 and exhibits in his own Artists Open House in the Brighton May Festival. He has exhibited in the Royal Academy and Whitechapel galleries, the Penwith Gallery in St Ives, and other venues throughout the South East. He is currently exhibiting at the Chalk Gallery, Lewes.

David is inspired by perspective and atmospheric light. His subjects range from views of Sussex and the South Downs Way to exotic world locations and dramatic coastal landscapes. He travels widely, taking many photographs and sketches for reference material. Some of David's latest work has been inspired by recent trips to St Ives, Dorset, Cambodia and Vietnam. He works in acrylics, oils, watercolours and mixed-media.

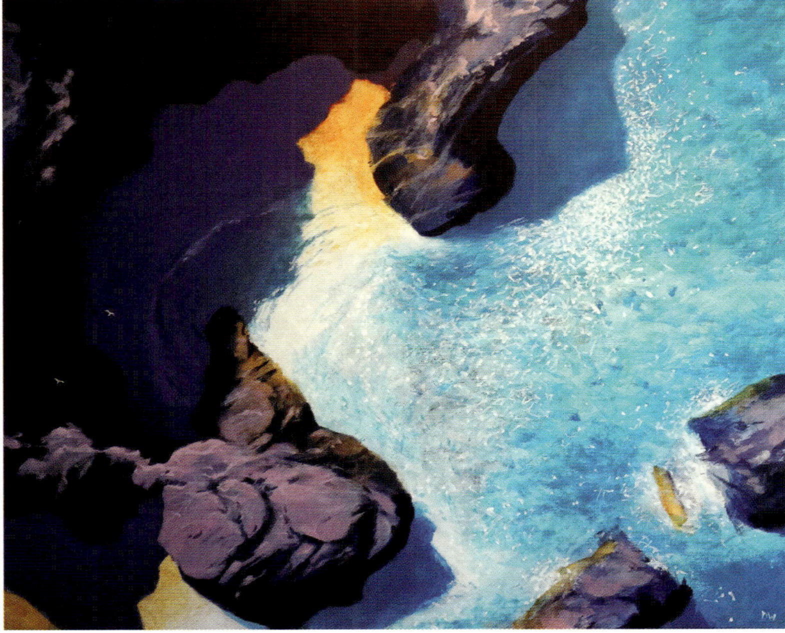

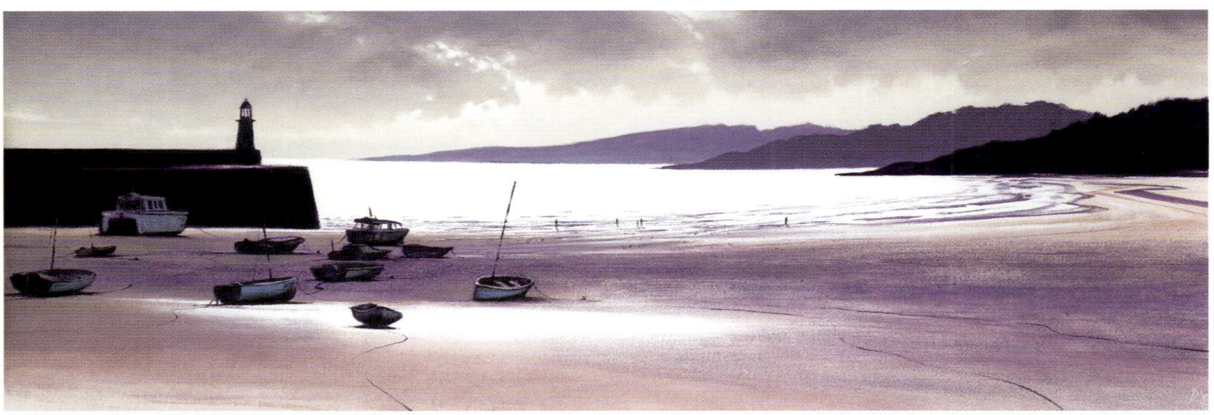

Catriona Millar

Artist
www.catrionamillar.com

Left to right: Trilby; Wodwo

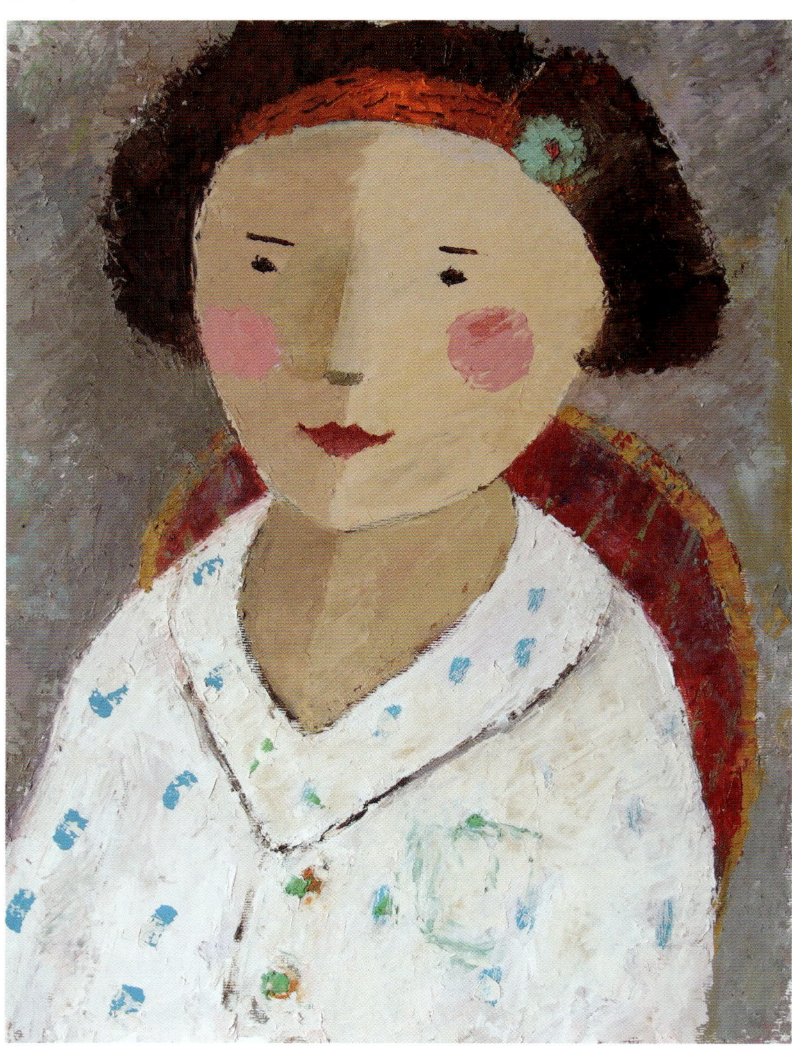

There is a classical and indeed an ancient voice lying beneath Catriona Millar's figures. It smiles or stares out, telling us familiar yet half-forgotten stories about ourselves. It is this connection on a hidden level that brings Millar's oil paintings into our lives with such a potency and lasting vigour

Scotland on Sunday

Ever since her 2005 Degree Show at Aberdeen's Gray's School of Art sold out within a few hours, Catriona Millar's work has earned critical and public acclaim.

She is now recognised as one of Scotland's foremost figurative oil painters. The *Sunday Herald* newspaper has ranked her in the top five most collectable Scottish artists and her work is admired and collected throughout Europe, the Far East, Australia and America.

Catriona Millar's paintings speak a universal language to all ages, and over the past four years many schools around the world have studied her work.

In 2012 Catriona relocated to Eastbourne and has been enjoying painting and tutoring in what she calls 'the beautiful south'. She has also been exhibiting regularly in London, Bath and Devon.

Catriona describes herself as a 'people painter' who loves being surrounded by so many colourful, exciting people. As a figure painter, she strongly believes that her move from Scotland has had a positive effect on both her work and her creative spirit. She is also enjoying the camaraderie of her art class, being surrounded by so many interesting, talented people.

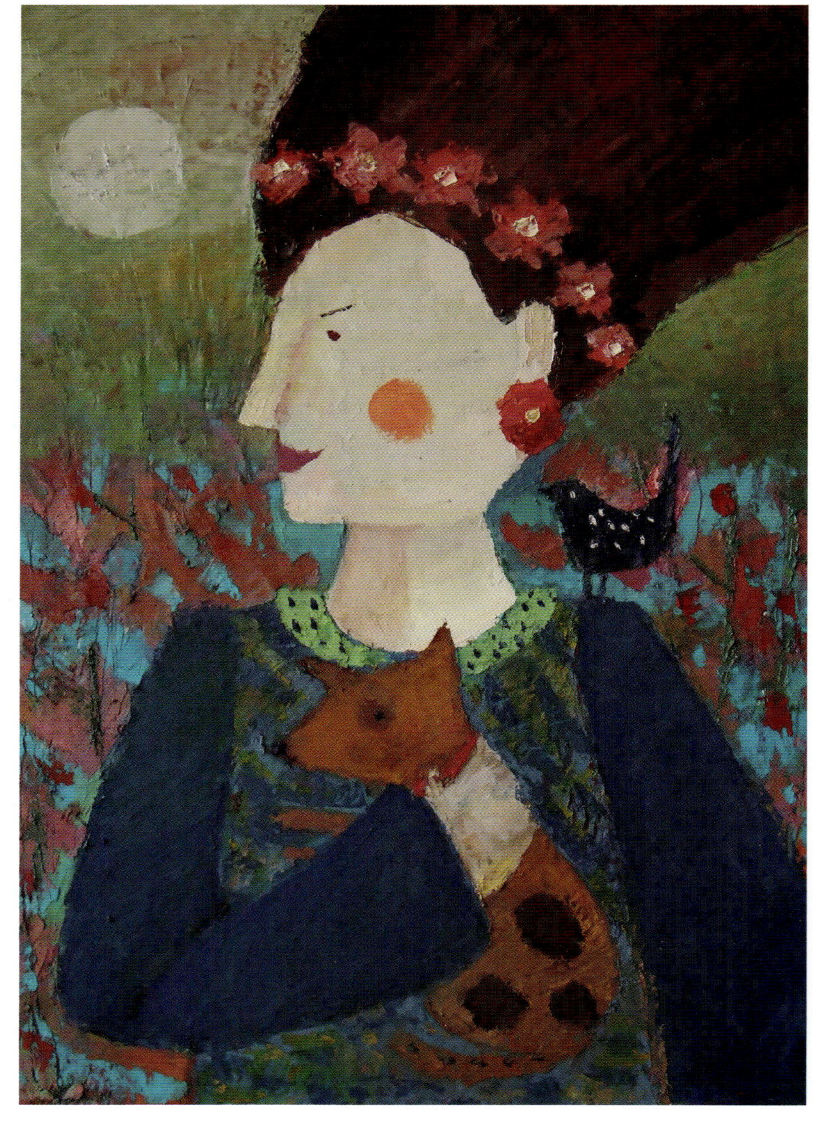

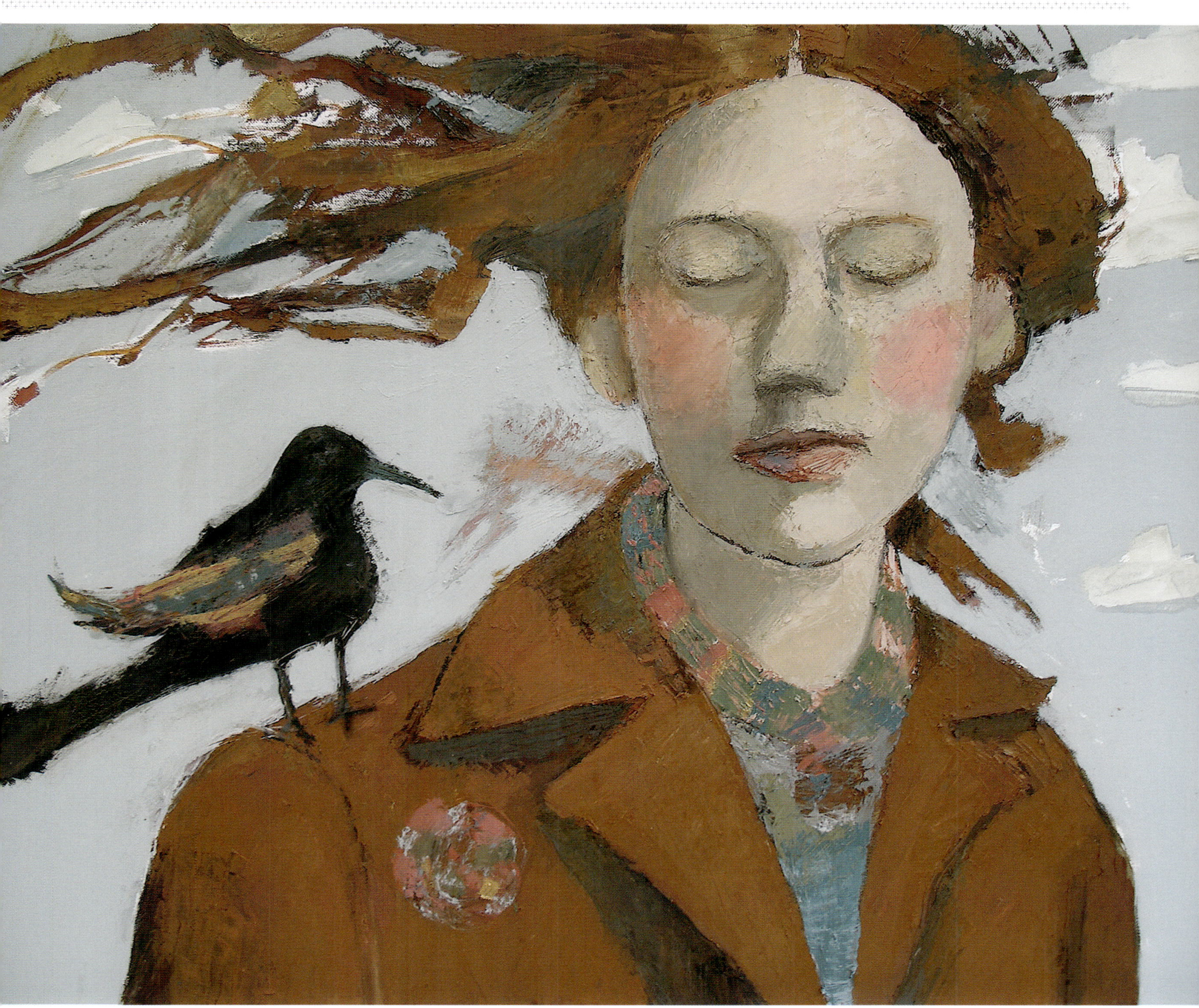

David Moore

Landscape Artist
davidscottmoore.wordpress.com

Clockwise from left:
Sussex Downs Sunset Crimson I; Sussex Downs Spring Storm I; Sussex Downs Sunset XXV

The Big Heart Auction Team 2015 on 'Sussex Downs Sunset Crimson'. "We love the dramatic and intensely colourful sky!"

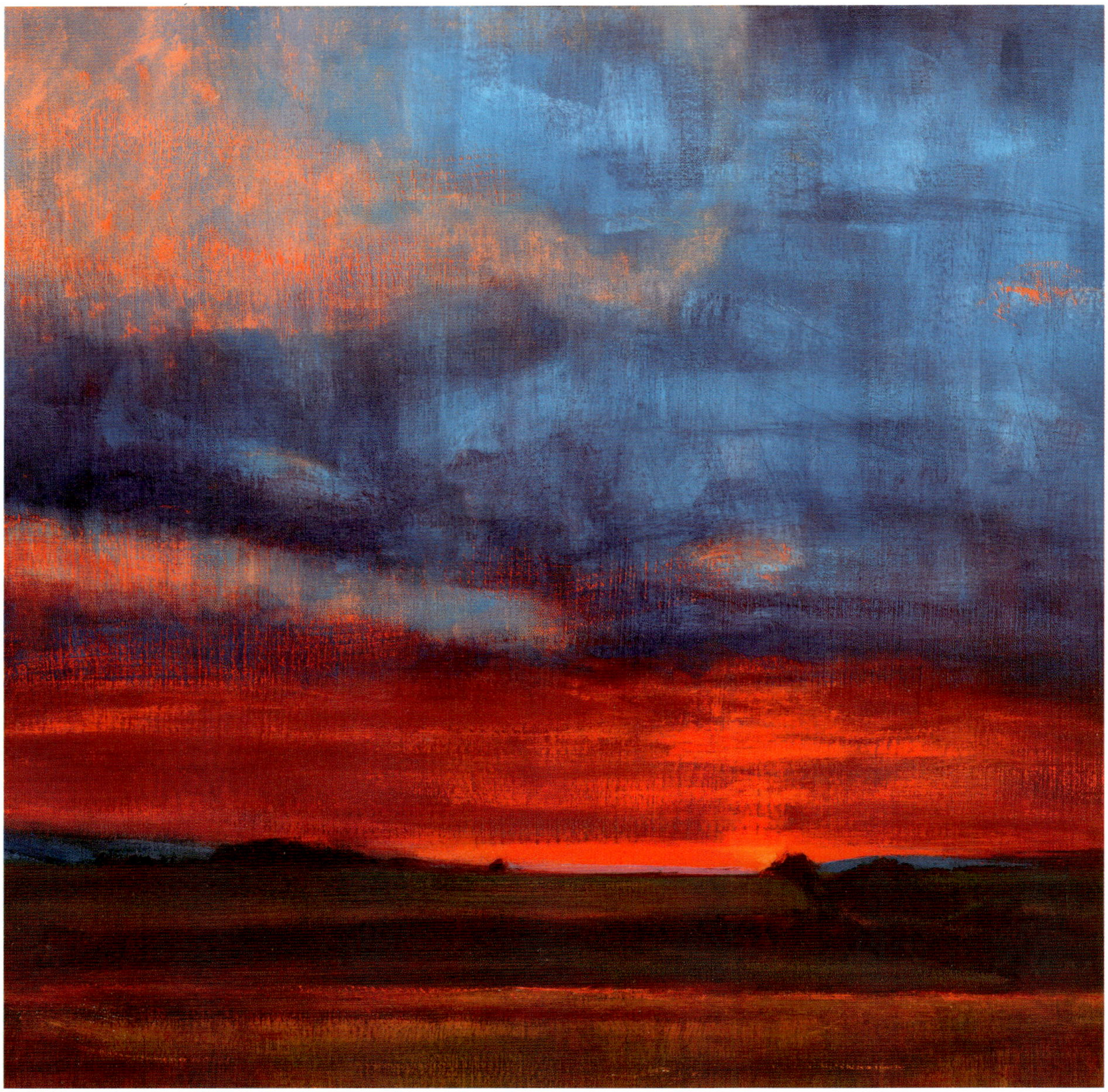

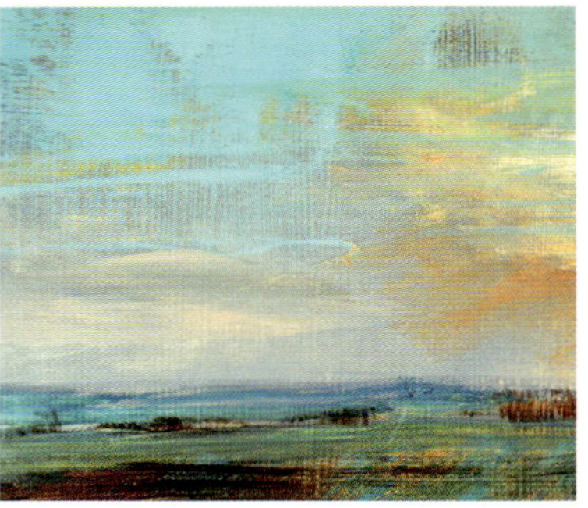

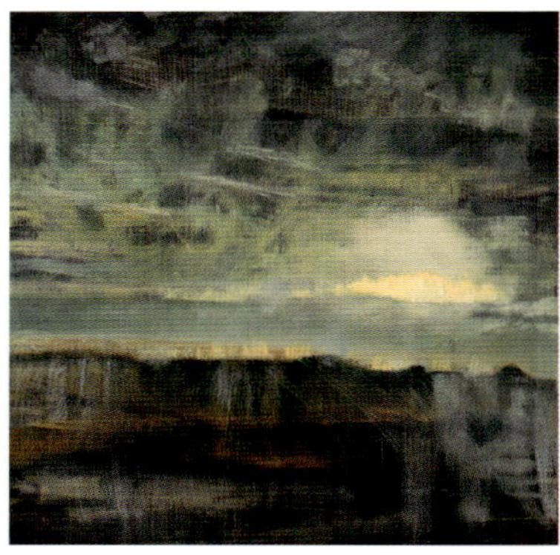

David Moore is a studio landscape painter of oils, based at Phoenix Arts Brighton, who produces paintings and prints. His bold experiments in light, colour and contrasting tones convey the drama and atmosphere of British landscapes.

David's recent panel landscape 'Sussex Downs Sunset XXV' reached the final judging stage of the Lynn Painter-Stainers Prize 2015.

Sheila Marlborough

Artist
www.sheilamarlborough.co.uk

Clcckwise from top left:
Trees; Enumeration; Flight; Moonset

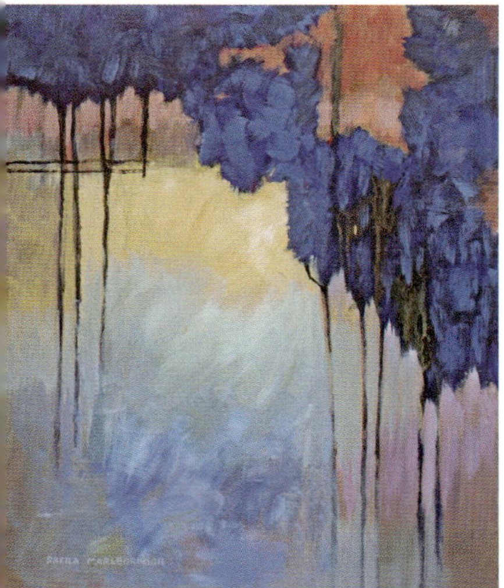

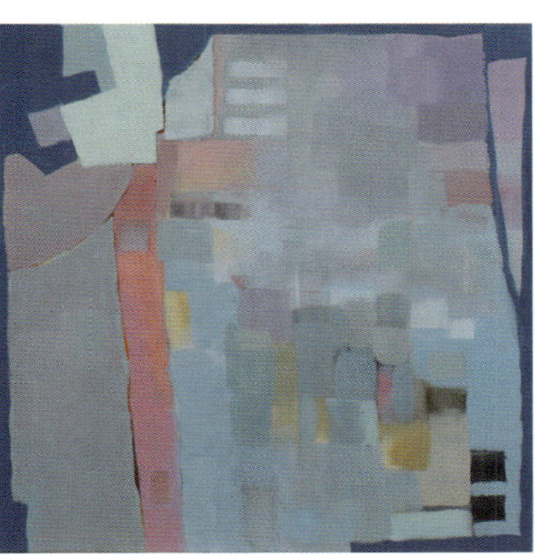

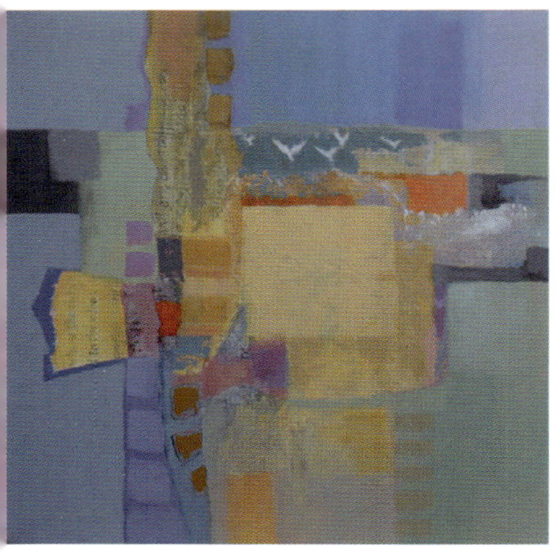

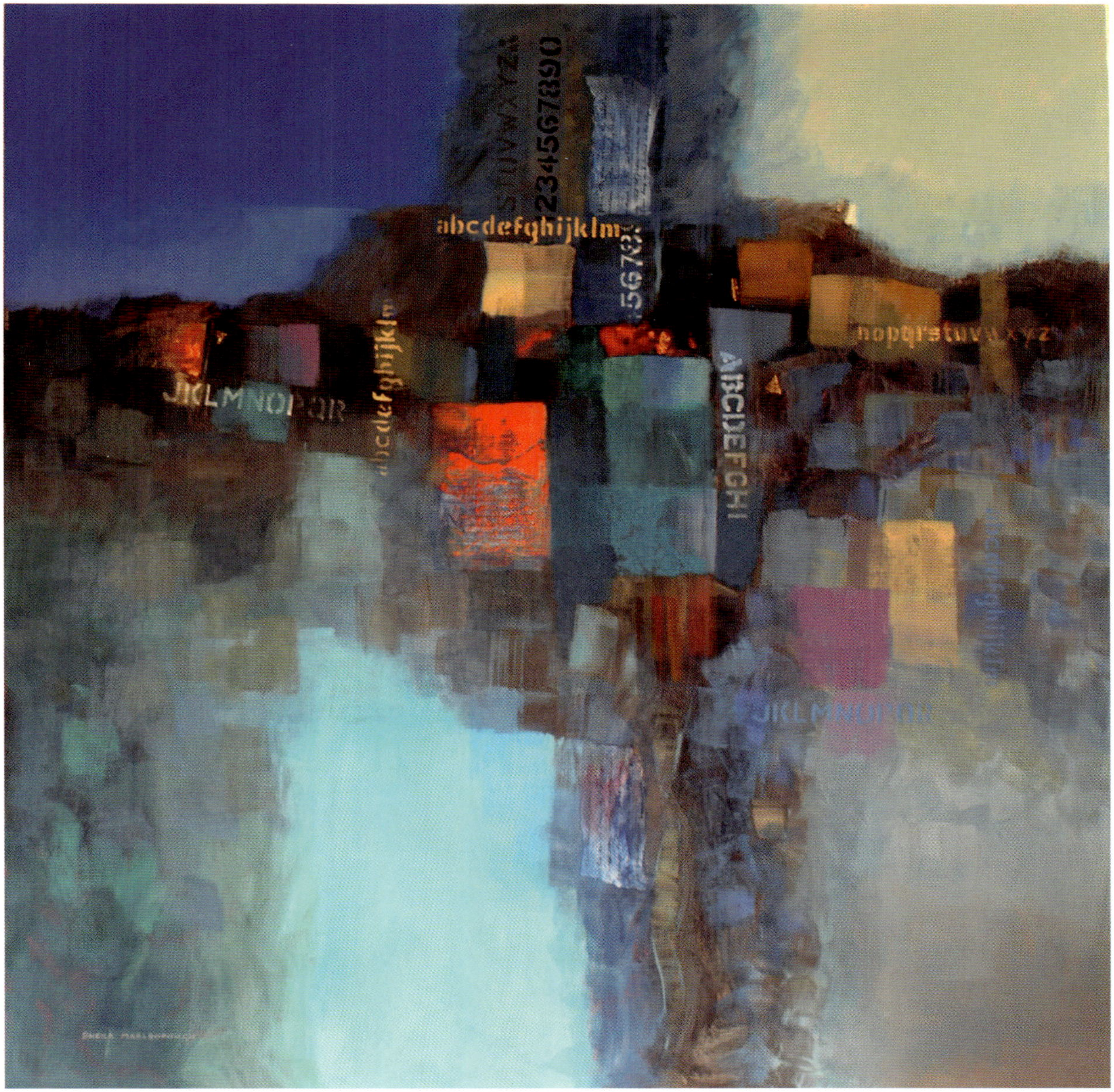

Sheila Marlborough's painting spans many years. She attended courses at Brighton Polytechnic and St Ives School of Painting between 1978–1985, and later taught art to adult students for 15 years.

Sheila has had work shown at the Mall Galleries, London, and won the RWS Open Exhibition Award at the Bankside Gallery in 2002. She was a member of Chalk Gallery, Lewes, for six years and President of the Sussex Watercolour Society from 2005–2014.

Working in acrylic and mixed media, Sheila is inspired mainly by the landscape combined with her imagination. She concentrates on shapes, colour and texture, executed either in applied paper collage or paint. Frequent visits to St Ives have influenced her abstract paintings, while her love of colour stems from many different sources.

Sheila sells her work in exhibitions, art fairs or from home. A selection of her work can be seen on her website (see above).

Claire Fearon

Artist
www.clairefearon.com

The 50 Heads Project. All paintings acrylic on paper (size either A1 or A2)

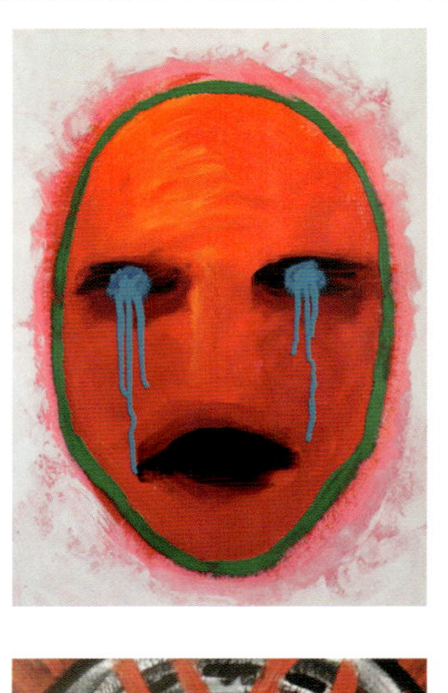
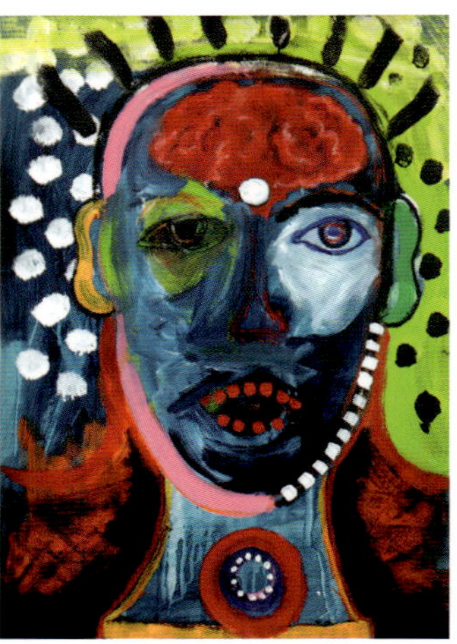
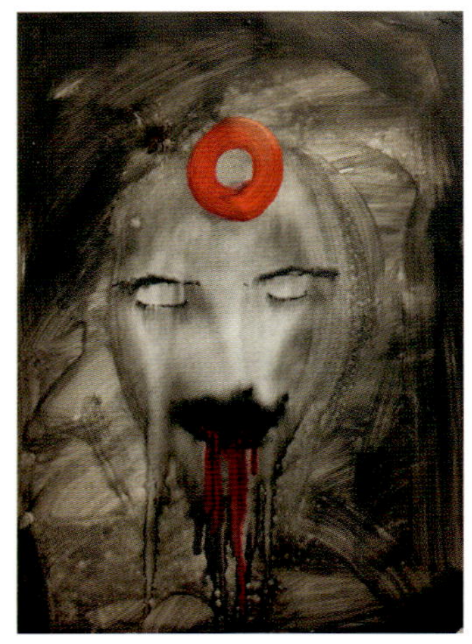
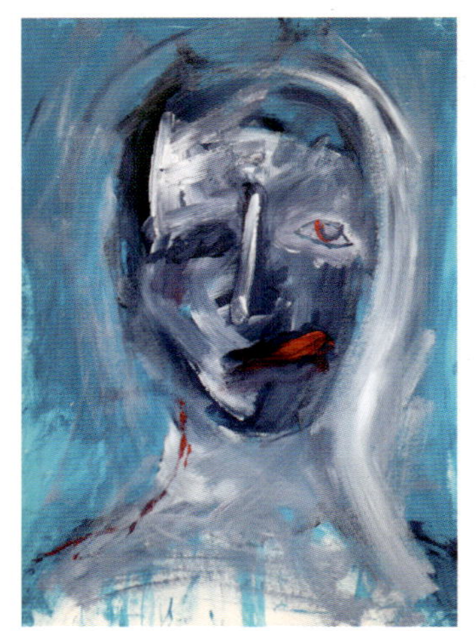
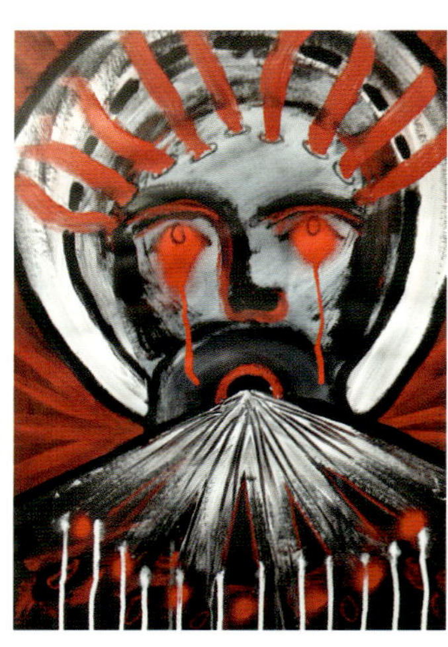
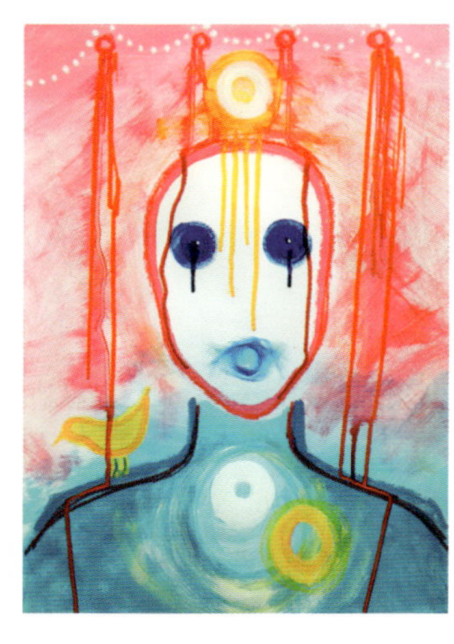
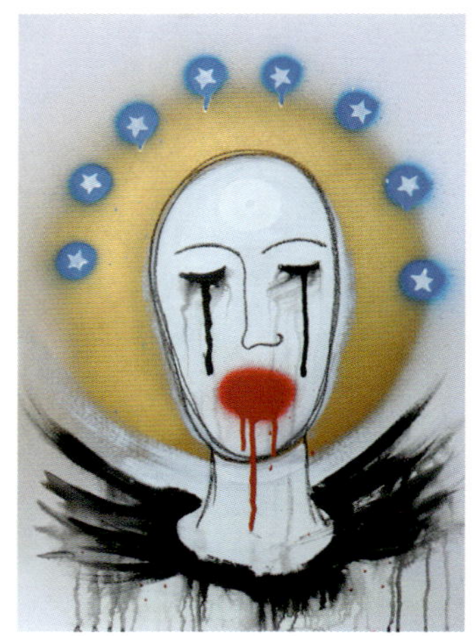
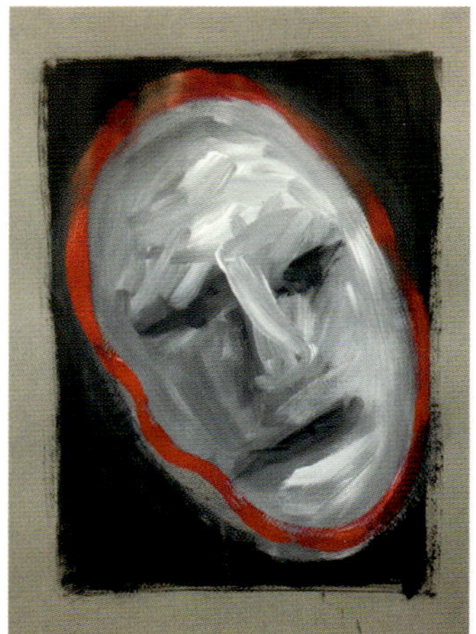
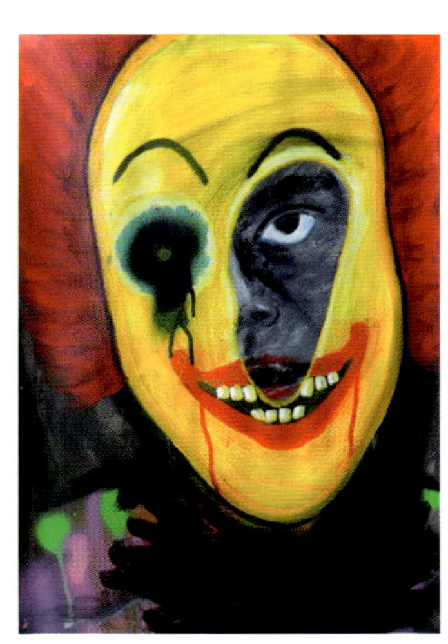
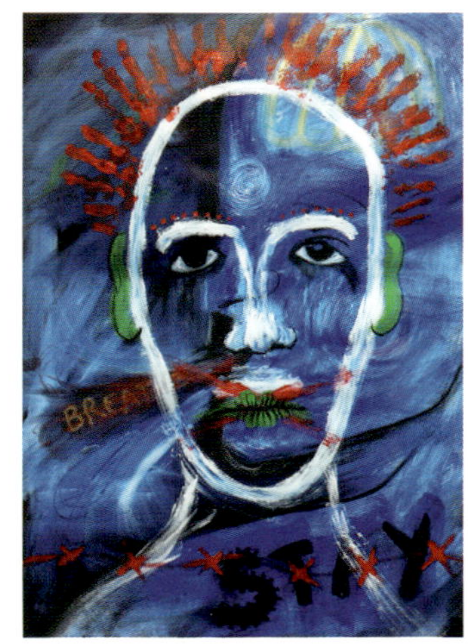
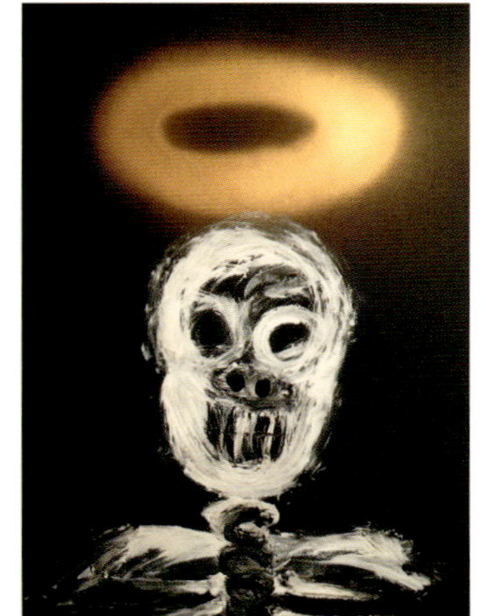
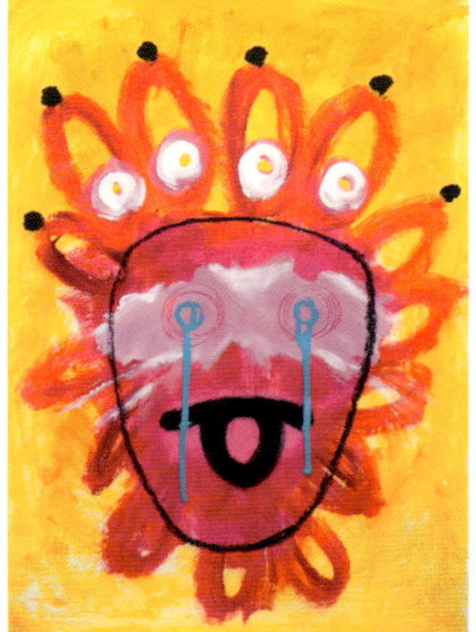

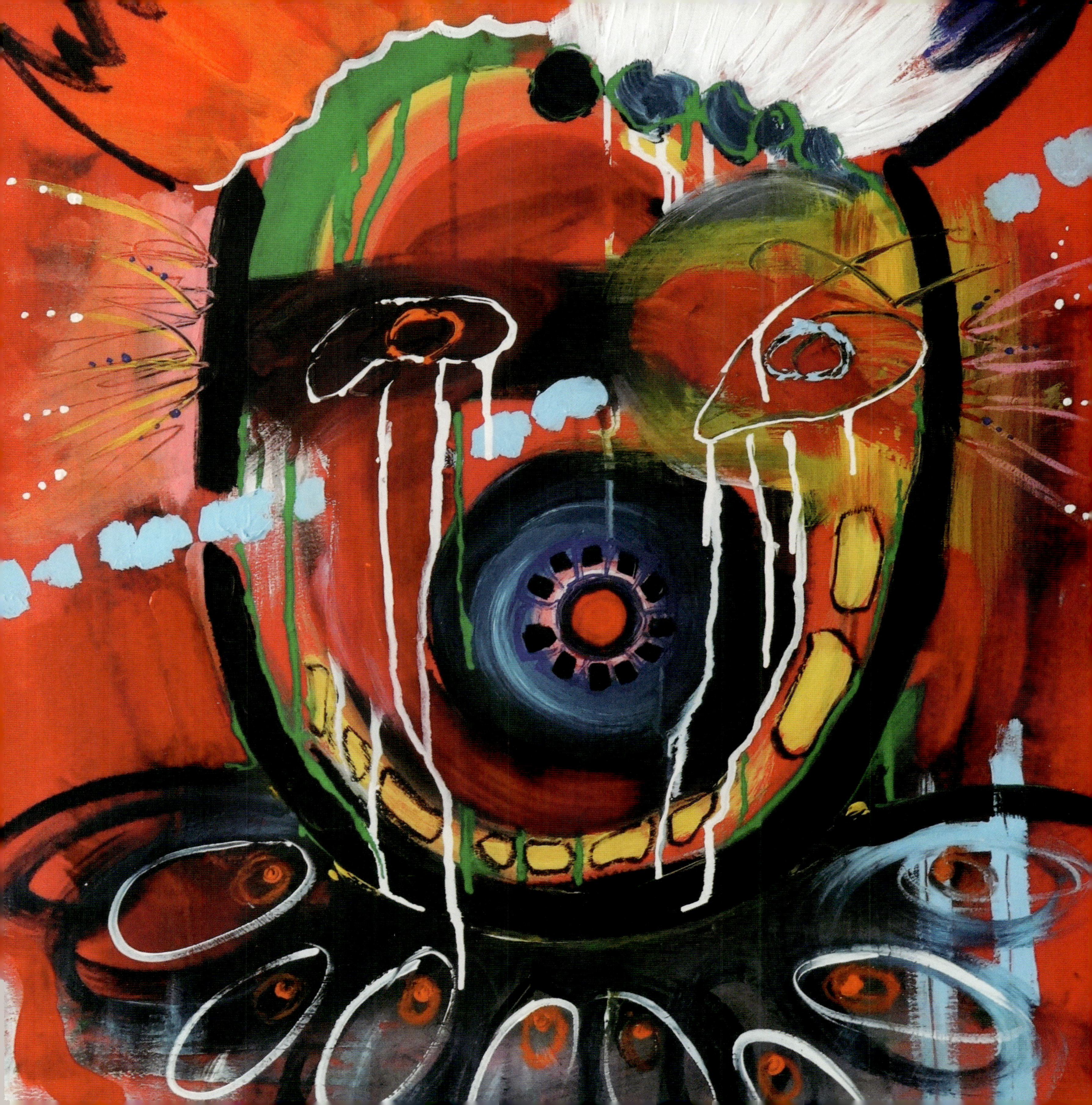

Romany Mark Bruce

Artist & Sculptor
www.romanymarkbruce.com

1219 (pencil, ink and acrylic on paper)

Irish-born Romany Mark Bruce is one of Brighton's most highly regarded artists, whose paintings are sought by collectors worldwide.

Whether working on vibrant canvases in acrylic, or – as here – in pencil, ink and acrylic on paper, his unique, sculptural palette strokes are challenging, charged and bold. A successful exhibition in South Australia has led to a number of large-scale commissions, as his reputation grows.

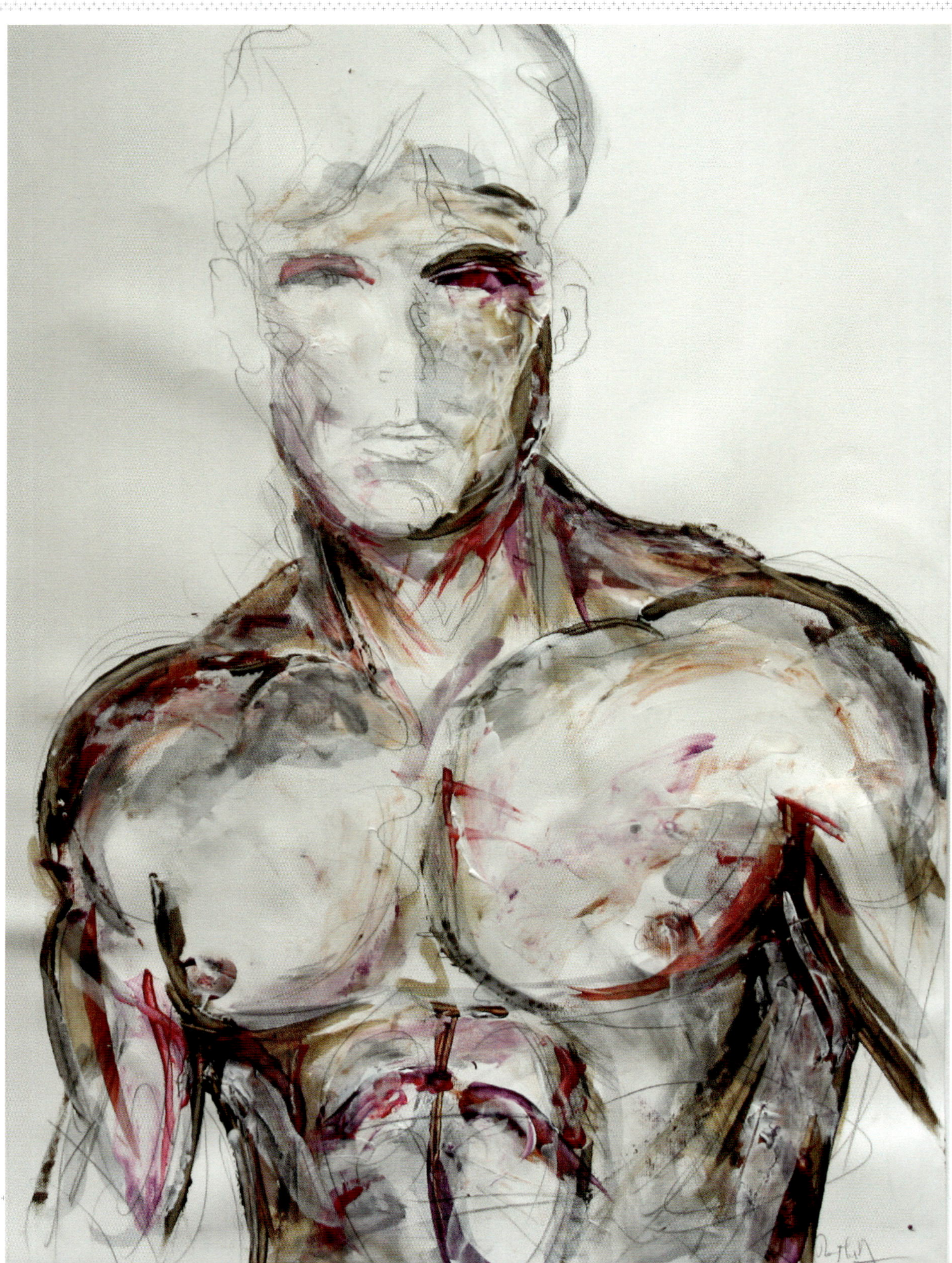

Alex Grey

Fine Artist
www.alexgrey.co.uk

Clockwise from top left:
Inner Sanctum; Big Idea; London Sky; Homecoming

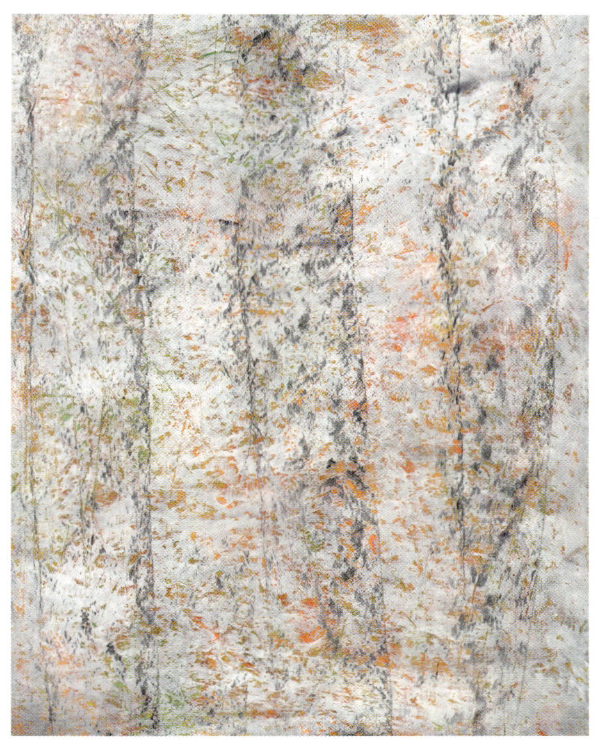

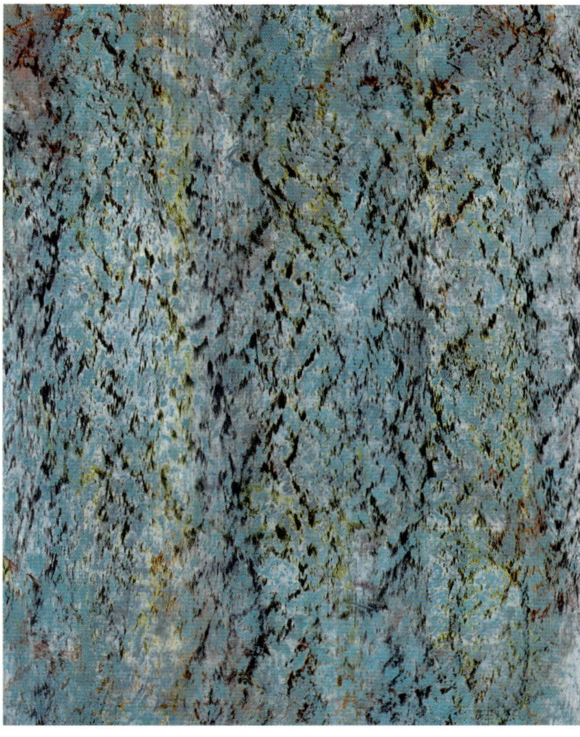

Synaesthesic artist Alex Grey emerged on to the UK art scene in 2013, showing her contemporary abstract work in curated exhibitions in London and all over the South East in her first year as a professional practitioner. Originally trained as a lighting and special effects designer, Goldsmiths alumna Alex works with oil pastels to create emotional landscapes using the language of shape and colour. Following solo exhibitions *Maiden Voyage* (2014) and *Homecoming* (2015), she is currently focusing on developing a range of silk scarves and ties based on her work, which will be available later in the year.

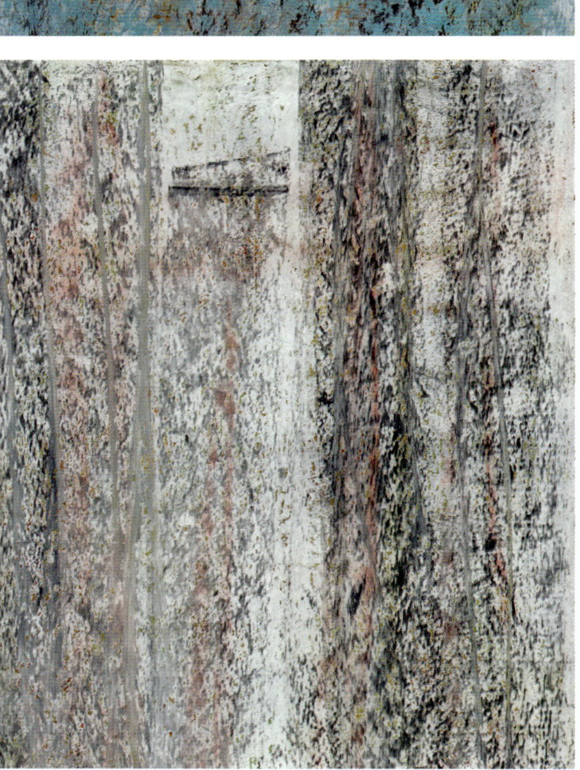

Tina Allonby

Artist
www.tinaallonby-artist.co.uk

Clockwise from top left: Lily Fish (50cm x 50cm) oil on canvas; Honesty (18in x 14in) oil on canvas; Orange Tree (61cm x 46cm) oil on canvas; Rhodi (100cm x 76cm) oil on canvas

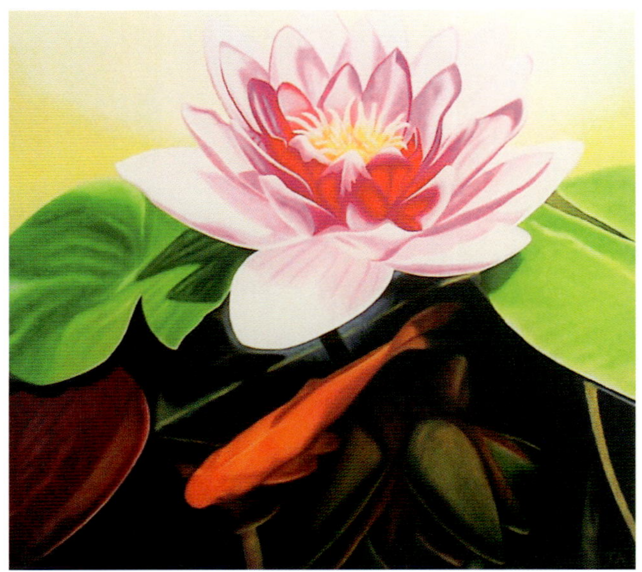

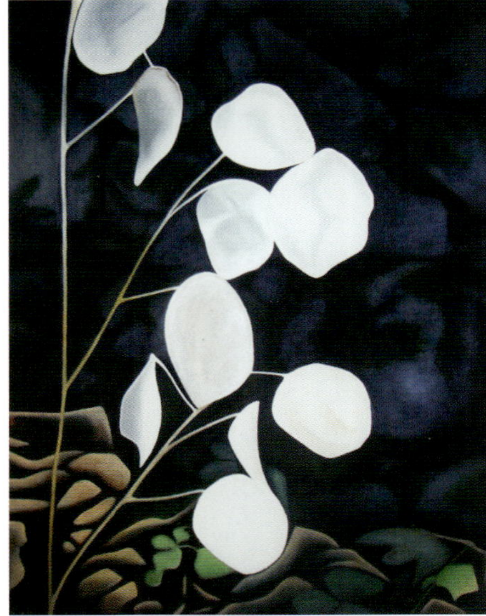

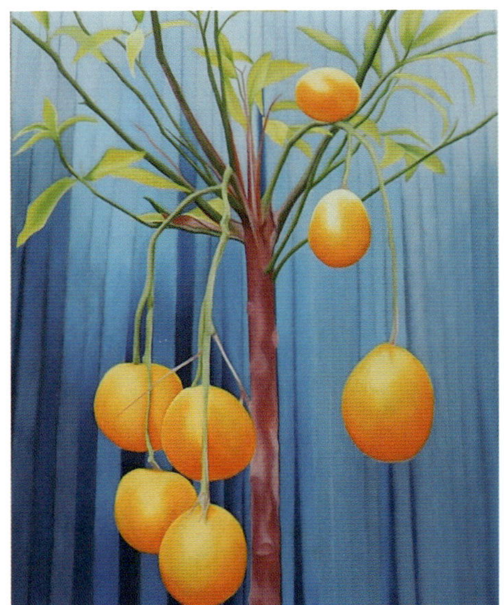

Tina is interested in conveying the dynamic between what's hidden and what's being shown and the space between. She develops her work through writing, drawings and photographic images that explore a combination of shape, colour and her relationship to a particular subject's physical form, presence and space; sometimes conveying emptiness, spaciousness and less concerned with form. Other times there will be more of a conceptual idea or significant feeling as the basis, and always a personal story connected with each piece of work.

Nature, environment, relationship, story and the healing power of art making

Tina originally trained as a printmaker using photographic silkscreen and etching print-making processes in her previous work. Now working mostly in oil, she has since developed her distinctive painting style, layering thin glazes for a light and stylised linear graphic effect. Tina is also an art therapist and a community-based art tutor. She has her studio on Brighton seafront at The Open Studios, 168 Kings Road Arches.

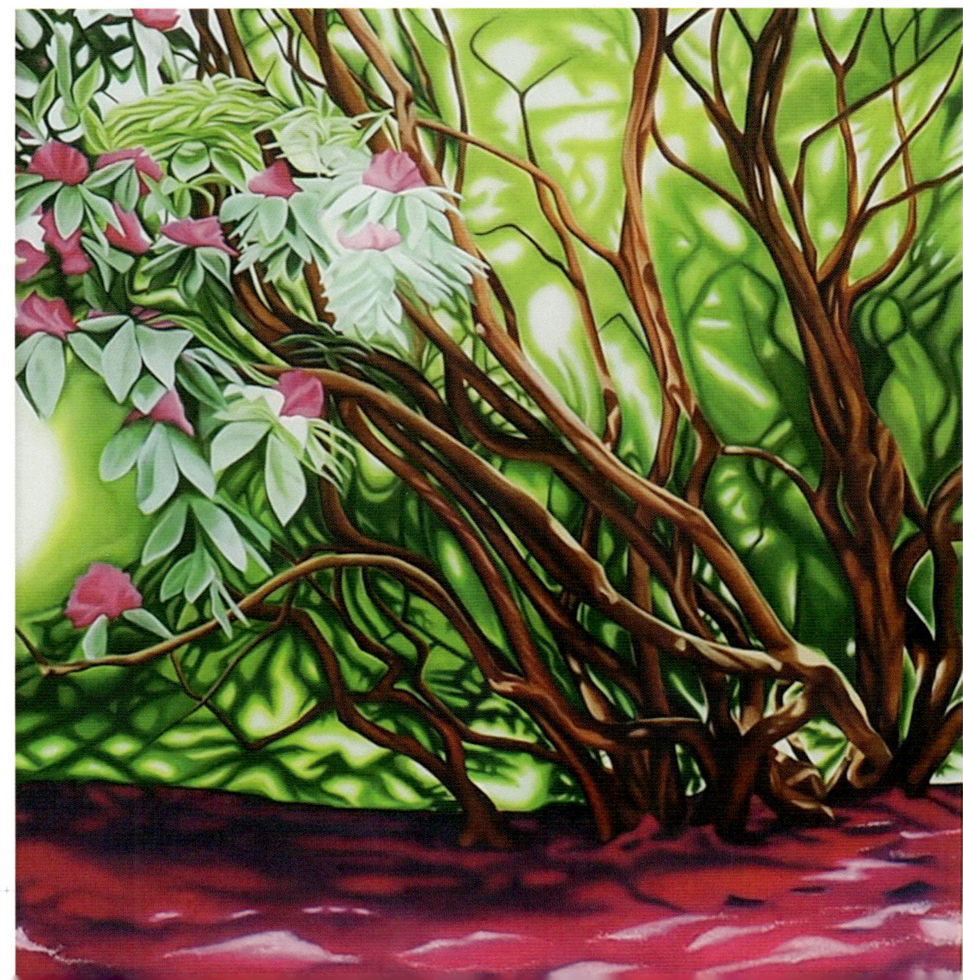

Auricula

12 Turner Dumbrell Workshops, North End, Ditchling BN6 8GT
www.auricula.co.uk

Clockwise from top left:
Himalaya; Jaipur; Tassilaq; Circe

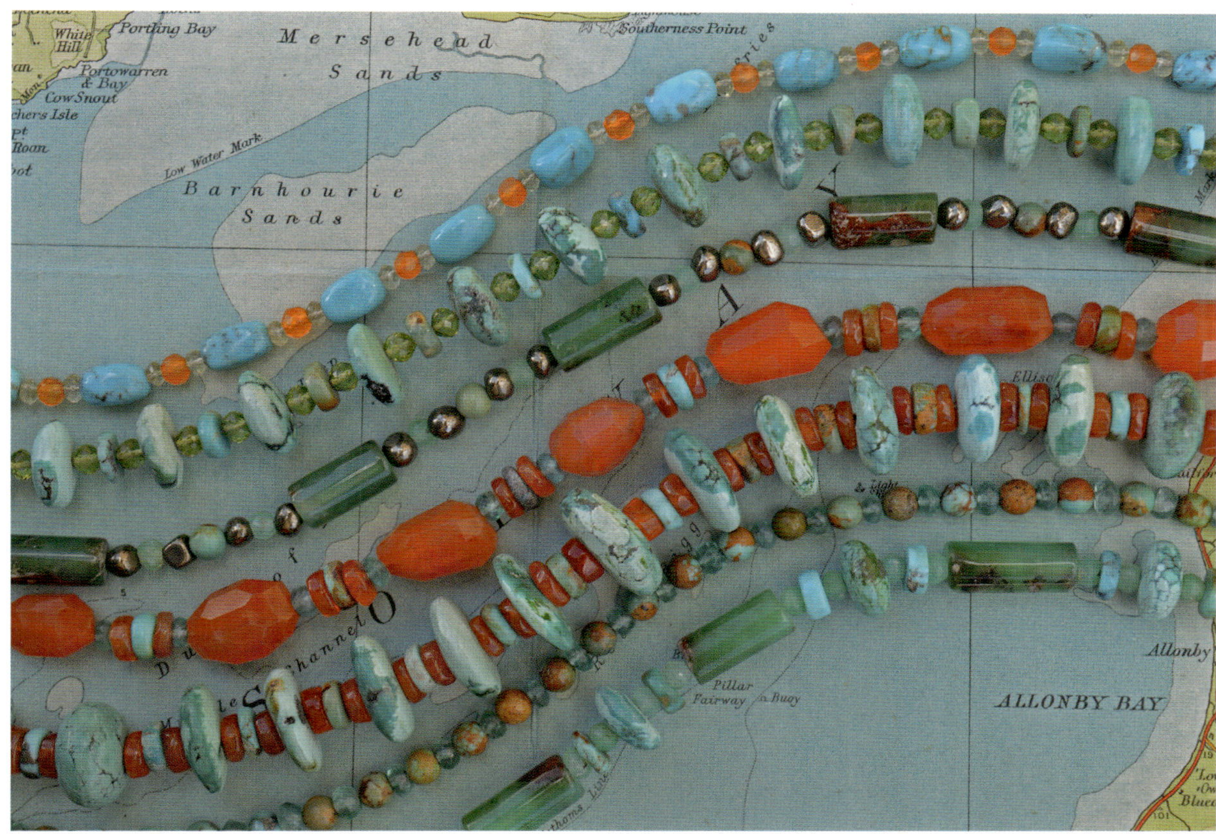

Auricula is a treasure trove of tempting beaded gemstone jewellery tucked away in Ditchling's Turner Dumbrell Workshops. From here, Natasha Caughey designs and makes her fabulous jewellery collections. She started trading in Ditchling in 2006 after five years working as a jewellery buyer and designer in central London.

Natasha loves to experiment with colour and texture in her designs. She hand-selects the gemstones and freshwater pearls on her trips to China and India and is always on the look-out for unusual cuts and colours. The selection of jewellery on offer is constantly evolving and Natasha welcomes commissions.

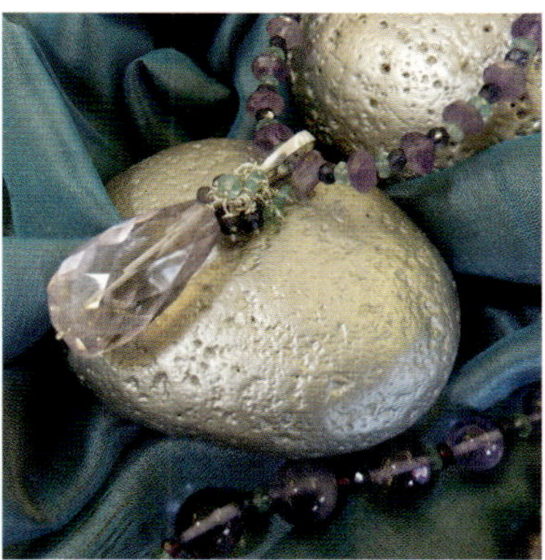

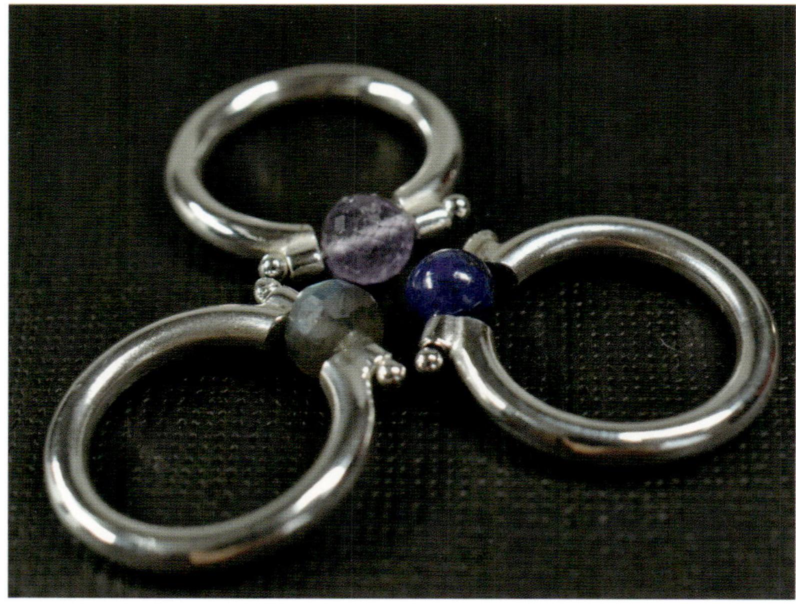

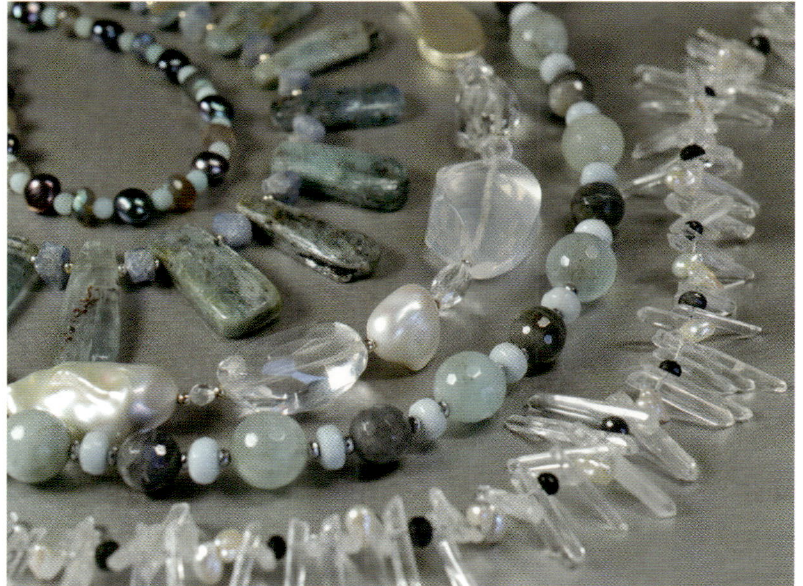

Alexander Johnson

Artist
www.alexander-johnson.com

Clockwise from top: Fuji Dream; Hiroshima Tricycle; Atomic; Life in Tokyo 3
Opposite page: Puerta 2

Professional artist Alexander Johnson produces hand-made silkscreens in small editions of six or fewer, and paintings on canvas. The images are distilled from memory and meant to provoke an emotional response from the viewer. There is much scraping-back and over-painting, and he likes this process to be apparent in the finished work, an antidote to the slick digital imagery that swamps us.

Look out for a solo show in September 2015 at The Project Gallery in Arundel.

I want an image that will make you stop and look, but also one that has a depth and will keep you coming back for more, just as I have returned to paintings by Rembrandt and de Kooning throughout my life

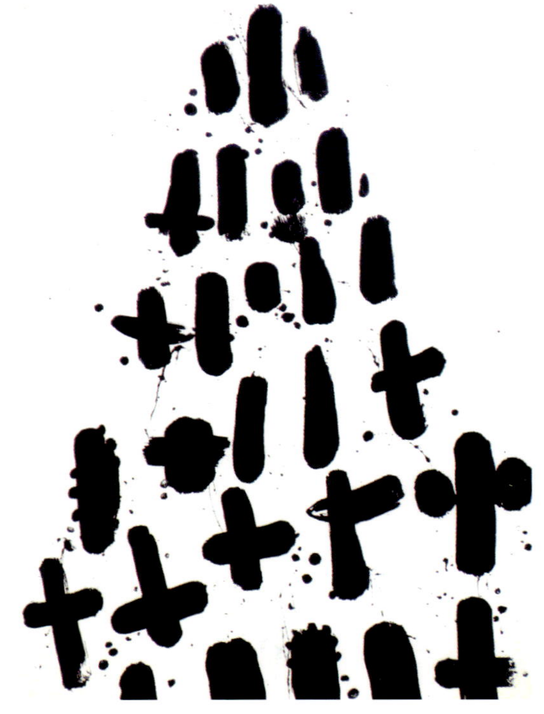

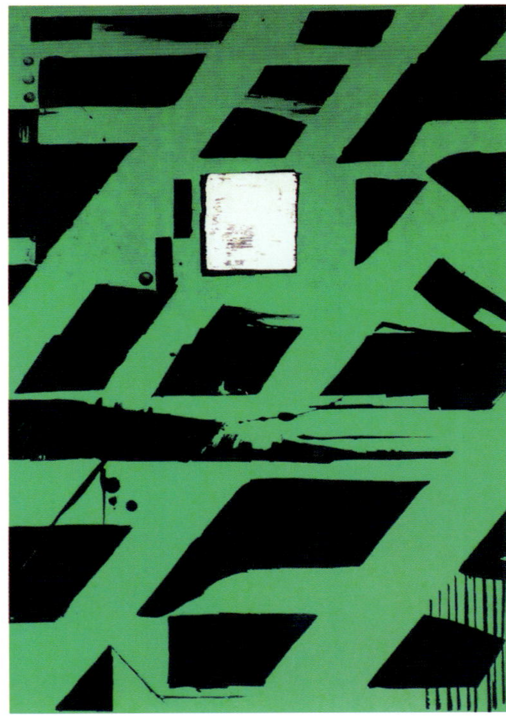

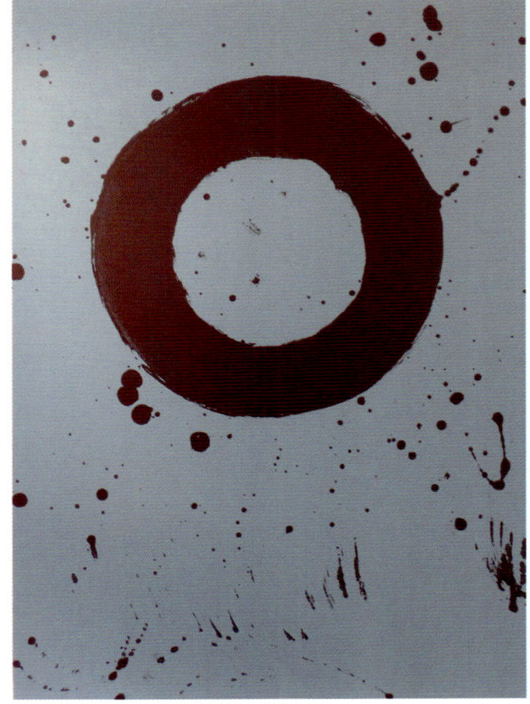

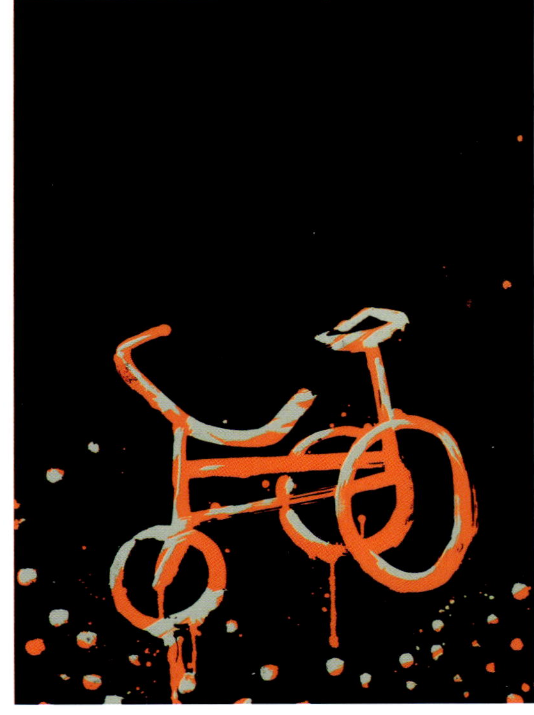

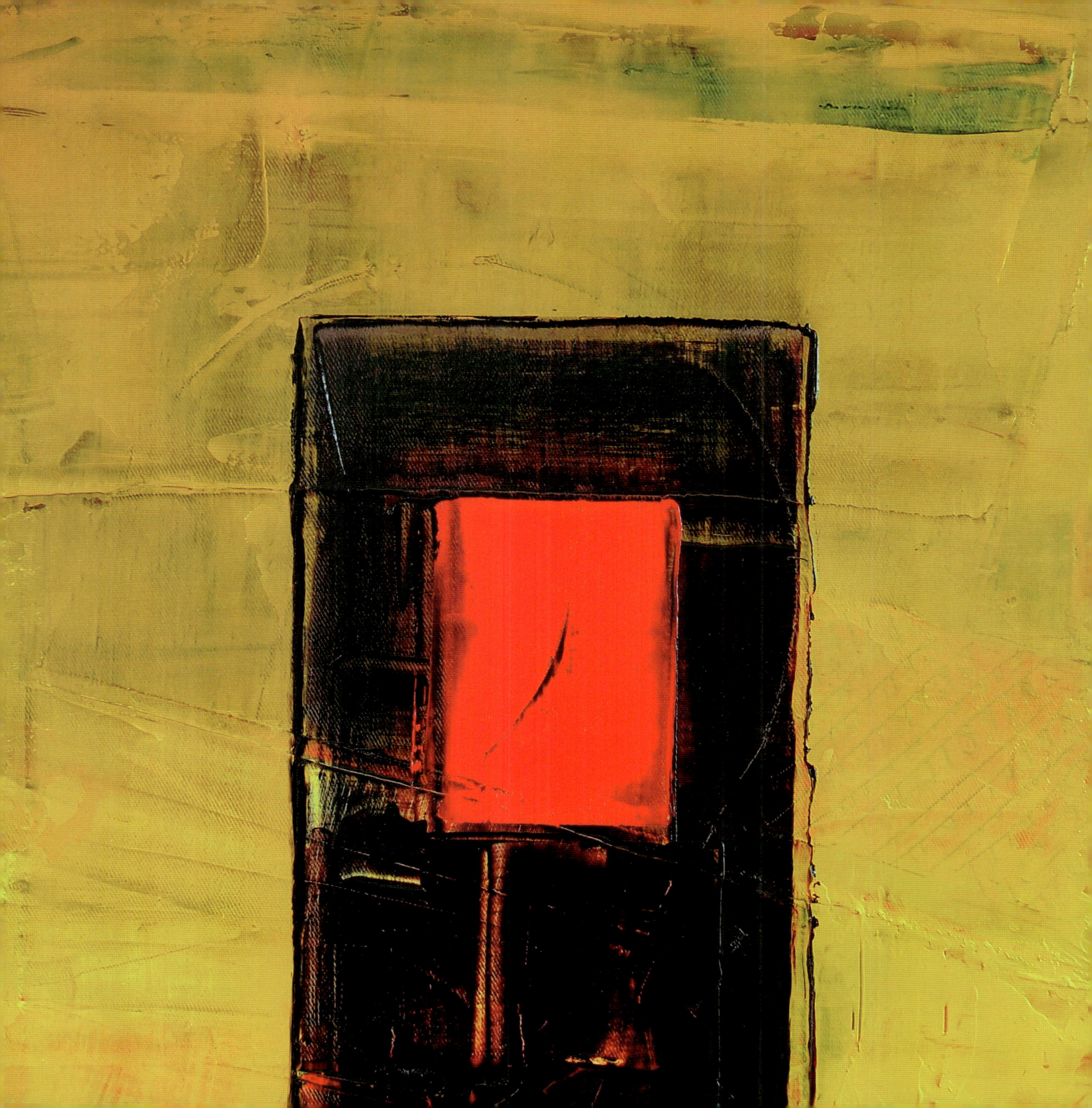

Holly Rozier

Soft Sculpture Artist
www.hollyrozierartist.com

Clockwise from left: The Open Studios; Unnatural Forms; Knobbly Bobbly; Bleeding Scabby Blob
Opposite page: Untitled (detail)

Manipulation and transformation of the body is the main focus of Holly Rozier's work. Exploring the juxtaposition of beauty and the grotesque, her work has the ability to intrigue, attract and repel the viewer simultaneously. Though intimations of the human form are the inspiration for her sculptures, the selected body parts have been reworked to a different extent in each of her pieces. She contorts, inflates and extends the body parts into a new breed or hybrid of a being. These surreal anthropomorphic forms could be human, animal, plant or alien; genetically engineered or naturally evolved, alive or dead?

Holly's chosen field of practice is soft sculpture – a highly controlled exercise that allows her to create voluptuous, fleshy forms that remain malleable and tactile, while the challenge of using soft materials to create substantial forms keeps creation exciting.

Everything susceptible to transformation is cut and sewn. Contrasting 'wet' and 'dry' fabrics, hessian sacking and nylon tights are used to create the appearance of skin. Alongside, rich silky fabrics are used to create intricate and beautiful, yet putrid and wet, sections of innards exposed through the 'skins' of the forms.

Heavily decorative and time-consuming processes are what the artist enjoys most. The act of repetitive hand-sewing and adorning the surface of her sculptures with bead after bead, and transformed fabric, is similar to the act of making a Frankenstein-style creation.

She operates on the creatures, slicing them open, resulting in fluids pouring out, and stitching them back up to fix them. The time spent on each humanoid form results in the development of a strong connection between the artist and the creatures, each one developing its own individual personality and quirks.

Holly's recent work is focusing on the idea that these living organisms are growing in a permanent site, fixing themselves to surfaces with limb-like extrusions or roots. She aims to create the thought that these equivocal, parasitic creatures are invading the space, feeding off the location they have fixed themselves upon.

Holly graduated from the University of Chichester in 2013, before becoming an Artist-in-Residence at St George's School, Ascot. She recently moved to Brighton, where her work can be viewed at The Open Studios on the seafront (see page 134 for map). Commissions accepted.

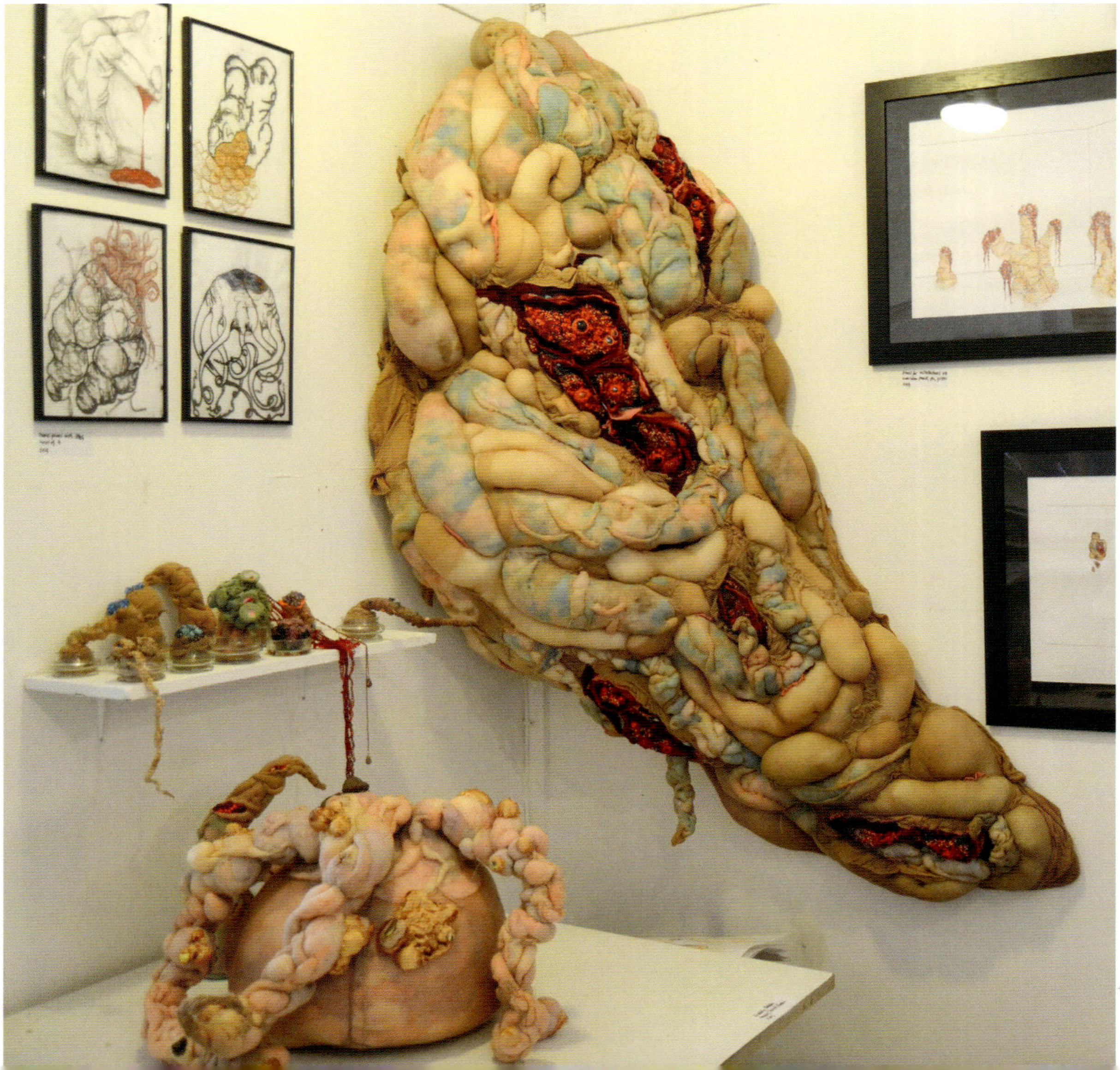

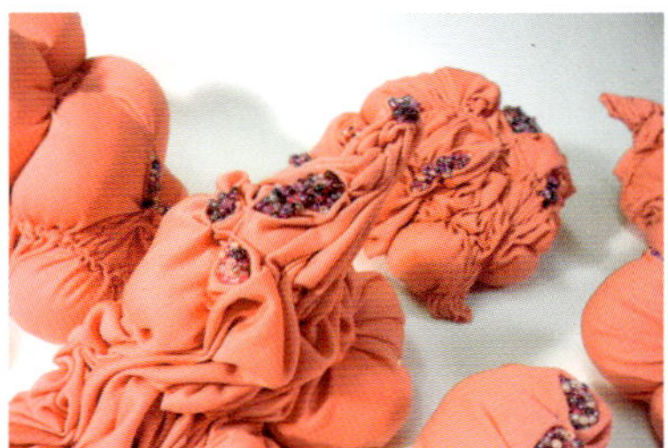

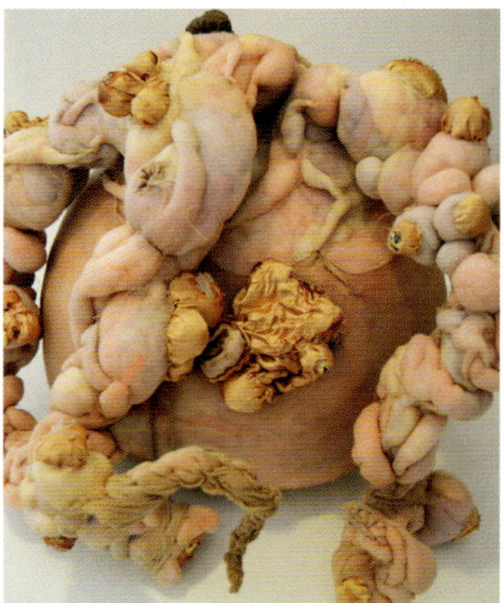

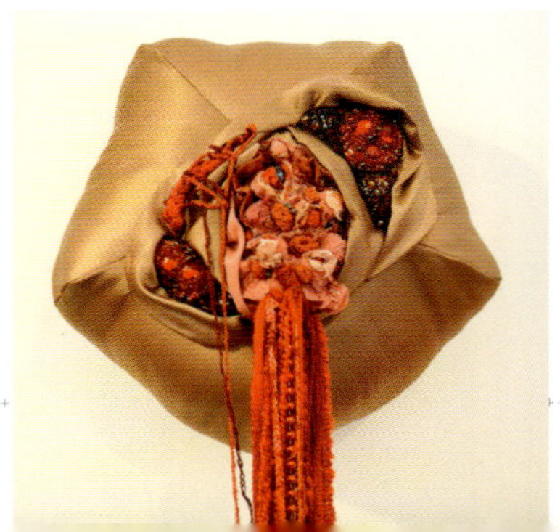

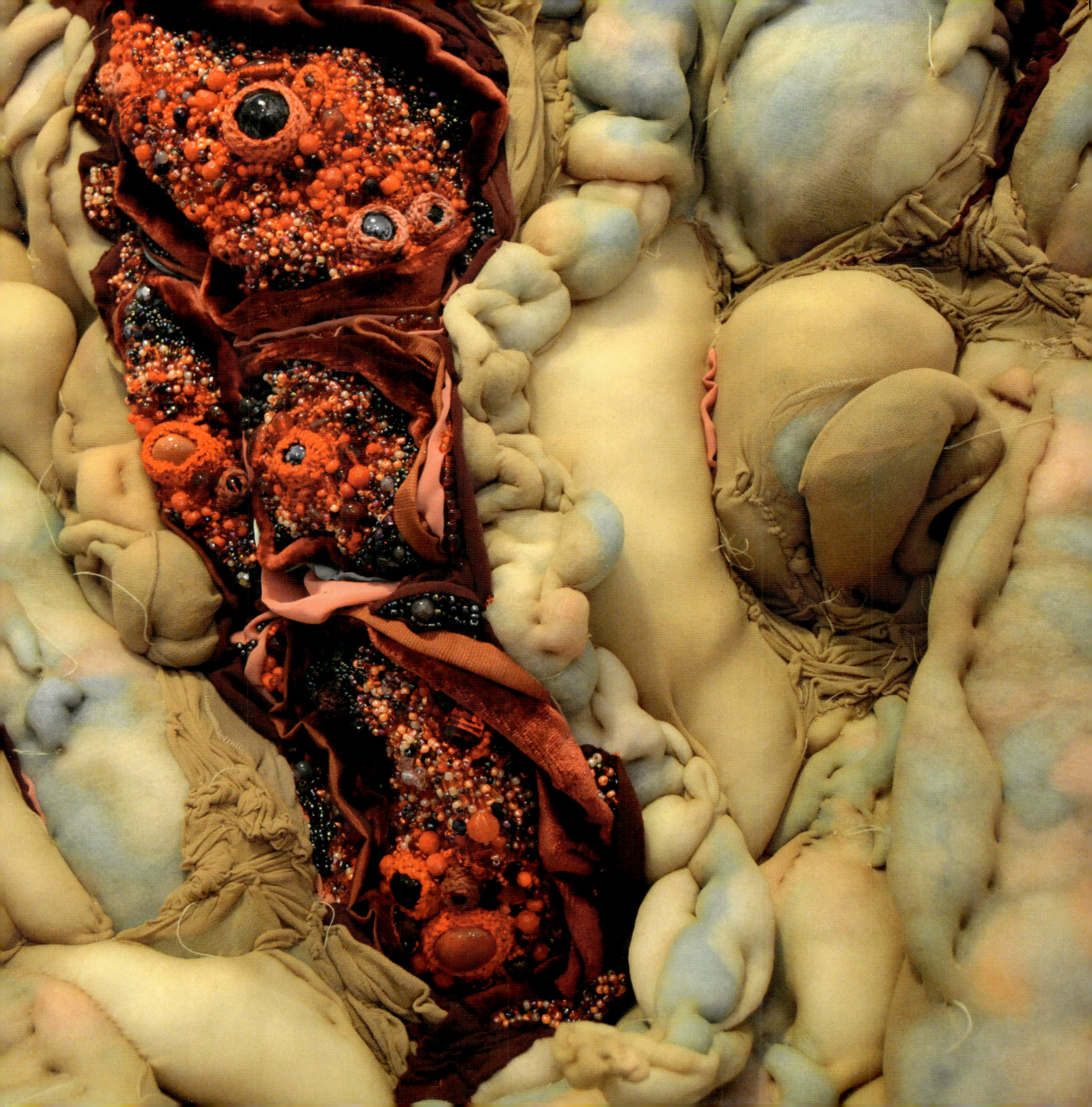

Linescapes

Architect & Illustrator
www.linescapes.co.uk

Clockwise from top left: House Portrait Commission; Textured Notebooks; Brighton Pier; Camera Notebooks; Abstract Print Pattern 6

Amalia Sanchez de la Blanca, the creative brains behind Linescapes, is an independent designer with more than 20 years' experience in Spain, USA and UK. After training in architecture and obtaining a master's degree at the Royal College of Art, she now spends her time designing products featuring digital illustrations, as well as lovingly restoring and hand painting furniture.

Her Architectural Collection consists of handmade blank cards, calendars, notebooks and prints that feature illustrations of well-known buildings. She's constantly expanding this collection by adding buildings from her adopted Brighton and across the UK, as well as undertaking house portrait commissions for private clients.

Amalia's Vintage Collection features illustrations of antique cameras and other objects that she then uses to produce prints, notebooks and cards.

The same products can be found in her Abstract Collection, where architectural details are abstracted, resulting in beautiful and colourful patterns.

Finally, the Textured Collection is made of elegant pocket-sized notebooks with luxurious textured covers.

Amalia sells her work through Etsy, local and London shops and markets, and has recently taken part in her first Brighton Open House by opening her newly-refurbished flat to showcase her work with five other artists. She's planning to take part again in the 2015 May Festival.

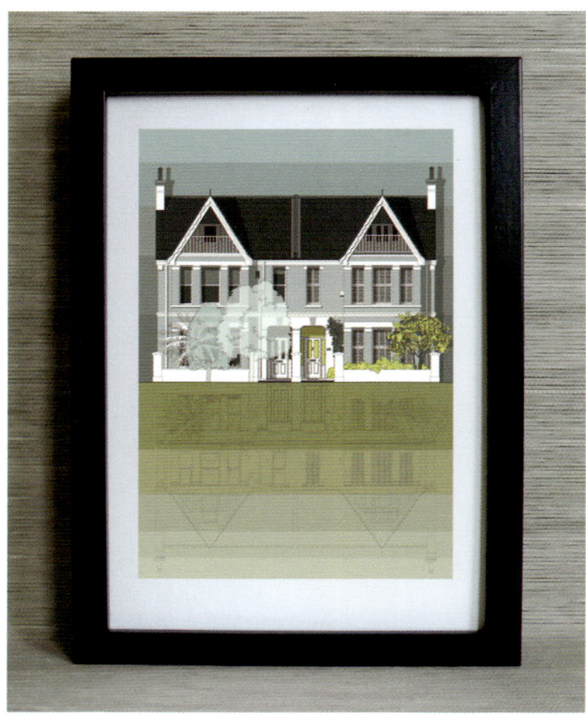

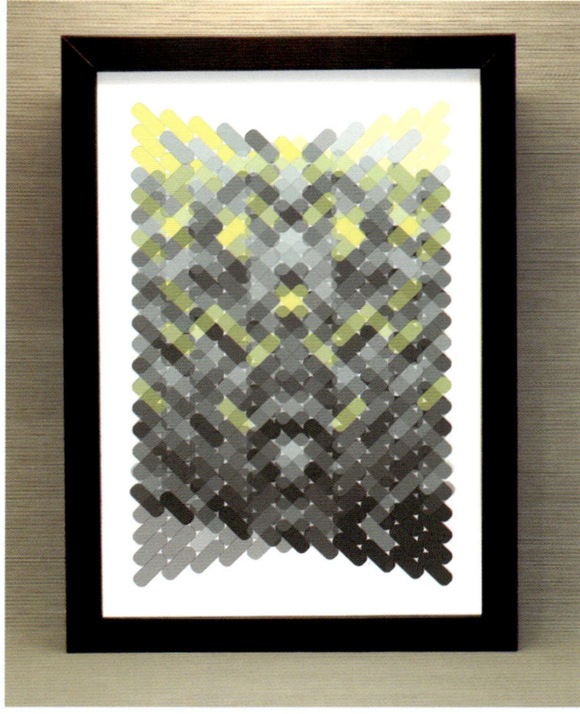

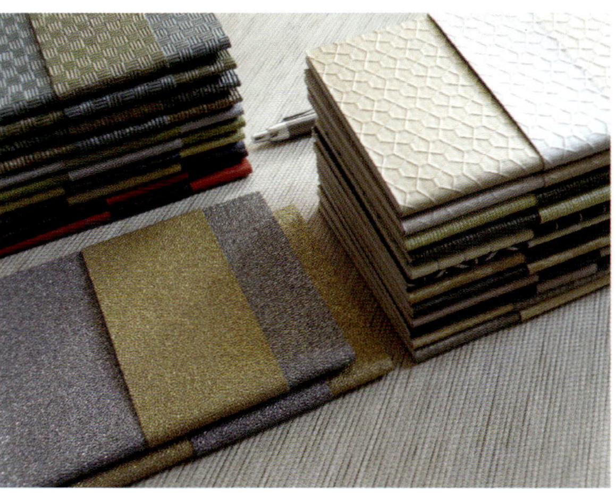

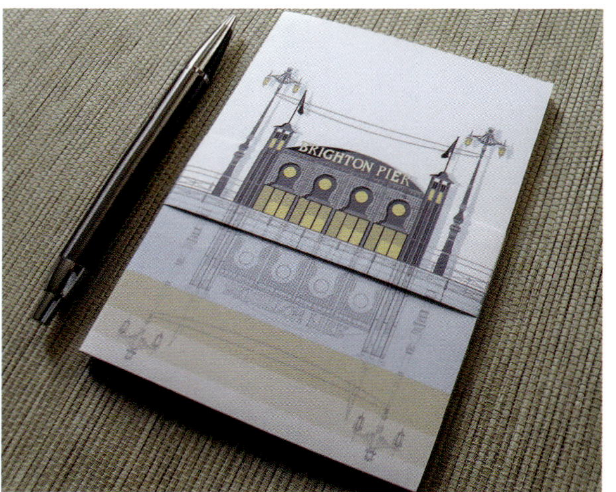

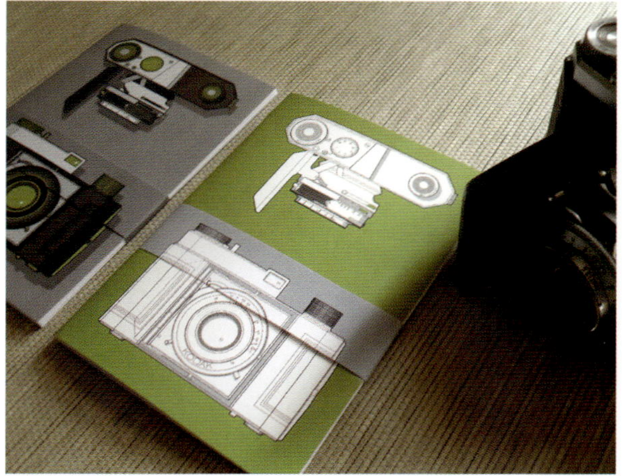

Janet Brooke

Artist/Printmaker
www.janetbrooke.com

Clockwise from top left:
Brighton Bits 9; And the Rains Came; Brighton Bits 2;
St Peter's in the Snow

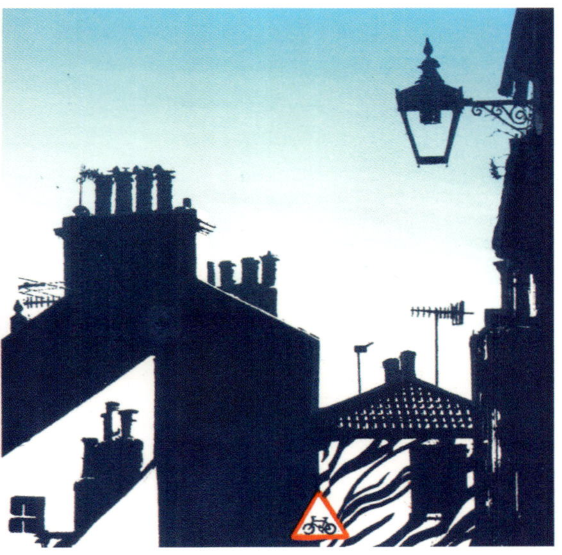

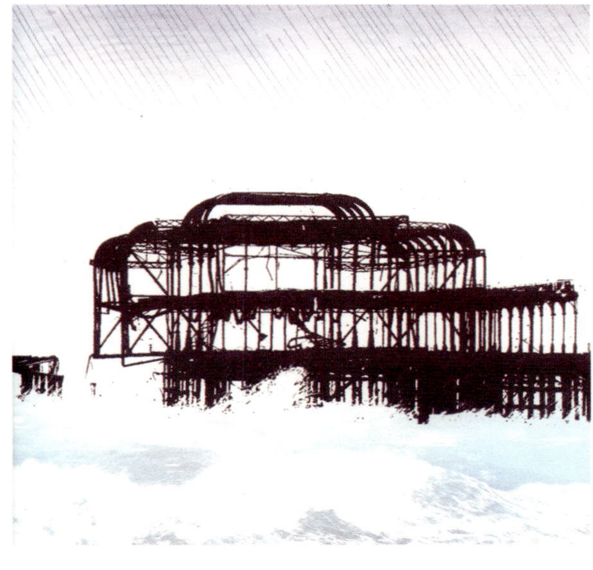

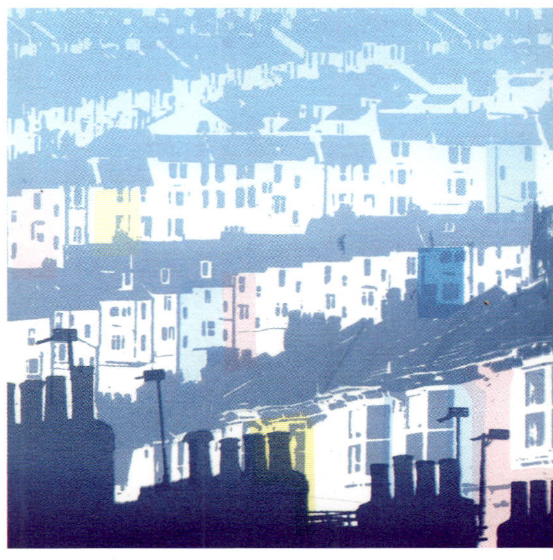

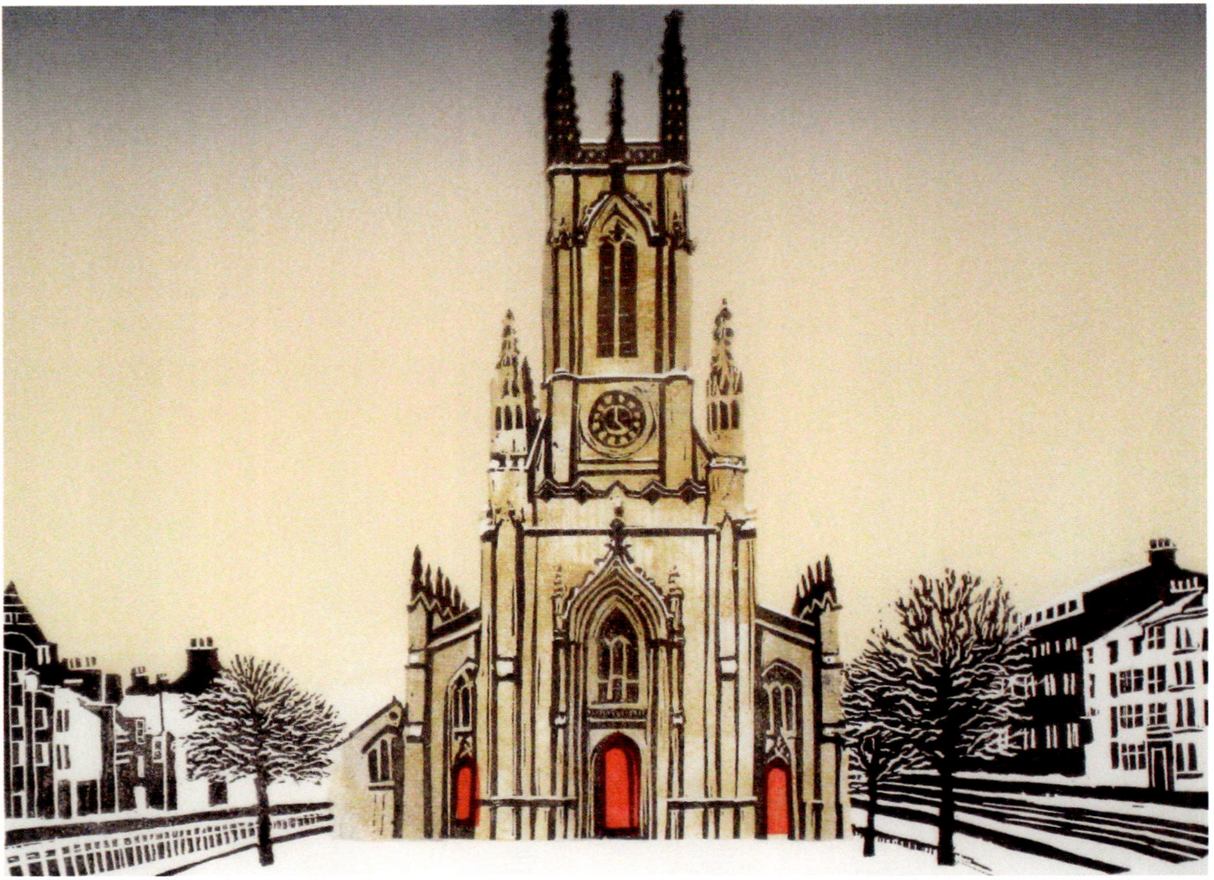

Janet Brooke is a printmaker specialising in the urban landscape. Her work can be seen at Orso Major and Bankside Galleries in London and during her Open House in Brighton. Visits to her studio can also be arranged.

In her linocuts and screen prints, Janet tries to evoke a clear sense of place – wherever it may be. During her long career, she has been inspired by many and varied locations, from the East End and City of London to cities in the Far East such as Hong Kong and Singapore.

But since her move back here, the place that has fired her imagination most has been Brighton, and in a short period of time she has produced an impressive catalogue of local work. Janet's prints of this many-faceted city aim to capture something of its essence without resorting to cliché.

During the past year she has split her time between working on a long-running series of linocuts of the Wren Churches in the City of London and continuing her exploration of Brighton.

All work is hand-printed in small editions and each print is signed and numbered.

Jo Watters-Pawlowski

Artist
www.jowatterspawlowski.com

Clockwise from top: Dawn; Last of the Snow; The Gallops; Dungeness Light; Downland
Opposite page: Dungeness Dark

The paintings of Jo Watters-Pawlowski are essentially driven by abstract expressionism. Using surrounding land or seascapes as her subjects, she plays with the figurative elements to create an emotional, abstract response.

Her aim is to evoke a reaction, rather than depict a scene, with each artwork carefully built up layer by layer using oil, acrylics and resist-work techniques that lend a spectacular intensity to the end results.

Jo's paperworks and smaller canvases, also available for sale, allow the public to experience the preliminary sketches and ideas that she works from when out and about. Back in her studio, Jo will replicate sensory and memory characteristics to translate into larger-scale paintings.

The artist's persona is depicted in the range and styles of her work: sometimes bold and brash, at other times soft and subtle. Each year her paintings evolve to create new work that can be refeshingly unexpected or simply familiar.

Jo's paintings are bought by private collectors, are specifically commissioned or are available through her annual Artists Open Houses exhibition in Ditchling.

Visitors are welcome to her Open House at 37 High Street, Ditchling, during the Brighton Festival in May. At other times, studio visits are by appointment only.

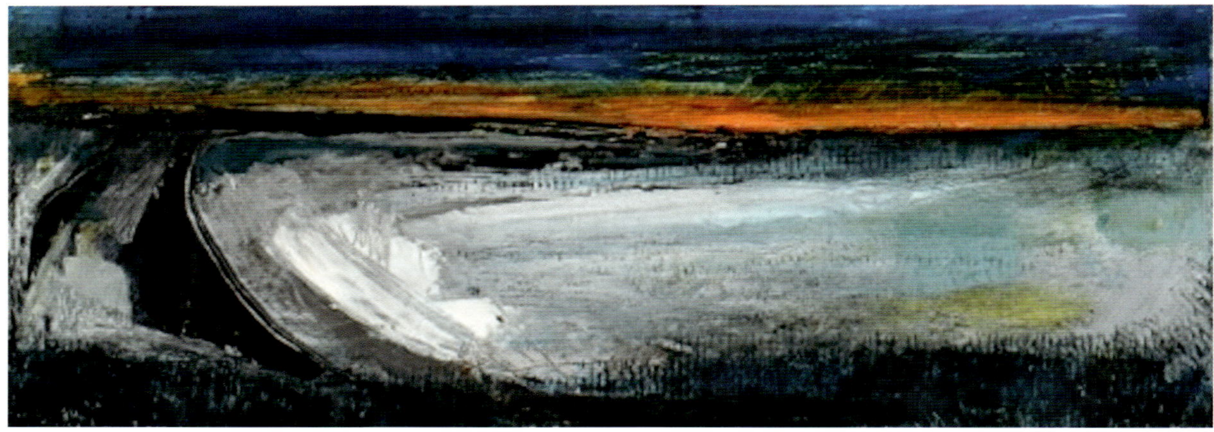

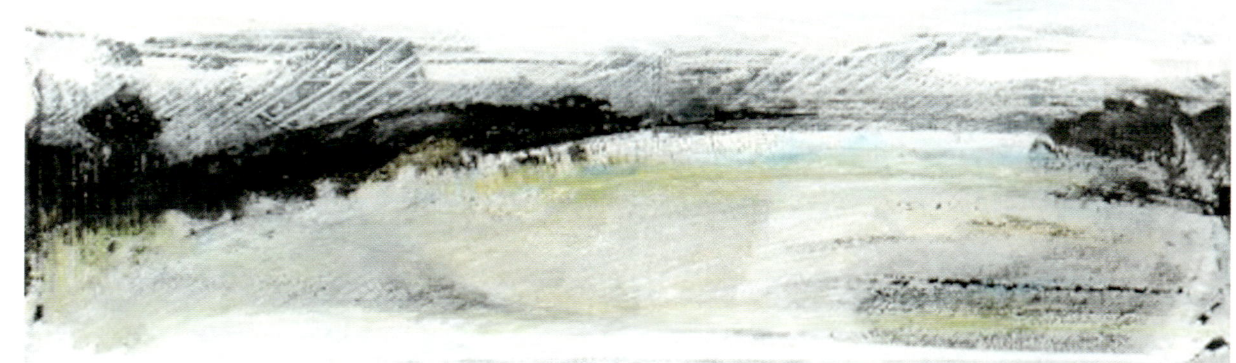

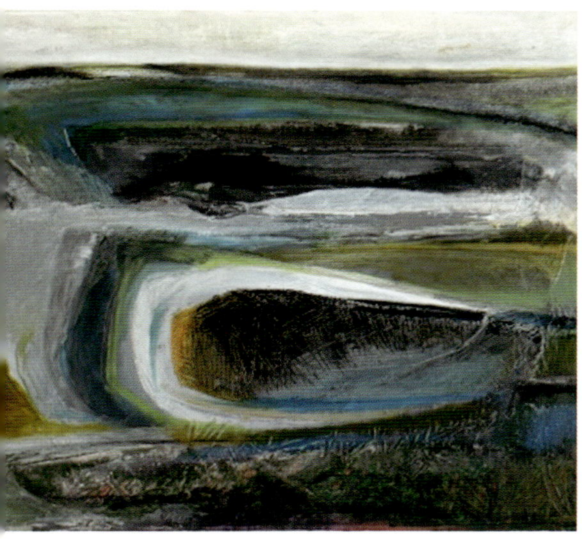

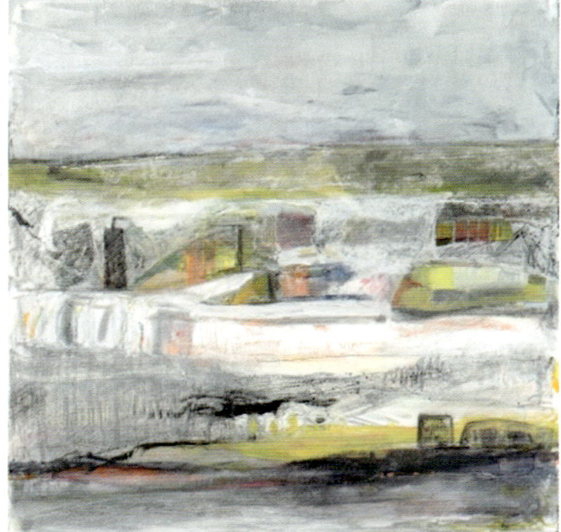

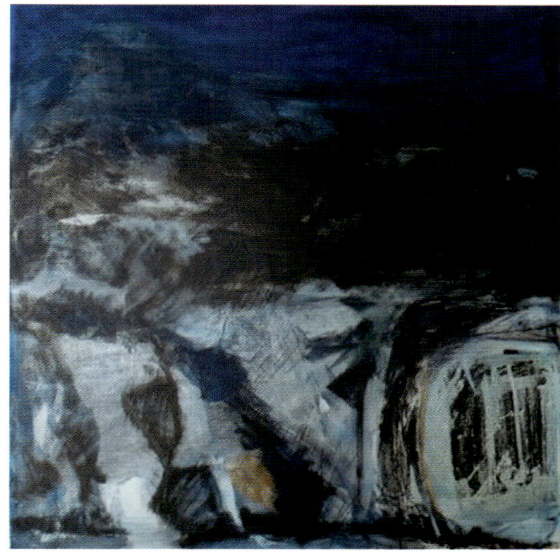

bip-Art Printmaking Workshop

1a Arundel Mews, Arundel Place, Kemptown, Brighton BN2 1GG
www.bip-art.co.uk

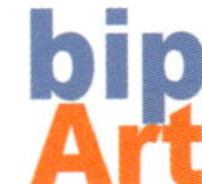

Clockwise from top left: Columbian Eagle; Cuckmere Haven by Helen Brown; bip-Art Printmaking Workshop

bip-Art is an open-access printmaking workshop situated in a flower-filled mews in Kemptown. The workshop, bathed in orange and blue, blossoms into a two-tier space that houses intaglio, relief and lithography departments.

Visitors enter through the etching area to be greeted by two presses: a hand-turned Rochat, made of cast iron and sporting an elegant wheel, and an electric Polymetaal press. The gentle heat and clicking of the hot plates accompanies visitors past the aquatint room and up the stairs to be greeted by the golden eagle perched on top of the hand-pulled Columbian relief press, circa 1844. The upper tier of the studio opens out to the right into the relief area. Here, roll-up tables and the wood/vinyl cutting area share the space with a hand-pulled, Albion relief press that is topped with a golden crown. The workspace to the left is the lithography area, housing four offset presses, three Globes and an enormous Hunter Penrose 'Deffa'. Each area offers a different set of processes and approach, but a similar sense of satisfaction at the creation of an image that has evolved as a result of the richness of the printmaking tradition.

Ann d'Arcy Hughes, Helen Brown and Hebe Vernon-Morris opened the doors of bip-Art in the Mews in May 2010 and continue to create a space where enthusiasts of traditional printmaking can learn and work in a relaxed and creative environment. Specialising in etching, drypoint, mezzotint, collagraph, wood/vinyl cut, block fabric printing and lithography, there are weekly evening and morning courses, weekends and summer schools available. The team welcomes all – from the beginner to the advanced – and groups are small to ensure maximum tutor support. Open access facilities are available for those confident enough to work independently.

bip-Art Brings Inner Peace

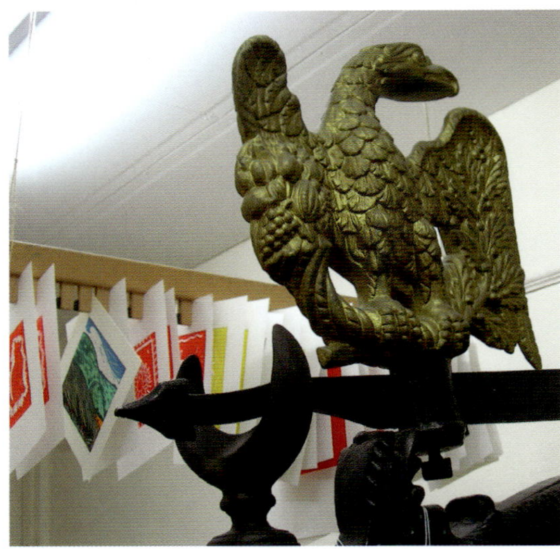

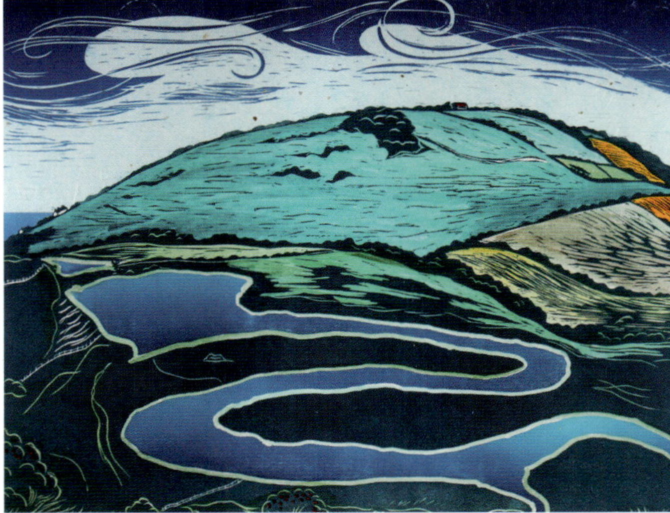

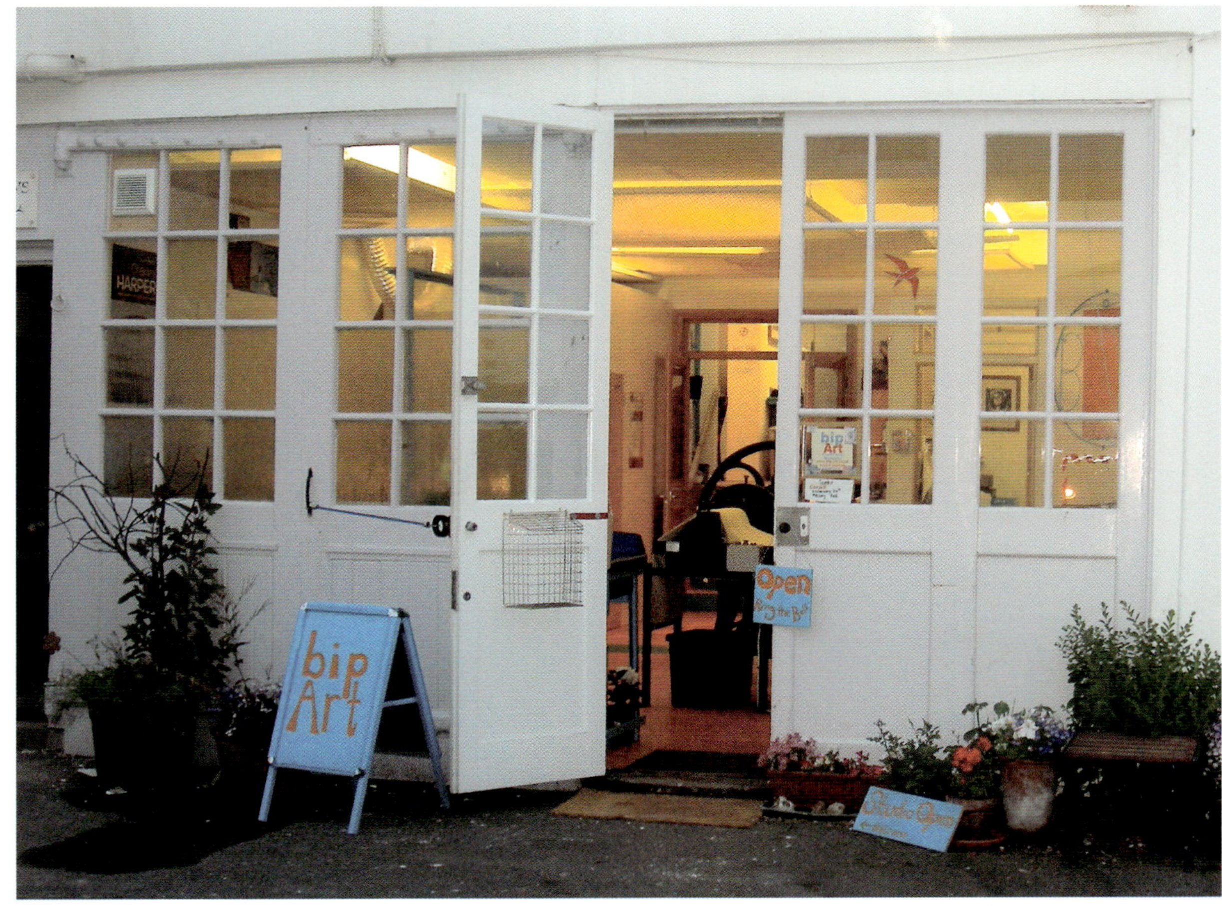

Left to right: Happily Attuned by Ann d'Arcy Hughes;
The beginnings of a plan... by Hebe Vernon-Morris

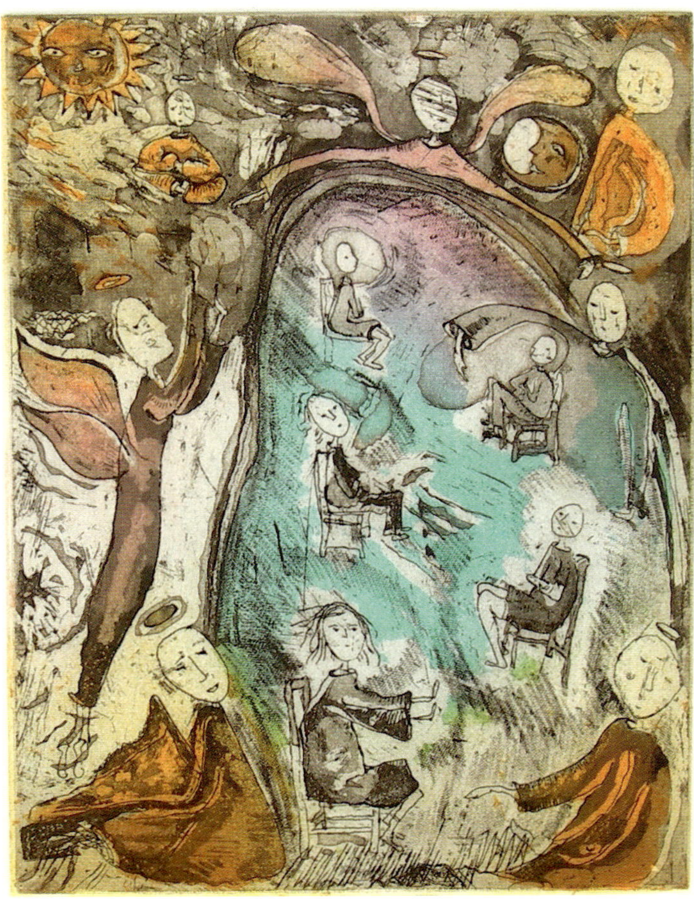

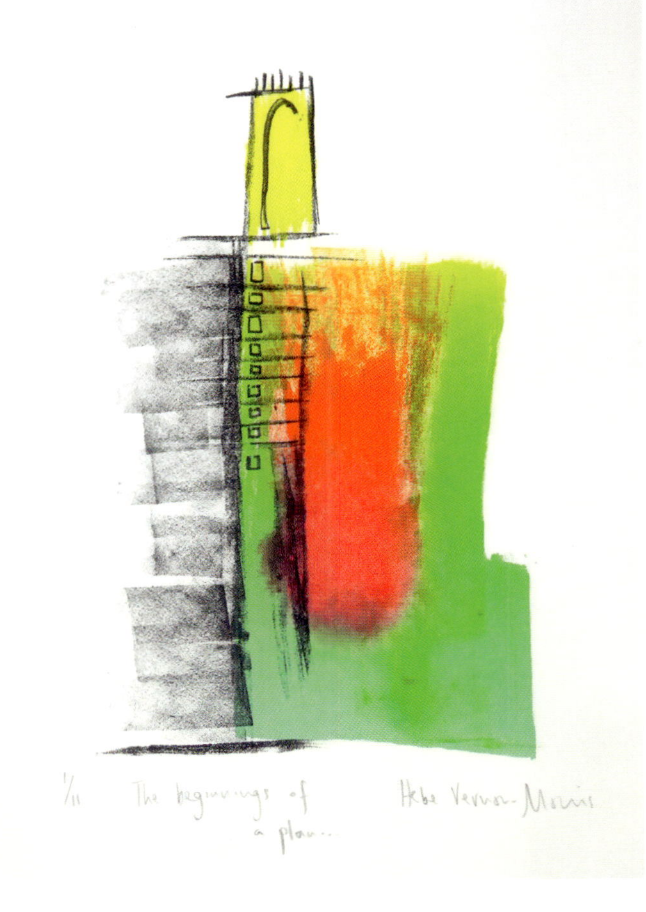

Helen Brown's work is inspired directly from the landscape. She works outside with woodblocks, drawing and carving from life. Working outdoors enables her to capture the line and fluidity of scenes and localities. A great lover of the South Downs and Sussex, many of her blocks are cut in the local area.

The time of day or year can dramatically change the landscape colour and form. Helen uses methods such as blends, jigsaw blocks and chine-collé to give each of her pieces individual life.

Helen teaches woodcut, along with the other areas of relief printmaking here at bip-Art, happily sharing her knowledge and love of this artform. For more details see www.helensprints.co.uk.

Ann d'Arcy Hughes uses the language of art and imagery, through printmaking, to express what cannot be easily relayed verbally. The constant theme running throughout her work is the depiction of the human passage through life. The symbolic use of the boat is that of the journey one takes from birth to death, alone at times, or with others. The stormy – or still – waters are the troubles or times of joy that one experiences on the way. Angels and spirits represent the forces of guidance that steer one through.

There are differing levels of perception and understanding and there are wave lengths, creating changes of time and scale. Ann's recent prints are more narrative and tend to depict one's experience on this journey. However, each image is open to the viewer to see what they comfortably relate to.

Ann has been a printmaker her entire life, with experiences that span student years taught by SW Hayter, Antony Gross, Jennifer Dickson and Harvey Daniels, and more than 40 years' teaching experience at the Slade, OCA and the University of Brighton. She initiated the printmaking workshop from a desire to uphold, teach and promote traditional techniques so vital as a balance in the digital age.

Hebe Vernon-Morris is inspired by the way that architecture mirrors the culture, character and soul of the human environment. Through years of travel – abroad and in Britain – she has developed a fascination for the details that tell the hidden story of a building. Humans build to create a space to survive, rest, love, work and worship, and these spaces hold the spirit of the lives that have been led within the boundaries of these structures.

Within her works, Hebe uses buildings to reflect the human condition. She imbues them with a soul and a personality, reflecting the idiosyncrasies of the human experience in the colours and marks, and the way in which they are clustered. There is humour and pathos in life, and Hebe's work encompasses both in her enduring fascination with the way humans overtly and inadvertently express their needs and dreams in the structures that populate the landscape. Lithography introduced Hebe to printmaking, and it has remained her enduring passion for the past 20 years. She teaches this technique at bip-Art and is constantly inspired by the spectrum of marks, colour and sensitivity that can be achieved.

Ann and Hebe co-authored *Printmaking – Traditional and Contemporary Techniques,* published in 2009.

Louise Dear

Artist
www.louisedear.com

This page, clockwise from top left: Coo..ee! Splash; Coo..ee! Blush; Coo..ee! Bloom; Water Babies
Opposite: Frisson ... Blush

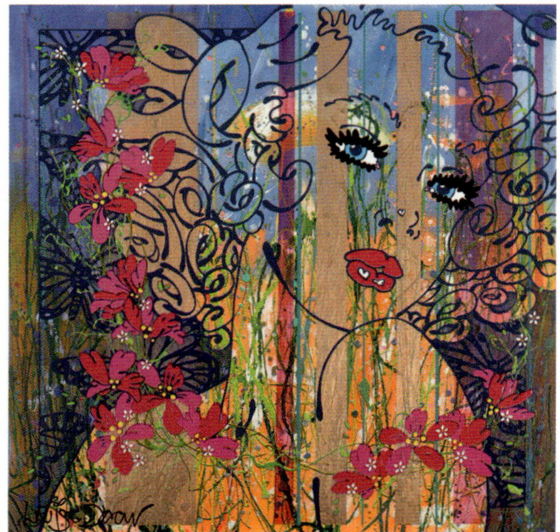

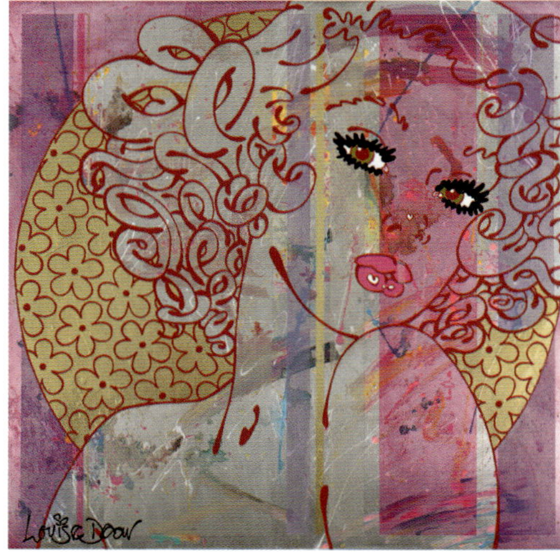

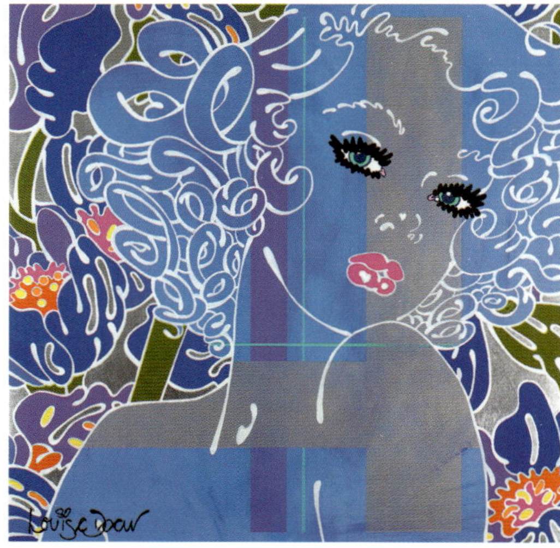

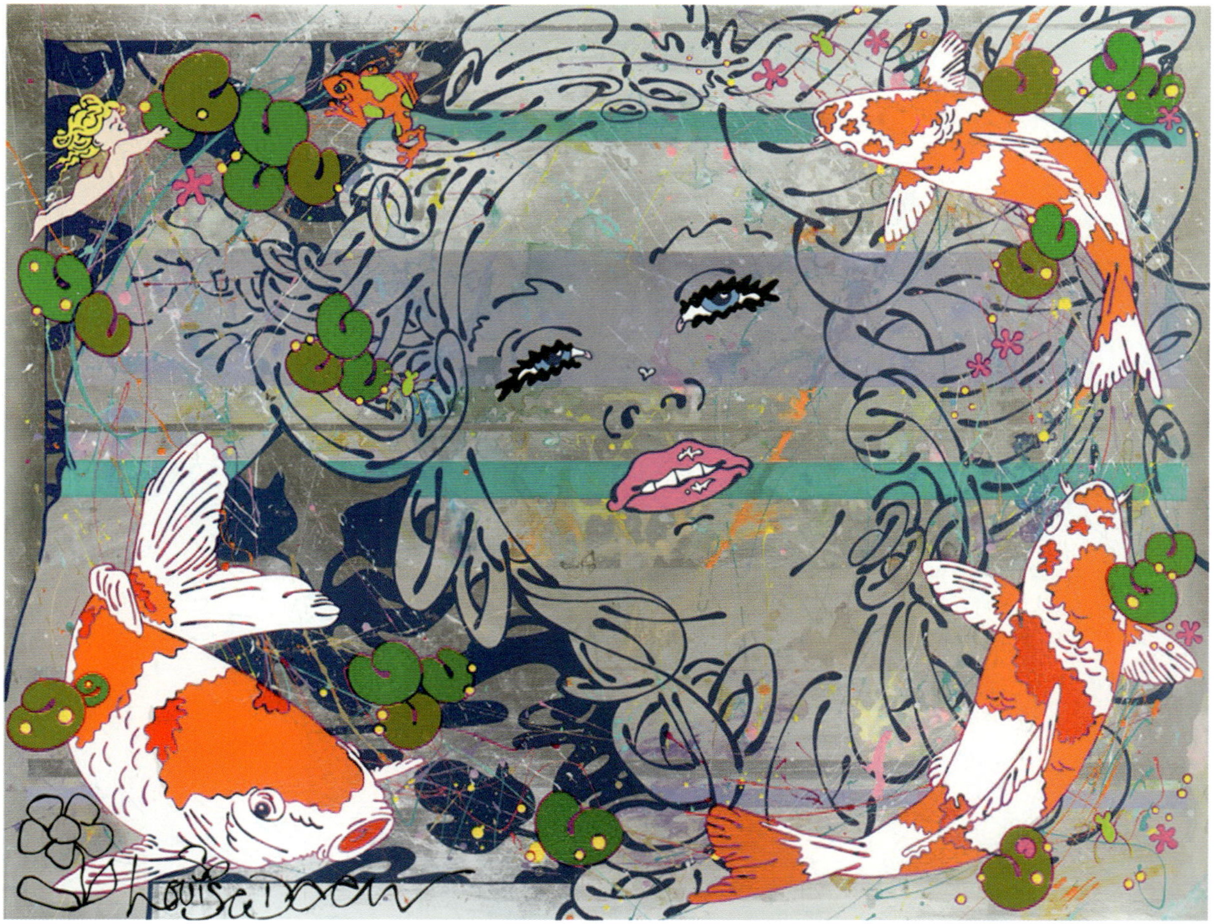

Louise Dear's paintings are a sumptuous feast. Seduction is her aim, and her works skillfully demand that their audience experiences the delight with which they have been created.

These neo-pop infused works are expertly fashioned using a multitude of media: golds, glitters and glosses layered on panels of distressed aluminium. Lavish, richly textured figures are sensually erotic, luminous and powerful, overlaid with flowers and frivolity that entice and seduce the viewer. In some works, elements of nostalgic kitsch emerge and storybook-beautiful children, their unique spirit captured, secure tender moments – snatches of childhood memory.

Louise Dear's works are addictive, and many of her collectors become obsessed with surrounding themselves with the pure pleasure they portray. Having been exhibited extensively, these vibrant paintings have sparked the interest of several major museums and are held in numerous collections, including those of Rick Stein, Qatar Holdings (the owners of Harrods) and Sir Elton John.

After a decade in Devon, Louise has returned to the heart of Brighton and set up a studio in the North Laine. Here you can view original works as well as beautiful prints that have been hand embellished with gold, glitter and gorgeousness.

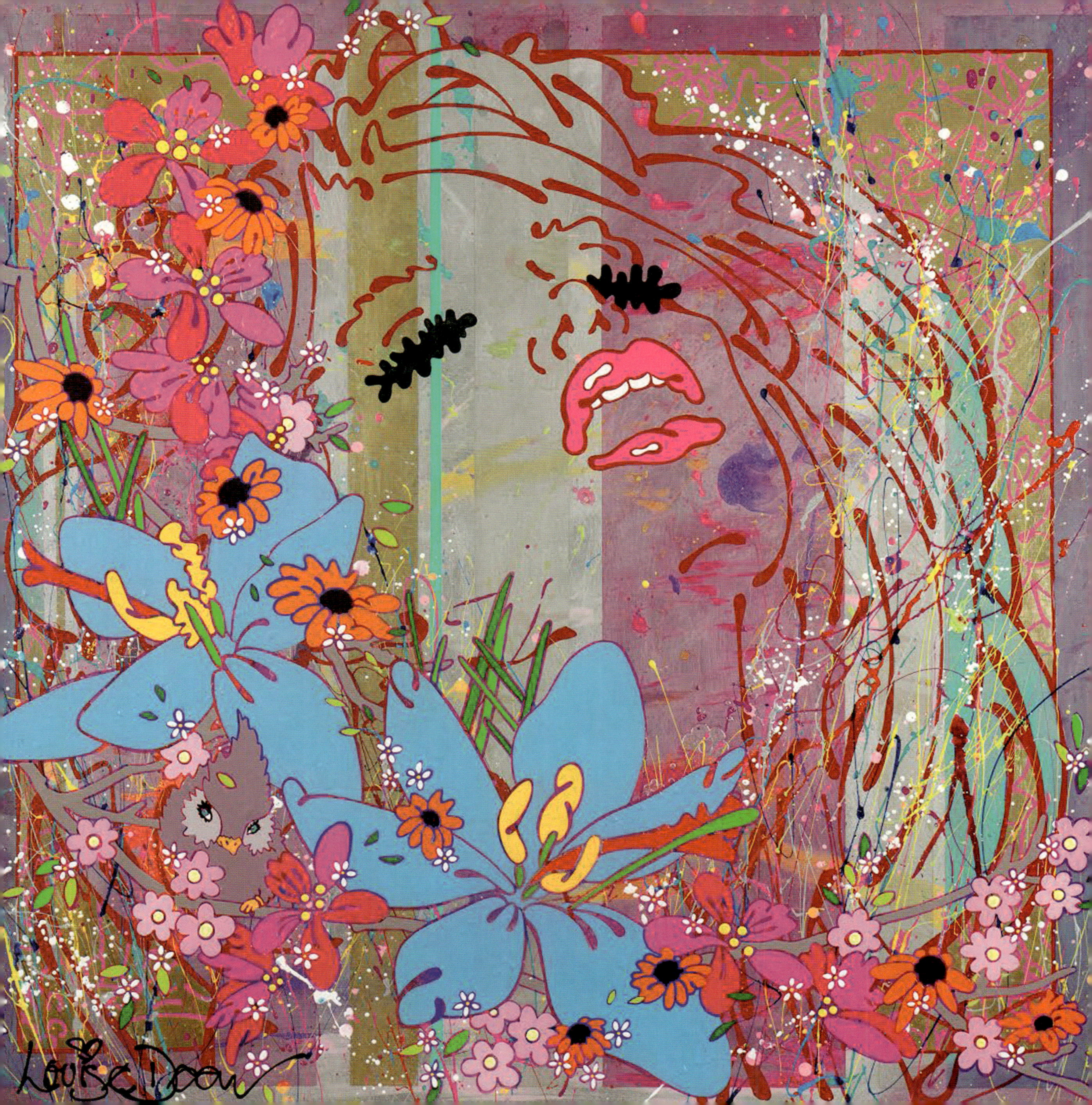
Louise Dear

Ellie Hipkin

Textile Artist
www.freyelli.com

Left to right: Wild Beach Sea Campions; Wild Beach Flora with Sea Views in Blues; Sea Kale with Sea View

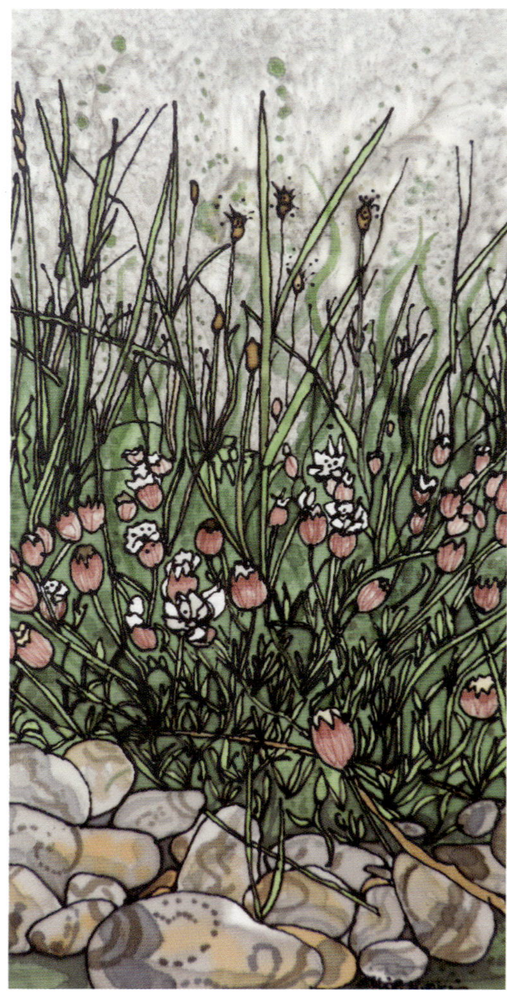

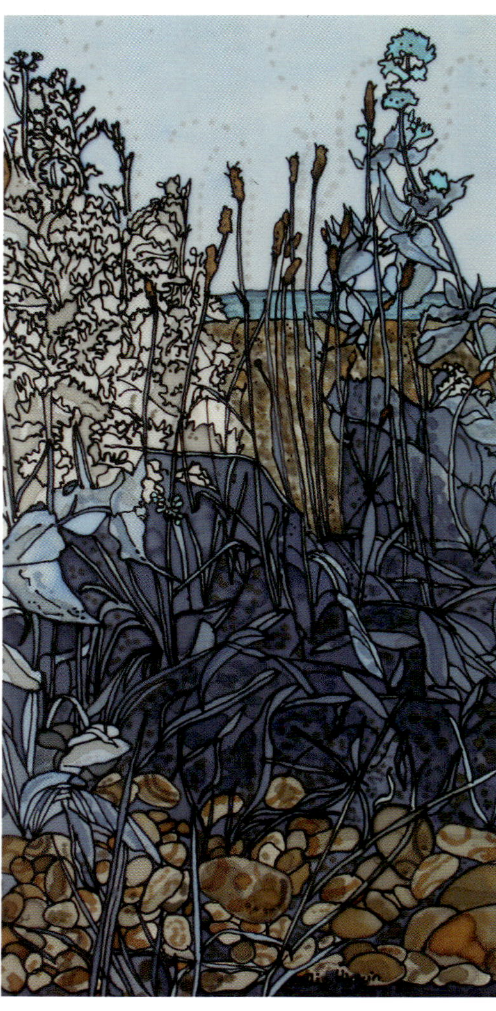

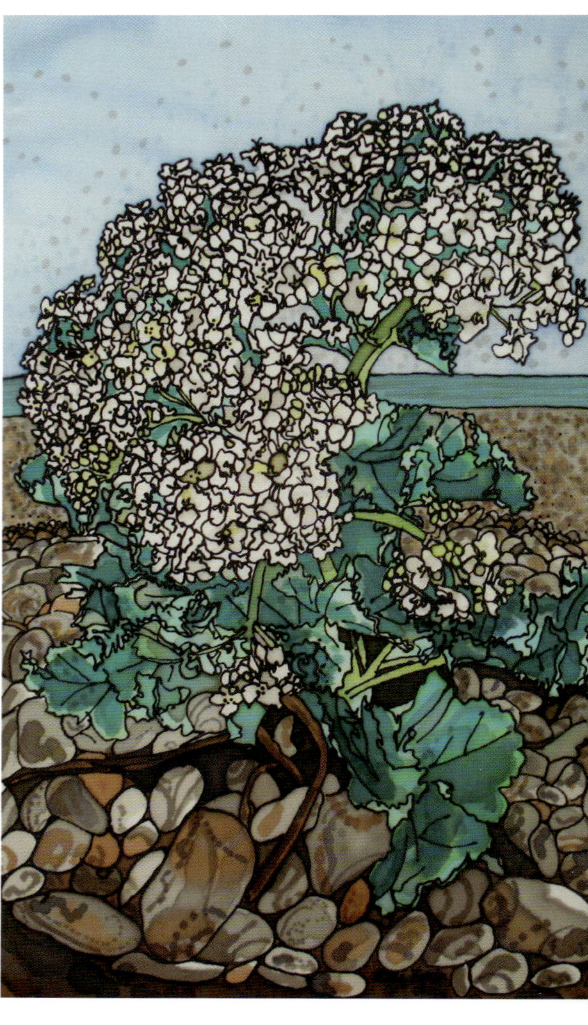

Ellie Hipkin is a textile artist who predominantly paints one-off pieces directly onto silk. Her work is inspired by the local flora and fauna that grow wild on the pebble beaches around Brighton and the south coast, including local iconic scenes and landscapes.

Ellie studied Fashion Design at Nottingham Trent University then worked in the fashion industry for 12 years before she started to paint. Her time working as a fashion designer saw her travel extensively across the globe, and the plethora of cultures she experienced has strongly influenced her current work. Through the subtle use of textile print, embroidery, embellishment and hand-painted techniques, her work brings to life the natural beauty of the south coast and Sussex Downs.

Alongside Ellie's paintings, she also paints one-off fashion pieces such as tops, dresses and clutch bags. She has recently diversified into homeware with cushions. Each piece is beautifully hand painted, and she takes much of her inspiration from the natural world around her, the sea being a major influence.

You can find Ellie's work in local galleries in Brighton: iO Gallery, Sydney Street; Bellis Gallery, Kings Road; and online directly from her website (above) as well as etsy.com and folksy.com.

Through the subtle use of textile print, embroidery, embellishment and hand-painted techniques, her work brings to life the natural beauty of the South coast and Sussex Downs

Clockwise from top left:
Glade; Miniature; Walk

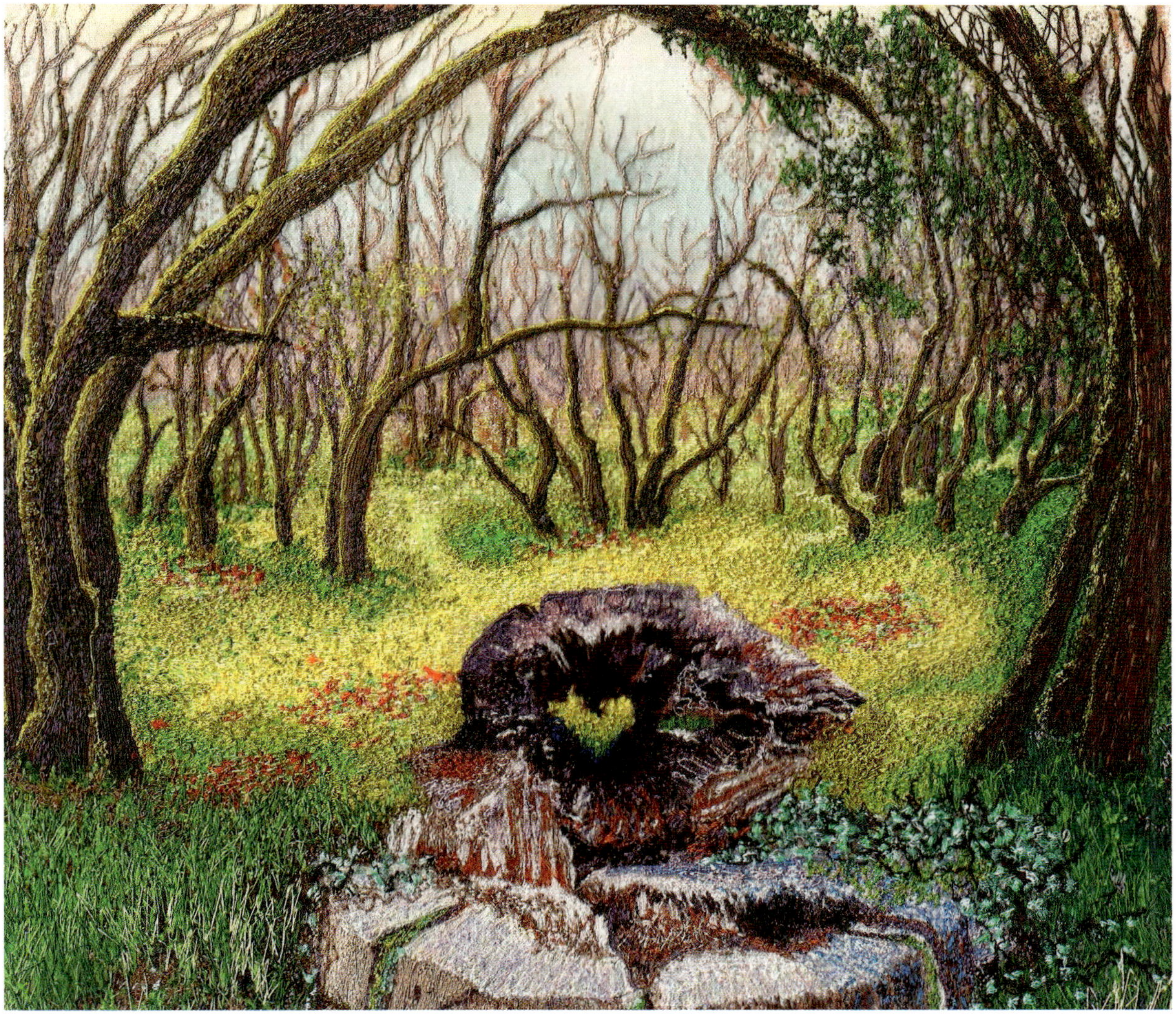

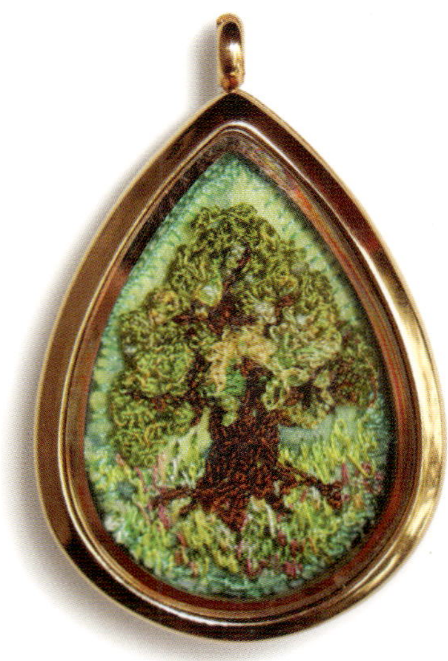

Agnes Chevalier graduated with a degree in Fine Art in 1984 in Rouen, France. Specialising in textile sculpture, she continued further studies in art at the Sorbonne in Paris and Goldsmiths College, London.

She pursued her art, exhibiting in France, Belgium, Canada and England, while working as a theatrical set and costumes designer and maker in France and later at the world-renowned costumier 'Angels' in London.

In 2008 Agnes resumed studying, turning her focus to sculpture and creative machine embroidery. She has since developed an extensive portfolio of fine art embroidery.

Her inspiration comes from the beautiful English countryside, focusing specifically on ancient forests and extraordinary trees. To create her embroidery artworks, she uses photos, which she then redesigns. Agnes paints the image on to fabric. Then, using her best friend – an old Bernina sewing machine – she draws with the needle, and just as she would paint, she stitches several layers of vibrantly coloured embroidery threads to produce an amazing 3D effect.

Since 2010 Agnes has been exhibiting and selling her work in Artists Open Houses in Brighton every year. In 2013 she opened her own house to the public under the name 'Chevalier House'.

Her inspiration comes from the beautiful English countryside

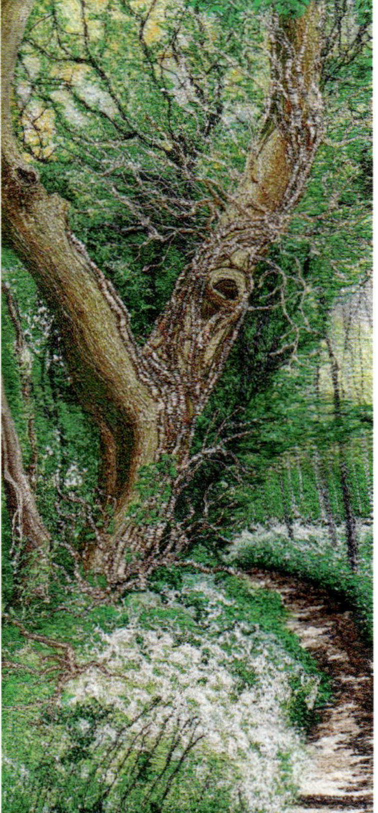

Amanda Davidson

Artist
amandasdavidson@gmail.com

Left to right: Poster image for The Adventures of Jane; Pen drawing of Carluccio's, Brighton; Watercolour of student drawing at the Skyros Centre

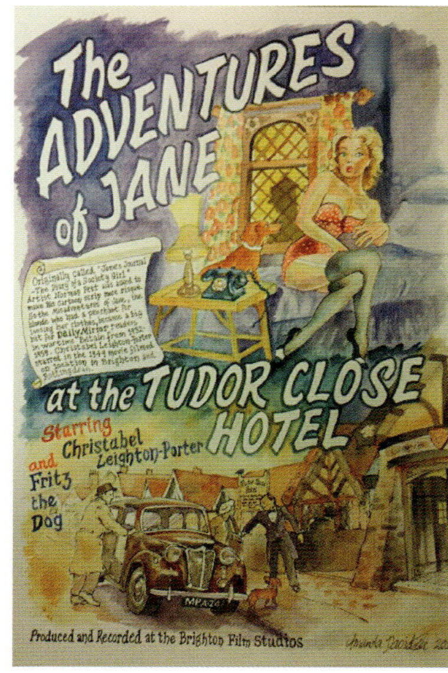

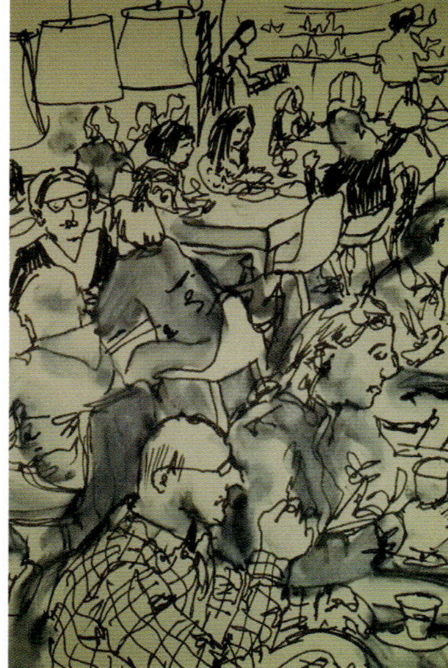

Amanda Davidson's journey through the world of art is a continual flow. From detailed architectural drawings in pencil, pen and ink to three-dimensional puppet theatres worked on cardboard and wood, Amanda will never turn down a new commission. It is joined-up thinking to her. Each project has its own medium, and just needs to be approached from a different angle. The excitement is in the challenge of meeting each client's brief.

Amanda studied at Brighton College of Art with inspirational tutors such as John Vernon Lord, Raymond Briggs and Justin Todd, and graduated into the all-encompassing world of publishing children's books and adult crafts.

From 1981-2000, she wrote and illustrated 21 titles for Harper Collins, Methuen, David & Charles and various other popular craft magazines. But it wasn't always an easy ride. A spell in a few design agencies as a paste-up artist just helped pay the rent until the royalties kicked in.

When publishers hit a pricing crisis and magazines folded, Amanda changed direction to work on interior design projects as a paint-effects artist. First for private homes stencilling and marbelling, then shop-front murals and a triptych for Pizza Express in Kingston-upon-Thames. Her talents were called upon to create a window display for Liberty's of London, and she worked on a major period house restoration in Holburn called Pushkin House, where the architect also asked Amanda to create some pen-and-ink drawings of the exterior to display in the hallways. Other drawing and design work followed for local conservation groups, estate agents and the private sector.

After opening her shop/gallery *Arty phArty Studios* in Rottingdean, Amanda met Philip Sugg who, after a career as a museum curator, film-maker and cartoonist, was looking for people to collaborate with his puppet theatres.

So began *Madame Butterfly in a Suitcase*, a theatre prop for Ignacio Jarquin's touring one-man opera; *The Smugglers Story* with Brighton-based Touched Theatre company; and *Rikki-Tikki-Tavi* for the Kipling Festival.

Amanda teaches regular mixed-media adult art classes and life drawing sessions every Thursday at the Rottingdean Whiteway Centre. She also teaches art at the Skyros Centre in Greece each summer.

Amanda is available for illustration/ mural commissions and for theatre prop designs.

For Amanda, each project has its own medium and just needs to be approached from a different angle. It's joined-up thinking to her

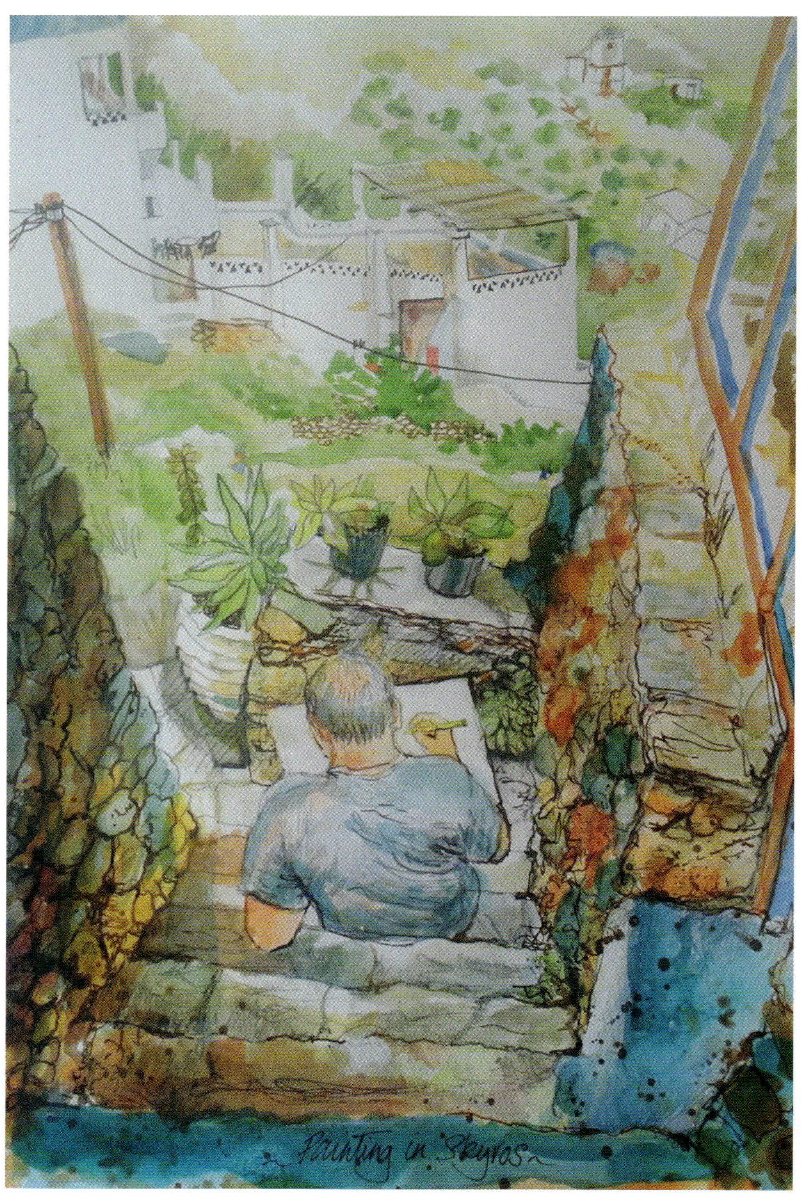

Clockwise from top left: Kipling Festival poster; Life drawing in pen & wash;
Rottingdean Smugglers Puppet Theatre Procenium (created with Philip Sugg); Pen & watercolour of Brunswick Square

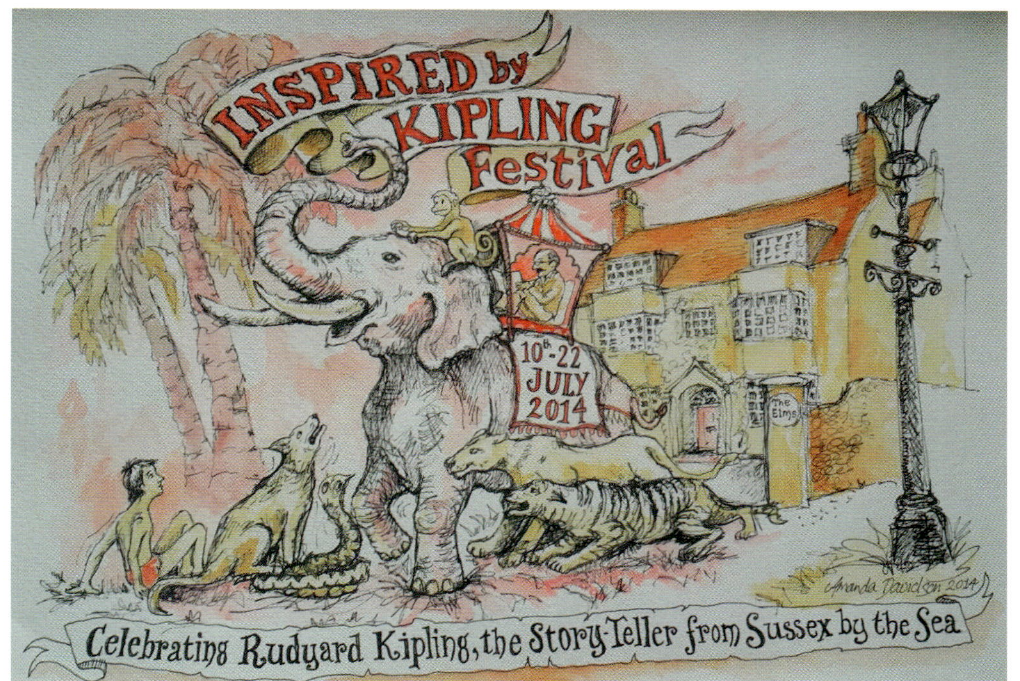

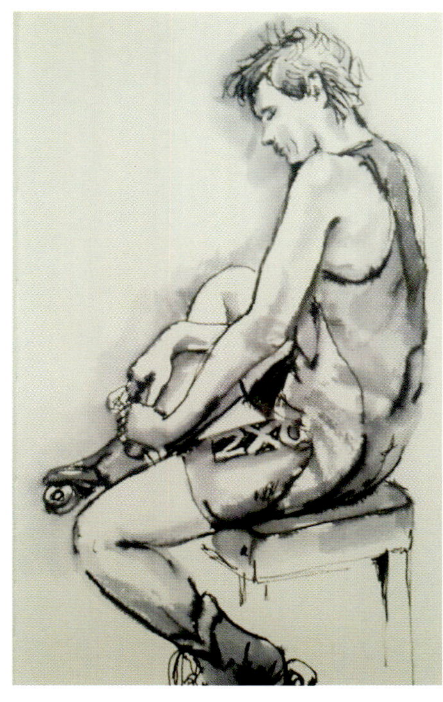

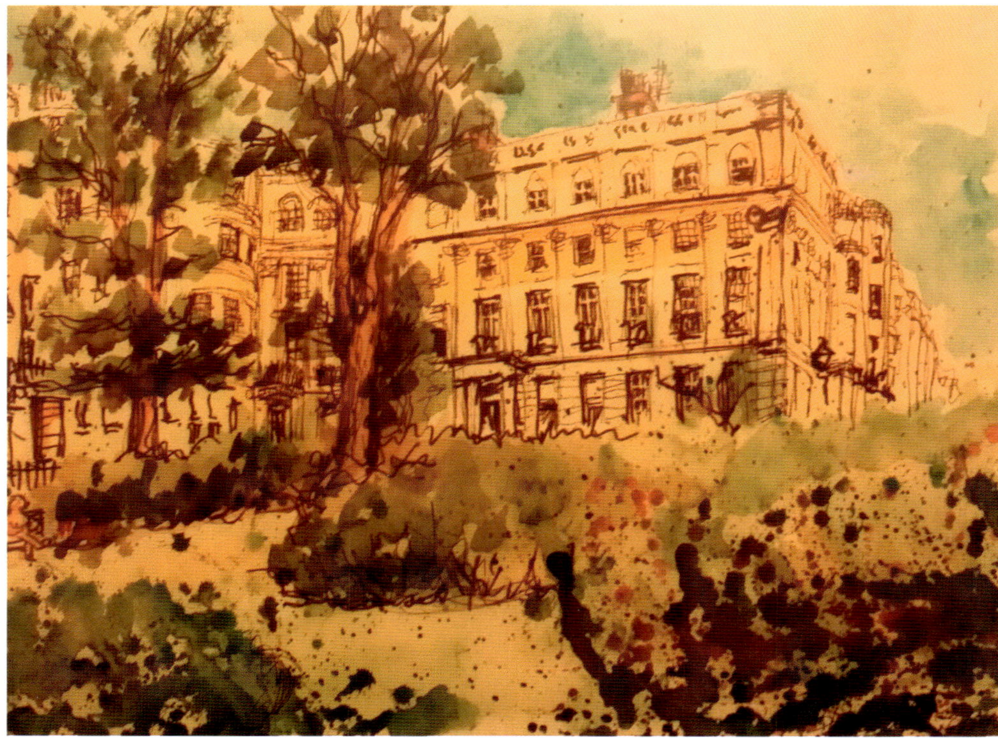

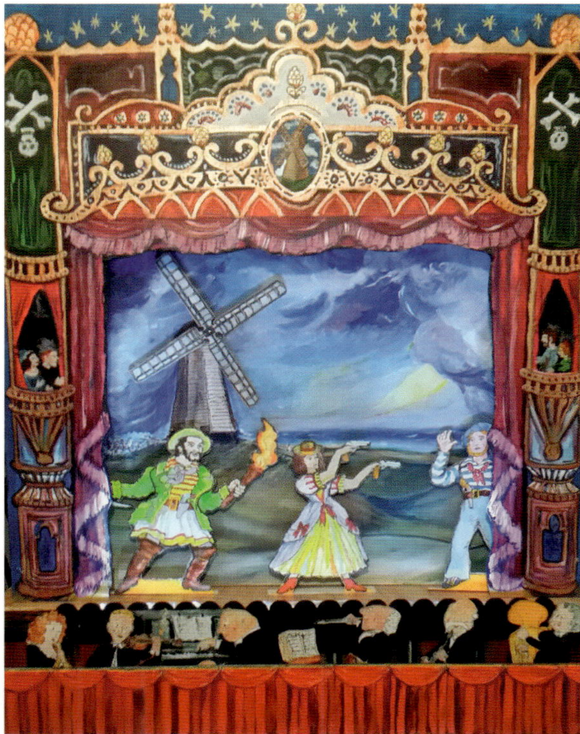

Richard Heys

Artist
www.richardianheys.co.uk

Clockwise from top left: Gravity's Rainbow; Remembering Tuscany; Summer Dreaming; Return; Nightfall
Opposite page: The Door at the End of the Earth

Richard Heys grew up in West Yorkshire at the foot of the Pennines. The bleak beauty of the rocky crags and moors surrounding his family's farm continues to inform his work. Richard has lived in East Sussex since 1997 and is particularly inspired by the shapes and moods of the South Downs.

Richard strives to create paintings with presence; paintings that have atmosphere and countenance. For the past couple of years he has been working in a beautiful, light-filled studio in Forest Row exploring tools and techniques that disguise the hand of the artist. From this limitation and challenge, he has found a greater freedom. In his painting Richard explores light and darkness and pure lyrical colour journeys, working with transparency and glazing to create vibrant surfaces. He is engaged in a passionate personal journey to rediscover beauty and uncover the unknown.

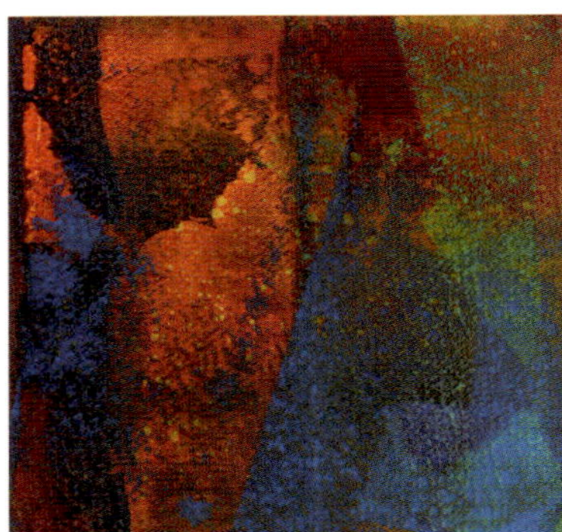

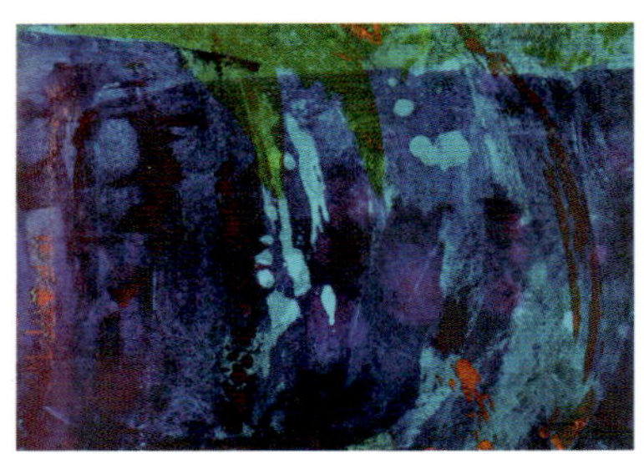

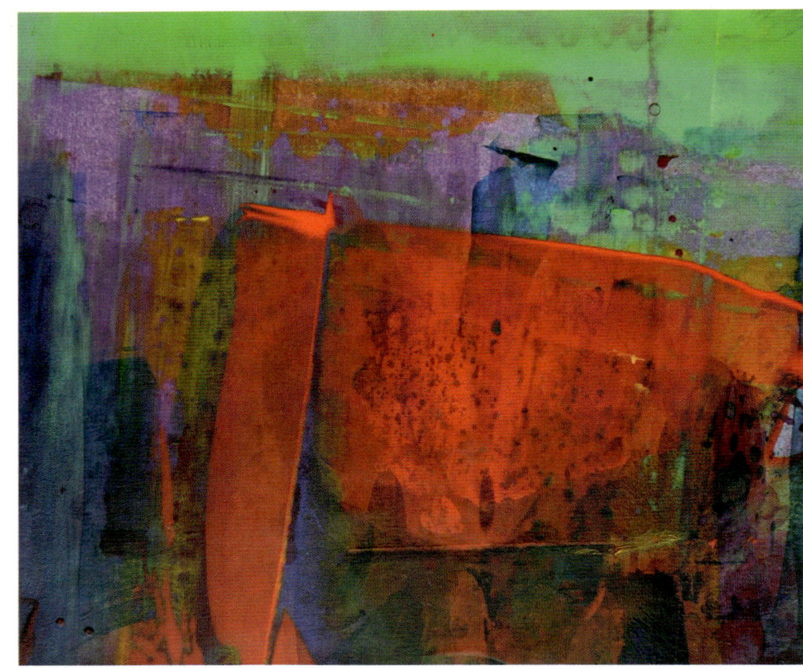

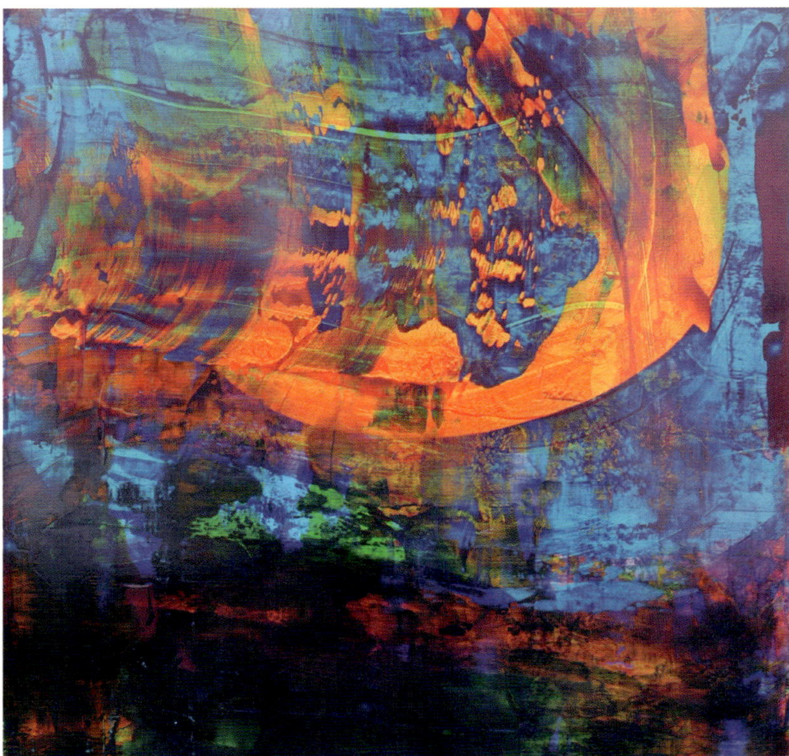

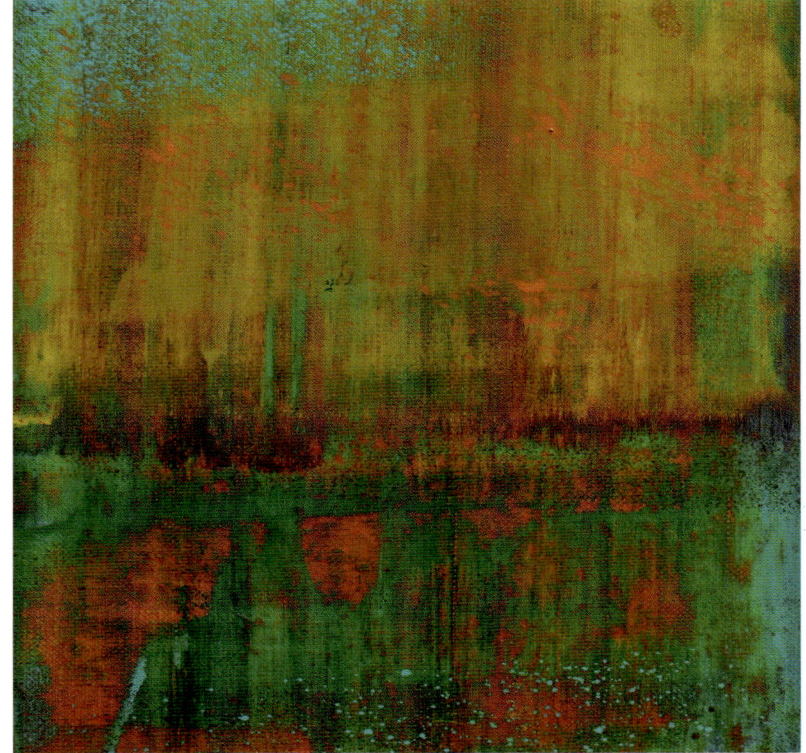

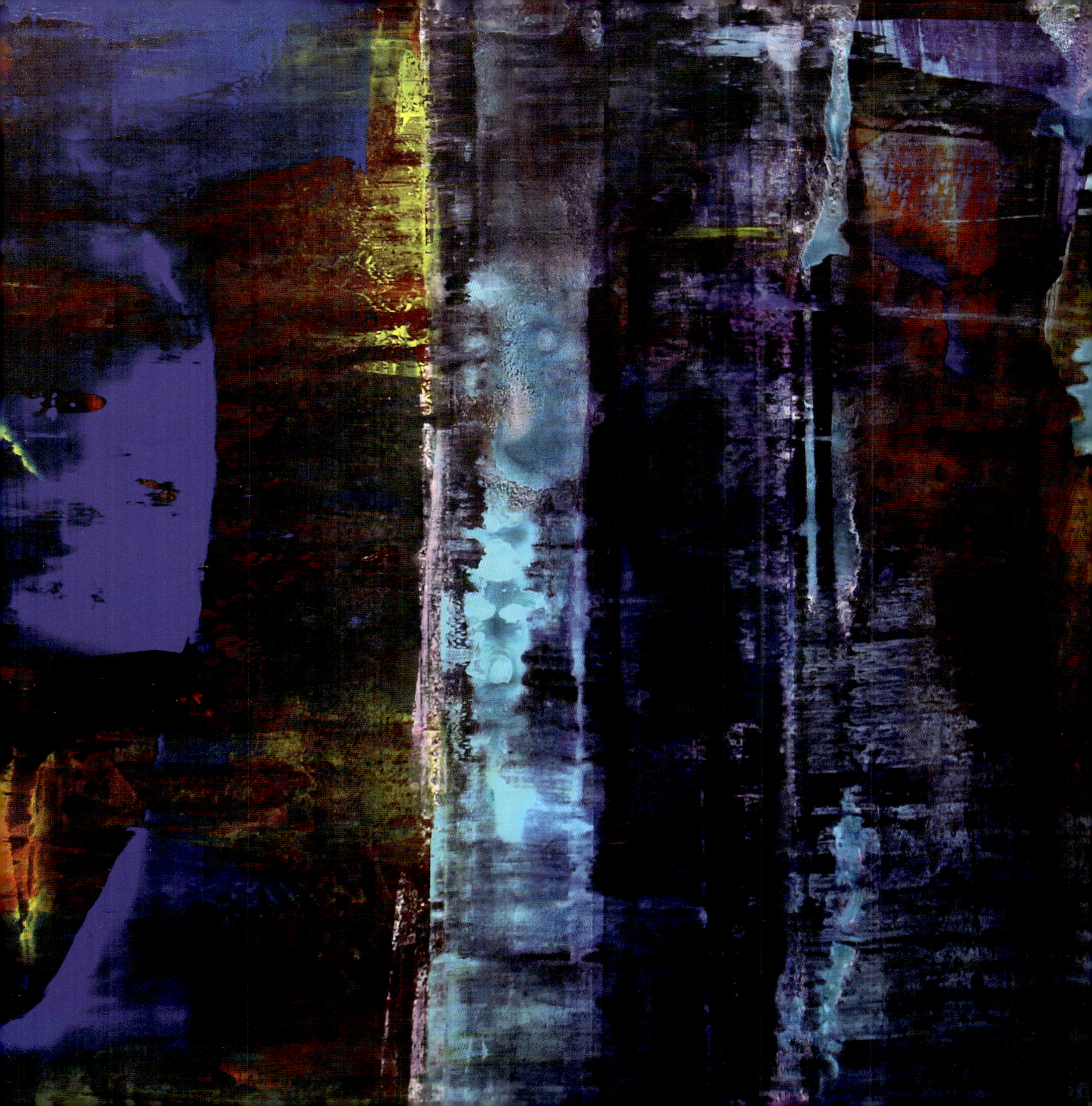

Ian Hodgson

Artist
www.ian-hodgson.co.uk

Clockwise from top left:
Boundary; Suspend; Acanthus

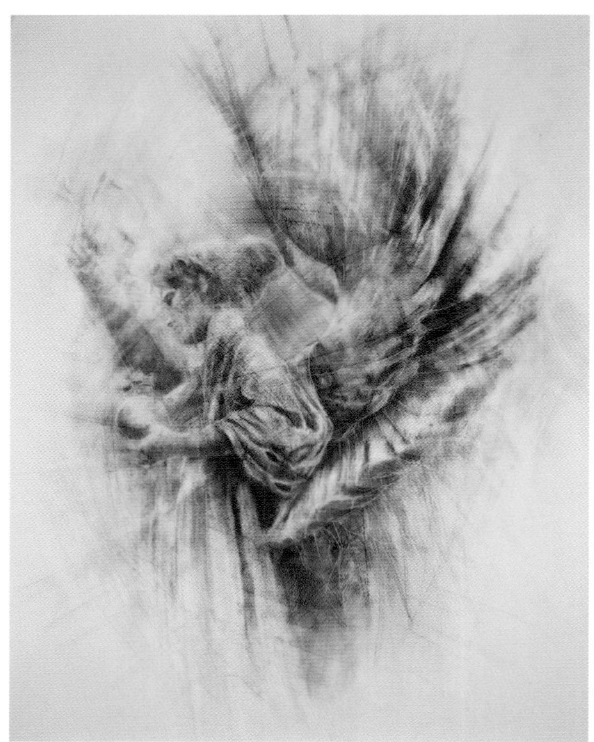

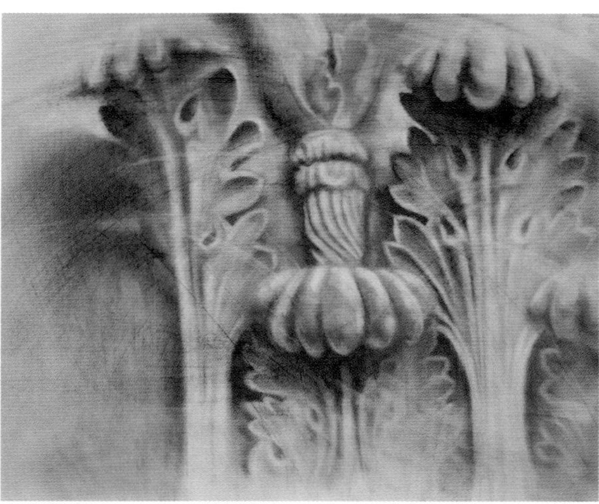

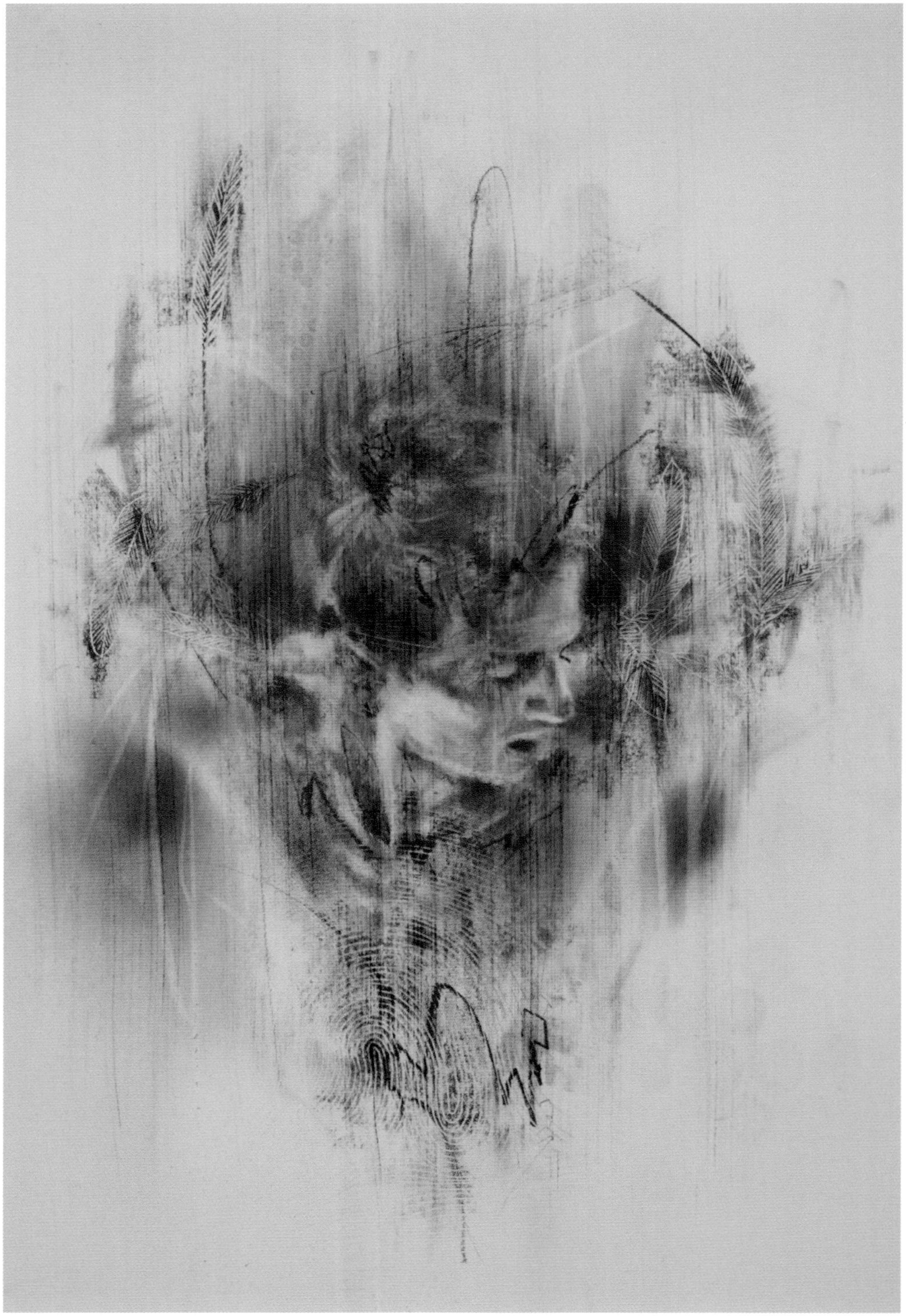

Engaged with identity and place, Ian's work explores the transformative process of journeys filtered through memory. His drawing process often leads to re-visiting objects, figures and spaces, and this reworking of the familiar has allowed his drawing practice to develop with each new approach, shedding fresh light on his subject matter.

Xavi Dom Buendia

Fine Art Photographer
www.xdbphotography.com

Clockwise from top left:
284; Self-portrait; The Kiss pt II

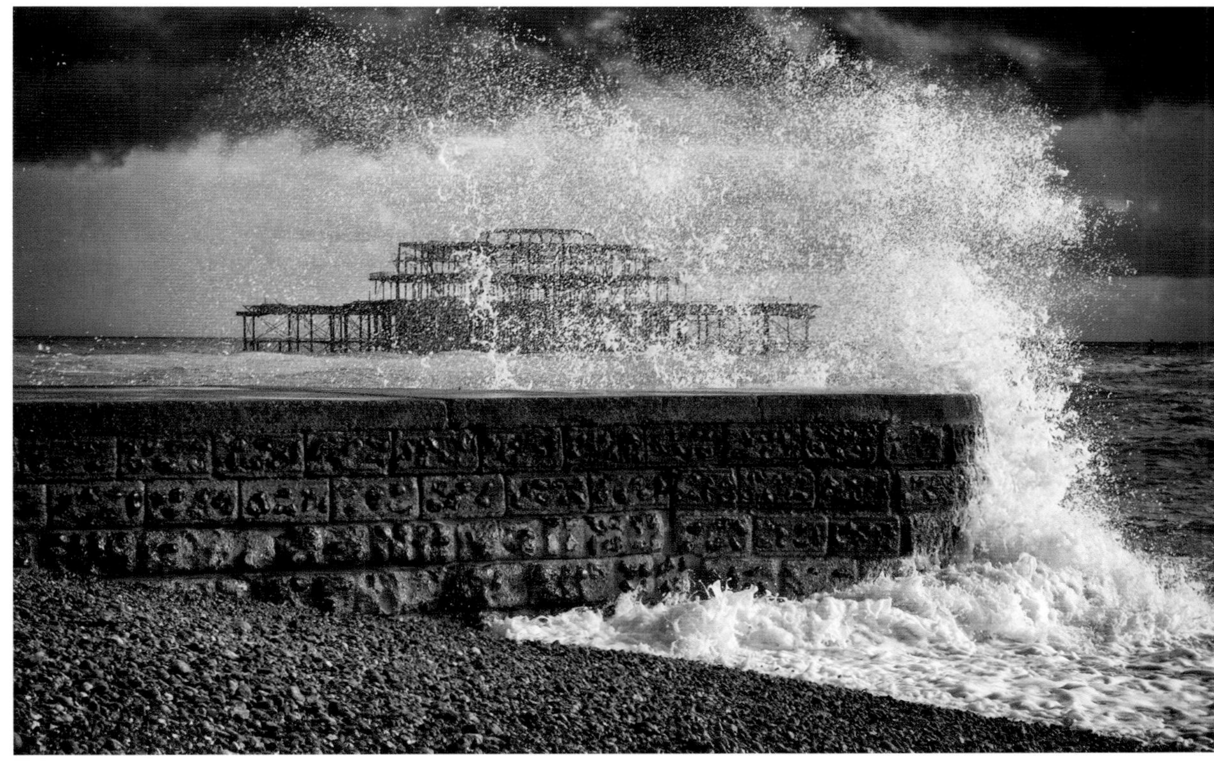

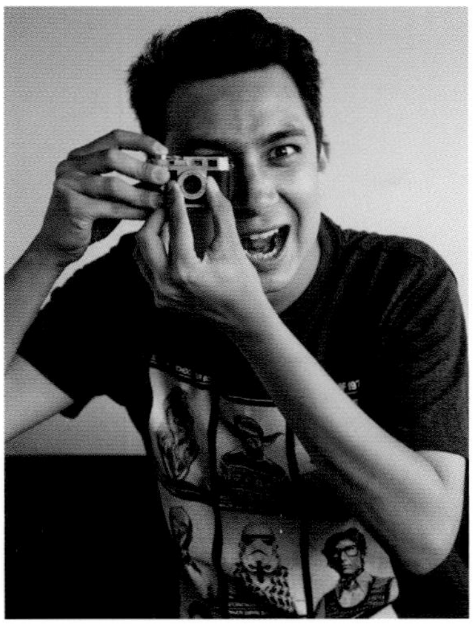

Xavi Dom Buendia is a fine art photographer who works on personal and commissioned projects.

Working mostly in monochrome, he likes to tell stories based on ideas and emotions of everyday situations found on the streets. His use of natural light is a big part of the creative process he follows to achieve such strong images.

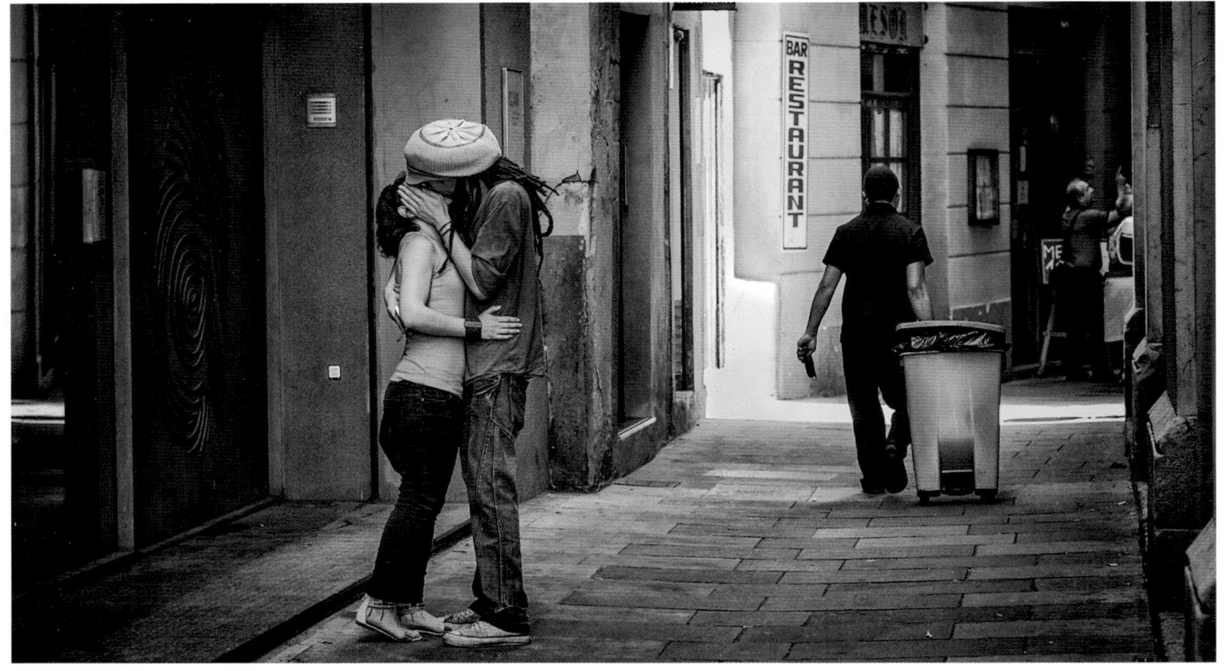

Luella Martin

Painter & Printmaker
www.luellamartin.co.uk

Clockwise from top left: Trees, Sky (solar etching); Hill, Trees (solar etching); Dark Woods (solar etching); River (solar etching)
Opposite page: Low Tide (oil on paper mounted on wood)

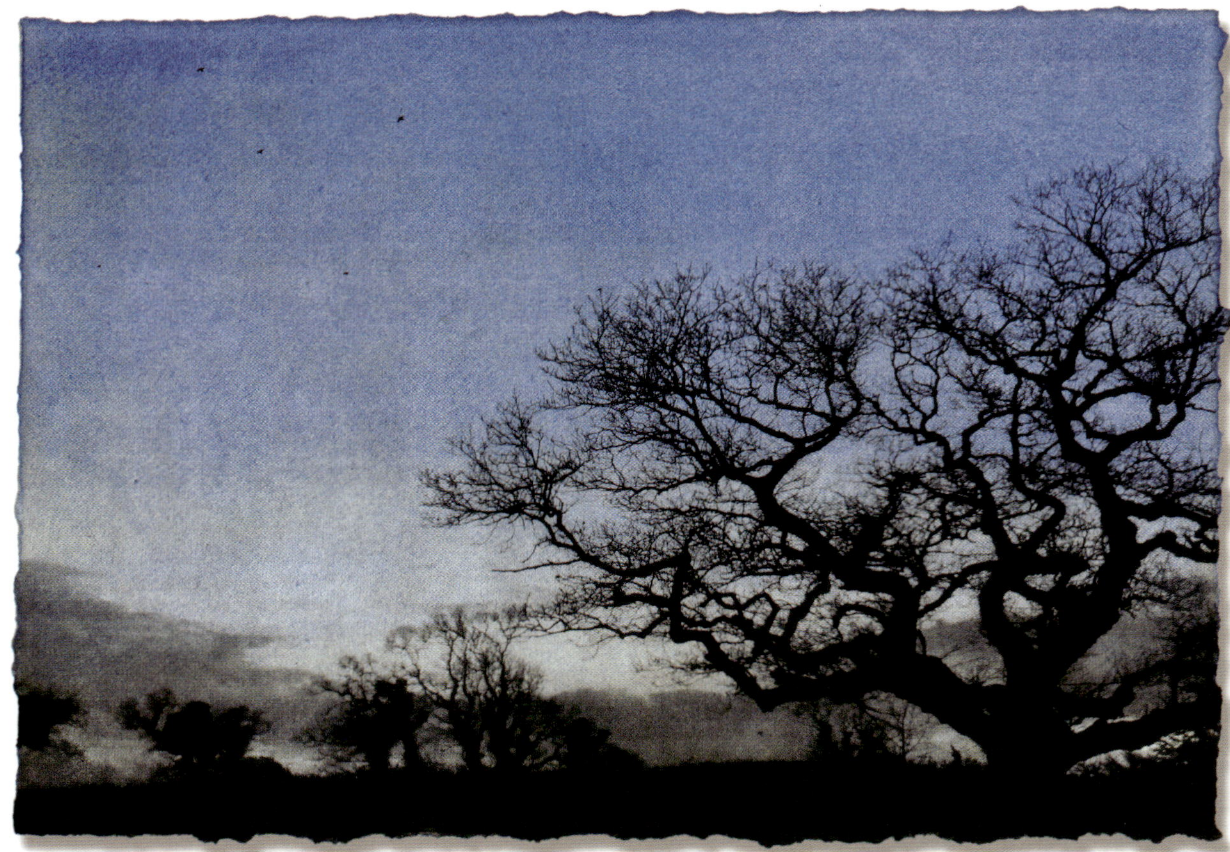

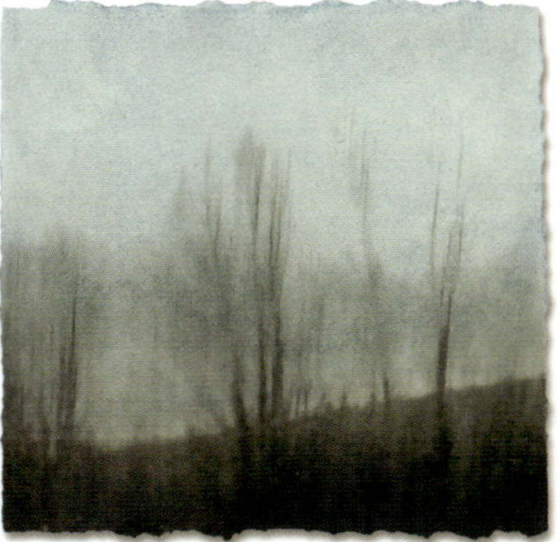

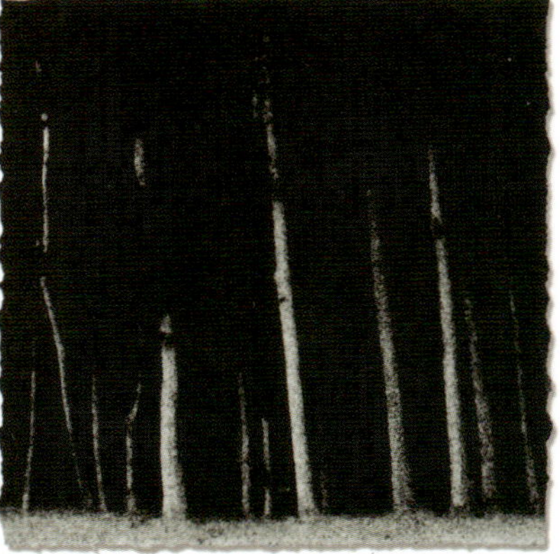

A painter and printmaker, Luella Martin is based at her Phoenix Brighton studio in the centre of the city. She exhibits in various galleries and art fairs in London, Brighton and the South East, and has pieces in many private collections around the world.

Luella's recent work focuses on landscapes and skylines, usually Sussex, painted in oils or using the medium of 'solar etching'. This is an exciting, versatile, non-toxic way of working using sunlight (or UV lamp) and tap water to make the etching plate.

Her etchings are all hand-made limited editions, often printed over the edge of the paper with no border, which gives the prints an almost sculptural quality. In addition, Luella sometimes paints the hand-made paper before or after printing, blurring the distinction between painting and printmaking.

During May this year Luella will be taking part in Artists Open Houses at 'The Dog House', 15 Hampstead Road, Brighton. She will be the 'featured artist' at iO Gallery, 39 Sydney Street, Brighton (page 106), from 9 to 21 June 2015. Then from 2 to 14 October 2015, Luella will be part of the group exhibition 'Chalk at the Towner' – the 10-year anniversary exhibition of past and present artists at the Chalk Gallery (page 112).

For the latest news about open studios, art fairs, exhibitions and events please see her website (above). Studio visits are welcome by prior arrangement.

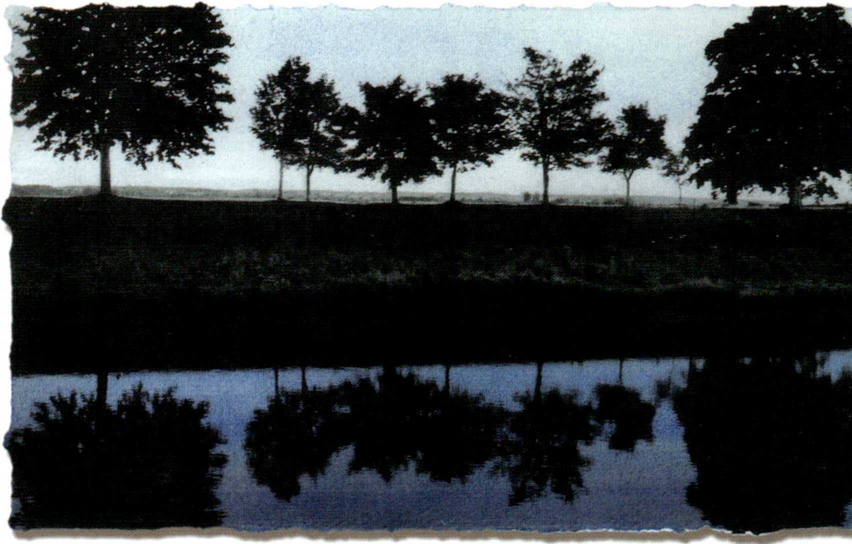

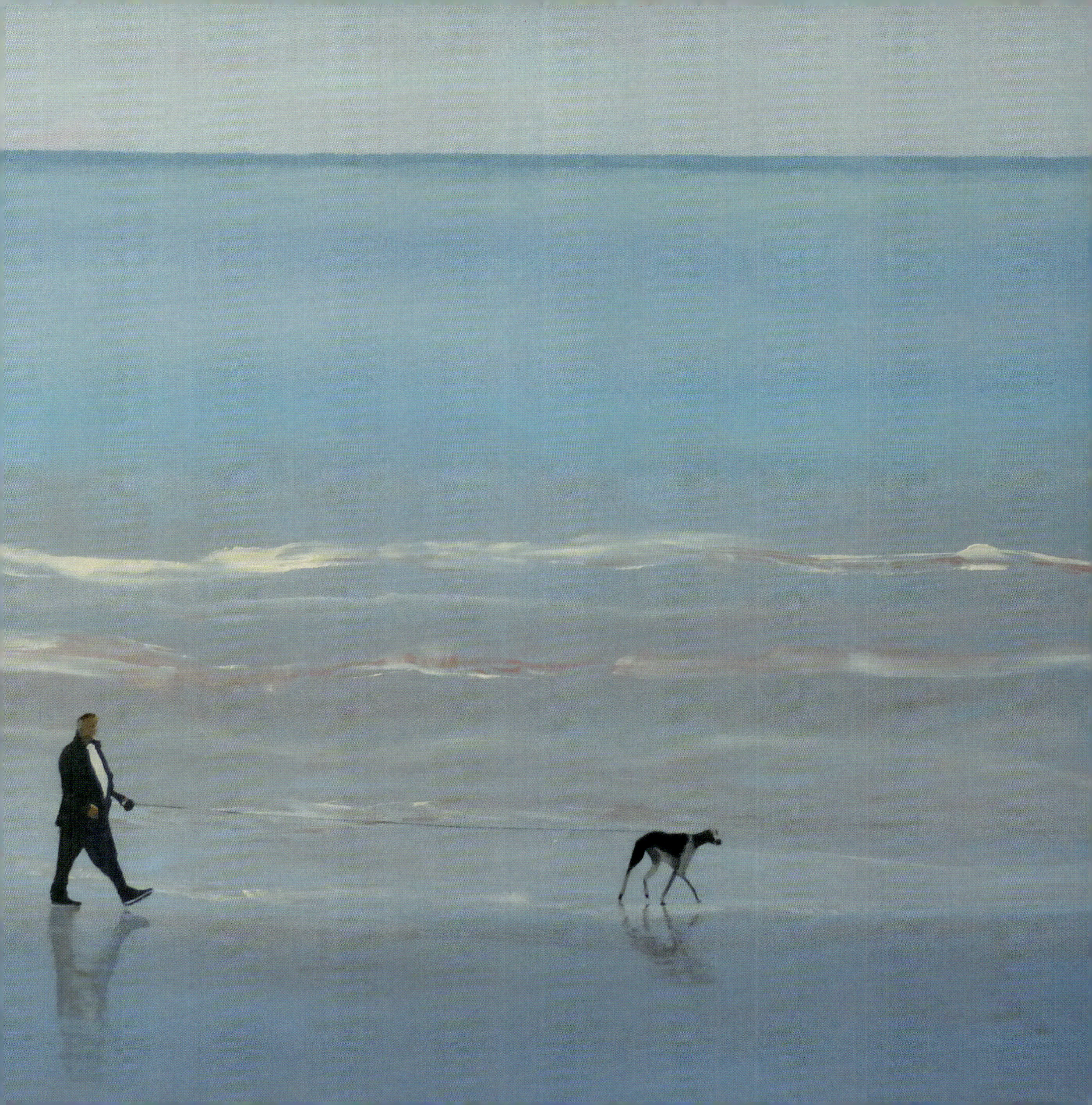

Veronica van Eijk

Artist
www.vaneijkarts.com

Clockwise from top left: Belgian Billy at Turnout I; Joy at Turnout IV; Belgian Billy at Turnout II

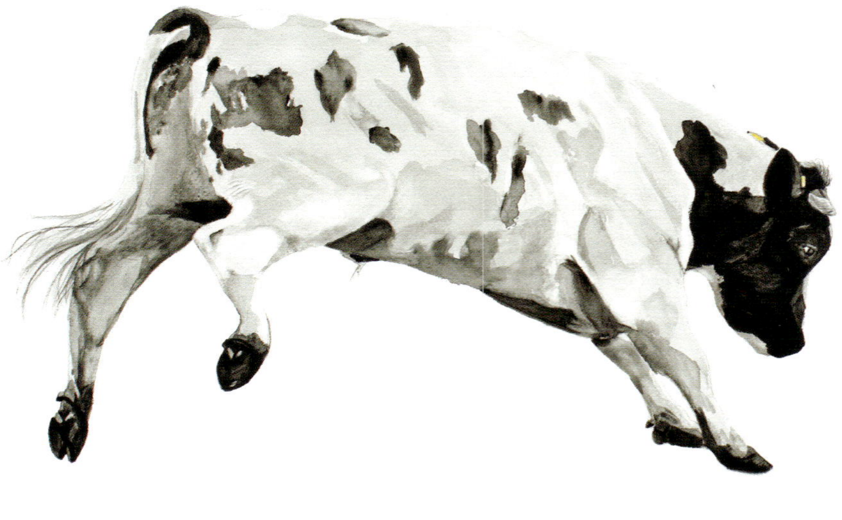

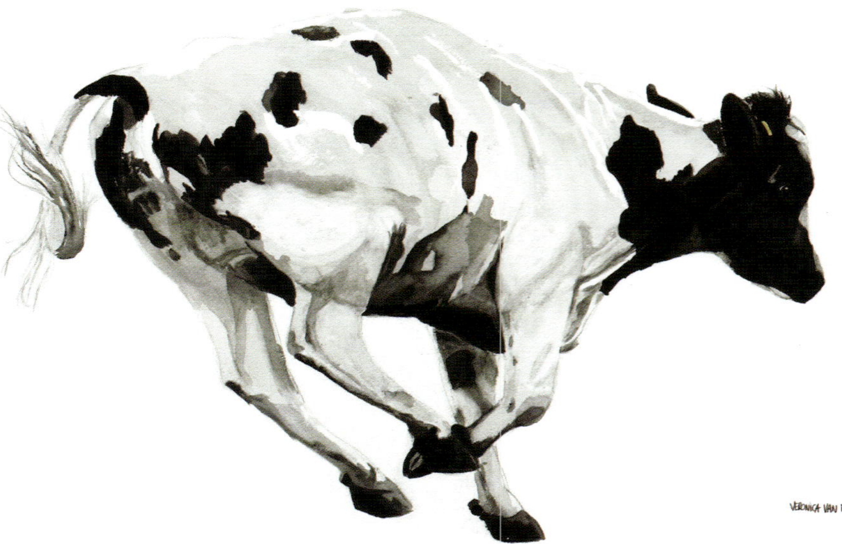

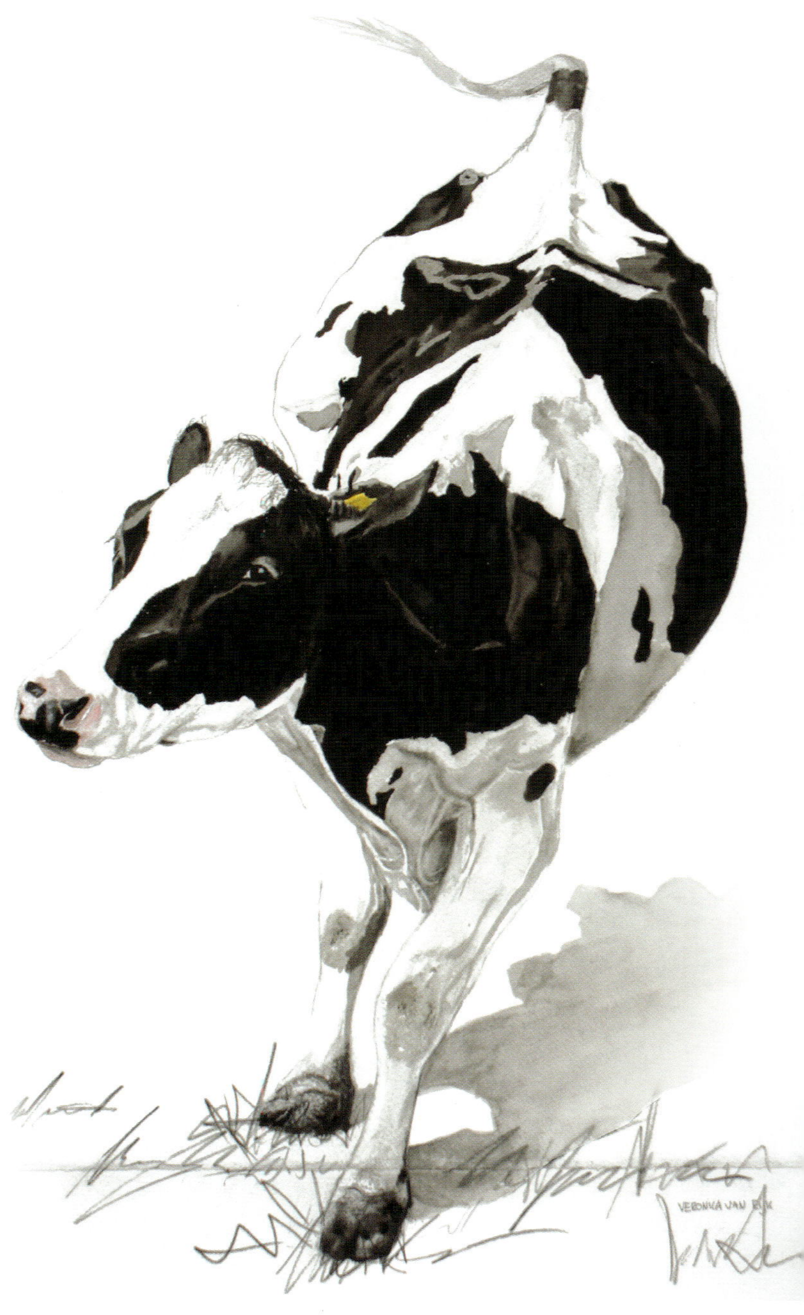

Cows have such strong expressions in their faces, they have a way of looking at you: curious, interested, haughty, frightened, timid, relaxed; and this is what Veronica van Eijk likes to capture in paints.

Fortunate to live next door to an organic dairy farm, Veronica has her subjects close by, enabling a very detailed observation of all their behaviours. Her latest work is a series of large paintings of running and leaping cows: behaviour observed especially at 'spring turnout' when the herd is very excited to return to fresh air and fresh grass.

Veronica is a member of the Chalk Gallery collective in Lewes and opens her Longleys Studio Barns to the public every June and September. Her work is in collections in several European countries, the USA and Australia.

This page:
Ruby Sem at Longleys Farm

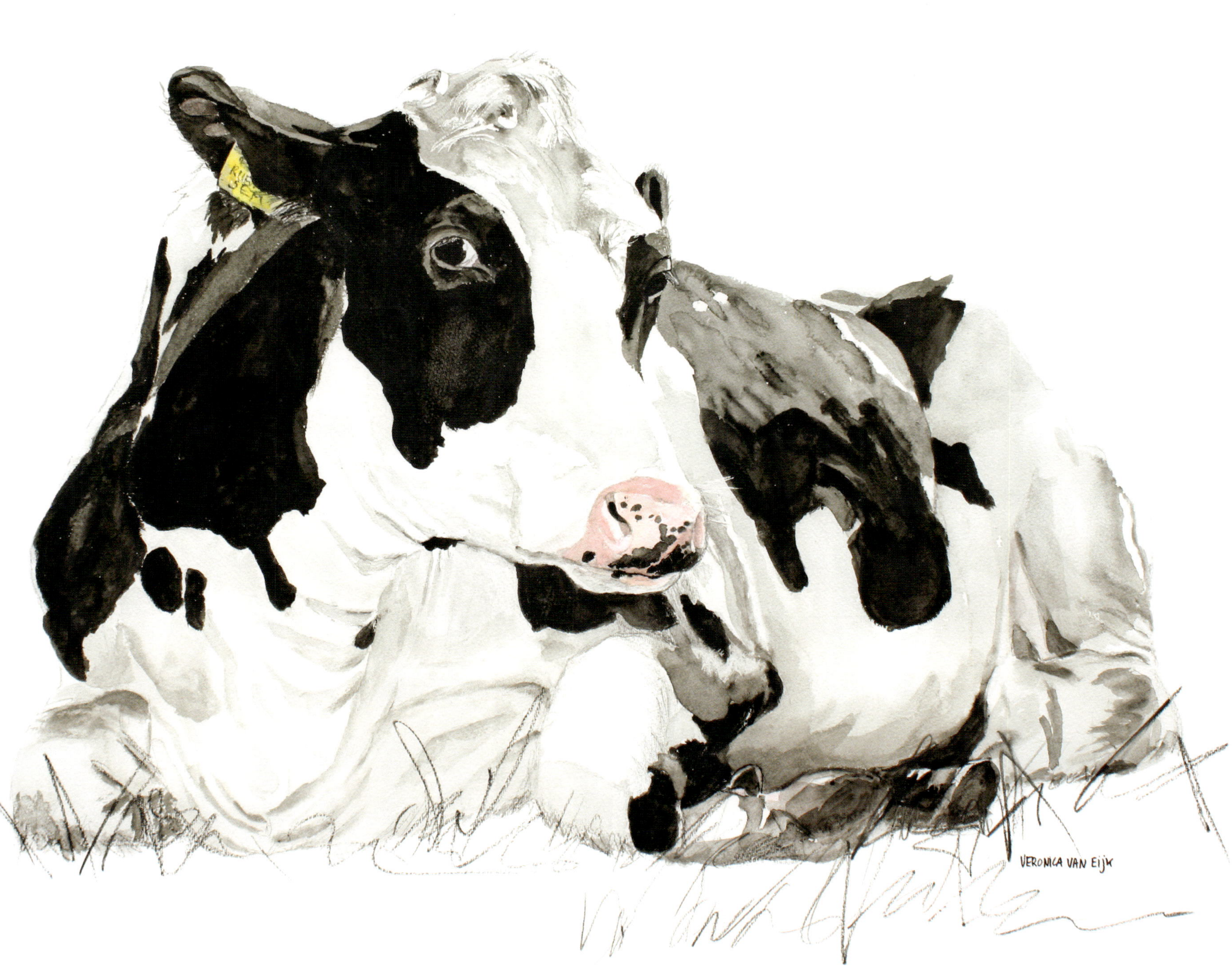

Sophie Abbott

Artist
www.sophieabbott.net

Clockwise from top left:
Clifftop Dunes; White Clifftop; Crantock; Blustery Beach

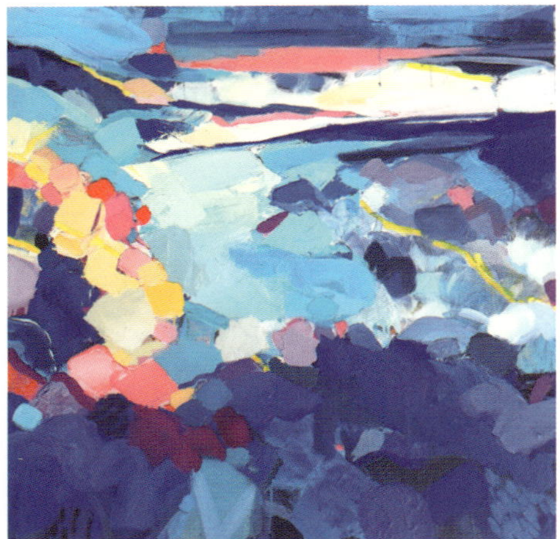

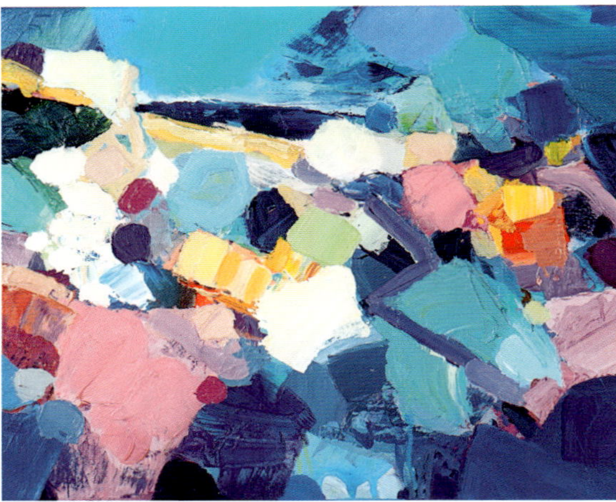

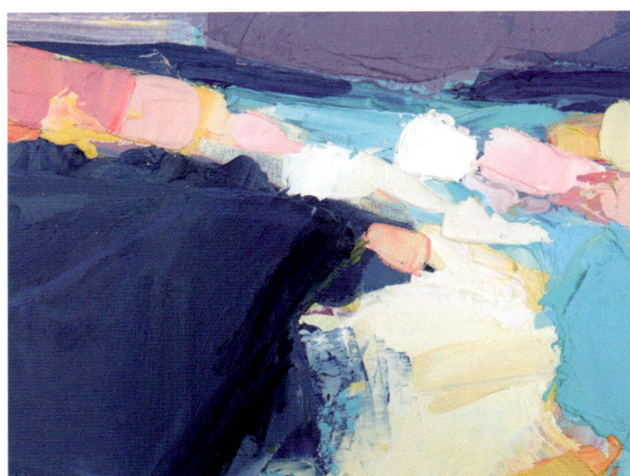

Sophie Abbott creates vivid, strong and atmospheric paintings that all stem from visual snapshots she records on her camera phone, in her sketchbook or keeps in her mind's eye.

Sophie's inspiration comes from many places: perhaps the seaside, a market stall, a beautifully shot film, local allotments or the landscape on a clifftop walk. It's not the factual elements of the scenes that excite Sophie, but the composition, shape and colour. She has a knack of finding the extraordinary in the ordinary, and capturing that in her paintings.

Sophie loves being surrounded by the landscape and feeling physically involved within it. She has been taking many walks along the same stretch of coastal path recently, and is always looking for something new emerging from the familiar. Often Sophie paints outdoors and creates a rapid response to her environment; something immediate that she can relate back to in the studio. These spontaneous, semi-abstract landscape paintings are full of layers of colour, texture and mark-making.

Sophie's paintings have appeared on TV and in interior design magazines.

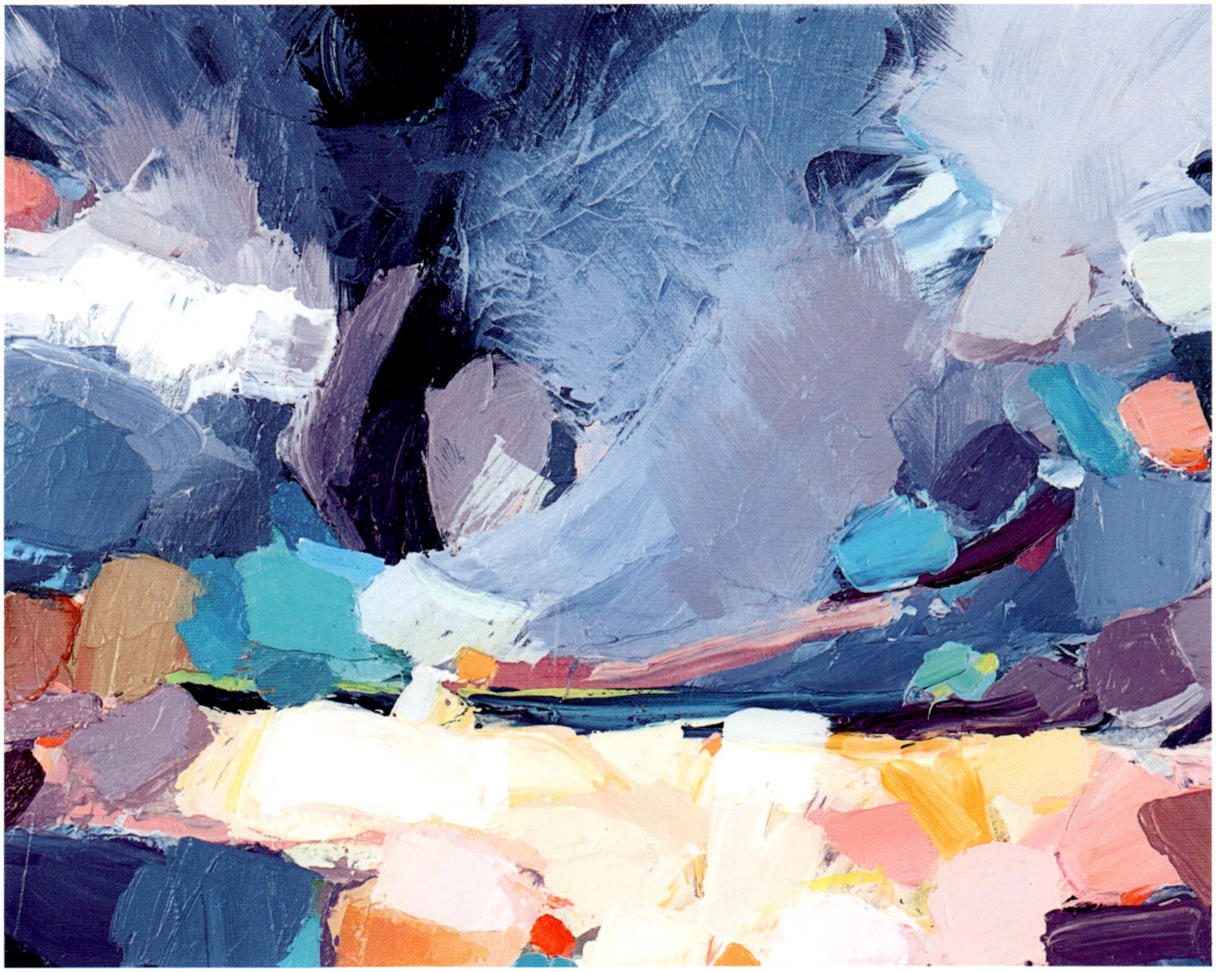

Mia Underwood

Illustrator and Artist
www.miaunderwood.co.uk

Clockwise from top left: Silver Birch Wood Pigeon; Two Turtle Doves; Character study for a children's picture book; Needle Felted Tiger 'My Felted Friends'; Needle Felted Squirrel 'My Felted Friends'

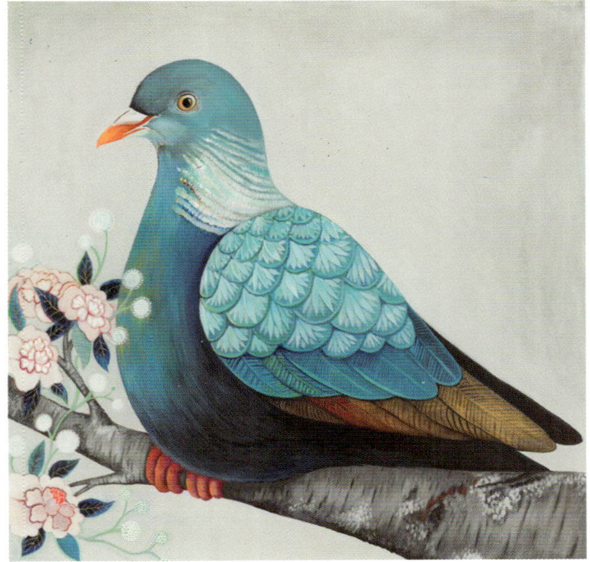

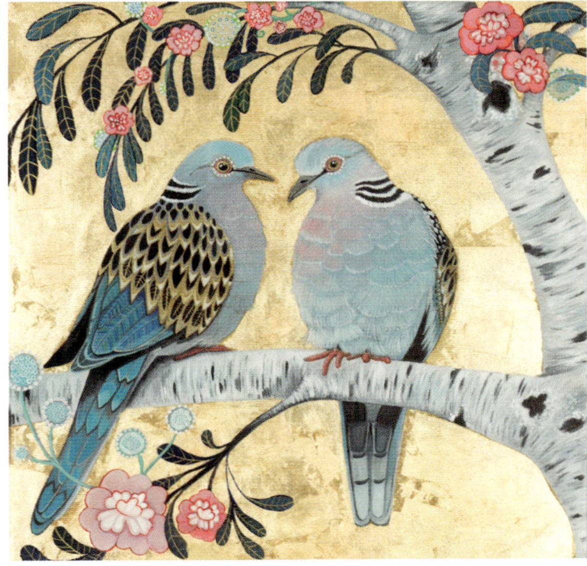

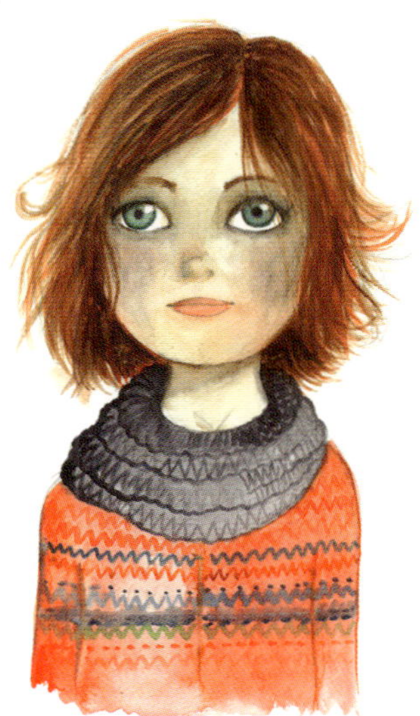

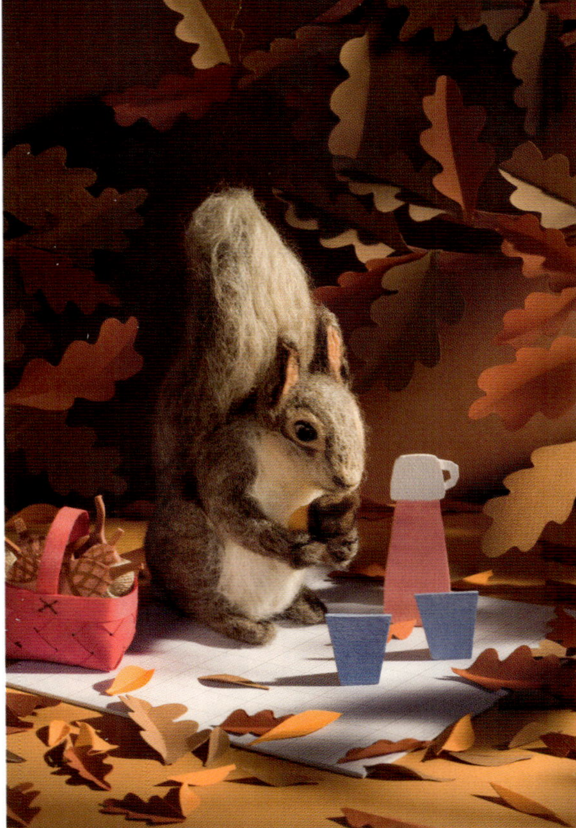

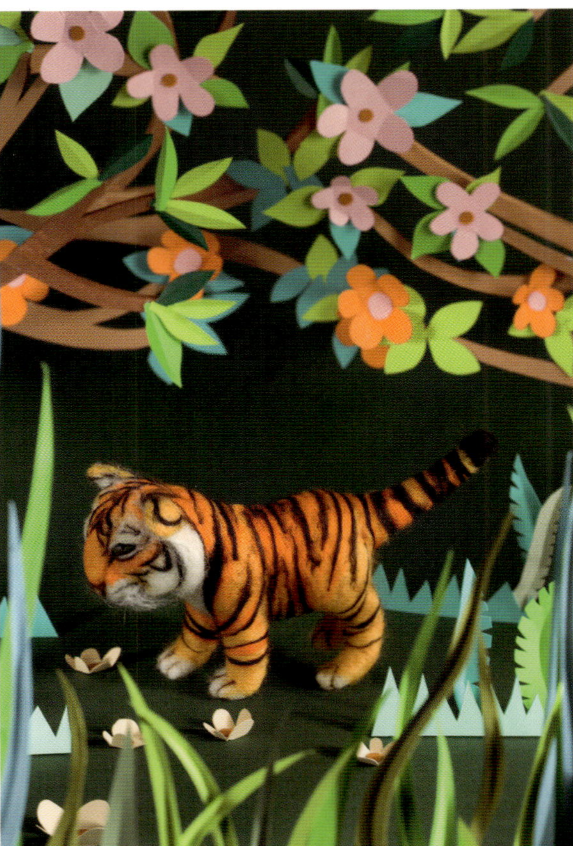

Brighton-based artist Mia Underwood creates multi-media drawings, paintings and soft sculptures inspired by the natural world, woodland creatures and mysterious folk tales.

Since completing a BA degree in Graphic and Media Design at London College of Printing, Mia has been experimenting continuously with new techniques; from painting on wood with gold leaf to digital illustration, working with spray paints and even making three-dimensional needle-felted animals.

Mia was taught to draw and paint by her father, world-known fine artist George Underwood. His encouragement introduced her to an incredible collection of artists, opening her mind to the wonderful world of creation through imagination.

Mia's works are often filled with fantastical scenes that capture the viewer's imagination, creating worlds where wild flowers grow from the kitchen floorboards and serene faces watch out from green hills, as birds carry three-storey town houses upon their heads. She has been curating the art exhibition Into the Woods in Brighton since 2009, and has published two books, *Nordic Crafts* and *My Felted Friends.*

Phil Dobson

Illustrator
www.magicpen.co.uk

Phil Dobson has been scribbling away for quite a few years now, producing illustrations for most of the top ad agencies, design companies and publishers. Signed prints of this Brighton map are available from The Open Studios, 168 Kings Road Arches, Brighton Beach, on the slope near the Fortune of War pub.

We love Phil's map so much we've begged him to let us turn it into a guide to the city's Arty-est shops and galleries. See the results on pages 134-5

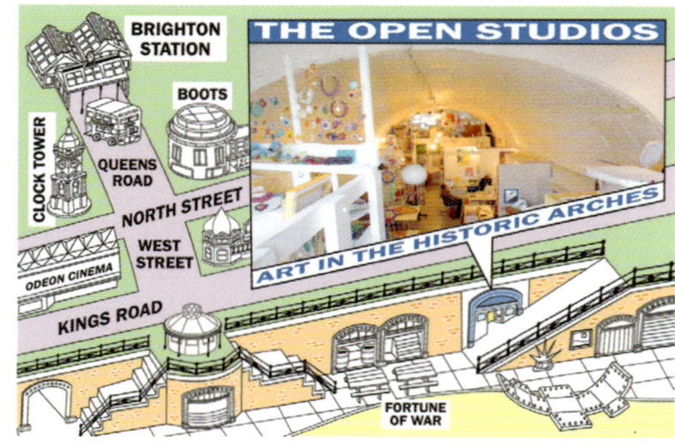

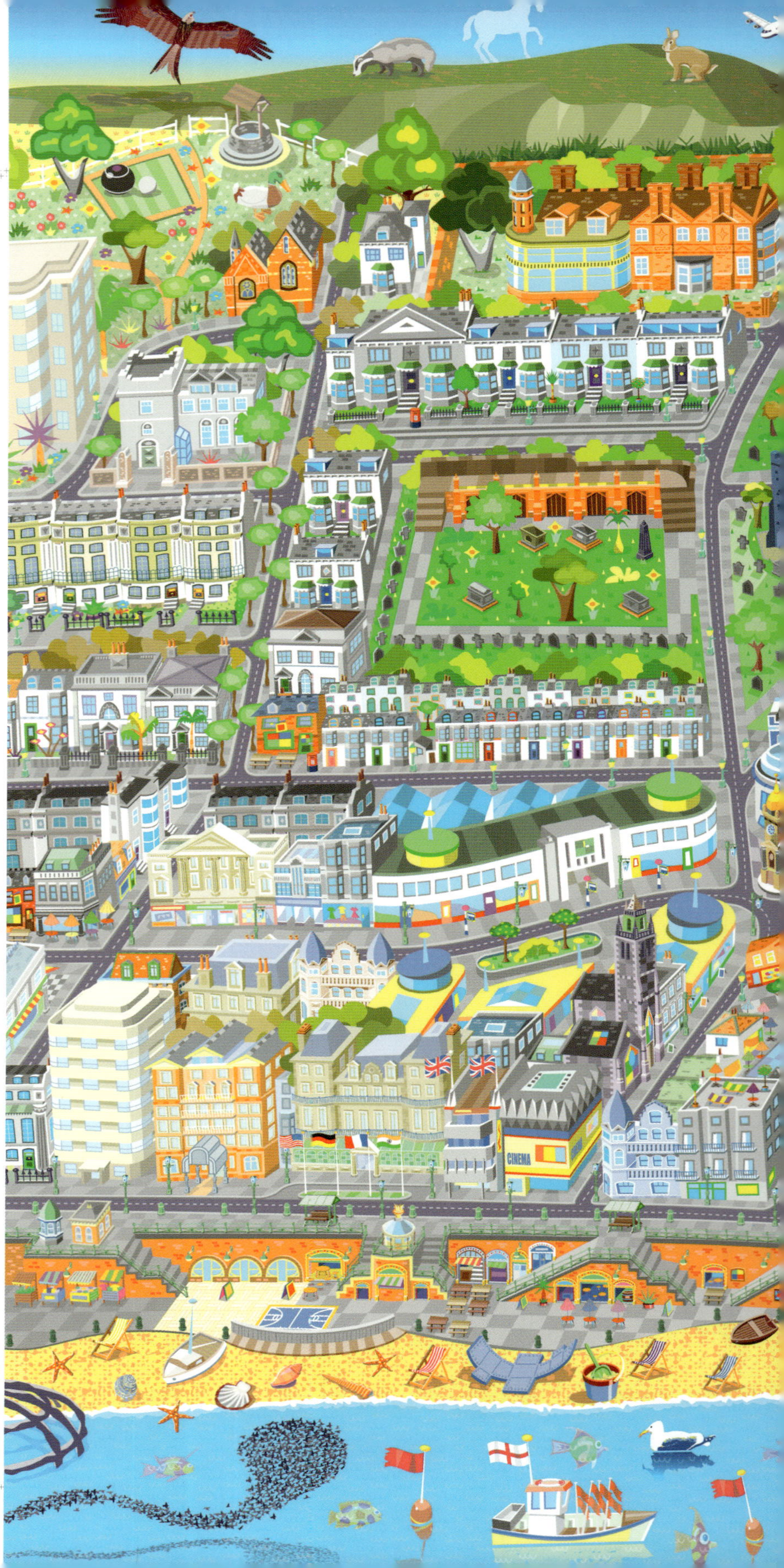

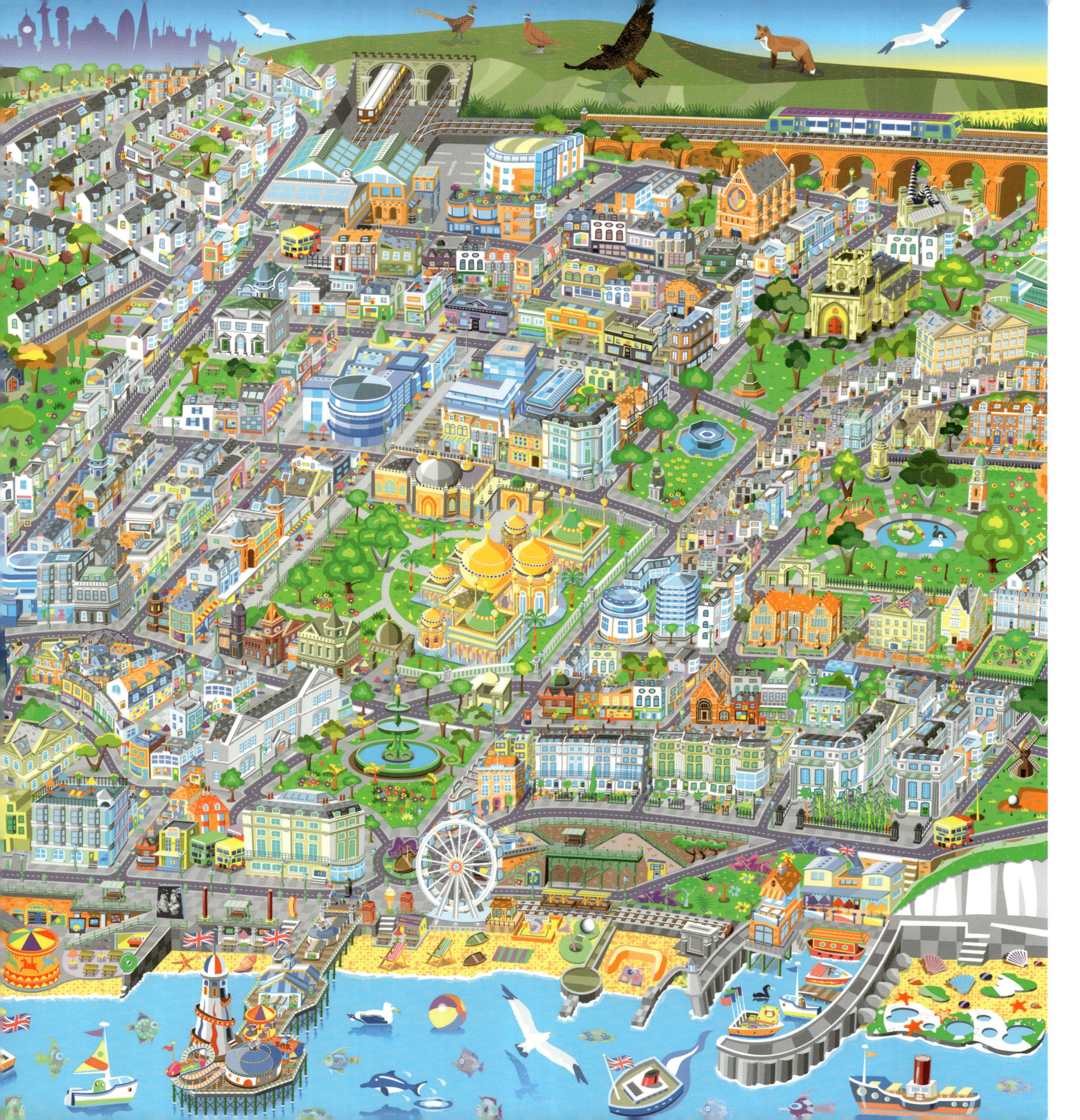

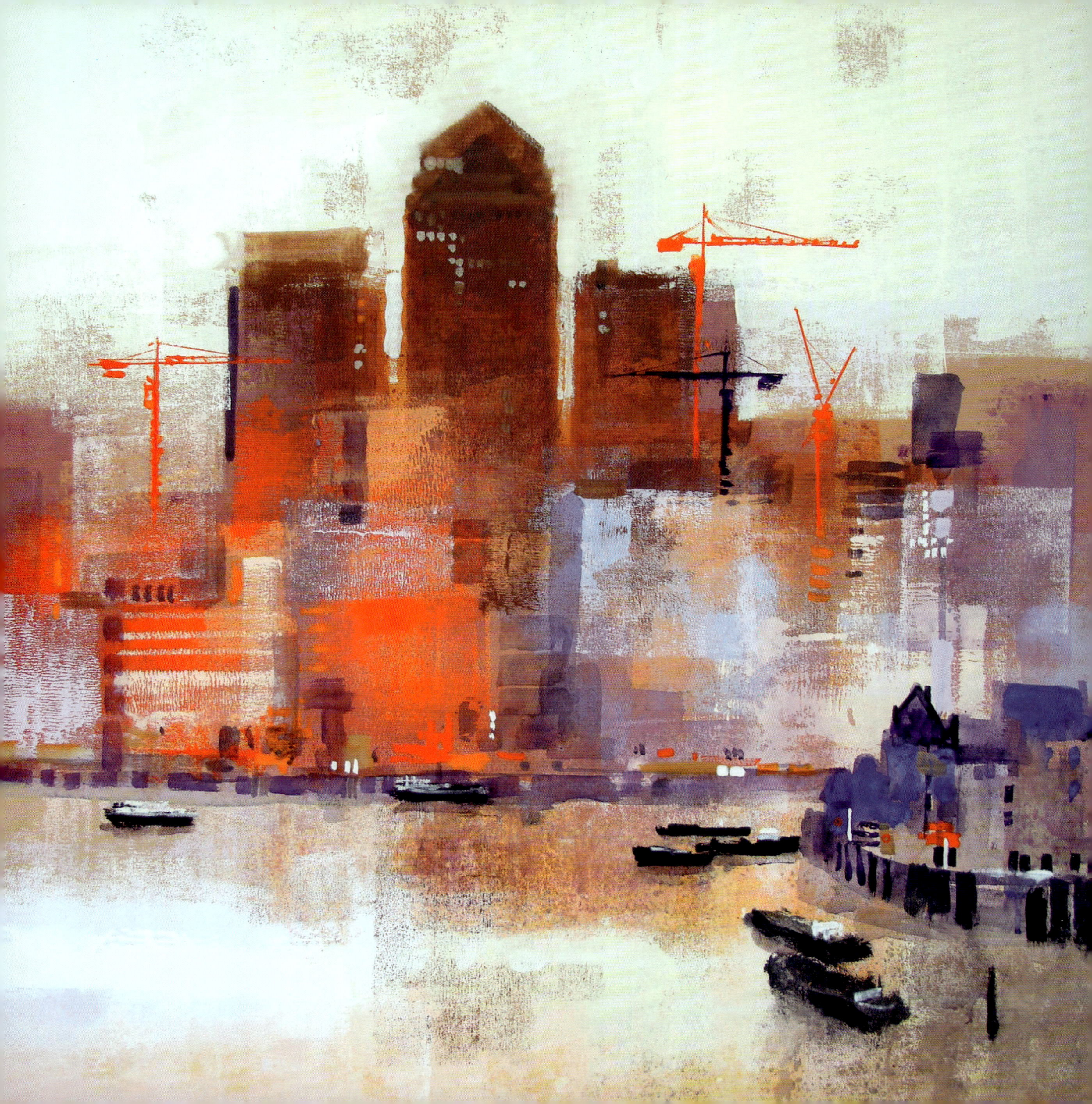

GALLERIES & SHOPS

Independent art spaces and boutiques where you'll find brilliant work & a friendly welcome

35 North Gallery
See page 104

35 North Gallery

35 North Contemporary Fine Art, 35 North Road, Brighton BN1 1YB
35northgallery.com

Clockwise from top left: Limehouse Reach by Colin Ruffell; Newlyn Stripe by Philippa Stanton; Seated Nude by John Whiting; Dreaming River by Monica Macdonald Ralph; City by the Sea by François Blosseville. Opposite page: Skaters by John Whiting

35 North Contemporary Fine Art opened its doors to the public for the first time in September 2014 with an exhibition entitled 'Images of Brighton' featuring the work of local artist John Whiting.

35 North is owned by Brighton residents John and Sharon Whiting. The gallery has a full programme of exhibitions lined up for 2015 featuring a variety of artists of both national and international renown. Painters, sculptors, photographers and illustrators are all part of the programme for this inaugural year.

Recent exhibitions include painters Philippa Stanton, Colin Ruffell and Kate Osborne as well as etcher Monica Macdonald Ralph and Dieppe-based sculptors Johanna Häiväoja and François Blosseville.

In June 2015, 35 North hosts a retrospective of the work of sculptor Pam Taylor, featuring artist's copies direct from her studio. Pam's best known works include public commissions at Tobacco Dock, Plymouth Hoe, Shakespeare's Globe and Felix Dennis' The Garden of Heroes and Villains.

The gallery is open Thursday, Friday and Saturday 11am-5.30pm. For all enquiries please contact Sharon Whiting (see page 132).

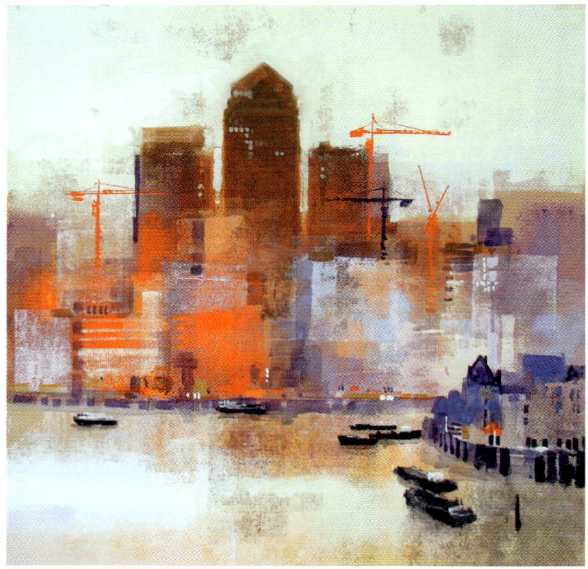

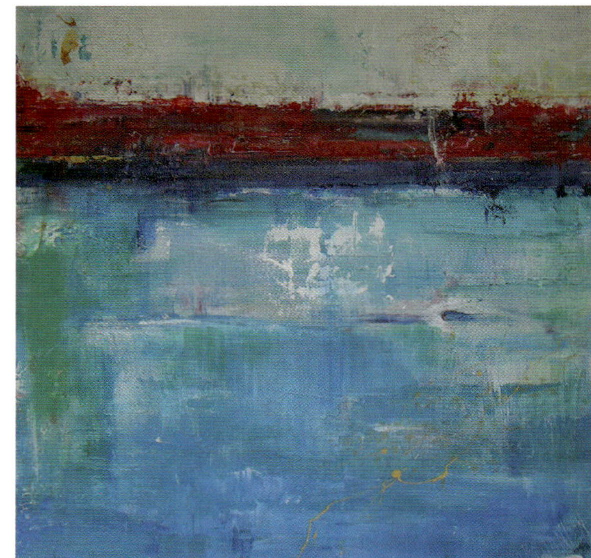

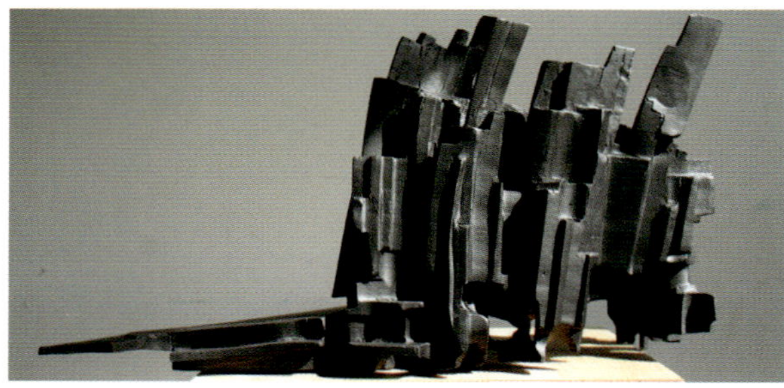

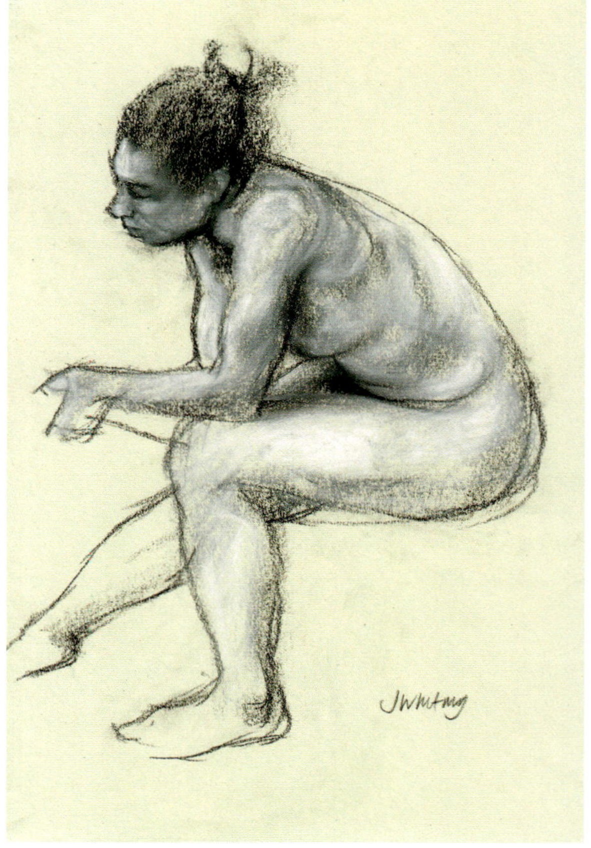

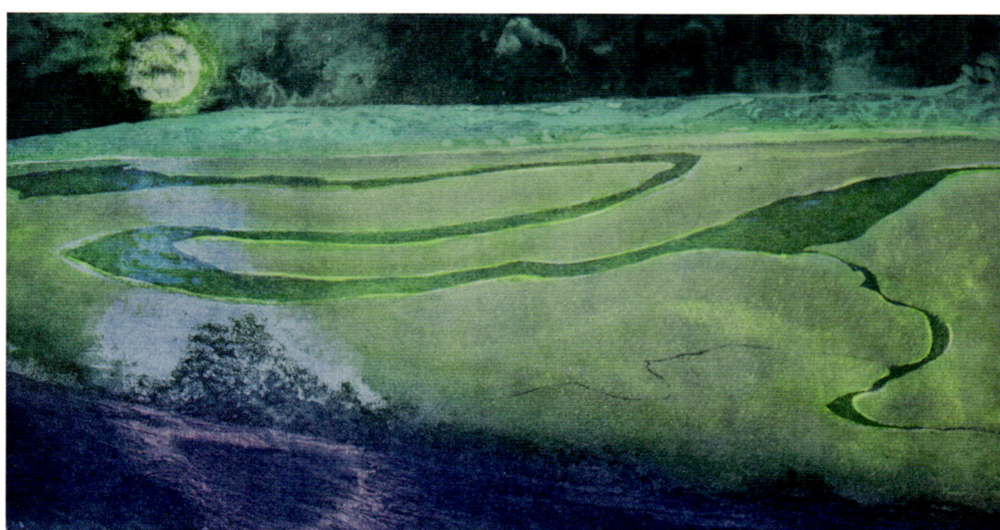

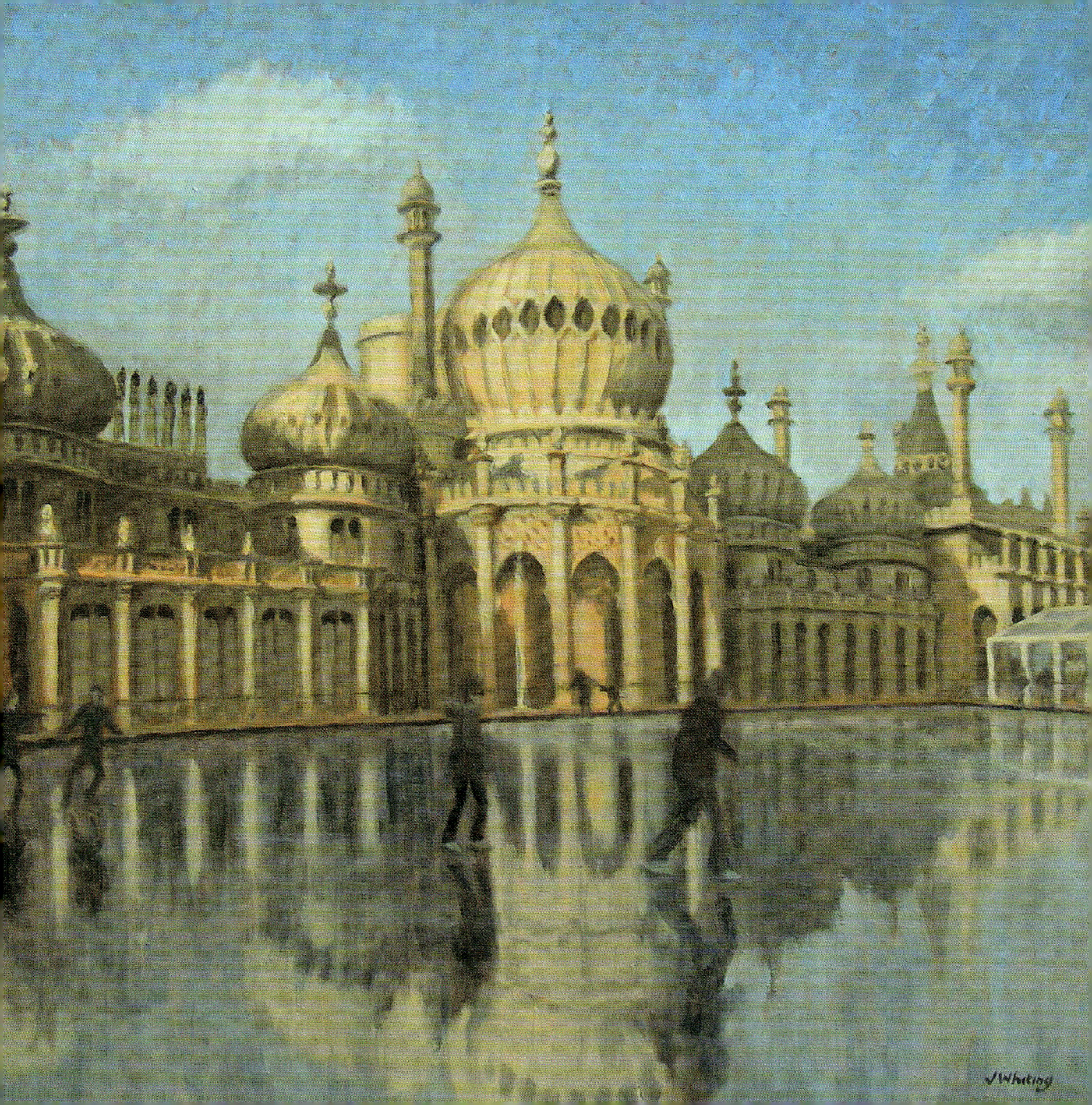
J Whiting

iO Gallery

Brighton Designers & Makers Ltd, 39 Sydney Street, Brighton BN1 4EP
www.iogallery.co.uk

Clockwise from top left: Reef Perfume Bottle by Peter Layton; Kitten stud earrings by Cath Laffan; Day Moon painting by Tania Corbett

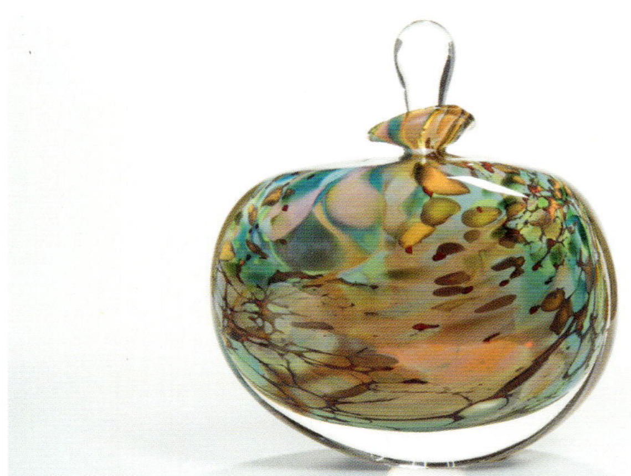

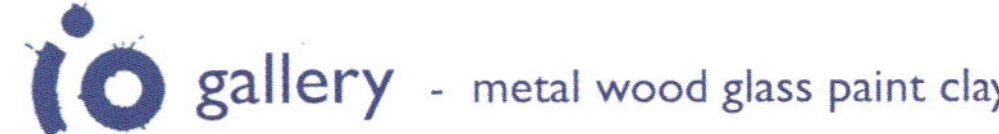

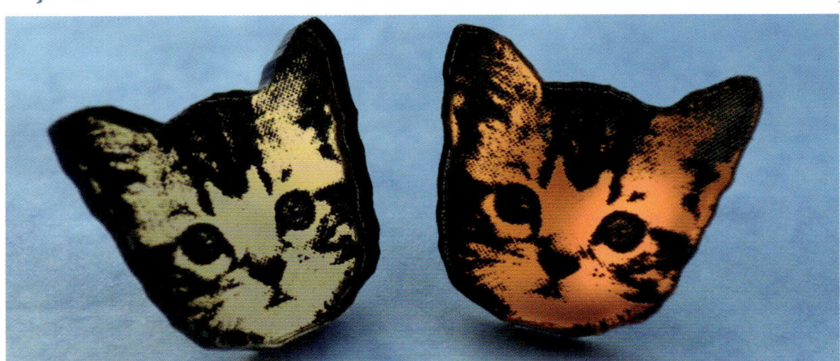

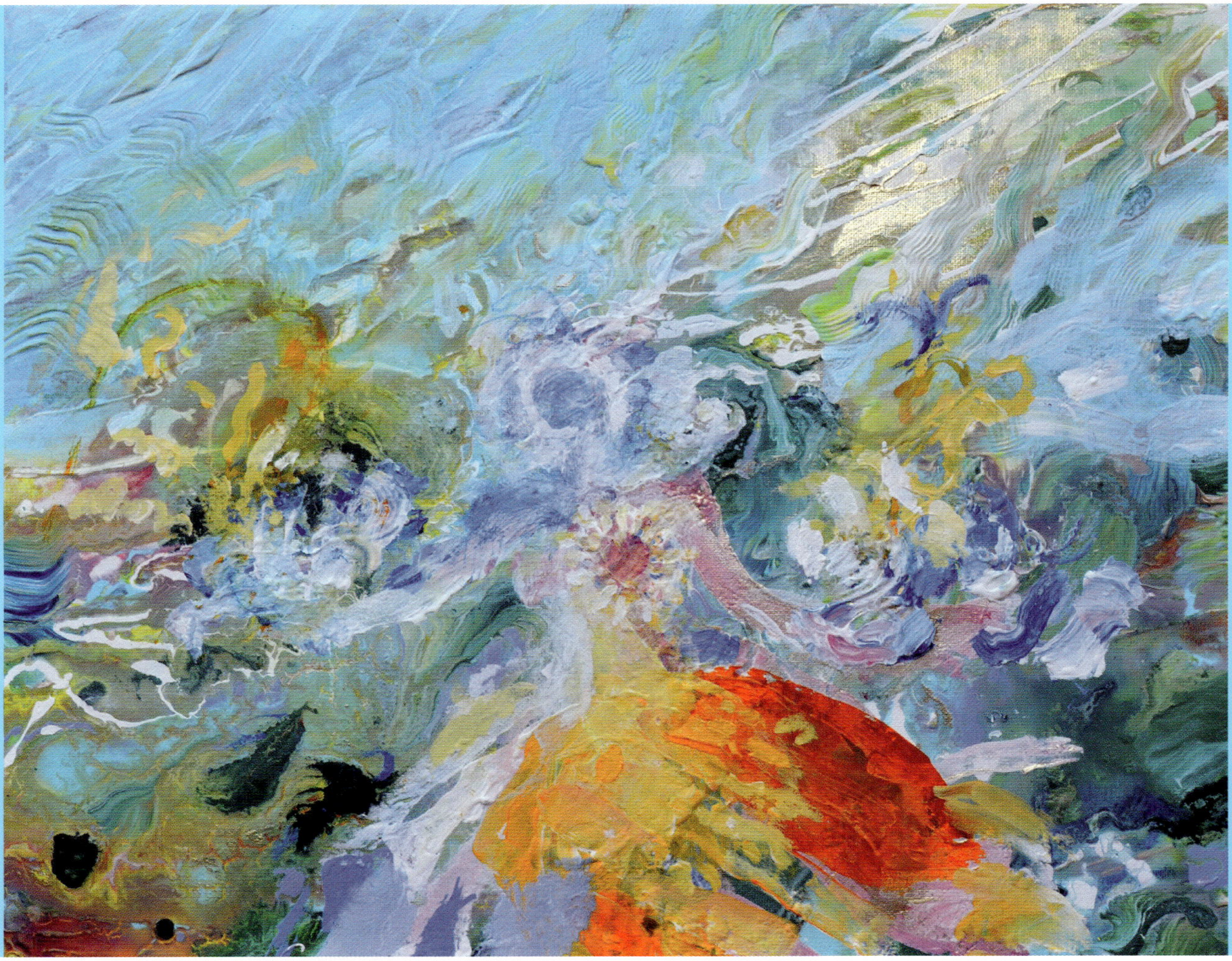

Kellie Miller Arts

20 Market Street, Brighton BN1 1HH
www.kelliemillerarts.com

Clockwise from top left: Conversation I; Interior Kellie Miller Arts gallery space; Mandorla Bianca; Winter Trees

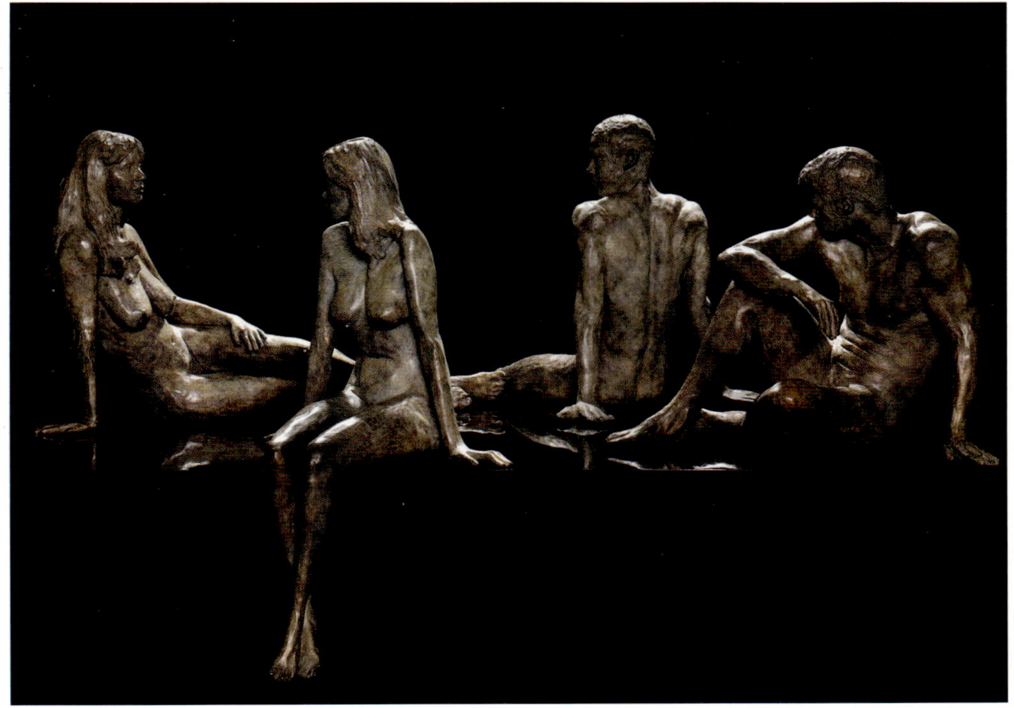

Kellie Miller Arts is an independent gallery situated in Brighton's prestigious Brighton Lanes area, a fitting location for a space sympathetic to the art of storytelling.

The artist-owned gallery exhibits works by local, national and international artists. Sculptures, textured paintings, mixed media and ceramics are Kellie's passion. Marrying different art forms allows her to present artworks that are approachable, engaging and enjoyable.

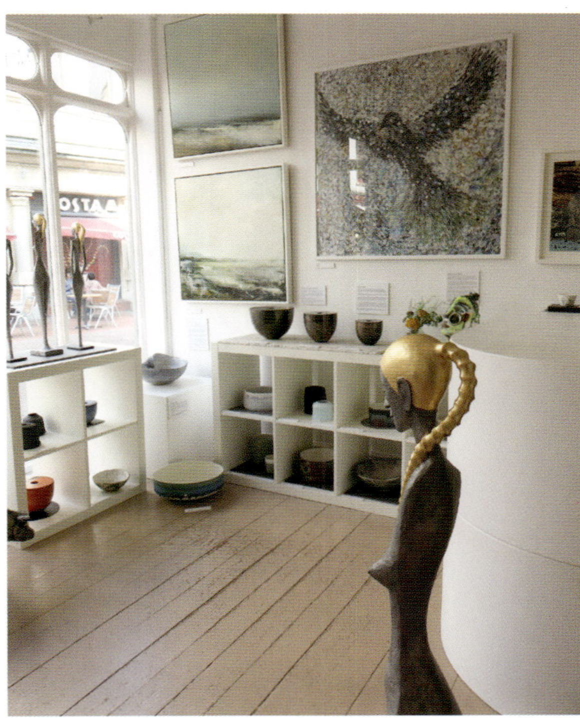

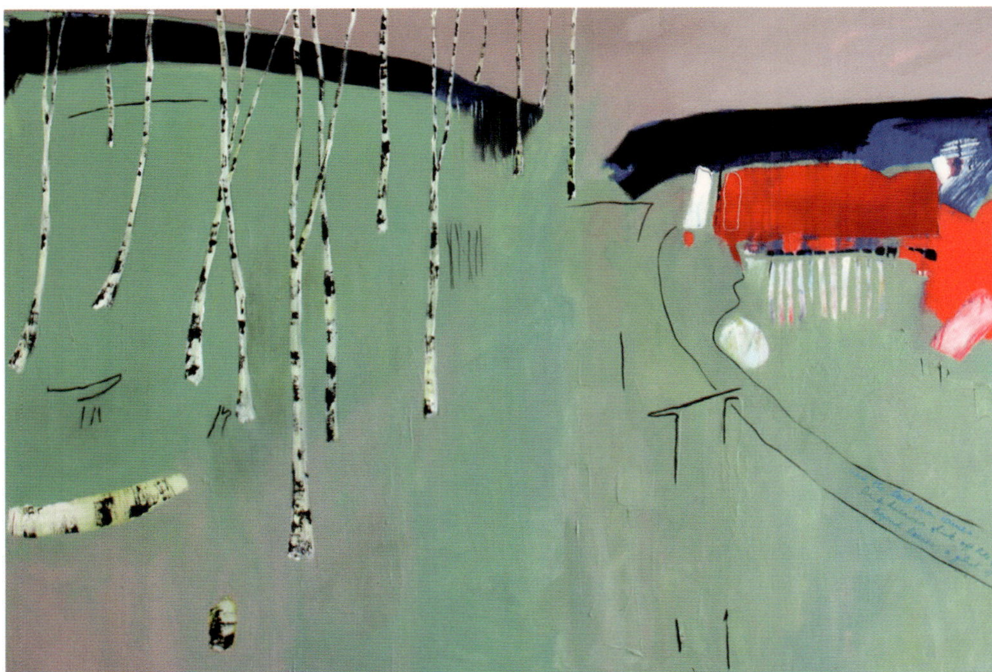

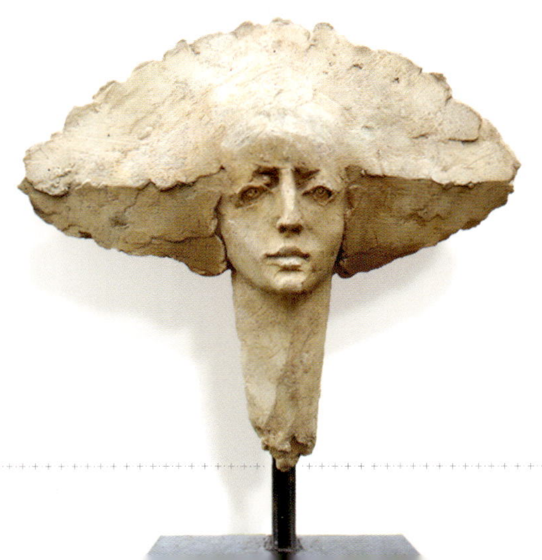

New Steine Hotel

The New Steine Hotel, Bar and Bistro & Gullivers Hotel, 10, 11 &12a New Steine, Brighton BN2 1PB
www.newsteinehotel.com

Clockwise from top left: We are the Dogs I; We are the Dogs II; Deluxe room; From the menu; Inside the bistro

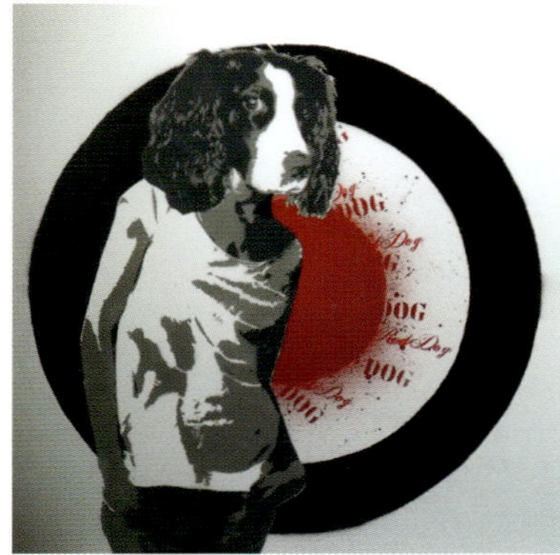

The New Steine Hotel is an elegant and fashionable Georgian Townhouse located in the centre of Brighton. This boutique hotel exudes warmth and style, with a hint of French influence.

New Steine has two passions: food and art. Its bistro is famous for mixing local produce with traditional French recipes. The atmosphere is cosy and continental with contemporary design, ideal for a romantic dinner or a night out with friends.

But while you are visiting, look up at the walls. The New Steine holds regular art exhibitions and will be showing 'We are the Dogs' – a solo show by the Funky Red Dog – as part of the Brighton Fringe Festival in May 2015.

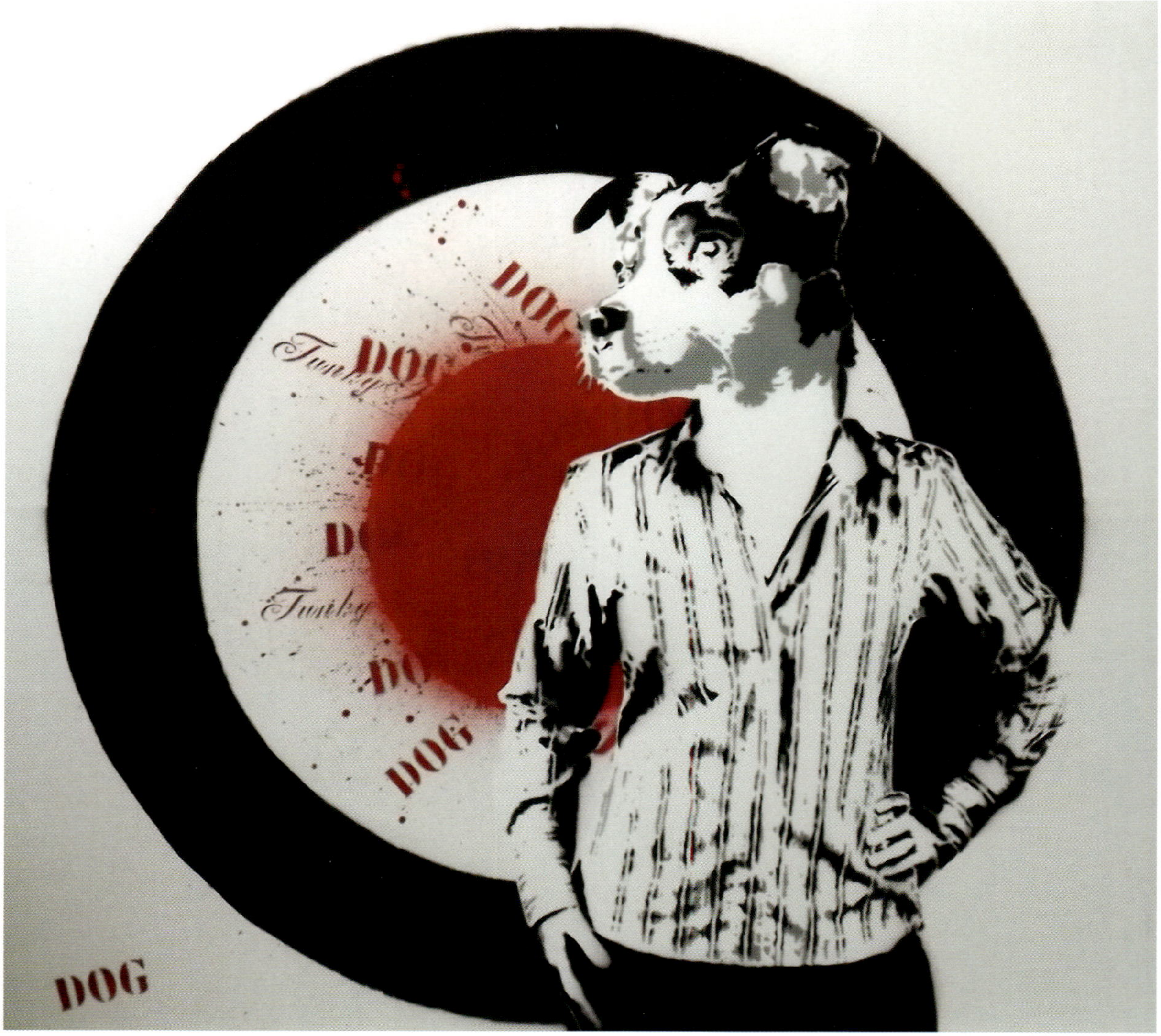

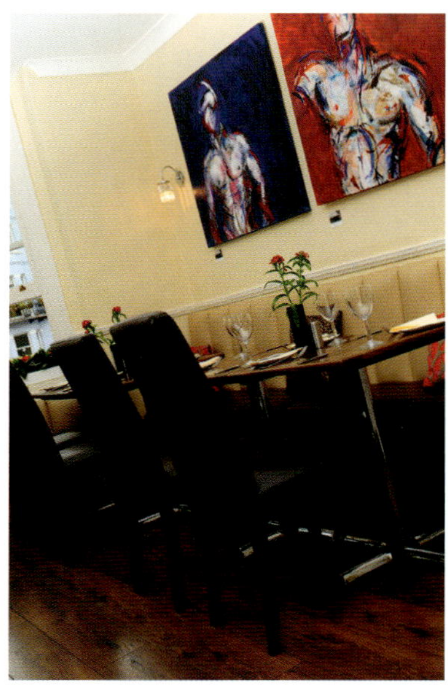

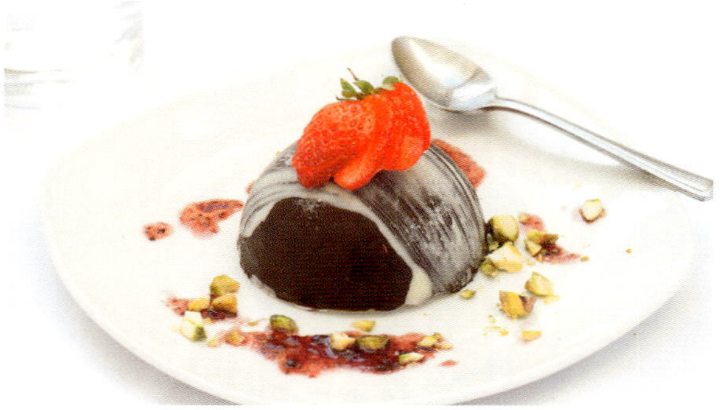

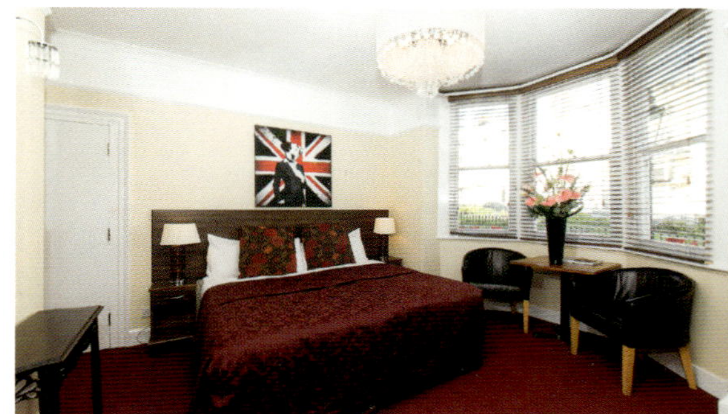

ART5 Gallery

5 Bartholomews, Brighton BN1 1HG
www.art5gallery.com

Clockwise from top left: Dappled Lights by Sarah Pye; Tower Bridge by David Wheeler; Autumn Watch by Louise Brooks; Evening Light, Brixham by Nagib Karsan; Off The Beaten Track by Tina Davies; Psychedelic Cow by Liz Chaderton

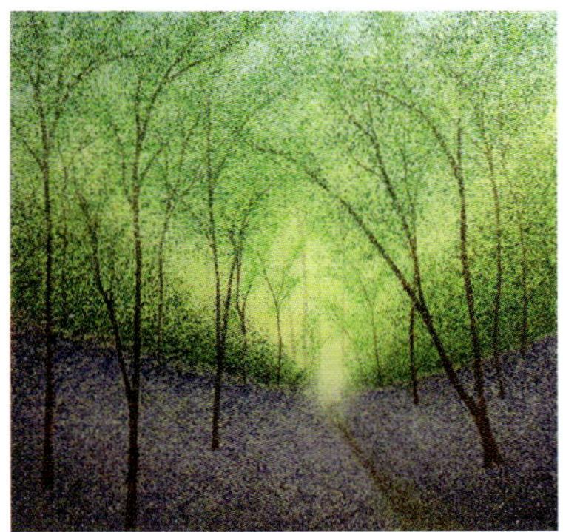

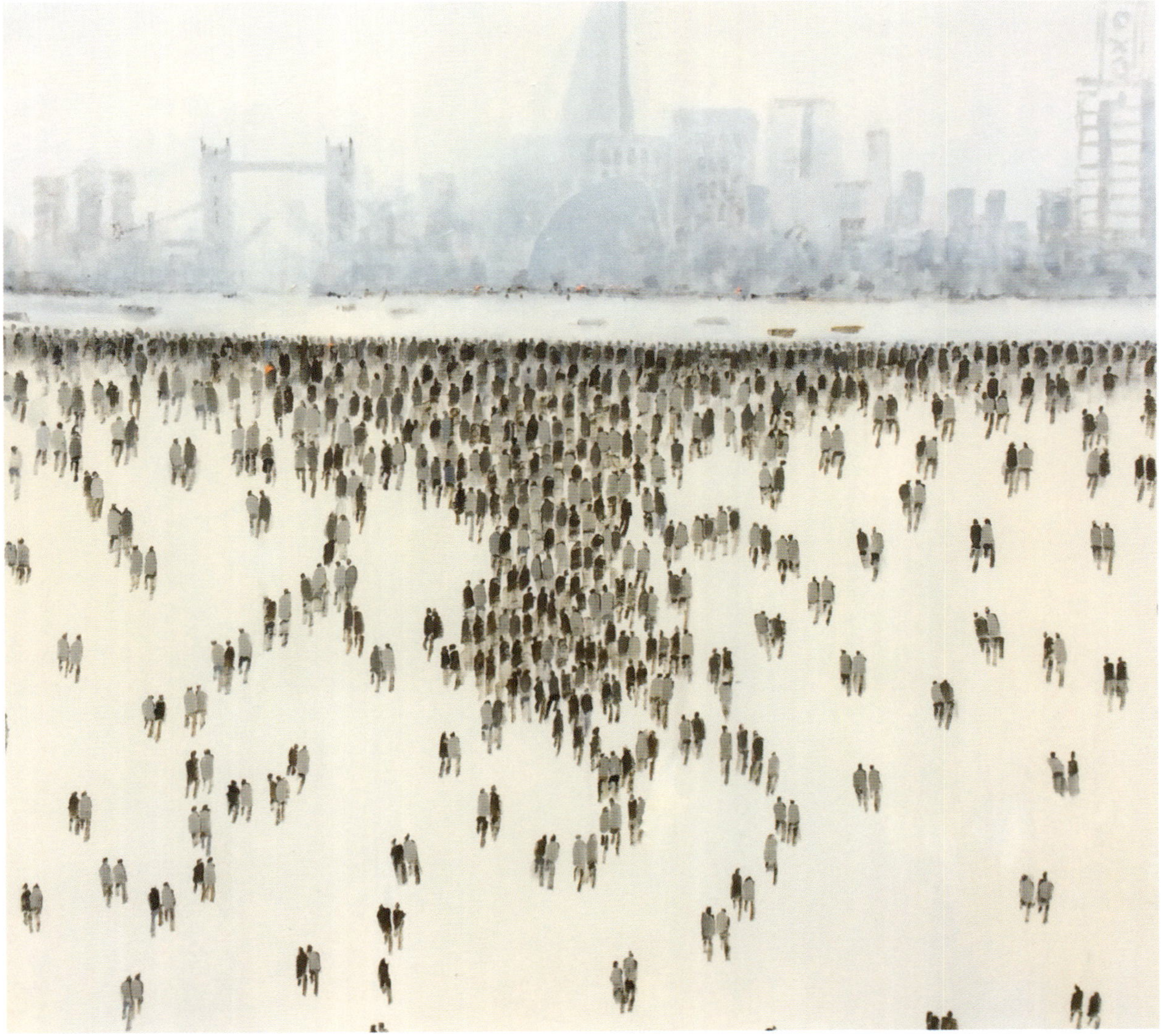

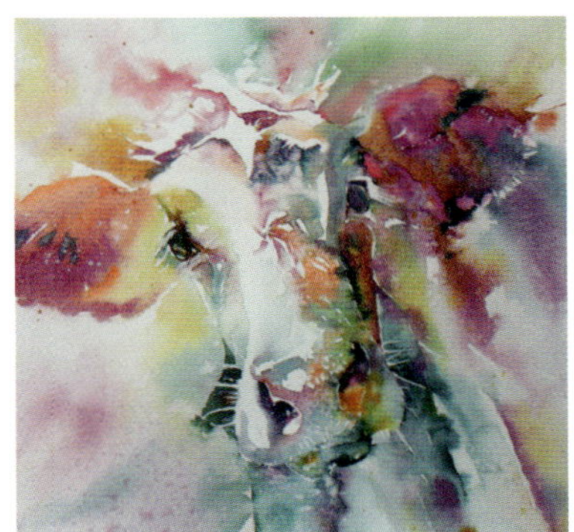

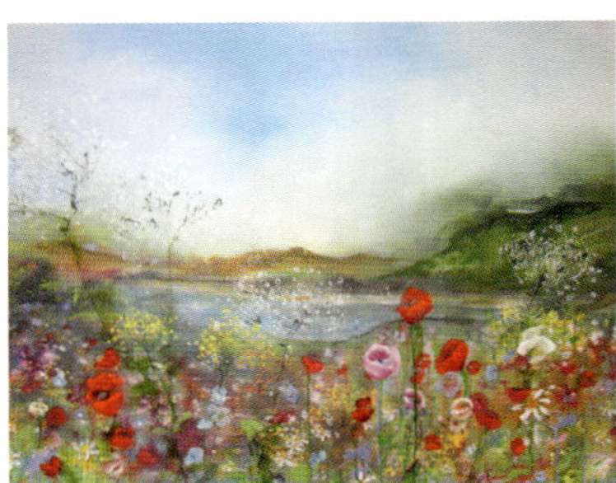

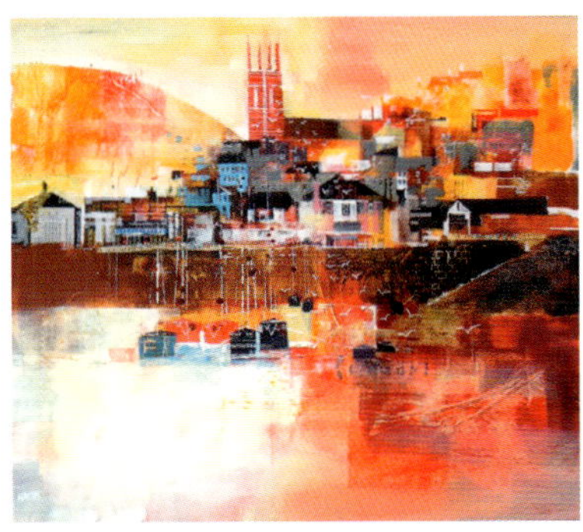

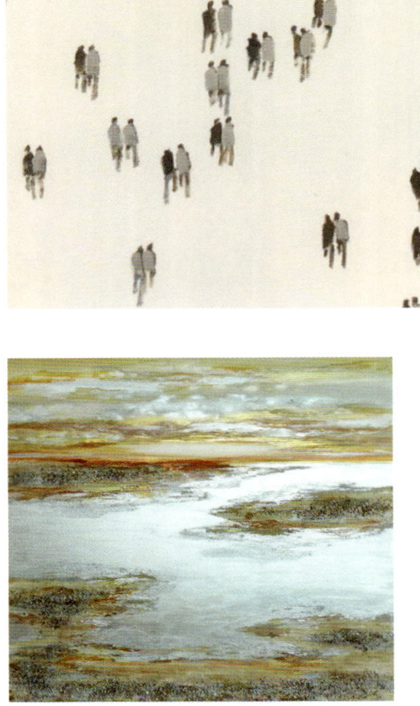

ART5 Gallery is situated in the heart of Brighton, in the fashionable South Lanes, and over the past 11 years has established itself as one of Sussex's leading contemporary galleries. The gallery represents a diverse selection of national and international artists, showcasing an extensive range of quality art at affordable prices, from original paintings and limited-edition prints, to unique ceramics and sculptures.

ART5 Gallery offers a free home and business consultancy service, giving you the opportunity to view the artwork in situ. The gallery's art consultants can provide practical and creative advice on choosing artwork that reflects personal style and taste, while complementing and enhancing your space.

ART5 Gallery is also an established member of Own Art, the Arts Council's interest-free loan scheme, which is designed to make it easy and affordable to acquire contemporary works of art. Visit the gallery and enjoy browsing its fantastic art collection in a friendly and informal environment.

Zimmer Stewart Gallery

29 Tarrant Street, Arundel, BN18 9DG
www.zimmerstewart.co.uk

Left to right: Mother and Child I by Tom Farthing; Red Path to the Gurnard's Head by Elaine Pamphilon

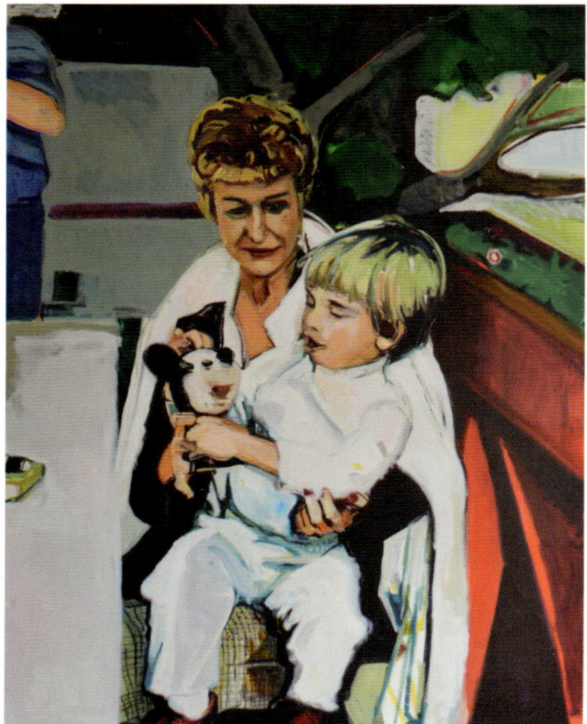

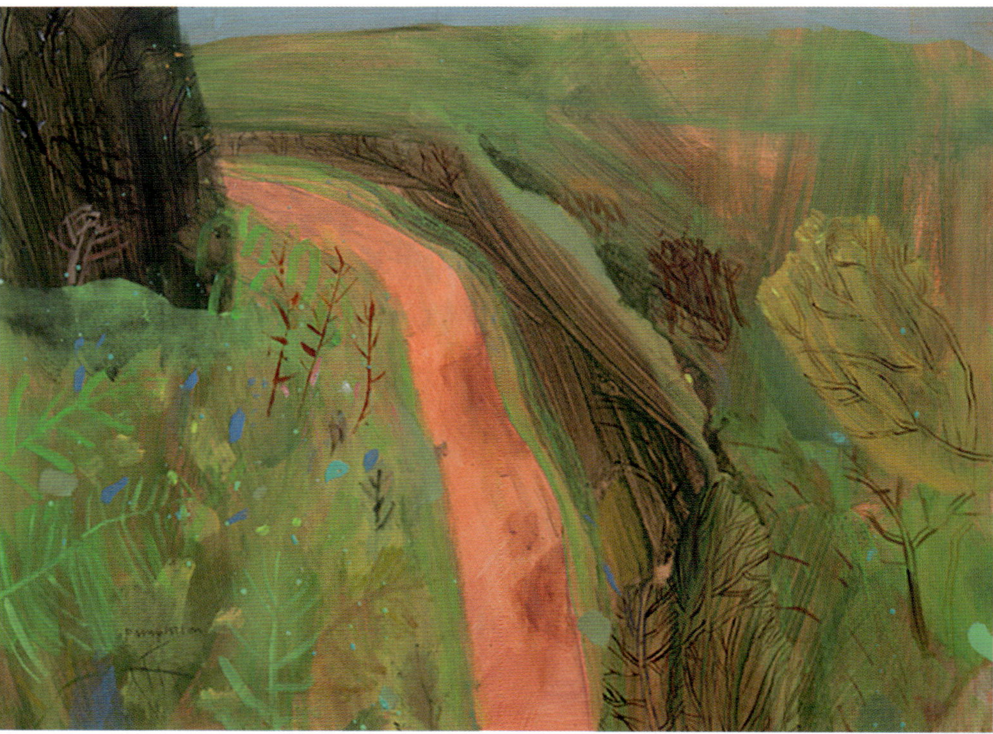

Arundel, just 20 miles or so west of Brighton, is a cultural centre for drama and music as well as visual arts.

Zimmer Stewart Gallery, which was established in 2003, has built up a following of collectors from across the South East, as well as delighting the casual art buyer with its varied programme of 8-10 solo and group exhibitions each year. The gallery is in the heart of Arundel, and exhibits contemporary paintings, original prints, ceramics, sculpture and textiles.

Zimmer Stewart has more than 25 artists listed on its website, with two new artists exhibiting for the first time in 2015: Tom Farthing paints from found (mainly American) photographs, which he then re-imagines the human figure in a contemporary context; while Elaine Pamphilon paints the landscape around St Ives and her Cambridge home in a naïve, almost folk art style with bright, vibrant colours and confident brush strokes.

Artists want their work to be seen by as many people as possible – and we enjoy showing it!

James Stewart, curator at Zimmer Stewart Gallery

Nick Bodimeade has exhibited every two years since 2005 and this year presents his 'American Travelogue', a new series of road-views from his recent trip to the USA.

Caron Penney and Katharine Swailes, both master weavers, have created hand-woven tapestry commissions for established artists such as Tracey Emin and Gillian Ayres. Here they will show their own work, which is based on their observations of New York and other places.

For Zimmer Stewart's Arundel Festival exhibition in late August, Spanish abstract expressionist Felix Anaut will exhibit his series of 'Visual Music' sculptural ceramics as well as paintings. Anaut is better known in France, Italy, Spain and Ireland, where he has exhibited in large spaces such as Museum of Contemporary Art, Naples; Ulster Museum; Instituto Cervantes (Bordeaux and Dublin); Musea de Isaba (Navarra, Spain); and the Abbaye de Flaran in south-west France.

The Zimmer Stewart exhibition programme ends with two popular, but quite different, landscape artists: Katharine Le Hardy and Piers Ottey. The former paints semi-abstract coastal scenes with broad impasto brushstrokes, whereas Piers Ottey paints both urban and country scenes with his idiosyncratic geometry overlaid on top of the subject.

Some of the work is displayed here on these pages. But you will be able to see more with the full exhibition programme and list of artists shown on the gallery's website (see above), including the printmakers, ceramicists and sculptors, whose work is always in stock.

Zimmer Stewart Gallery provides an extremely useful 'search and selection' service for offices, as well as a gift list service that can be used for wedding lists, significant birthdays, retirement gifts and other group art-related purchases. See the website for full details.

Clockwise from top left: Fire Mountain II by Nick Bodimeade; Evening Walkers, Bantham by Katharine Le Hardy; Intersection 55th & 7th NYC by Caron Penney; Into the Light - Redchurch St II by Piers Ottey

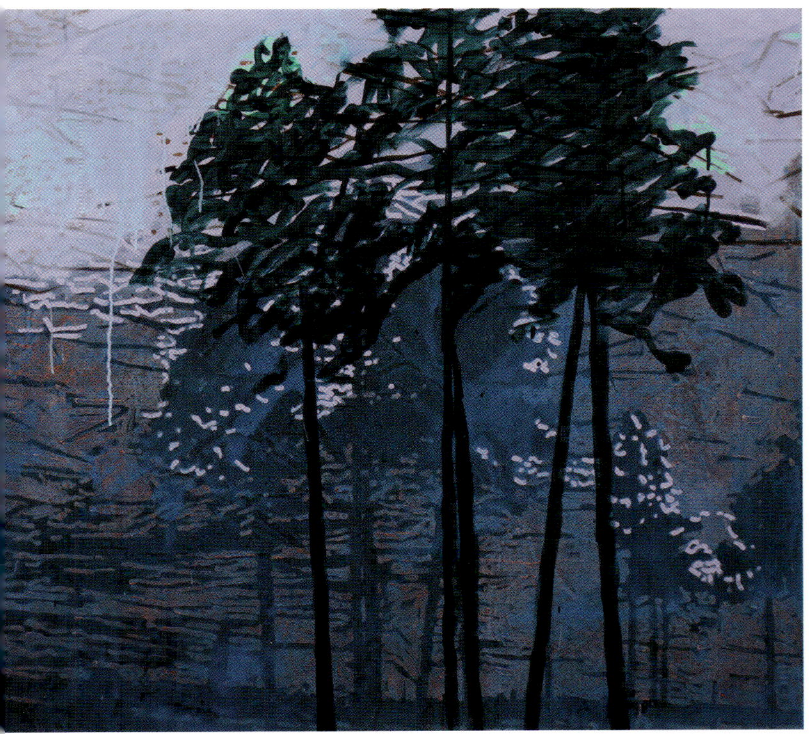

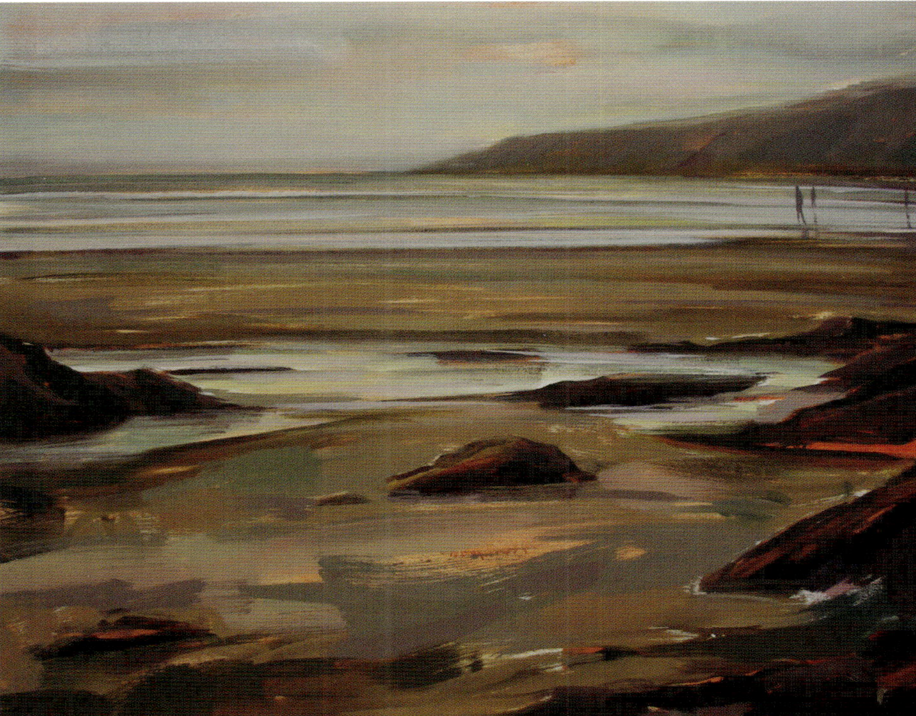

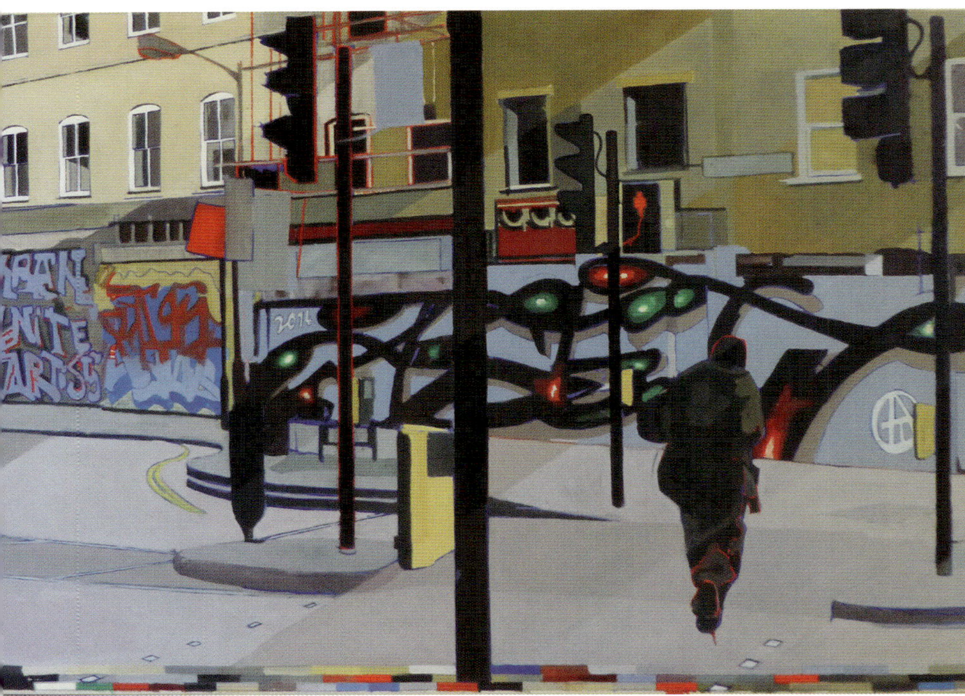

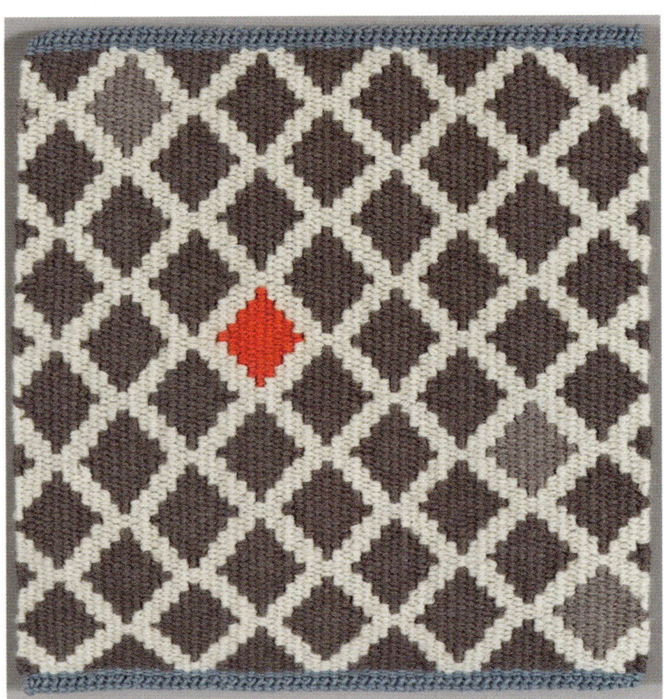

Chalk Gallery

4 North Street, Lewes BN7 2PA
www.chalkgallerylewes.co.uk

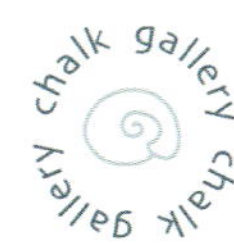

Clockwise from top left: The gallery; Secluded Bay by David Williams; Bird on the Wing by Janie Cochrane-Stewart; September Sunlight by Janice Thurston; Awakening by Louise Chatfield; Downs at Sunset by Gus Harrison; Trillion Strata by Kat Zahran; Peace by Tony Parsons

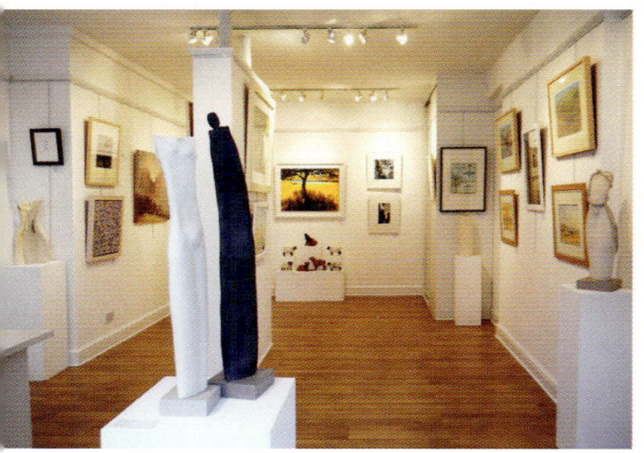

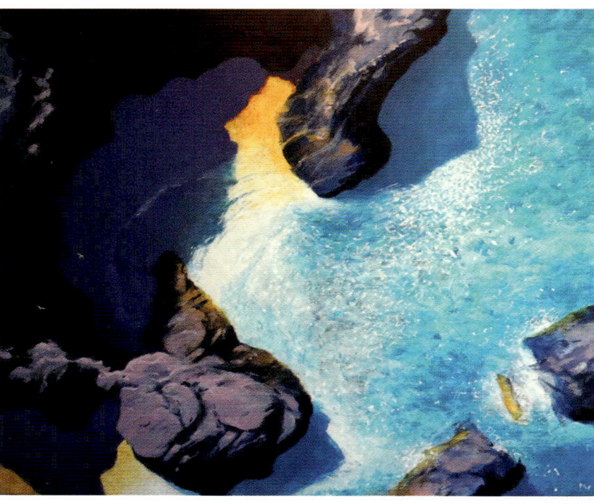

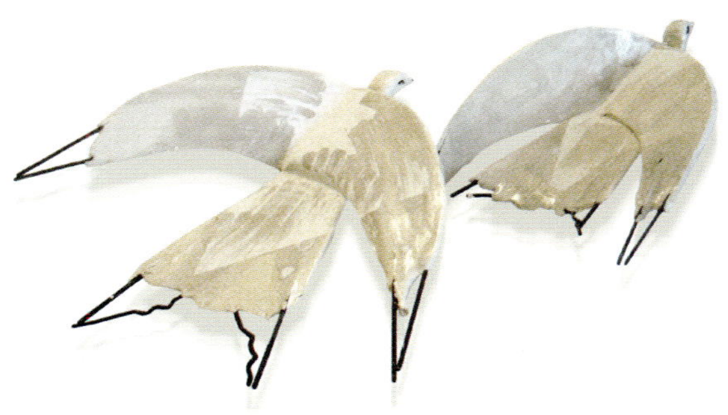

Chalk Gallery in Lewes celebrates its 10-year anniversary this year. Over the past decade it has built up a reputation for 'beautiful art at affordable prices', with a friendly welcome from one of the 21 artists who run the gallery in attendance when you visit.

There's a brand new exhibition every six weeks, and a different artist featured every three weeks, so there's always something new and exciting to see. Open seven days a week, with members changing from time to time, there have been more than 100 artists involved since the beginning. To celebrate this achievement – and the contribution of all the artists over the years – there will be a very special exhibition in the large Exhibition Hall at the Towner Gallery, Eastbourne, in October 2015, which will include art from members past and present.

For its customers, Chalk Gallery offers paintings, original prints, drawings, ceramics, sculpture and jewellery. There is also a selection of unframed original works and prints in the browser, plus greeting cards. Many of the artists also exhibit regularly in London.

For artists, the gallery provides a chance to exhibit in a beautiful, contemporary space and be part of a vibrant group of professional artists. Guest artists are invited when space permits.

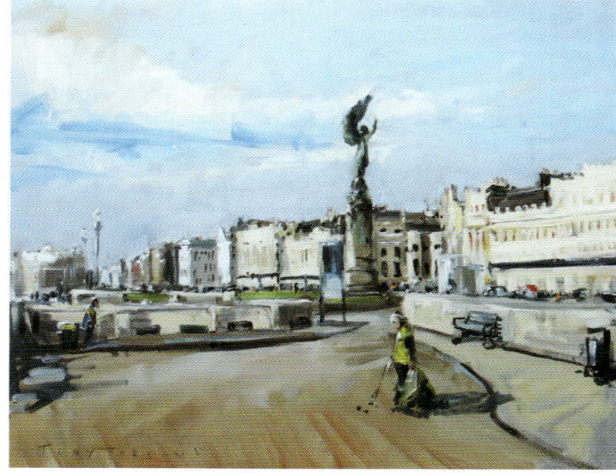

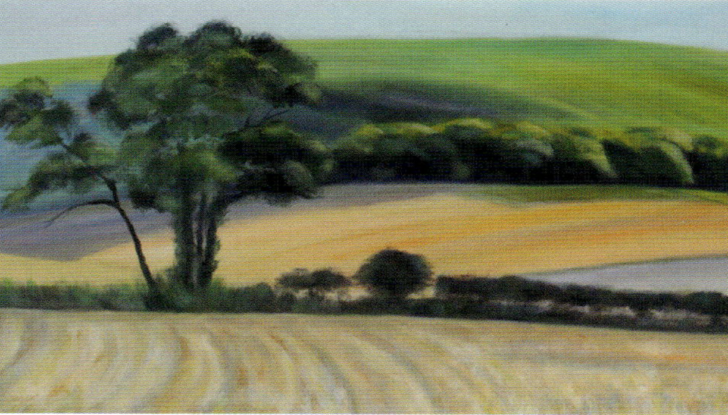

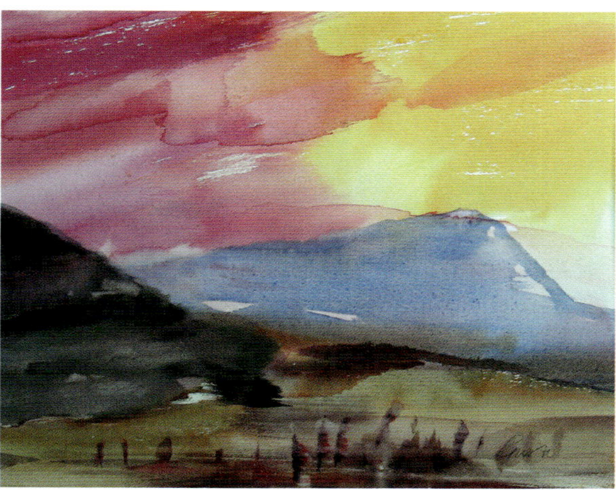

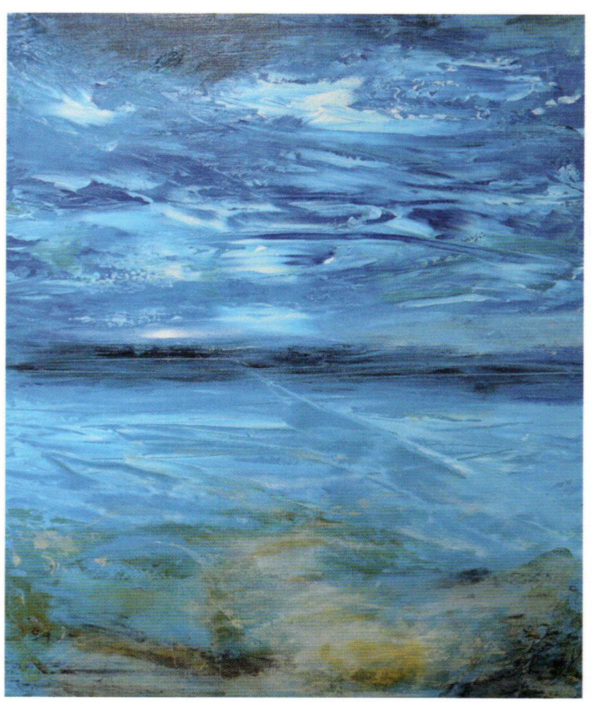

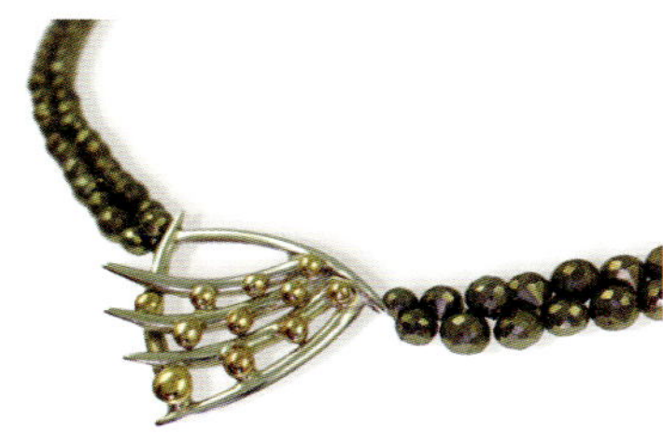

Clockwise from top left: Autumn Colour on the Downs by Gail Gibson Tait; Food and friends by Lyndsey Smith; Cow 1 by Mary Clarke; Tree of Life by Orna Schneerson Pascal

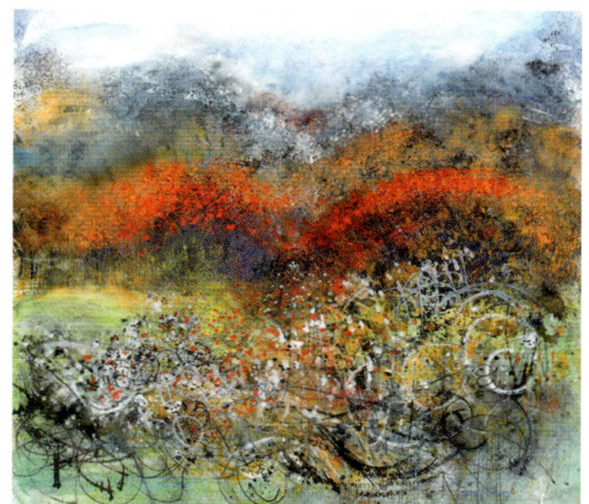

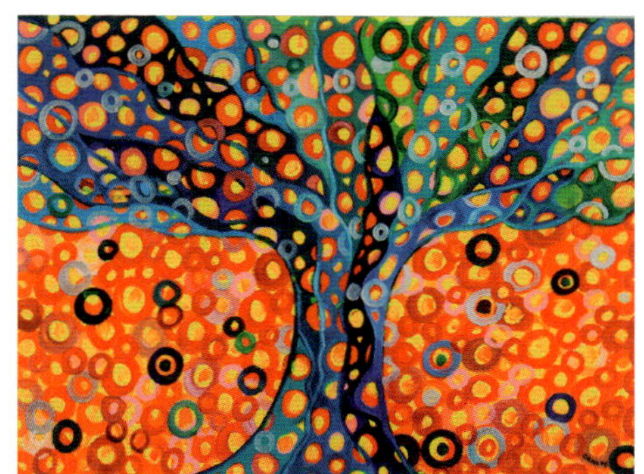

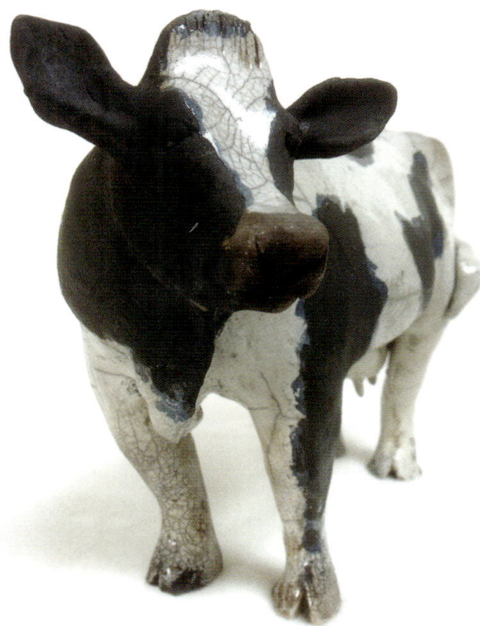

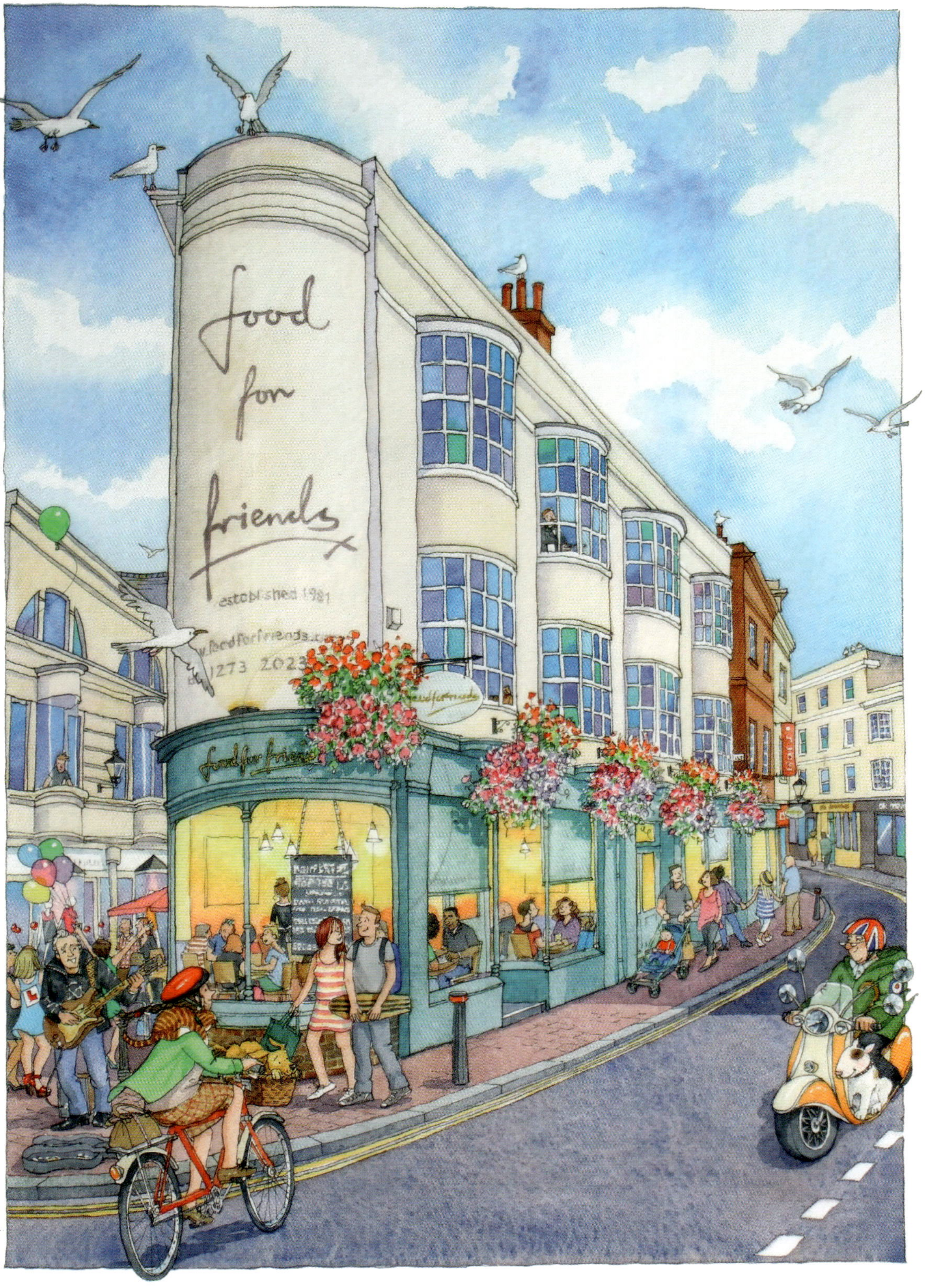

Hop Gallery

Star Brewery, Castle Ditch Lane (off Fisher Street), Lewes BN7 1YJ
www.hopgallery.com

Left to right: Angel by Julie Snowball;
Skoter 2 by Joseph Davey

Hop Gallery is a delightful, light and calming visual arts exhibition space situated in the 18th-century Star Brewery building, with its ancient brickwork, massive beams and echoes of a fascinating industrial past in Lewes, the vibrant county town of Sussex.

Considered one of the most significant and prestigious visual arts venues in the South East, Hop Gallery is multifunctional – complementing traditional and modern art, sculpture and installation equally well.

The Gallery is proud to host exhibitions by regional, national and international artists, and showcase accomplished as well as up-and-coming artists and makers, enabling it to offer a diverse programme of exhibitions.

Within the Star Brewery building, visitors will discover a variety of studios, including the renowned Mohamed Hamid Pottery Studio. Through the higgledy piggledy streets between the Gallery, the Castle and the River Ouse, enjoy exploring a huge array of atmospheric coffee bars and eating houses along with unique shops all less than five minutes' walking distance away.

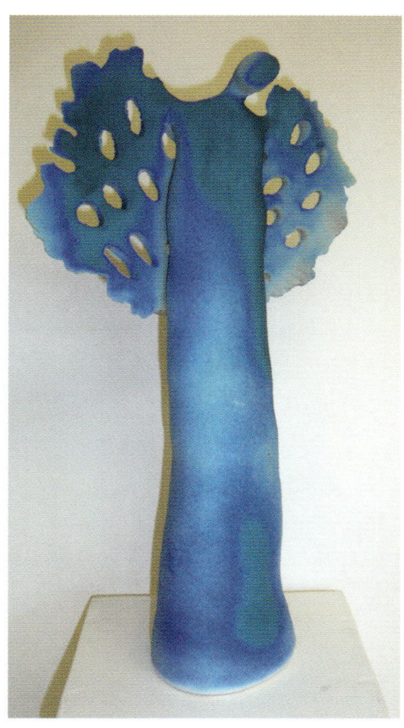

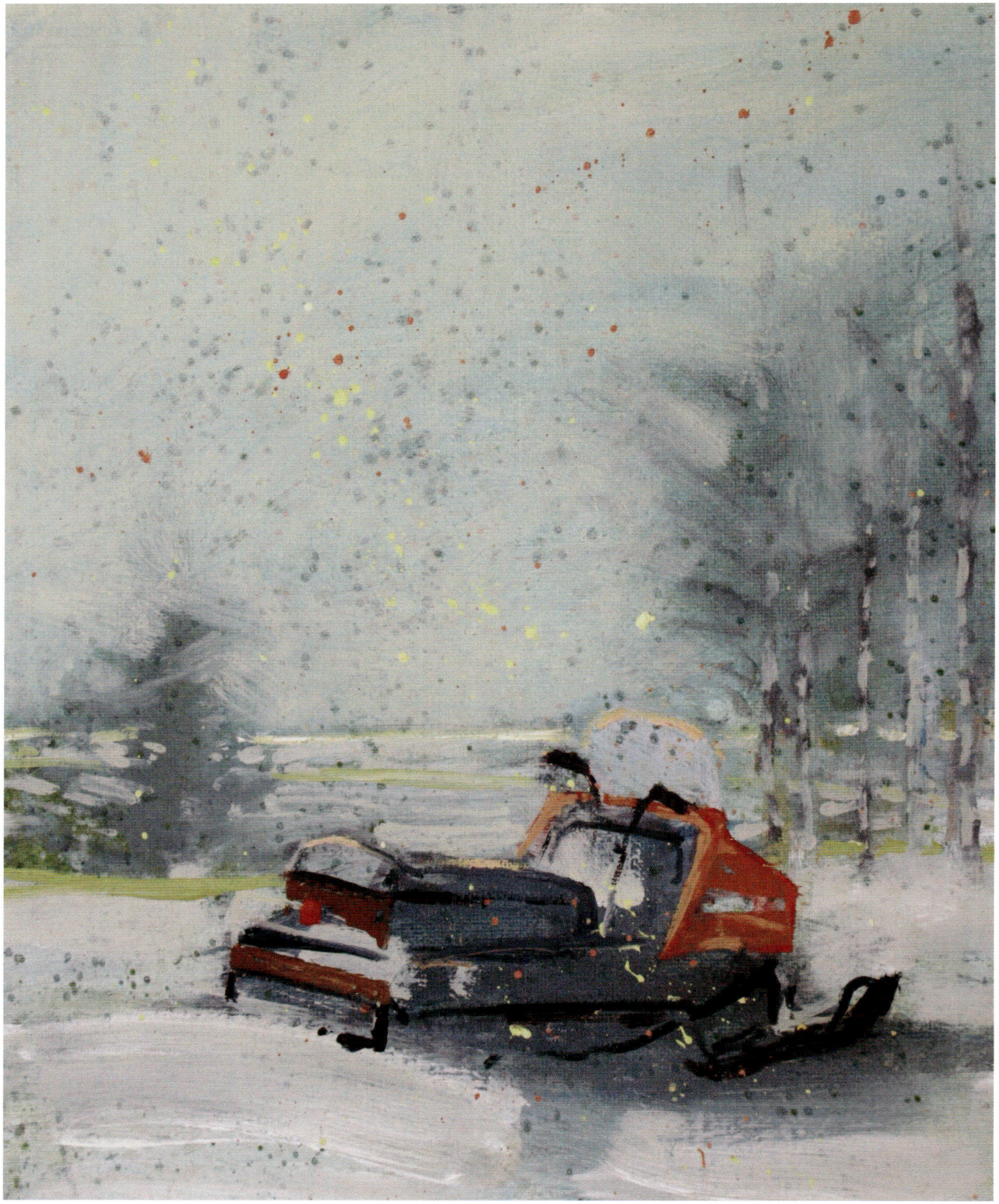

Window Gallery

Studio 9, Turner Dumbrell Workshops, Dumbrells Court Road, Ditchling, Hassocks BN6 8GT
www.windowgallery.co.uk

Until We Meet Again by Philip Dunn

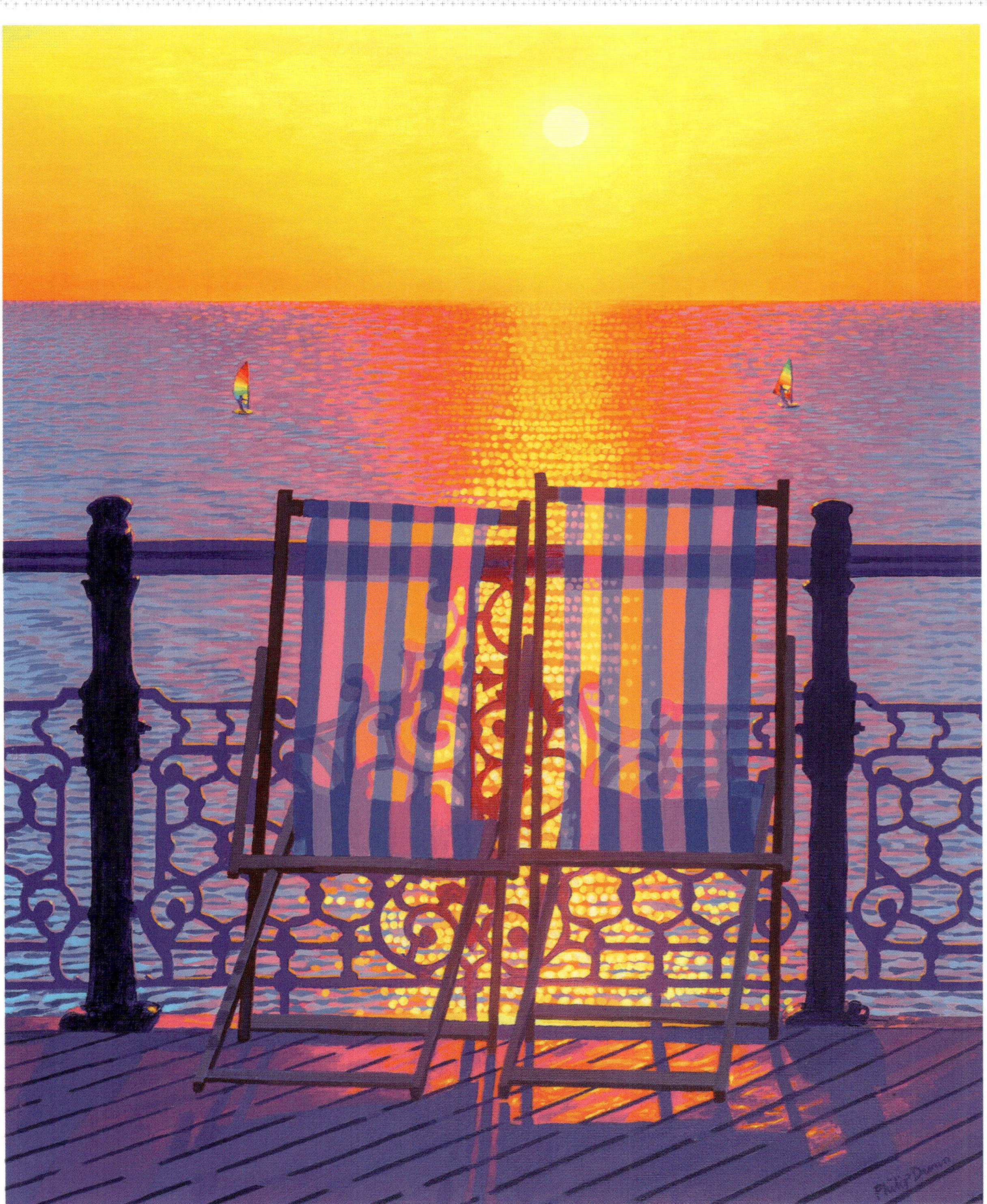

Philip Dunn's deckchair paintings have become a symbol of the city

Located in the Turner Dumbrell Workshops in Ditchling, the famous Window Gallery shows paintings and prints by Philip Dunn – who has earned a reputation as Brighton's favourite artist, due to his abilty to capture the spirit of the seafront and his particularly evocative deckchair scenes. The gallery also offers a bespoke picture framing service.

Gallery 40

40 Gloucester Road, Brighton BN1 4AQ
www.gallery40.co.uk

In the popular North Laine, Gloucester Road continues to rise as a vibrant destination for art lovers thanks to its eclectic mix of galleries and shops. If you're in the area, a 'must visit' is Gallery40, which provides two floors in a well-lit space with plenty of natural light.

Providing an opportunity to showcase local East Sussex artists is extremely important to Gallery40, and throughout its annual pop-up programme work in disciplines as varied as painting, photography, sculpture, stone carving, performance art and installations add to its unique feel. The gallery is also keen to continue its relationship with new and emerging artists from Brighton University.

Keep up to date with what's happening at this unique space on Twitter @gallery40. You'll find information about hiring and availability on its website (above).

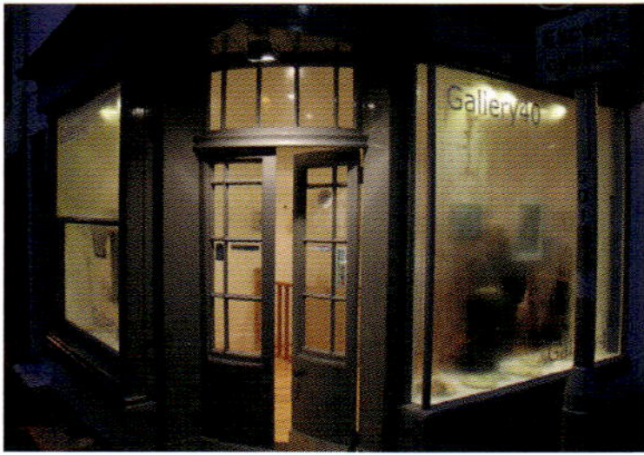

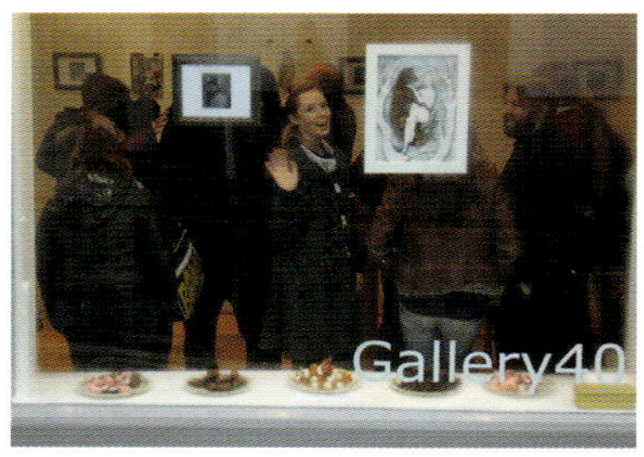

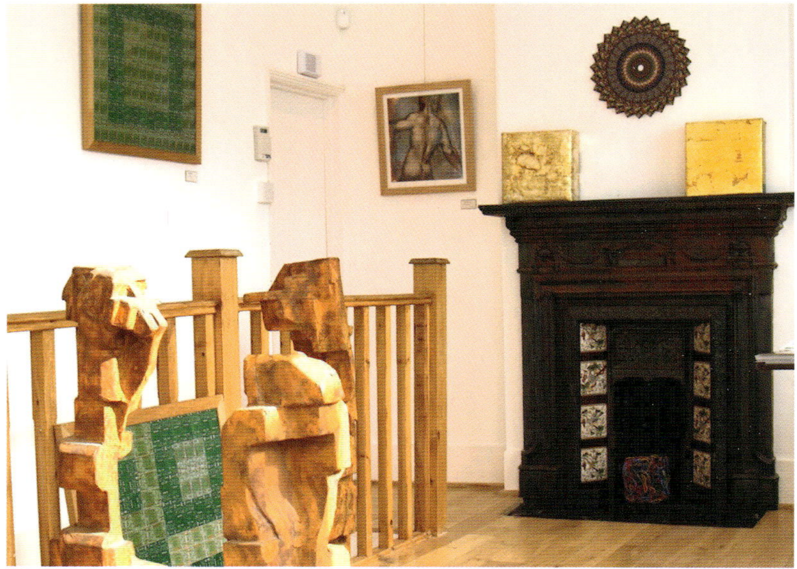

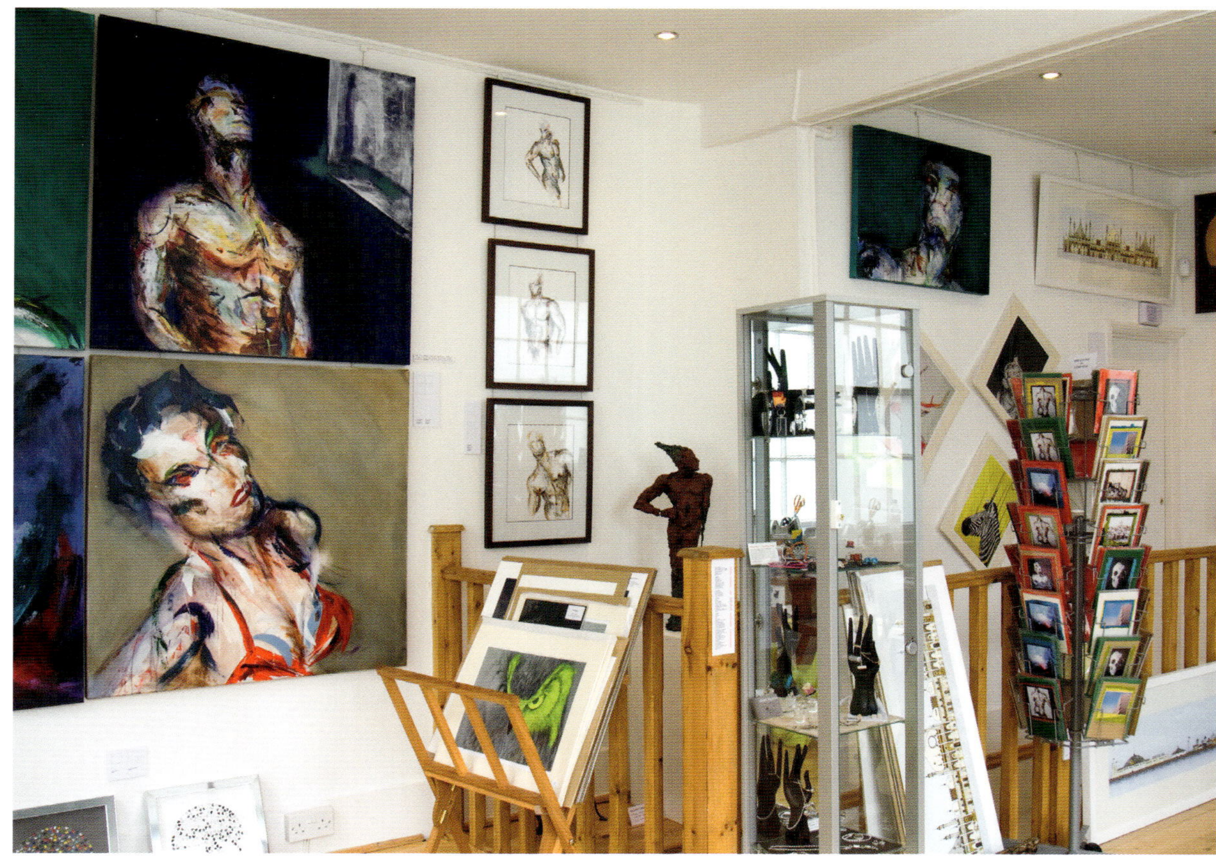

Kemp Street Corner

Art Schism, 87 Gloucester Road, BN1 4AP, www.artschism.net
White Rabbit, 88 Gloucester Road, BN1 4AP, www.facebook.com/WhiteRabbitMakersGallery

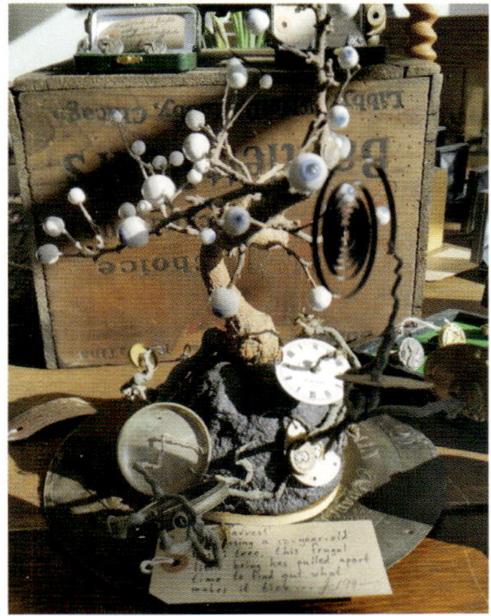

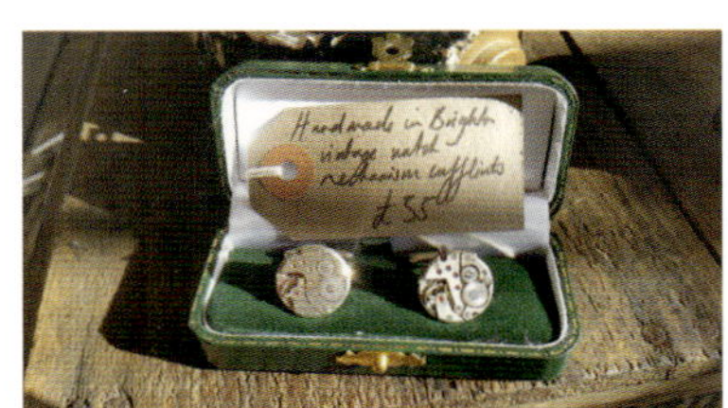

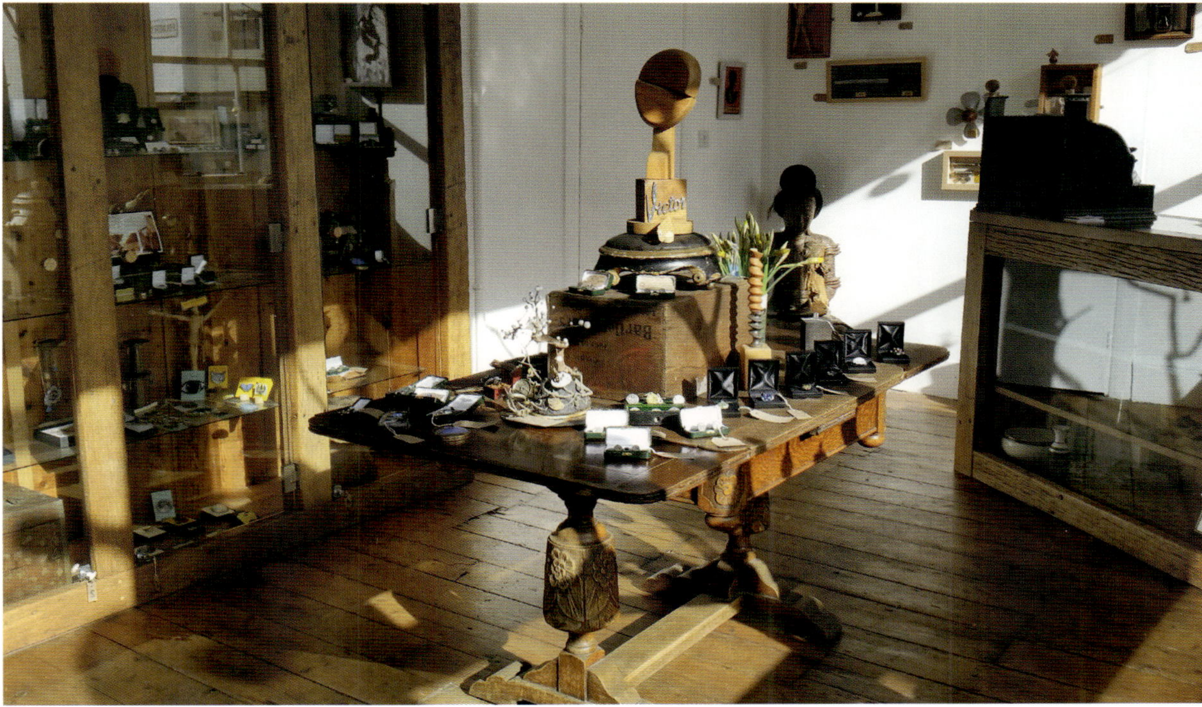

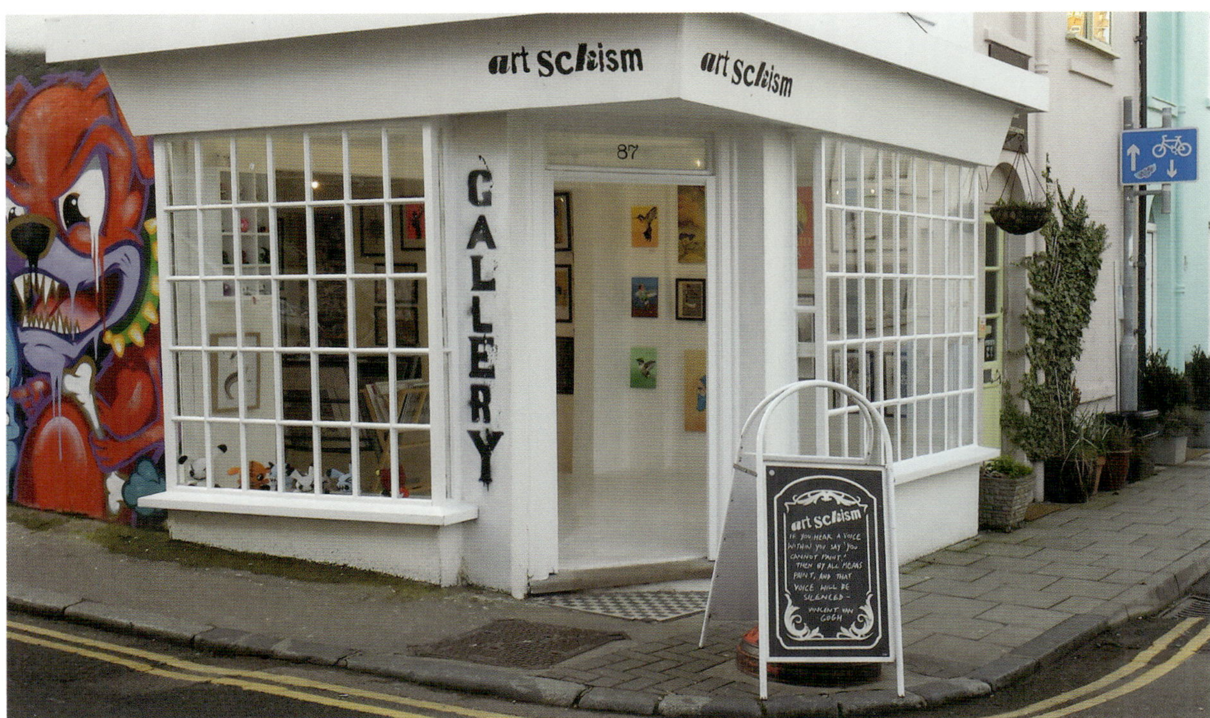

Opposite Gallery40 on Gloucester Road, glass-blower John King has established White Rabbit Gallery (above) as a quirky and enticing space for independent artists, designers and makers to show and sell their work.

Then just a stone's throw away across Kemp Street, the Art Schism co-operative and collective (left) have transformed the corner into an ever-changing work of graffiti art in itself and host a varied programme of artists' shows throughout the year.

Bellis Gallery

8-9 Kings Road, Brighton BN1 1NE

In this spacious and lovingly restored Victorian building just off East Street, Sema Ugur curates one of Brighton's most elegant and enticing gallery spaces. She brings together a fabulous mix of overseas, Fairtrade and local artists' work to ensure there truly is something for everyone – and surprisingly affordable prices.

The variety of individually sourced artwork, textiles, ceramics, jewellery and accessories is astounding. And the sense of harmony and calm the gallery exudes is a tribute to Sema's curatorial skill, ensuring everything takes its place beautifully. On permanent show, expect to see fantastical illustration by Harriet Butler and Heike Roesel's (page 9) extraordinary etchings.

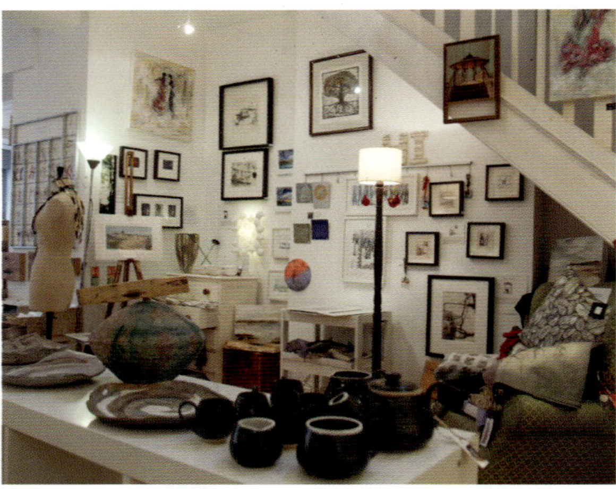

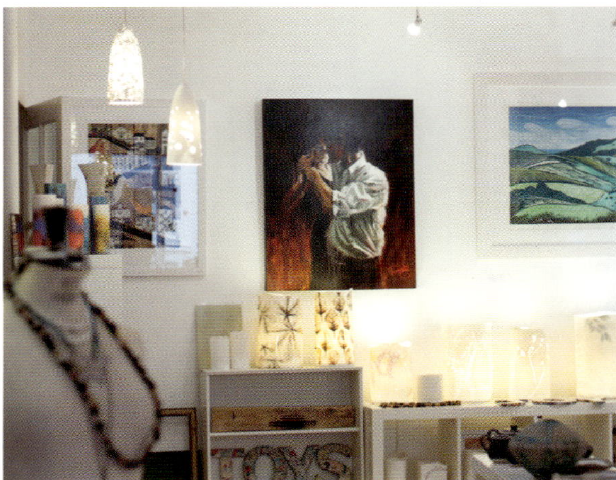

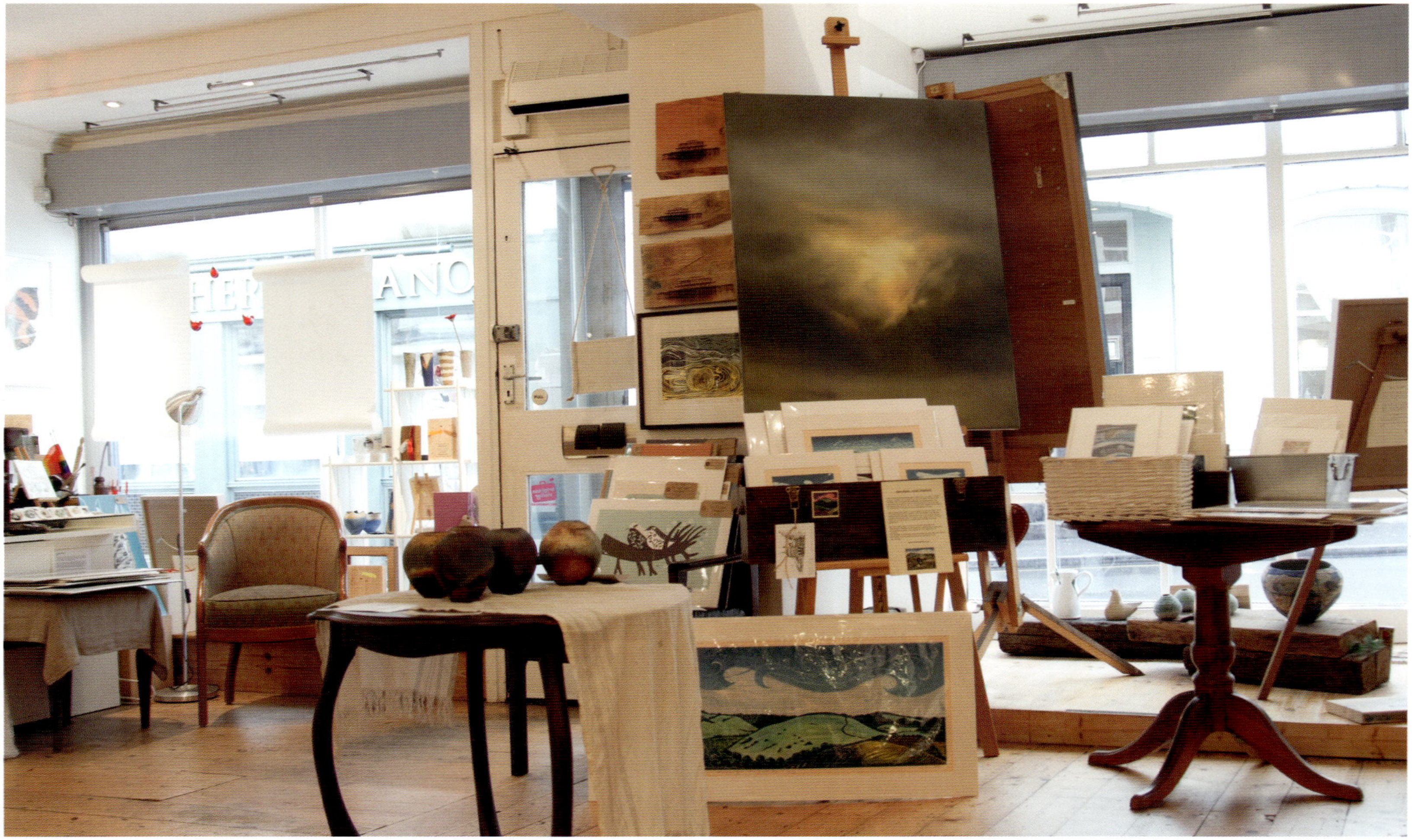

In My Room

35 Gloucester Road, Brighton BN1 4AQ
www.inmyroom.co.uk

Clockwise from top: Italian Atomic Nesting Tables; Brand New Wooden Landrover County; Czechlosovakian Art Deco Bedside Tables; GPlan Armchair

In My Room has been established for more than 12 years in the boutique district of Brighton's fashionable North Laine. It offers hand-selected vintage pieces, furniture and interior design from Art Deco to the present day, all lovingly restored or sourced in excellent original condition. Highlighting 20th-century design classics alongside a more unusual and idiosyncratic collection.

In My Room takes sourcing very seriously – but that also includes a large soft spot for fun and eccentric pieces. Owner Oliver Learmonth has a history in cabinet making and art, and has been collecting for nearly 30 years. His passion and appreciation for design has established his store as a leading purveyor of style. With a constantly changing selection of quality stock, it's a good idea to check in store or on the website (above) on a regular basis.

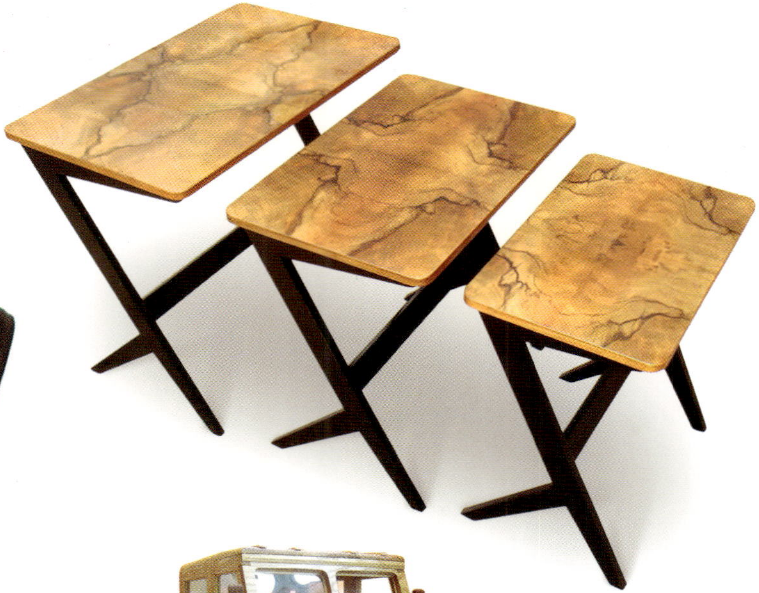

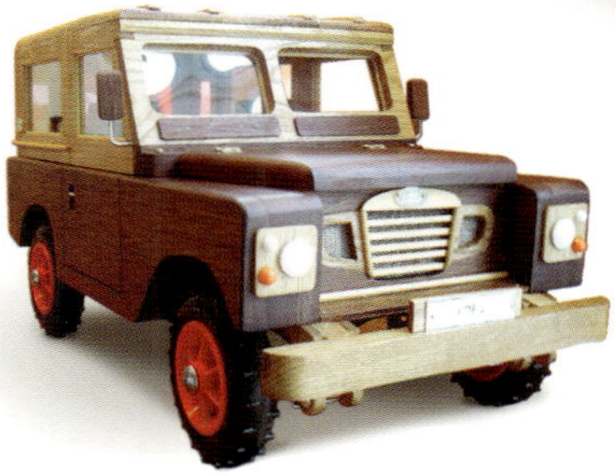

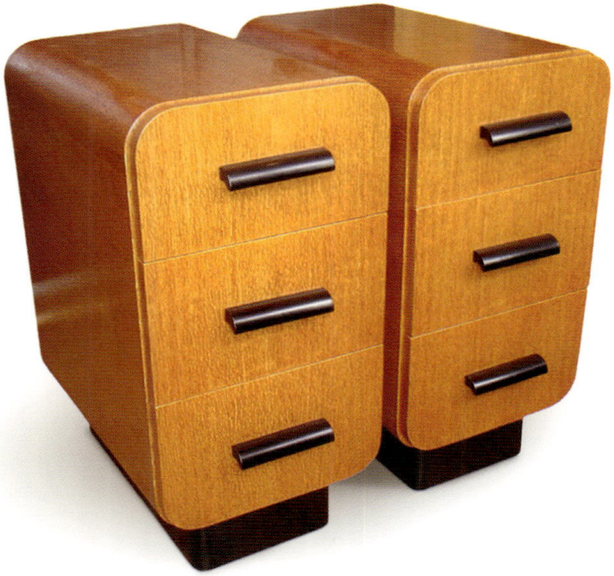

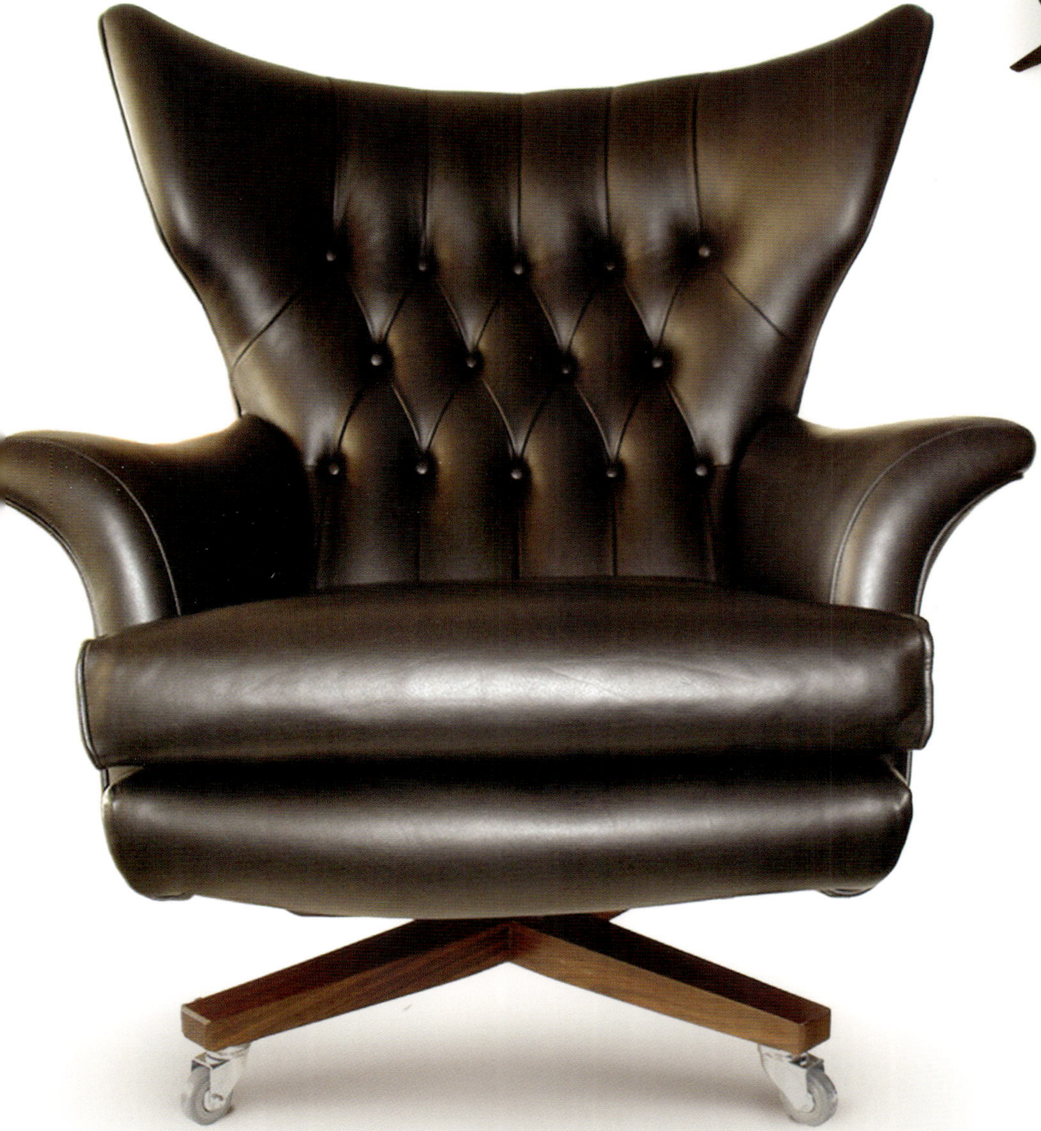

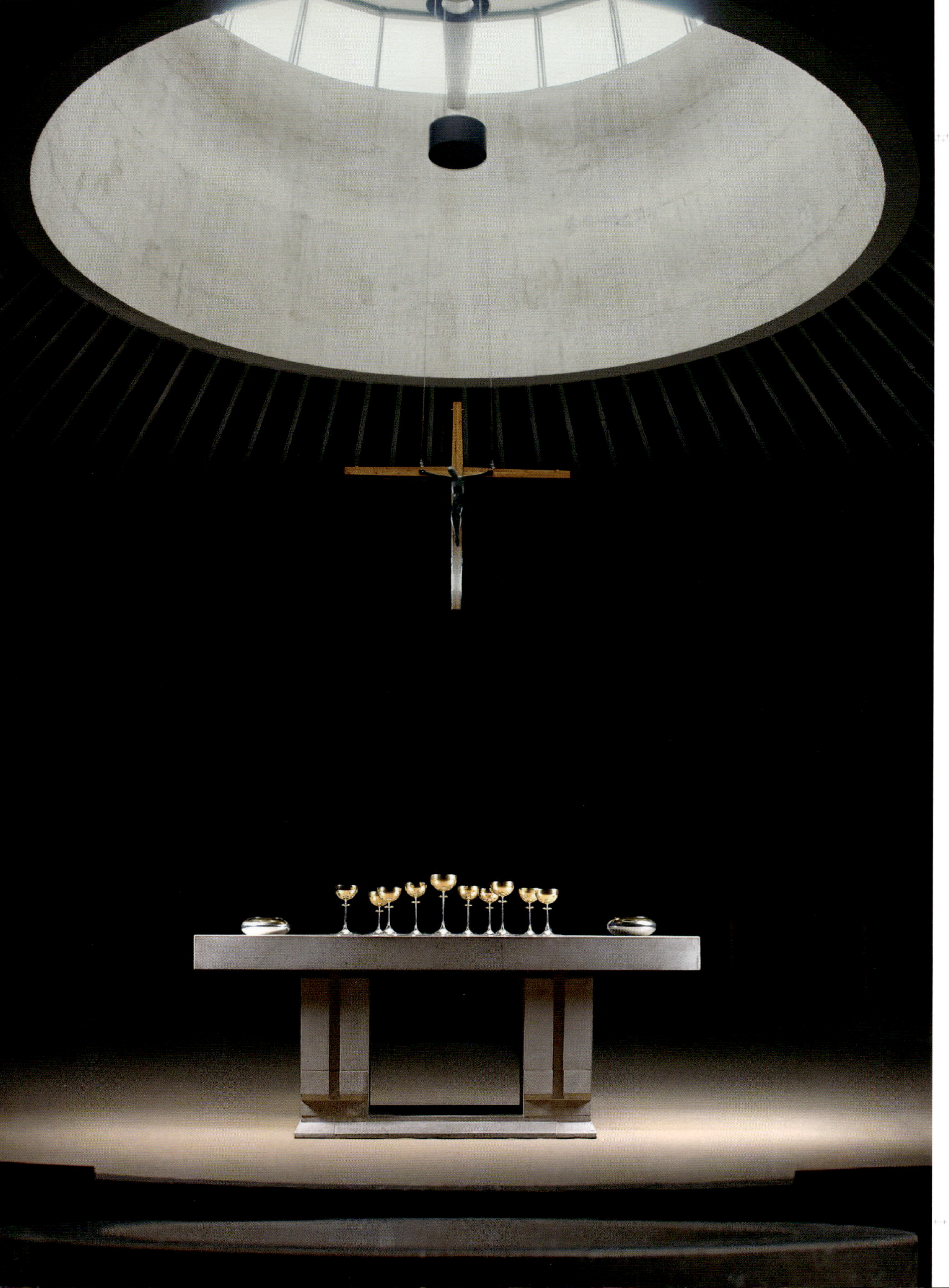

Pruden and Smith are established local goldsmiths, jewellers and silversmiths. Their gallery and workshops are located in the historic Arts and Crafts village of Ditchling, just five miles north of Brighton. You will find a fabulous array of contemporary precious jewellery, unusual gemstones and silverware. They are open every day or you could take a sneak preview online.

As well as a gallery full of stunning designs in silver, gold and platinum, featuring diamonds and sumptuous coloured gemstones, Pruden and Smith make a lot of work to commission, including the new silverware for Worth Abbey.

In 2011, Worth Abbey reopened after completion of the unfinished interior of the Grade II listed church, designed by architect Frances Pollen in the 1960s. New furniture designed by Thomas Heatherwick was commissioned, and Pruden and Smith were asked to design and make a sculptural silver and silver gilt altar set of 10 chalices and three stacking ciboria.

The space inside the church is dramatic, with the altar as the focal point. It was clear to designer Rebecca Smith as soon as she entered that it was not just a group of functional vessels that was required for this sacred space, but a single sculpture that worked with the altar, the lighting and the church building to further enhance its meditative focus, drama and sense of wonder.

The 10 chalices were designed with different heights to break up their uniformity. The stems were made as slender as possible with flattened knops to give the effect of the base of each chalice disappearing, leaving the brushed silver gilt chalice bowls floating above the altar in a golden cloud form.

Opposite page: Worth Abbey Chalices and Ciboria (photographer Henke Images)
This page: 18ct gold jewellery using recycled gold, gems and diamonds (photographer Clive Hadwin)

Pruden & Smith

The Crossroads, 2 South Street, Ditchling BN6 8UQ
www.prudenandsmith.com

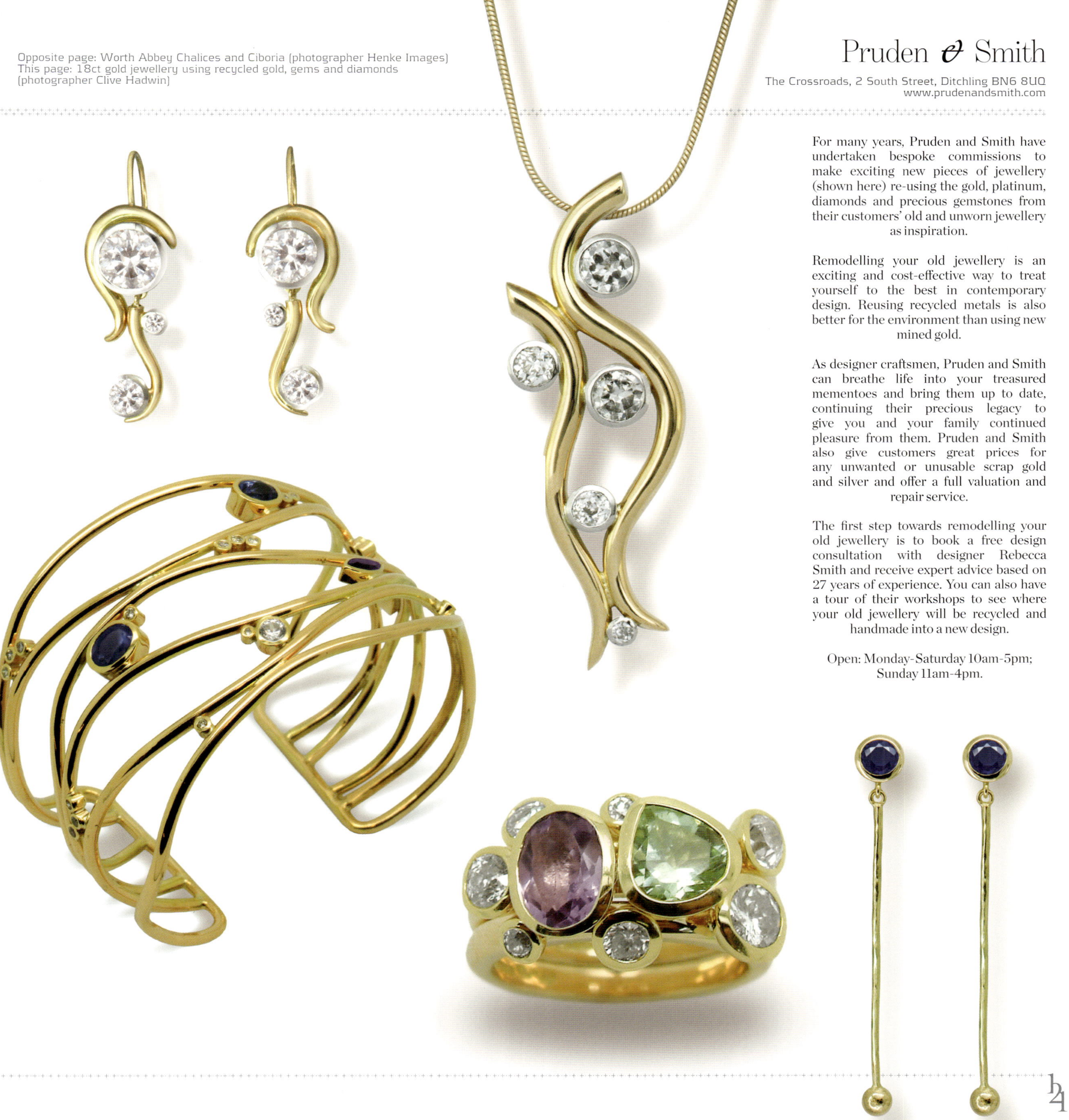

For many years, Pruden and Smith have undertaken bespoke commissions to make exciting new pieces of jewellery (shown here) re-using the gold, platinum, diamonds and precious gemstones from their customers' old and unworn jewellery as inspiration.

Remodelling your old jewellery is an exciting and cost-effective way to treat yourself to the best in contemporary design. Reusing recycled metals is also better for the environment than using new mined gold.

As designer craftsmen, Pruden and Smith can breathe life into your treasured mementoes and bring them up to date, continuing their precious legacy to give you and your family continued pleasure from them. Pruden and Smith also give customers great prices for any unwanted or unusable scrap gold and silver and offer a full valuation and repair service.

The first step towards remodelling your old jewellery is to book a free design consultation with designer Rebecca Smith and receive expert advice based on 27 years of experience. You can also have a tour of their workshops to see where your old jewellery will be recycled and handmade into a new design.

Open: Monday-Saturday 10am-5pm;
Sunday 11am-4pm.

Junkfunk

27 Gloucester Road, BN1 4AQ
www.junkfunk.com

Junkfunk is an independent design gift shop in the heart of Brighton's North Laine. The shop started life as a stall in London's Spitalfields market in 2003 selling its own-designed T-shirts, which are still available to buy in store and online. The T-shirts are the shop's main product selling all over the world with one NO PASARÁN (They Shall Not Pass) worn by 'Pussy Riot' Punk activist Nadezhda Tolokonnikova at her trial in a Moscow court room in 2012.

Alongside the Tees, there is an ecclectic mix of products from an exciting mix of designers and illustrators and makers. Prints by James Brown, cards by illustrators, Freya, 67Inc, Tom Frost and David Shrigley, with stationery, books, dresses and homeware also.

The unpretentious and quirky nature of the shop appeals to Brighton's creative community and is a great place to find something interesting at an affordable price. Open seven days a week, 10am-6pm Monday to Saturday and 11am-5pm on Sunday.

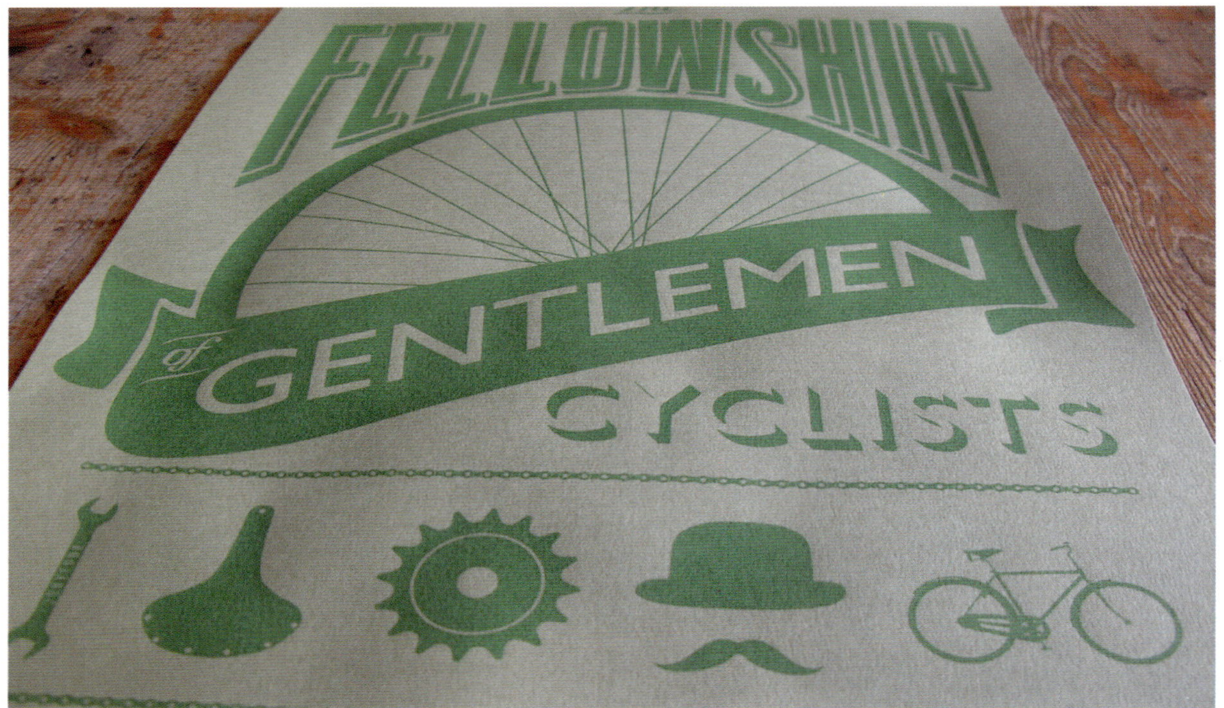

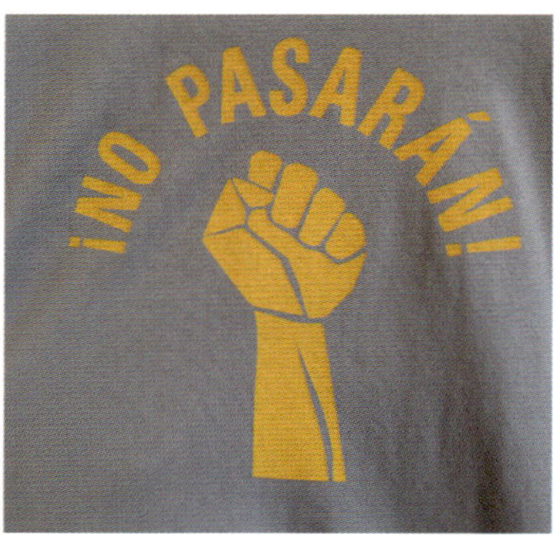

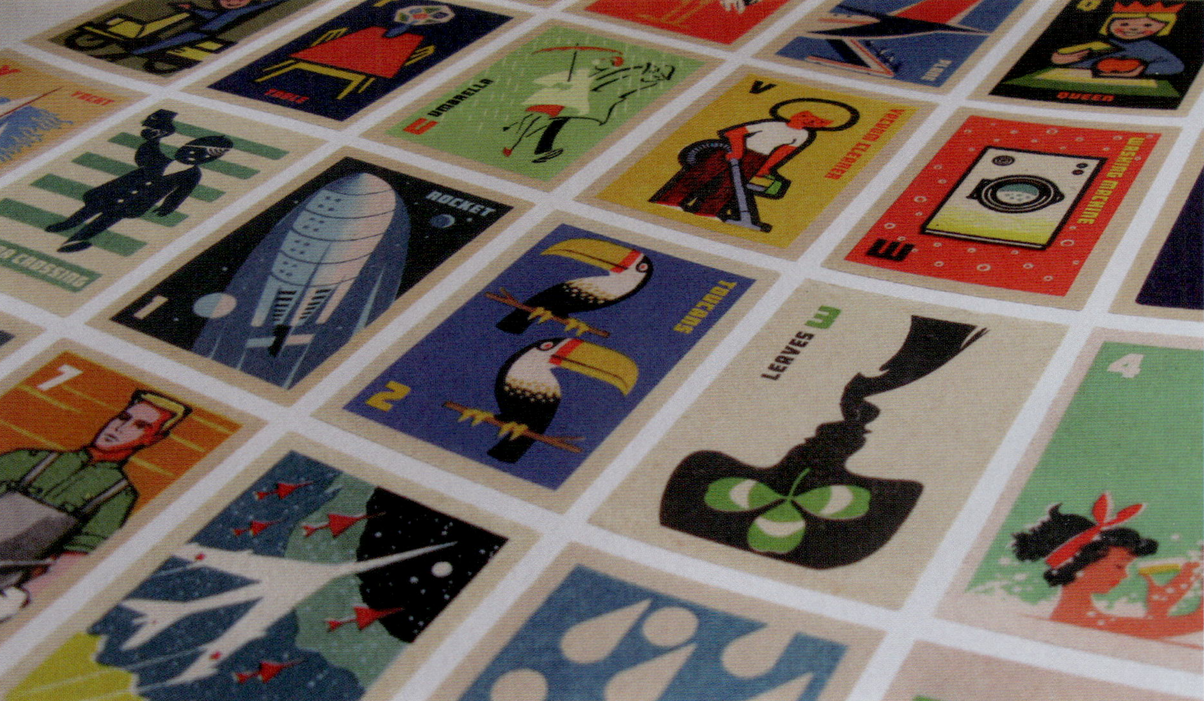

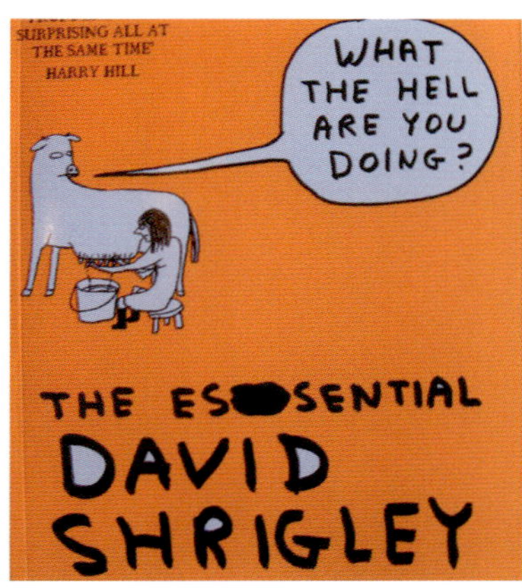

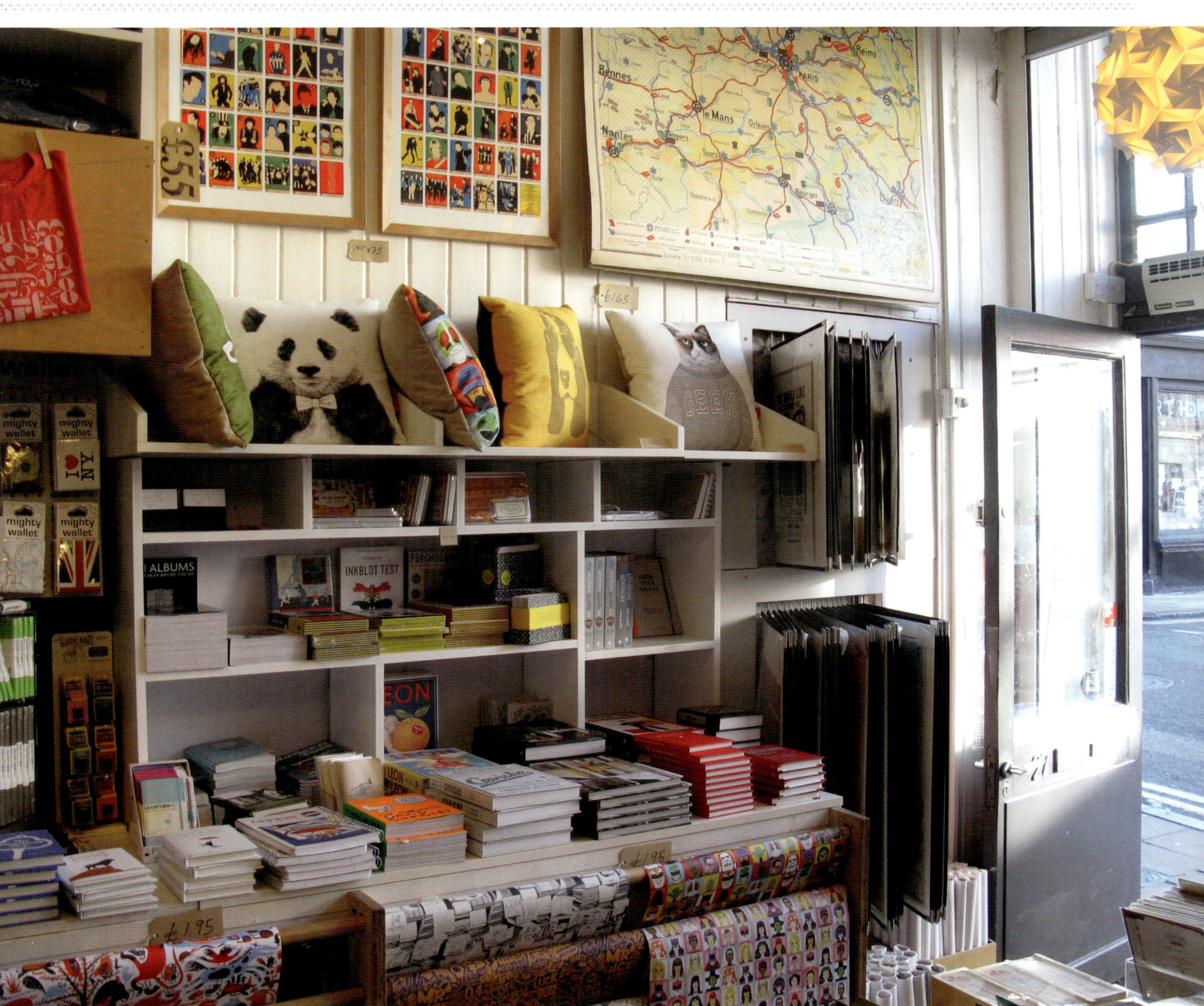
£55
Rennes
PARIS
Reims
le Mans
Orleans
Nantes
Angers
Tours
Troyes
Bourges
Dijon
GEEK
mighty wallet
mighty wallet
mighty wallet
mighty wallet
ALBUMS
INKBLOT TEST
LEON
£1.95
£1.95

Unlimited

10 Church Street, Brighton BN1 1US
www.unlimitedshop.co.uk

Unlimited is an independent design shop, gallery and studio based in Brighton. The design studio was founded in 2008 by husband and wife team Patrick and Sara Morrissey. In 2010 they began to showcase the work of a collective of like-minded contemporary illustrators, designers and makers from their weekly 'pop-up' studio shop. They participated in three years of Artists Open Houses exhibitions, and have also held a number of their own exhibitions showcasing new work from their designers.

In 2013 and 2014 Unlimited was selected to exhibit at *Pick Me Up* (the UK's largest and most prestigious annual graphic arts event held at Somerset House, London) to huge success. In August 2013, they opened their permanent gallery and shop in the heart of Brighton's North Laine.

Continuing to work closely alongside each other, Patrick runs the Unlimited design studio, while Sara focuses her energies on the shop and gallery – where they continue to curate, showcase and sell prints and unique, design-led products by an exciting and expanding collective.

Feedback over the past few years has been amazingly positive, and the gallery and shop has grown organically as a reaction to this. The couple aims to keep forging new connections with other skilled creatives, and to keep evolving as a business and be inspired by what's going on around them. The gallery space allows Unlimited to be a more visible and pro-active part of the Brighton creative and retail scene, and its main drive is to continue to source, provide and promote a great selection of concept-led, exciting and innovative work.

This year Unlimited is taking an exhibition of new and exclusive prints produced in collaboration with 40 artists, illustrators and makers on tour. Entitled *Four Play* it can be seen at Unlimited gallery for the whole of May as part of the Brighton Fringe Festival.

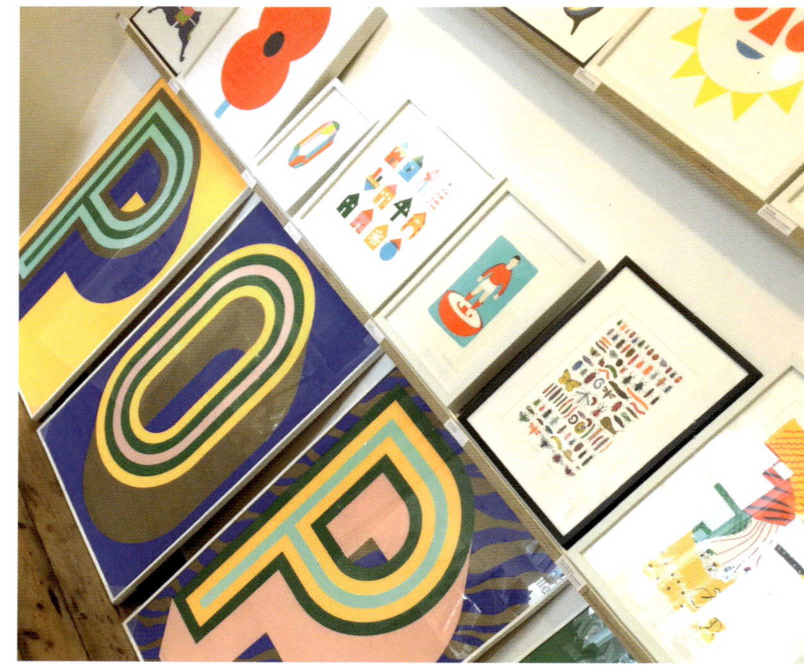

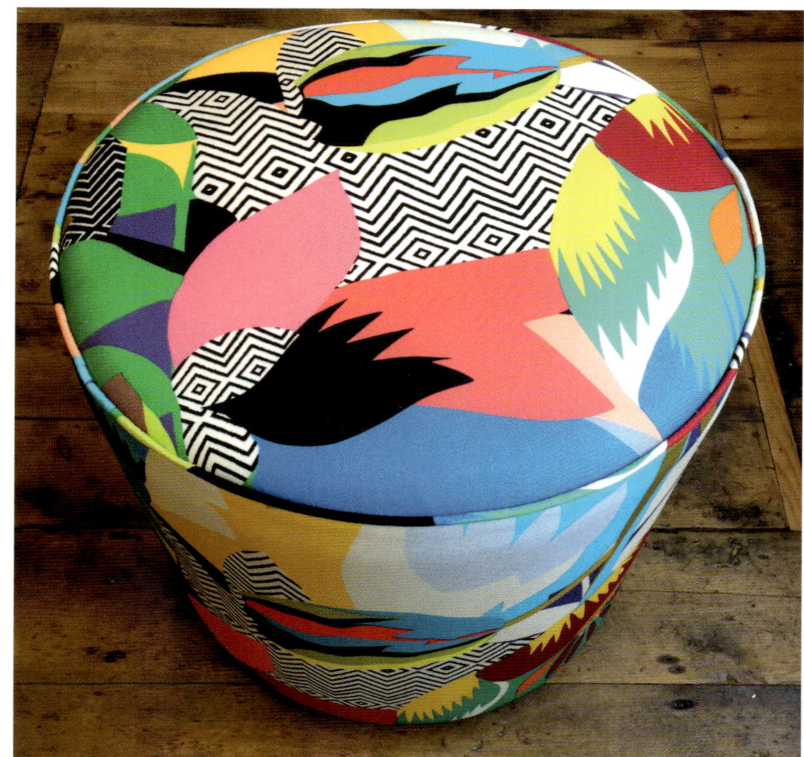

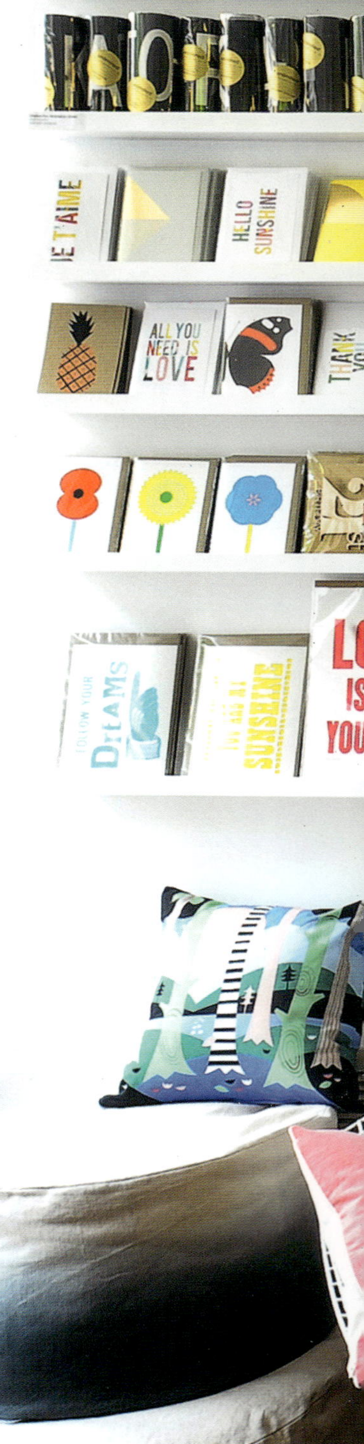

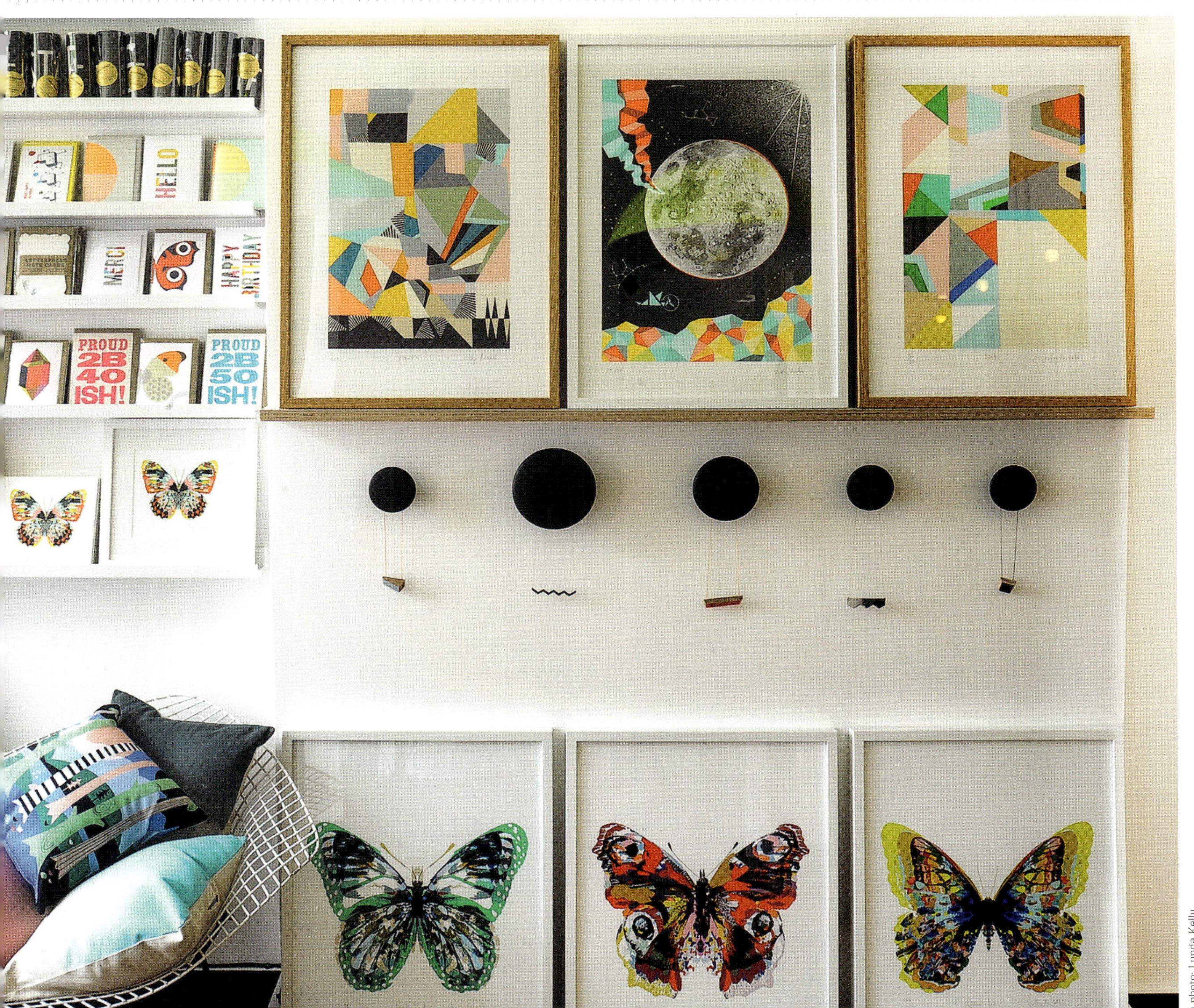

Main photo: Lynda Kelly

JONATHAN
ROGERS

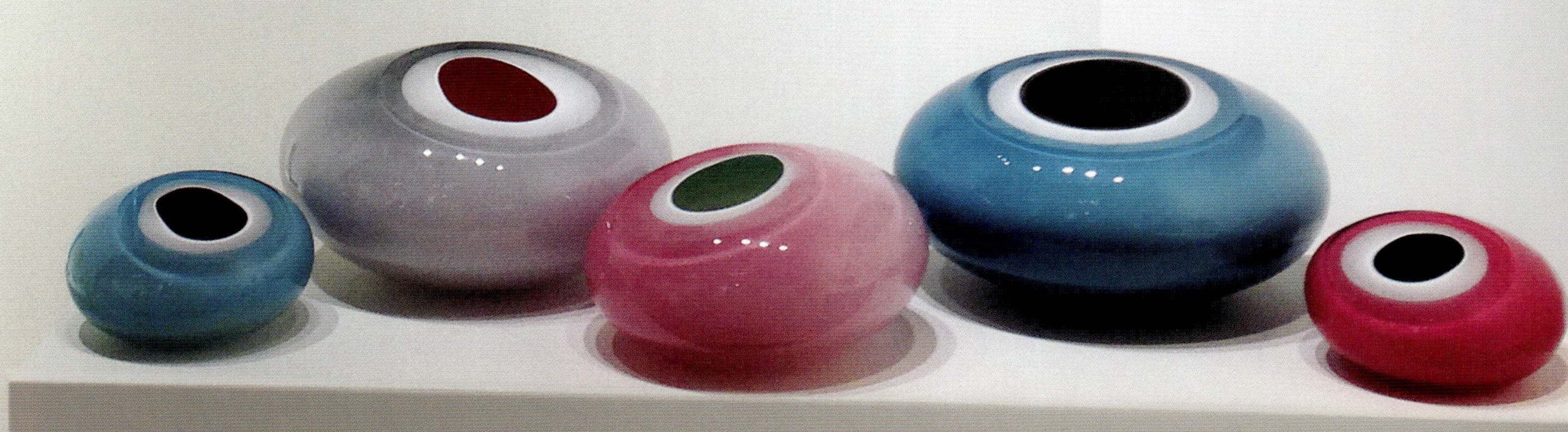

EVENTS

For art lovers, it's always a good time to visit Brighton. These are the shows and festivals you just can't miss

MADE BRIGHTON
See page 131

Artists Open Houses

May and November/December weekends, venues around the city
www.aoh.org.uk

Clockwise from top left:
The Art of Movement by Billy Cowie, Central trail; Joy Fox, Prestonville trail; Ravenswood, Beyond the Level trail (inside and outdoors); Have We Met by Lindy Martin, Ceramic House, Fiveways trail; The Dog Show by Gemma Rees, Brunswick Town trail

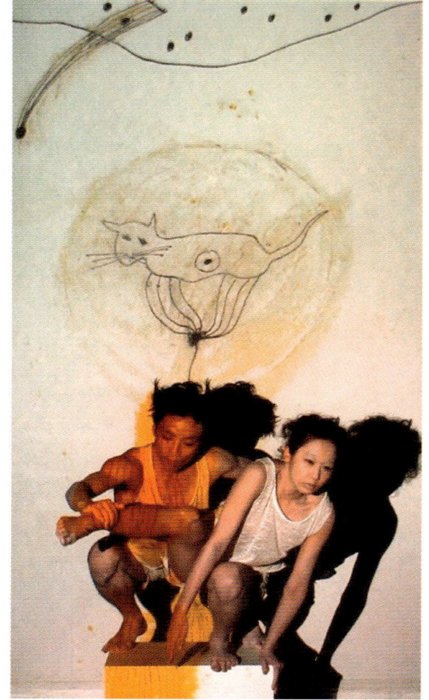

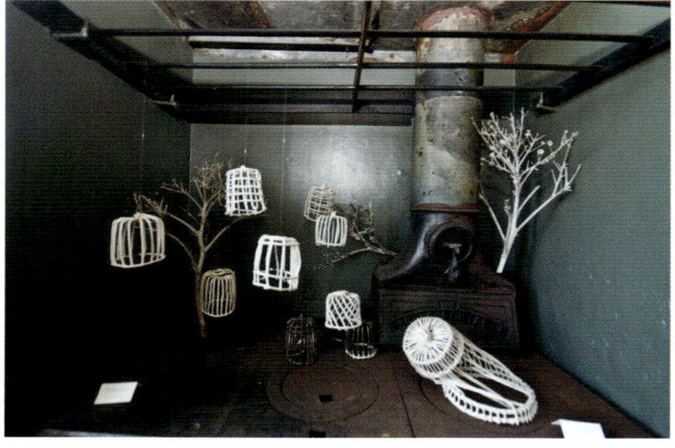

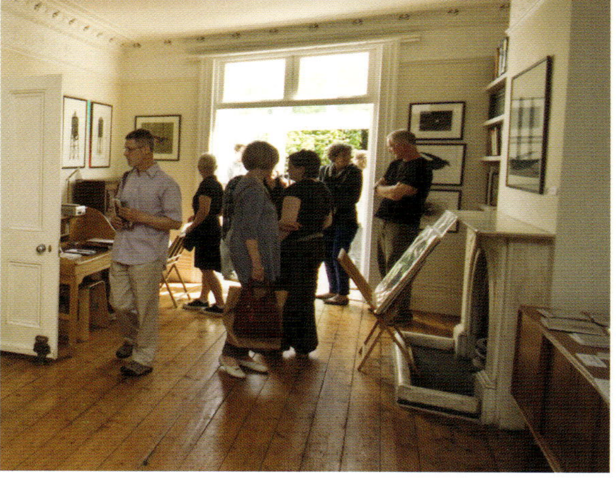

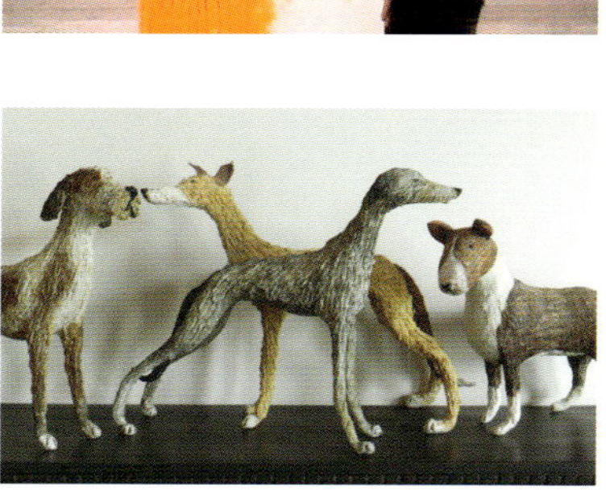

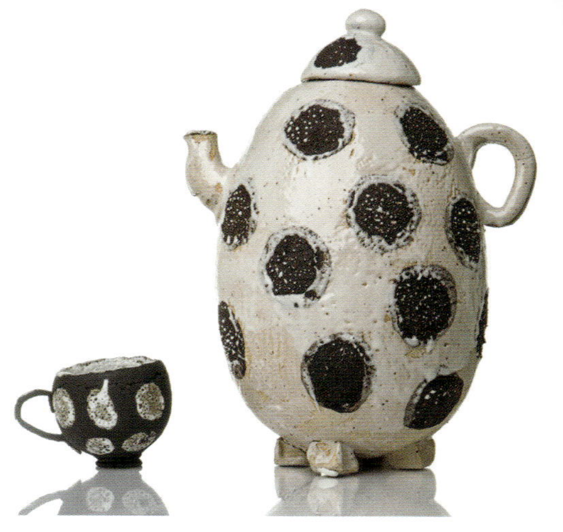

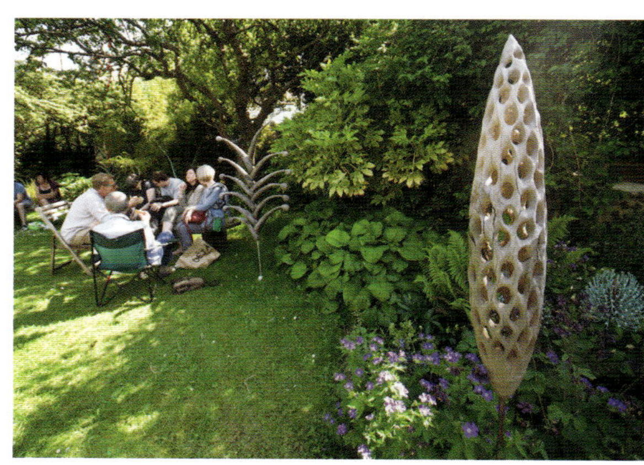

Text by Judy Stevens

Brighton & Hove Artists Open Houses festival is the oldest and largest Open House movement, proud of its roots within the city's diverse and vibrant artists' community. Constantly evolving, and innovating, AOH reflects the experience and professionalism as well as the youth and freshness, of the city's artists.

The phenomenon began in 1982, when Fiveways artist, Ned Hoskins, opened his front door to the public, inviting visitors into his home to view his own work and that of a group of friends. Other artists in the area followed, to form the Fiveways Artists Group. The idea proved very popular with the visiting public and soon other trails sprang up around the city, and the Artists Open Houses were born.

Artists Open Houses now stands as an important festival in its own right, partner festival to the city's established May Brighton and Fringe Festivals.

Open Houses provide a unique experience for visitors, offering the chance to visit artists and makers in their homes and buy artworks directly from them. The hugely diverse selection of works on offer includes paintings, prints, ceramics and textiles, photography, sculpture, jewellery and much more.

With approximately 200 houses and studio spaces across the city opening their doors to exhibit the work of more than 1,000 artists and makers, the Artists Open Houses is a great way to spend a day. Entry to the houses is free, with many offering homemade tea and cake. Houses are grouped geographically into trails around different areas of the city, with venues generally being in walking distance of each other. Trails range from the fishermen's houses of Hanover, to the urban warehouse spaces of the North Laine and cottages of the South Downs village of Ditchling. Many visitors buy their first piece of original artwork at an Open House and return year after year.

The Artists Open Houses has an ethos of inclusivity rather than selection; any artist can open their house as part of the festival, as long as they live within the 01273 telephone code area. Artists outside this area can still take part as 'guest artists' in someone else's Open House. The festival encourages participation from artists and makers of all ages, at all stages of their careers, and from all parts of the community including community groups, marginalised artists and school and college students.

The festival runs twice a year – weekends throughout May and for three weekends in November/December. With a focus on quality and value for money, the Artists Open Houses Festival brings a dynamic mix of arts and crafts to the widest possible audience, providing visitors and viewers with engaging and inspiring experiences.

For information on May and Christmas Artists Open Houses Festivals visit the AOH website (see above). And in the run up to and during the festivals, look out for AOH brochures in Brighton and Hove's museums, libraries, stations and many bars and cafes – as well as in all the Open House venues themselves.

Clockwise from top left:
Swansong by Dion Salvador Lloyd, Hove trail; Ceramic House, Fiveways trail;
Encounters, West Hove trail; Ceramic House, Fiveways trail

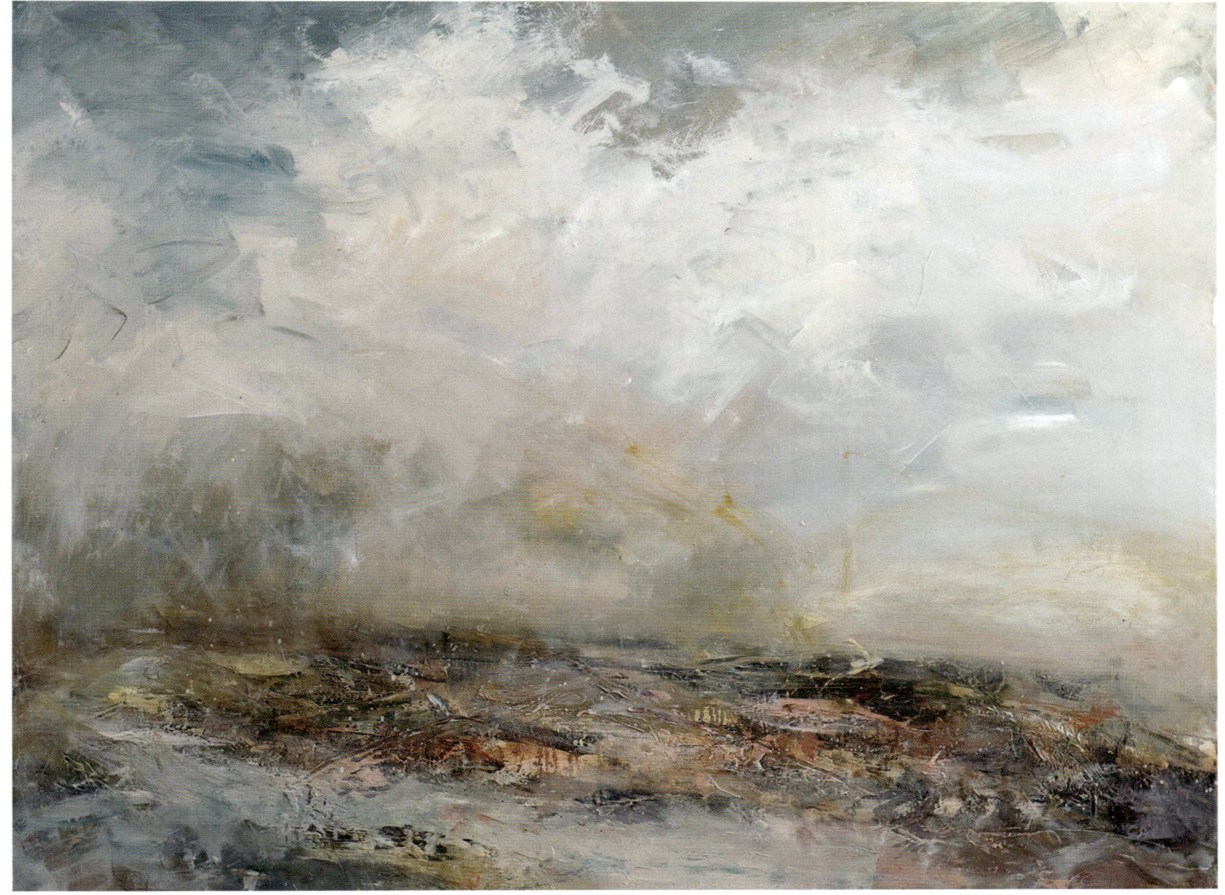

A unique opportunity to visit and buy from artists and makers in their own homes

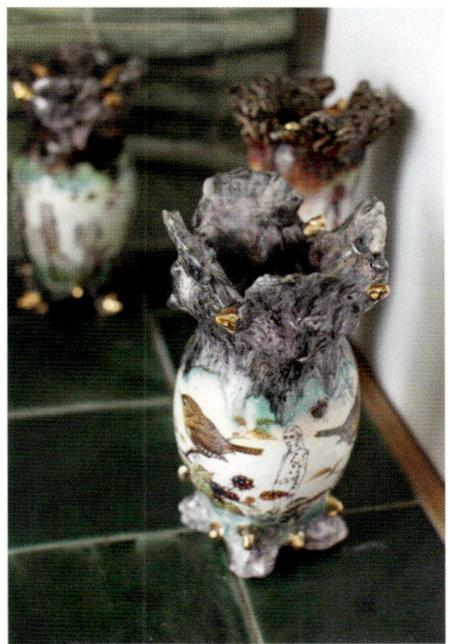

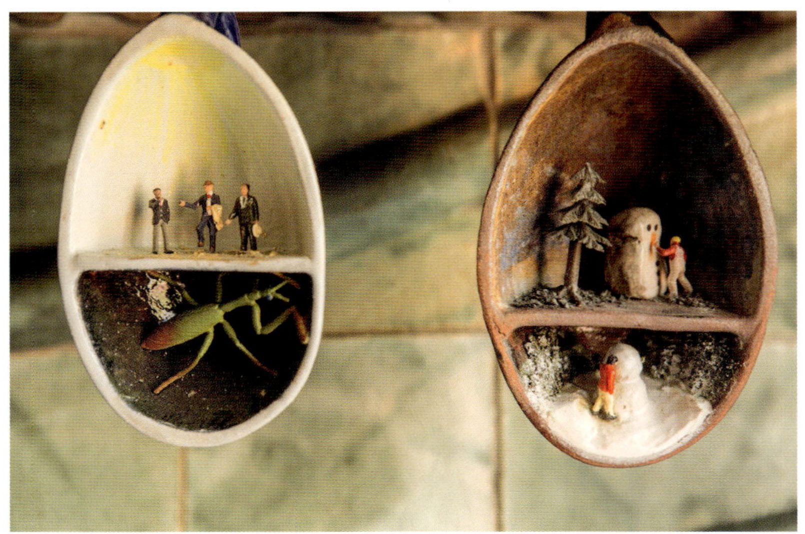

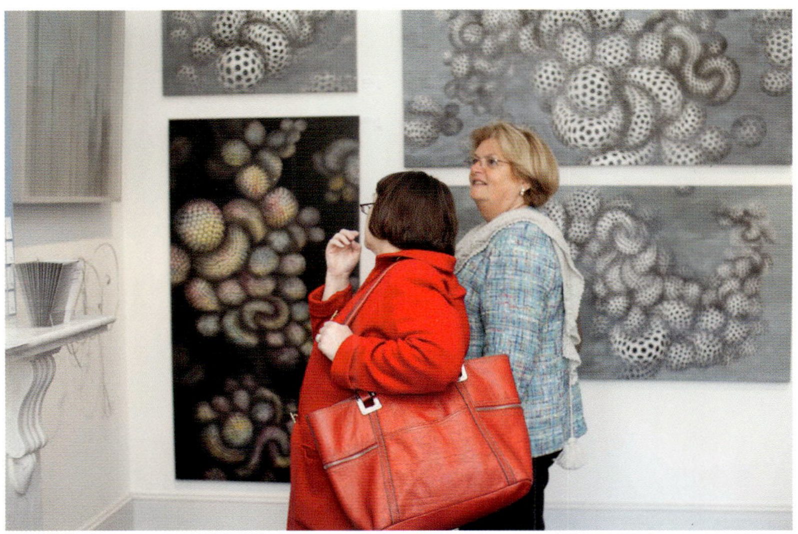

Brighton Art Fair

25-27 September 2015 at The Corn Exchange, Church Street, Brighton BN1 1UE
www.brightonartfair.co.uk

Clockwise from top left: Blind Man by Chris Murray; Seascape by Jane Skingley; At the Fair

Artists present their work to the public, bringing a personal feel to the viewing and buying process. The show welcomes over 5,000 visitors each year

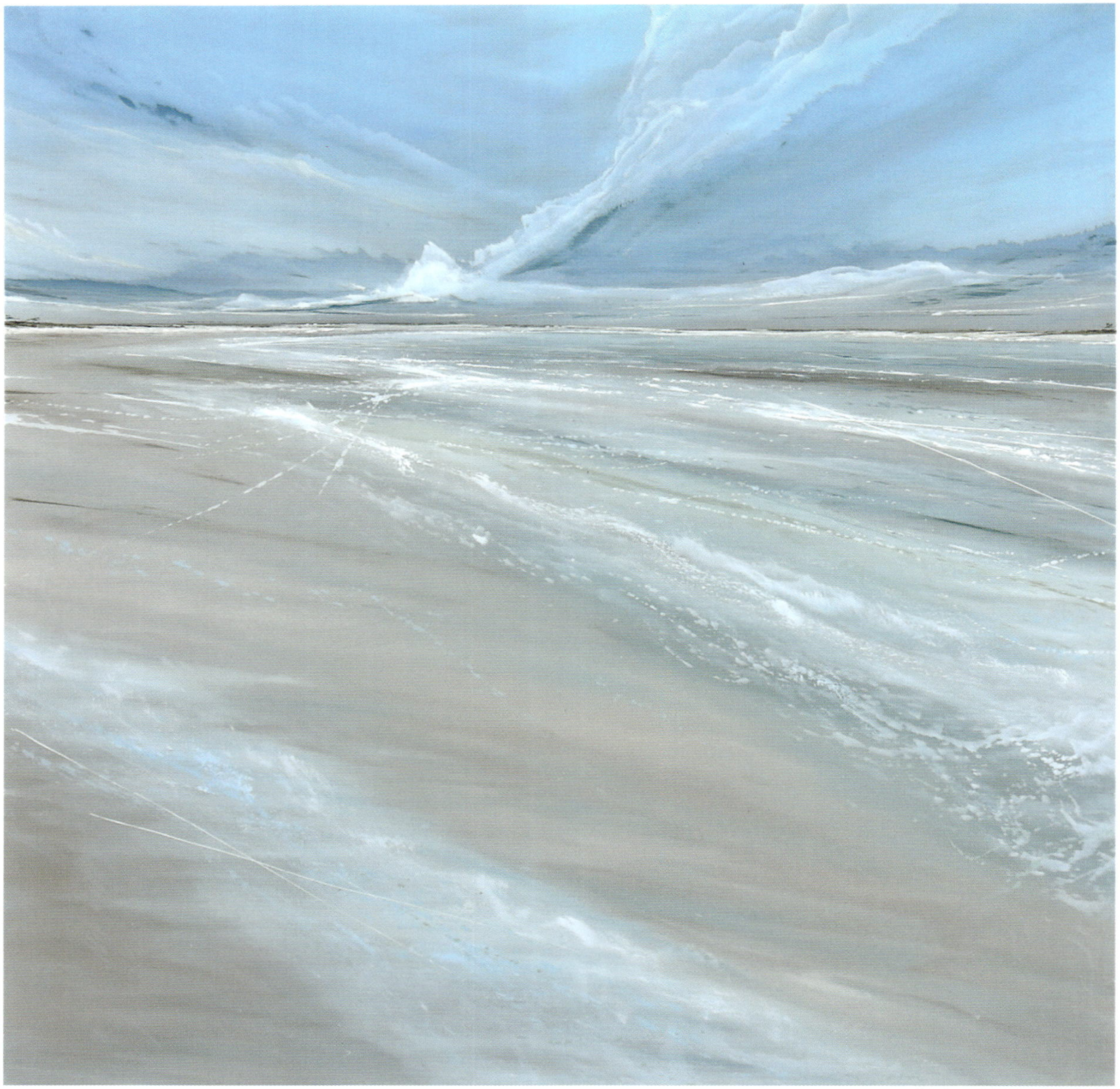

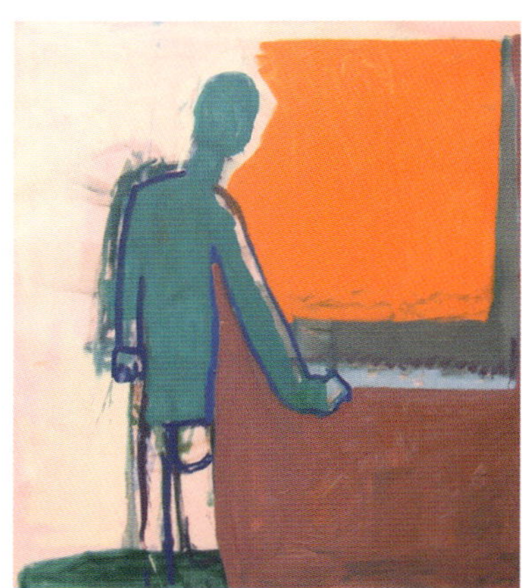

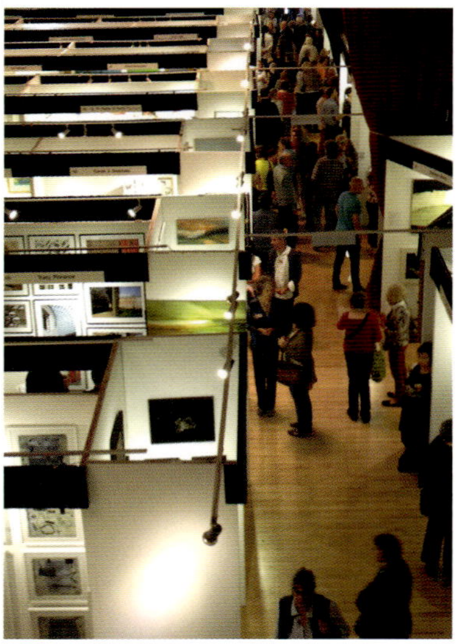

Now in its twelfth year, Brighton Art Fair is a premium selling event with 100 of the best contemporary artists from the UK and abroad showing and selling their diverse work direct to the public. The Fair always promotes a good balance between established and emerging artists, and insists that all work is exciting, fresh and exceptional. This is what keeps its strong reputation as one of the must-see visual arts events in the country.

Painters, printmakers, ceramicists, photographers and sculptors exhibit, with the work being an original and eclectic selection across as wide a variety of methods and subjects as possible. Artists themselves present their work to the public, bringing a personal feel to the viewing and buying process. The show welcomes over 5,000 visitors each year; buyers, collectors, galleries and curators, many of whom return year after year.

Artworks are shown in the majestic and historic Corn Exchange at the Dome in the heart of the city, in a relaxed, informal and friendly environment. A café provides space to take refreshment and contemplate the work.

Clockwise from top left: Jonathan Rogers Glass; Inside MADE; Yen Robinson Lighting

20-22 November 2015 at The Corn Exchange, Church Street, Brighton BN1 1UE
www.brighton-made.co.uk

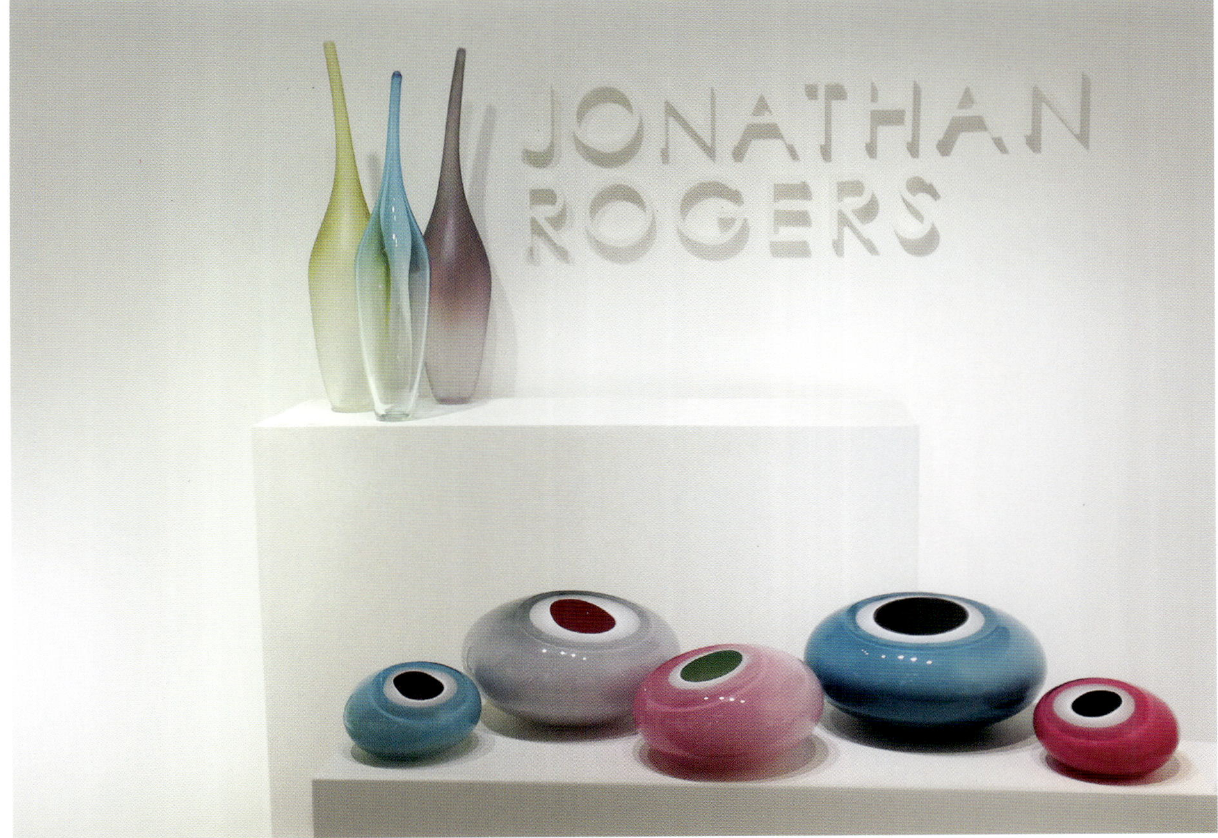

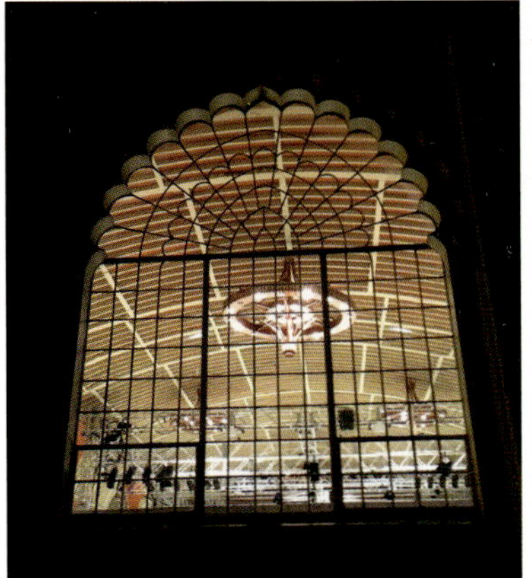

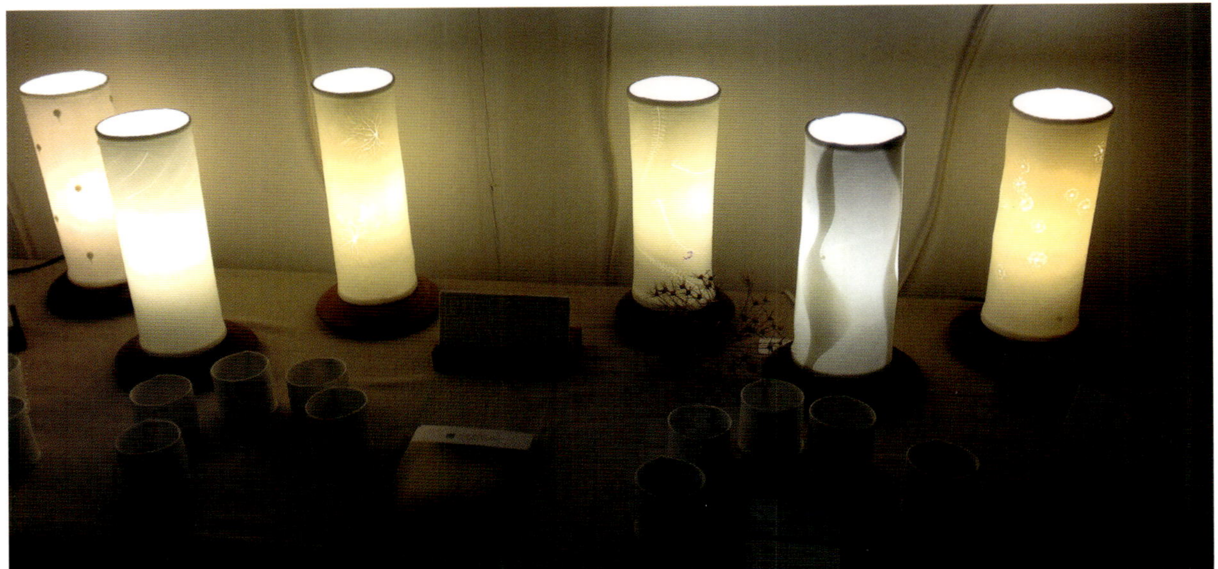

MADE BRIGHTON celebrates its 10th year in 2015. It's the city's annual contemporary craft and design fair, which takes place in the beautiful Corn Exchange at The Dome. MADE BRIGHTON is a selling event, offering the public the opportunity to buy original and exceptional pieces of craft and design direct from the best local and national makers, and has become firmly established as a friendly, accessible and top quality show. Over 5,500 visitors attend, the majority of whom return year on year knowing that the work on show won't disappoint.

MADE BRIGHTON showcases jewellery, textiles, ceramics, basketry, glassware, furniture, home accessories, fashion and much more. All the work is hand crafted, unique and often quirky.

A café provides a place for visitors to relax and take refreshment. With so much work to see, many people like to make a day of it, spending the morning viewing work, stopping for a bite to eat, then returning to continue shopping. It's wonderful!

Index

Please get in touch with us to discover more

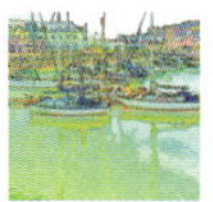
Jude Evans 50
www.judeevans.co.uk
judeevansart@yahoo.co.uk
07825 145044

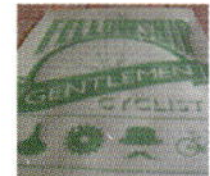
Junkfunk 122
www.junkfunk.com
info@junkfunk.com
01273 680555

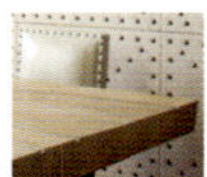
Karl Smith 59
www.carvedoak.co.uk
karl@carvedoak.co.uk
07717 740206

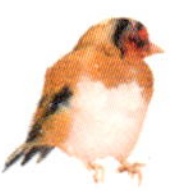
Kate Osborne 20
www.kateosborneart.com
kate@kateosborneart.com
07787 515714

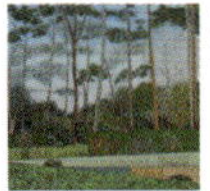
Kellie Miller 29
www.kelliemiller.com
info@kelliemiller.com
07803 589059

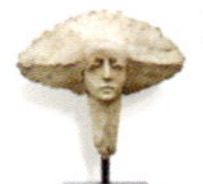
Kellie Miller Arts 107
www.kelliemillerarts.com
contact@kelliemiller.com
07803 589059

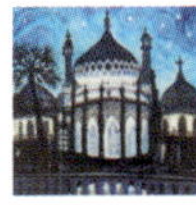
Kim Bodycombe 62
www.kimbodycombe.com
Facebook: Artonthebeach
Open Studios, Kings Rd Arches

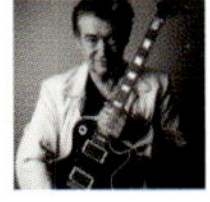
Kris Pawlowski 61
www.krispawlowski.com
kris.pawlowski@btinternet.com
07714 294125

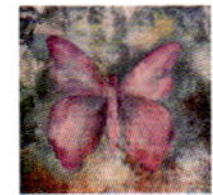
Laura Callaghan Grooms 53
tinyurl.com/pdwbpws
laura@handonheartarts.com
07775 964785

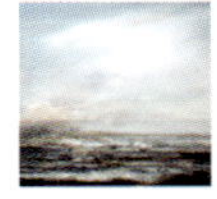
Leila Godden 22
www.leilagodden.com
leila.godden@btinternet.com
07837 965887

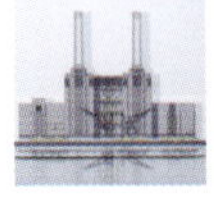
Linescapes 78
www.linescapes.co.uk
contact@linescapes.co.uk
07710 651172

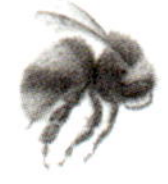
Louisa Crispin 30
www.louisacrispin.co.uk
louisacrispin@btinternet.com
01580 752139

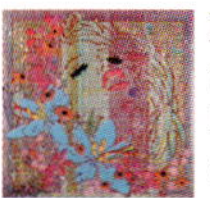
Louise Dear 84
www.louisedear.com
louise@louisedear.com
07900 117430

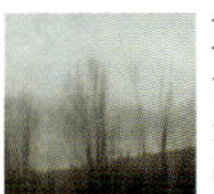
Luella Martin 94
www.luellamartin.co.uk
mail@luemartin.co.uk
07986 938751

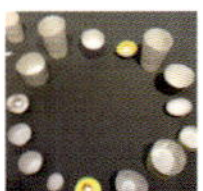
MADE Brighton 131
www.brighton-made.co.uk
info@brighton-made.co.uk
01903 608757

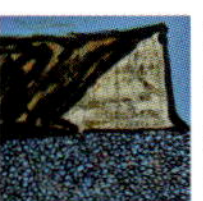
Mark Glassman 10
www.markglassman.org.uk
glassmarky19@gmail.com
01323 899296

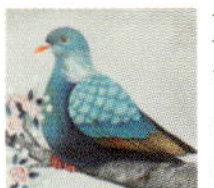
Mia Underwood 99
www.miaunderwood.co.uk
miaunderwood@gmail.com
07920 474784

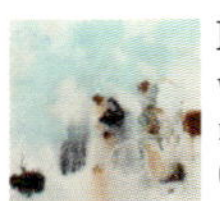
Michelle Cobbin 40
www.michellecobbin.com
michellecobbin@gmail.com
07960 694376

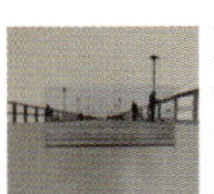
Monika Jakimauskaite 60
www.moniusia.eu
moniusia@ymail.com
07540 648108

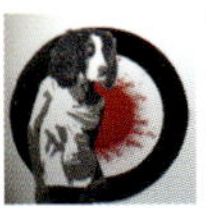
The New Steine Hotel 108
www.newsteinehotel.com
reservation@newsteinehotel.com
01273 681546

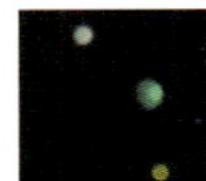
Patrick O'Donnell 28
www.patrick-odonnell.co.uk
mail@patrick-odonnell.co.uk
07763 190790

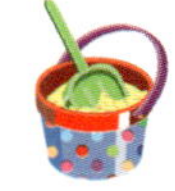
Phil Dobson 100
www.magicpen.co.uk
phildobson.art@gmail.com
07807 274672

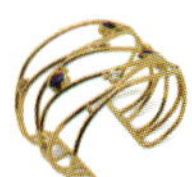
Pruden & Smith 120
www.prudenandsmith.com
info@prudenandsmith.com
01273 846338

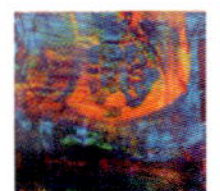
Richard Heys 90
www.richardianheys.co.uk
richard@richardianheys.co.uk
07818 624996

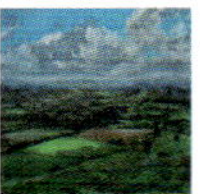
Rob Ollerenshaw 24
www.artymagazines.com
rob.ollerenshaw@btopenworld.com
01273 748338

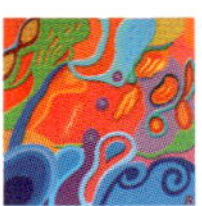
Robin Cooper-Hannan 35
www.robincooperhannan.com
r.cooperhannan@btinternet.com
07910 153517

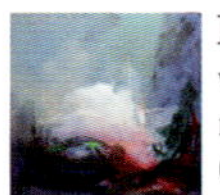
Romany Mark Bruce 70
www.romanymarkbruce.com
romanymb@mac.com
07799 600908

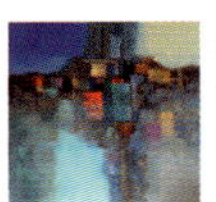
Sheila Marlborough 67
www.sheilamarlborough.co.uk
spmarlborough@aol.com
01444 246605

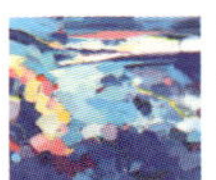
Sophie Abbott 98
www.sophieabbott.net
sophie@sophieabbott.net
07745 834066

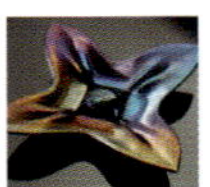
Stephanie Else 27
www.glassinfusion.co.uk
info@glassinfusion.co.uk
07887 975818

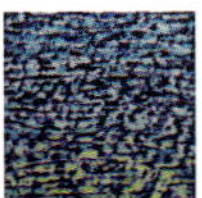
Stuart Dodman 11
www.stuartdodman.com
stuartdodman@gmail.com

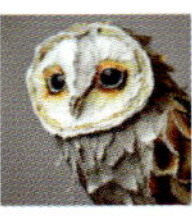
Suzanne Breakwell 21
www.suzannebreakwell.com
info@suzannebreakwell.com
07881 957056

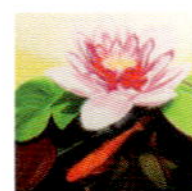
Tina Allonby 72
www.tinaallonby-artist.co.uk
tina.allonby@gmail.com
07765 448535

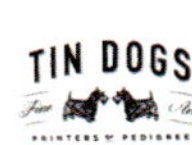

Tin Dogs 17
www.tindogs.com
hello@tindogs.com
07553 724475

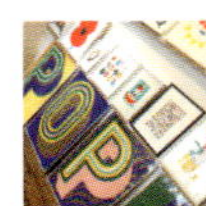
Unlimited 124
www.unlimitedshop.co.uk
Twitter @weareunlimited
01273 204423

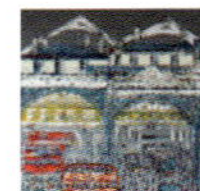
Val Fawbert 12
www.valfawbertcityretreat.com
vfawbert@hotmail.co.uk
01273 227191

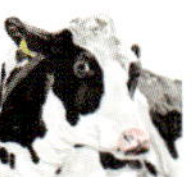
Veronica van Eijk 96
www.vaneijkarts.com
vaneijkarts@gmail.com
07740 104501

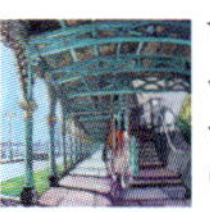
Vincent Donlin 8
www.vincentdonlin.co.uk
vincent1311@btinternet.com
07738 981805

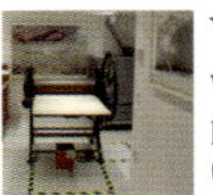
Volcanic Editions 55
www.volcaniceditions.com
printsianbrown@hotmail.com
07986 532161

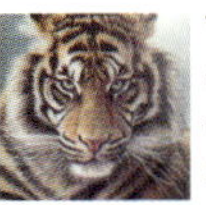
Wendy Standen 56
www.wendystanden.co.uk
wstandenart@gmail.com
shoreham.gallery@gmail.com

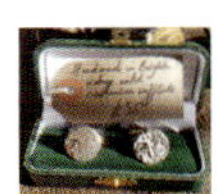
White Rabbit 117
www.facebook.com/
WhiteRabbitMakersGallery

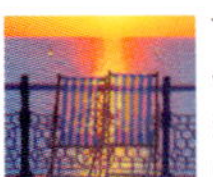
Window Gallery 115
www.windowgallery.co.uk
info@windowgallery.co.uk
01273 726190

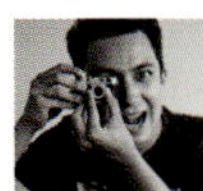
Xavi Dom Buendia 93
www.xdbphotography.com
xdbphotography@gmail.com
Facebook @XDBPhotography

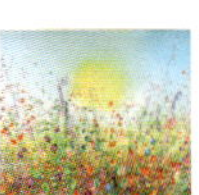
Yvonne Coomber 18
www.art5gallery.com
info@art5gallery.com
01273 774222

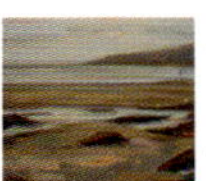
Zimmer Stewart Gallery 110
www.zimmerstewart.co.uk
james@zimmerstewart.co.uk
01903 882063

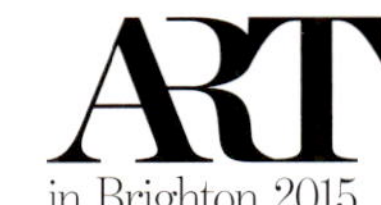

Kemp Street Productions Ltd
www.artymagazines.com
info@artymagazines.com
01273 670426
07768 638115

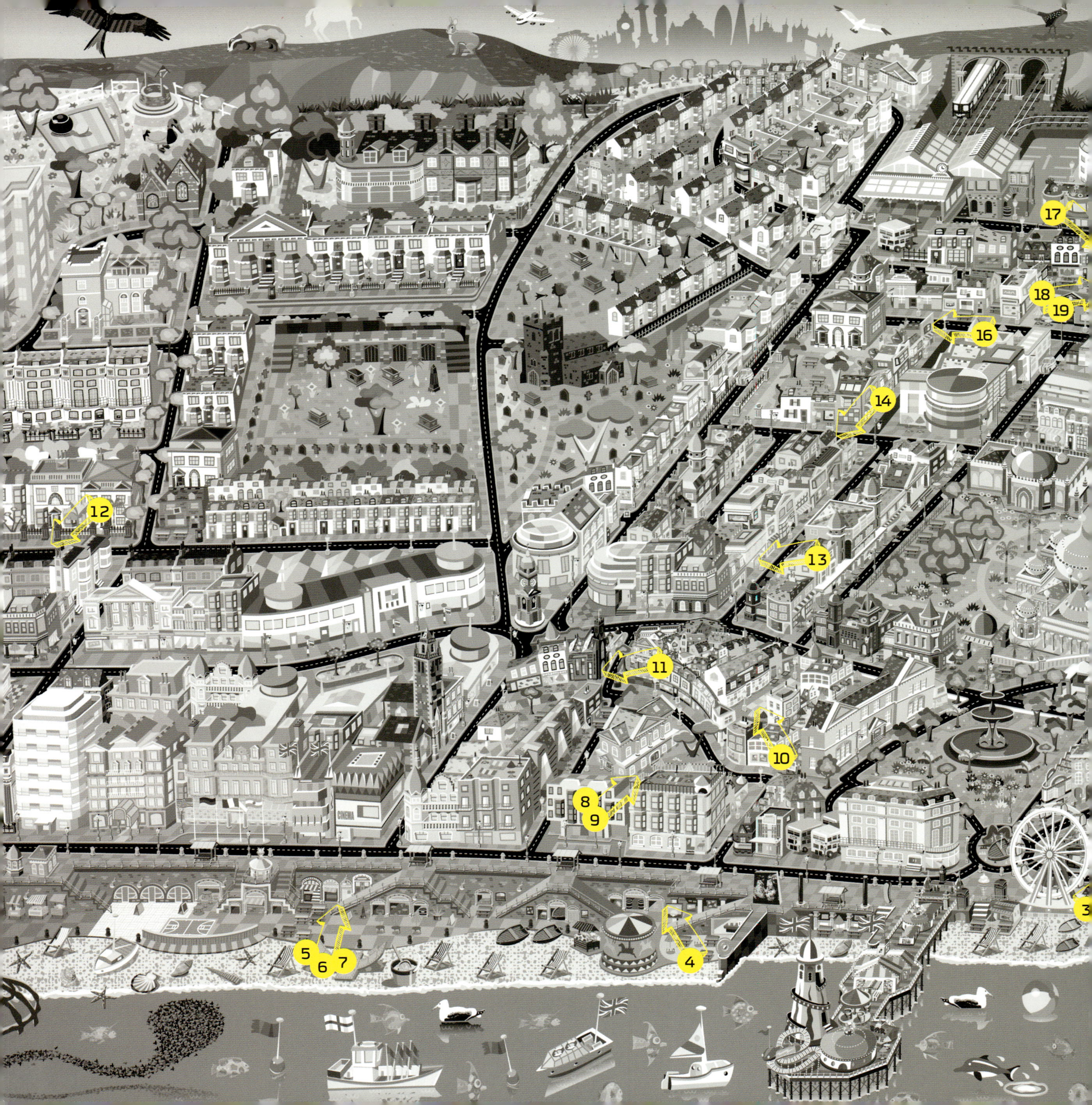
17
18
19
16
14
12
13
11
10
8
9
CINEMA
5
6
7
4
3

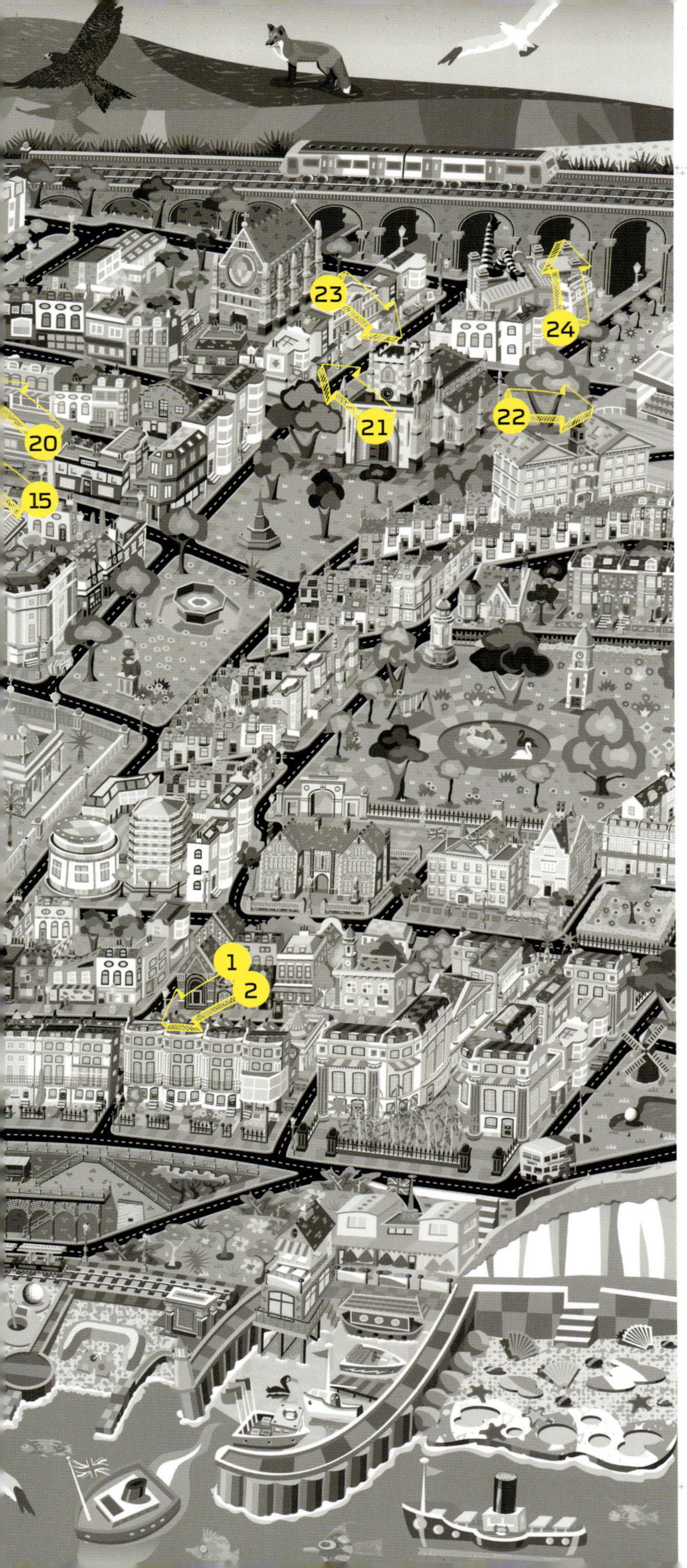

The Arty guide to central Brighton

Map by Phil Dobson
See his work in its full-colour glory on page 100

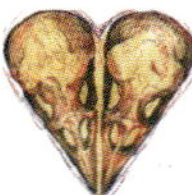

1. The Gilded Cage Tattoo
106 St James St
Tattoo studio and boutique, featuring James Robinson.

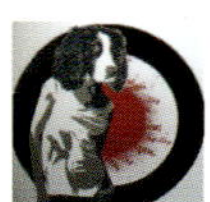

2. New Steine Hotel
10,11,12a New Steine
Boutique hotel, French bistro and gallery. See page 108.

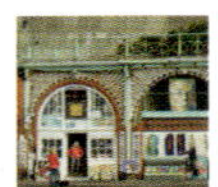

3. JAG Gallery & Open Studios
283a Madeira Drive
Artists' studios and art gallery on Brighton beach.

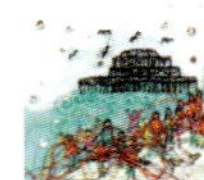

4. Naughty Pirates
Arch 237, Kings Road
Featuring the textiles of Heidi Jane Rhodes - and much more.

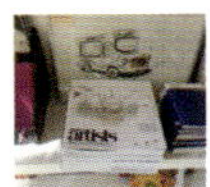

5. Castor+Pollux
165 Kings Road Arches
Brighton's favourite beachfront gallery and bookstore.

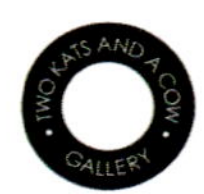

6. Two Kats & a Cow
167 Kings Road Arches
Katty McMurray and Kathryn Matthews' much loved venture.

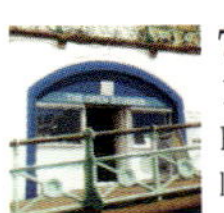

7. The Open Studios
168 Kings Road Arches
Home to an exciting group of local artists.

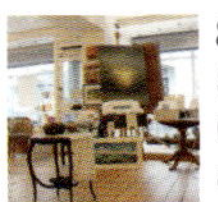

8. Bellis Gallery
8-9 Kings Road
One of the city's most elegant art spaces. See page 118.

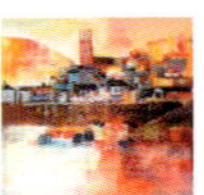

9. ART5 Gallery
5 Bartholemews
A wonderfully diverse selection of artists. See page 109.

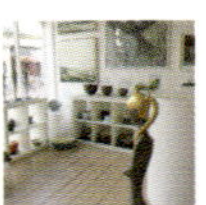

10. Kellie Miller Arts
20 Market Street
Sculptures, mixed media and ceramics. See page 107.

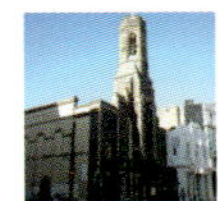

11. Fabrica
Duke Street
Visual arts organisation with an exciting annual programme.

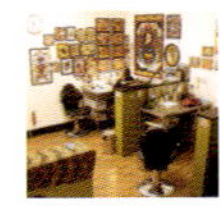

12. Magnum Opus Tattoo
33 Upper North Street
Tattoo studio with downstairs gallery space.

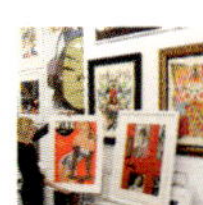

13. artrepublic
13 Bond Street
Collectable, cutting-edge and classic art prints.

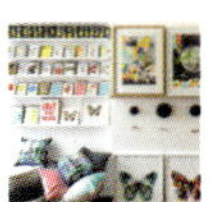

14. Unlimited
10 Church Street
Design shop, gallery and studio. See page 124.

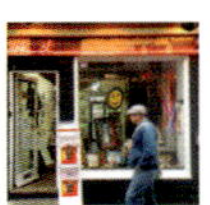

15. ink_d Gallery
96 North Road
Challenging and exciting contemporary art.

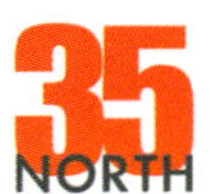

16. 35 North Fine Art Gallery
35 North Road
Owned by John & Sharon Whiting. See page 104.

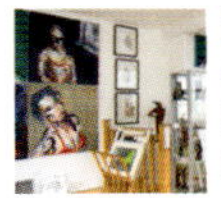

17. Gallery40
40 Gloucester Road
Pop-up gallery space in the North Laine. See page 116.

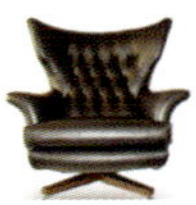

18. In My Room
35 Gloucester Road
Hand-selected vintage pieces - and toys! See page 119.

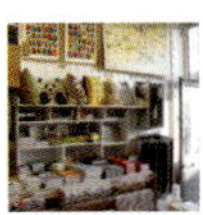

19. Junkfunk
27 Gloucester Road
Design gift shop with great T-shirts. See page 122.

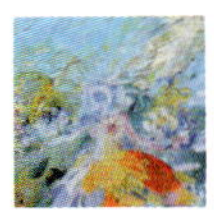

20. iO Gallery
39 Sydney Street, BN1
Eclectic and contemporary art and crafts. See page 106.

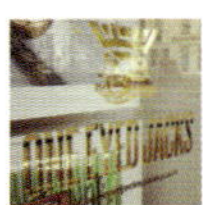

21. One Eyed Jacks
28 York Place
Showcasing photography with a flair for narrative.

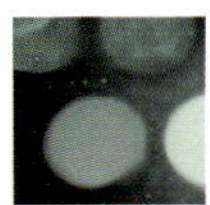

22. Phoenix Studios
10-14 Waterloo Place
Largest artist-led arts organisation in the SE.

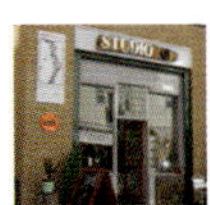

23. Open Market
London Road
Home to a host of local producers and creators.

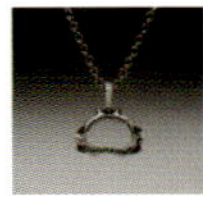

24. Chris Hawkins Jewellery
79 Beaconsfield Road
Exquisite bespoke jewellery for men, plus workshop classes.

About the book's creators

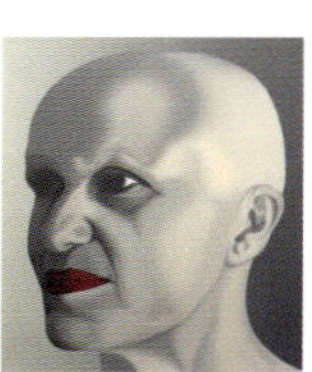

Alison Krog
EDITOR

Alison studied English Literature at the University of London, where she fell in love with Byron and went on to gain an MPhil in Romantic Studies at Oxford University. She had always dreamed of working in magazines, which didn't quite come true when she landed her first publishing role as Editorial Assistant for Professional Electrician & Installer Magazine. After 24 years' working on women's newsstand titles and a multitude of customer magazines, Alison now works for a content marketing agency writing lots of branded stuff.

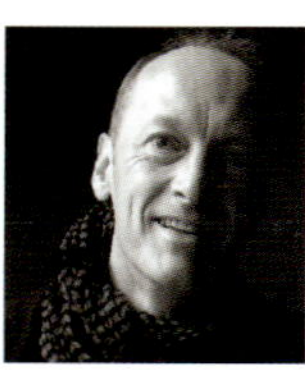

Torben Krog
CREATIVE

Danish-born Torben trained as a typographic designer and has worked in the advertising and magazine industries for the past 21 years. He first visited Brighton as a language student and swore never to return after a gang of local lads threw pebbles at him on the beach. After living in beautiful Japan – and not so beautiful Watford – he moved to London where he met Alison at the advertising agency Publicis. Alison and Torben became 'the Krogs' in 2011 and live in the North Laine with their two spoilt cats called Gilbert and George.